THE EIGHTIES

THE EIGHTIES

America in the
Age of Reagan

John Ehrman

Yale University Press
New Haven and London

Set in Galliard Old Style type by Achorn Graphic Services. Printed in the United States of America.

Library of Congress Cataloging-in-Publication Data
Ehrman, John, 1959–
The eighties : America in the age of Reagan
     p.   cm.
Includes bibliographical references and index.
ISBN 0-300-10662-9 (alk. paper)
  1. United   States—Politics   and   government—1981–1989.
2. Reagan, Ronald—Influence.   3. Conservatism—United
States—History—20th   century.   4. United   States—Social
conditions—1980– 5. Social change—United States—History—
20th   century.   6. United   States—Economic   conditions—
1981–2001. I. Title.
  E876.E344 2005
  973.927—DC22   2004024715

A catalog record for this book is available from the British Library.

The paper in this book meets the guidelines for permanence and durability of the Committee on Production Guidelines for Book Longevity of the Council on Library Resources.

10 9 8 7 6 5 4 3 2 1

FOR MOM AND DAD

CONTENTS

INTRODUCTION

Two inaugurations, two outgoing presidents. At the first ceremony, on January 20, 1981, Democrat Jimmy Carter was the departing
chief executive, his four-year term marked by political ineptitude, deteriorating economic conditions—inflation, in particular, appeared uncon-
trollable—and declining confidence in the federal government's ability to
deal with the country's problems. Running for reelection the previous
November, Carter had been beaten so badly that he conceded defeat
before the polls closed on the West Coast. Now he had to watch as
Ronald Reagan, the conservative Republican who had defeated him by
pledging to roll back decades of Democratic policies, took the oath of
office. Eight years later, however, the scene was dramatically different.
A smiling Reagan, reelected in a landslide in 1984, escorted his vice president and successor, George Bush, to the Capitol for his swearing-in.
Reagan's first two years had been a time of deep recession, but since early
1983 economic growth had been strong, inflation had been subdued, and
more than 15 million new jobs had been created. Reagan had numerous
legislative accomplishments to his credit, doubts about the effectiveness
of the government had disappeared, and he was leaving office with the
highest popularity rating of any outgoing president since World War II.
Bush, for his part, had won the 1988 election in large part because he
promised to continue Reagan's policies.

This book is about how American politics, economics, and society
changed during the eight years between those two inaugurations. My

central point is that the decade of the 1980s—the period from Reagan's election in 1980 through 1989—were the years when America made the transition from the political and social arrangements built by post–World War II liberalism to the highly competitive, fast-changing, and technology-oriented system we know today. At the center of this transformation was a political shift. Liberalism had been in decline since the late 1960s, but it still dominated American political life into the Carter years. Despite the growth of conservative institutions and grassroots organizations, moreover, even after Reagan's victory it was unclear if conservatives had the strength to govern successfully and win additional national elections. During the decade that followed, however, liberalism continued to lose intellectual and political strength. By 1989, conservatives not only had shown that they could govern successfully but also had established their movement as the dominant force in American politics.[1]

The story of the 1980s also is one of broad economic and social change. Virtually every area of American life underwent some type of transformation during the Reagan years, and often a drastic one. It was the time, for example, when taxes became a central issue in American politics and budget deficits precluded new government social programs, when corporate America began to be restructured through deregulation and takeovers, when technology started to change the way people work, and when the first of what became known as the culture wars began. These developments were closely related to one another, and events in one area often affected trends elsewhere. The changes also brought significant benefits to the majority of Americans, although substantial numbers failed to gain—or actually lost—ground during the 1980s. One of my purposes is to untangle the threads of the transition from the old to the new, identify winners and losers, and understand conservatism's—and Reagan's—roles in shaping and moving these changes.

My emphasis on change during the 1980s should not obscure the important continuities of the decade, however. Despite liberalism's decline and Reagan's success in establishing the dominance of conservative politics, most liberal achievements and institutions remained in place, and many of its assumptions continued to play large roles in American political and social life. Since World War II, Americans had become much more liberal and tolerant on social issues, as the ending of institutional-

ized racism, expansions of individual rights, and acceptance of the changing roles of women showed. Because of this, minorities and women had
gained a great deal of political power since 1945. Simultaneously, Americans had accepted, and then embraced, an enlarged role for the federal
government in many areas of their lives—especially when it protected
individual rights, health, or the environment. Little support existed for
reversing these developments and, in fact, most of them continued during the Reagan years on their pre-1980s trajectories. Even areas of change
showed some continuity with the past, as many of the policies of the
1980s had started as experiments during the 1970s.

Foreign affairs was another area that saw profound changes during the
decade when Reagan was in power, although I do not address that subject. The transformation of American politics and life did take place during the final years of the cold war and often was connected to events
abroad, but my focus is exclusively on domestic events. Reagan's foreign
and national security policies obviously deserve careful consideration, but
they would require a volume of their own and are well beyond the scope
of this book.

As these points suggest, this book covers a wide range of complicated
topics, and sorting through them means first understanding the terms in
which they are described. This begins with defining "liberalism" and
"conservatism," both of which are central terms in this book and, indeed,
in any discussion of recent American history. American politics, however,
is notorious for its ideological inconsistency and provides no clear definition of either term—liberalism is attached to the Democratic Party and
conservatism to the Republicans, but both parties are broad coalitions of
interest groups, politicians, and intellectuals that disagree on as many
points as they agree upon. The most useful way to approach the question
may be to describe the main characteristics of each group. Liberals generally seek greater social equality and look to the federal government to
take the leading role in addressing social problems, but prefer to avoid
intervention in the sphere of individual rights and privacy. Thus, for
example, they usually support expanded social welfare programs and
strong action to protect the civil rights of defined groups, but wish to
leave moral decisions—especially those regarding personal behavior and
sexuality—to individuals.

In contrast, conservatives emphasize individual responsibilities rather than rights. As a result, conservatives seek to limit the government's social role while promoting what they view as traditional morality. They usually support, for example, nongovernment or combined government-market approaches to social welfare, remedying individual cases of discrimination rather than trying to protect large classes of people, and—in one of the major fault lines of our politics—restricting abortion rights. Exceptions and contradictions abound within each group, however. Among liberals, moderates are inclined to favor the interests of the middle class and are more inclined to pursue market-based policies that require less public funding, while those further to the left emphasize using the government to help the poor, with less regard for cost; on the right, libertarians and religious conservatives clash over the question of government intrusion into personal affairs. Both groups' moderate factions, moreover, are more inclined to consider opponents' interests and work for compromises than are their more ideologically committed colleagues. As long as such inconsistencies always are kept in mind, however, these characteristics can serve as basic working descriptions of liberalism and conservatism.

For telling the story of the 1980s, however, perhaps the most important defining differences between liberalism and conservatism are their respective economic policies. Not only did Reagan's economic policies do much to stimulate the wide range of changes that marked the 1980s, but reactions to them were a large part of what defined liberalism, both internally and in the popular mind, during the decade. Liberals during the 1980s still held to the basic tenets of Keynesian economics—that the government, by manipulating demand through taxes, spending, and monetary policy, can promote steady economic growth and full employment with acceptable inflation. Liberals also still believed that government should play an active regulatory role in the marketplace, albeit a smaller one than it had before the 1970s. Conservatives rejected these approaches, believing instead that free markets, operating with minimal government regulation and low taxes, would bring prosperity on their own. Here, too, liberalism and conservatism had internal disagreements and sometimes overlapped. No liberals ever rejected basic capitalist ideas, although some advocated government-business partnerships for economic planning. Conservatives, for their part, divided into supply-side advocates, conservative Keynesians, and other schools of thought, and few were shy about interfering in the marketplace if it was politically expedient. Both sides, however, generally were more consistent in their beliefs and policies regarding economics than they were in other areas.

Ideological confusion and inconsistency combine with the enormous variety and complexity of American society to complicate any discussion of political and economic trends. Together, these factors create a jumble that makes it hazardous to describe change or experiences in general terms—and exceptions can always be found to any statement. One reason for this is that American culture houses many subcultures, and people often can fit, or be defined into, any of several. Thus, for example, working-class Americans whose economic interests might be expected to make them Democrats often hold religious and cultural values that lead them to conservatism; prosperous suburbanites frequently have moral and ethical views that bring them to liberalism; and immigrants are as varied as the countries they come from, having only their foreign birth in common. To sort through matters, commentators often divide Americans into broad categories—class, race, gender, geographical location, religion, and so on. Such categorizations make it easier to analyze data and identify broad characteristics, but they also lend themselves to oversimplifications that can hide more than they reveal. I intend to break down as many of these generalizations as possible and illustrate how the changes of the 1980s affected different people in different ways. As with the definitions of liberalism and conservatism, however, readers should still bear in mind perils of broad statements.

One generalization that is safe to make, however, is that this diversity pushes American politics toward the center. The American democratic system not only has to accommodate the competing demands of its wide variety of groups, but it must also find room for new actors as they emerge and organize to promote their interests—as blacks, Hispanics, and women have done during the past sixty years, for example. As a result, American politics operates by adaptation, compromise, decentralization, and deal making. Indeed, since the founding of the Republic, Americans have tended toward consensus on major issues, and the political system continues to operate by gradually creating broad agreements as new issues emerge. Consequently, change almost always is incremental and policy seldom is made according to comprehensive plans; rather, policies are stitched together in a search for workable solutions that can satisfy the demands of competing interest groups. Because of this, bold or radical ideas have to be moderated if their basic tenets are to achieve broad acceptance, and sudden change or drastic swings to the left or right are rare.

The centrism of American politics and culture is embodied in the attitudes of the suburban middle and professional classes. This group expanded dramatically in the years after World War II, and by 1980 it was the largest socioeconomic bloc of the population, making it broadly representative of the experiences and beliefs of Americans in general. Although they, too, can be subdivided the same ways as the general population—by race, religion, sex, income levels, and region, to name some—members of the middle and professional classes have many common characteristics and views. At the broadest level, they tend to place a high priority on maintaining a stable economic environment, and they are comfortable with social change and technological innovation. At the individual level, they tend to be well educated, tolerant and open-minded, and enthusiastic consumers. Political beliefs in the middle and professional classes, in the best American tradition, are flexible. These people are attentive to politics and are shrewd judges of candidates and issues, but they are interested more in results than in ideological consistency. Because of this, and again at the risk of some oversimplification, I will frequently illustrate the effects of change during the 1980s by referring to the experiences of the middle and professional classes.

This leads to what I see as the most intriguing question of the 1980s—how was Reagan able to push a nonideological political system, rooted in the center and dominated by a centrist class with many liberal tendencies, toward the right? The answer, which forms another important theme in this book, embodies all of the subtleties and inconsistencies of American politics. Although Reagan was a strong conservative, he was also, I argue, a shrewd politician and a man of moderate temperament and cautious political instincts that were similar to those of most other Americans. He was elected in 1980 not because Americans had swung to the right but rather, when liberal and centrist politicians seemed unable to cope with difficult times, because voters were willing to experiment with the alternatives he offered. In office, Reagan worked consistently to nudge policy and politics to the right, but he was careful not to go beyond the limits of popular support. He accepted and worked within the gradualism of American politics, took his victories where he could, and compromised or backed off when he had to. The voters, meanwhile, never turned conservative during the 1980s but, because Reagan's policies were generally successful—especially when compared with those of his immediate predecessors—they rewarded him with their continued support.

Reagan's success also shows that even if ideology matters little in American politics, ideas still are important because they give people something to believe in. Ideas provide intellectuals with a framework for interpreting the world that they, in turn, pass to politicians for use in public debate and decision making. Without a foundation of useful ideas—that is, those that can be grasped easily, make sense intuitively, and address the concerns of ordinary people—political success is difficult in the American system. During the 1980s, conservatives' basic ideas of promoting tax-cutting and free-market ideas generally were internally consistent, coherently presented, and promised to benefit the middle and professional classes. Liberals, in contrast, were unable to agree on a basic set of ideas, let alone present them in a way that attracted a majority of voters. The result was that, in the three presidential elections of the 1980s and on numerous occasions in between, Reagan and conservative ideas triumphed, even though voters had not moved from their centrist moorings.

I have tried to organize this book to make the threads of these arguments easy to follow. The Prologue is a short review of Reagan's prepresidential life and career that explains his character and connection to the American political tradition. Chapter 1 introduces the major themes of the book and briefly traces the shifts in American political and intellectual life that enabled Reagan to win the presidency. Chapters 2 and 4 examine the political and economic events of Reagan's first and second terms in the White House. In between, Chapter 3 looks at changes in how Americans lived and worked during the 1980s. Chapter 5 discusses the impact of change in the social sphere and identifies the major sources of discontent. Finally, the Conclusion looks at what the 1980s can teach us about change and continuity in American life. The tables referenced in the text can be found in the Appendix, and the notes provide suggested readings for detailed discussions of specific events or alternative points of view.

I finished revising this book six days before Ronald Reagan died on June 5, 2004, and, except for minor corrections, have not altered the text since then. As the eulogies, media accounts, and responses of ordinary Americans to the news of his death show, Reagan now is understood as a transformational president. In the days before his funeral—Reagan's most magnificently staged event, in a career filled with them—commentators frequently said that his effect on American life and politics was equal to that of Franklin Roosevelt. Such a comparison still is premature, I believe, but the chapters that follow may help clarify Reagan's role.

PROLOGUE: THE AMERICAN

Understanding the United States during the 1980s begins with understanding Ronald Reagan. But after a lifetime in the public eye—in radio, as an actor for twenty-five years, for eight years as governor of California, and for two terms as president—several biographies and autobiographies, countless articles, interviews, television appearances, and journalists' analyses, Reagan remains a mystery to many. Almost everyone who knew him had the same observation, that he was a reserved figure, gracious but not a man who was easy to know intimately. "He is the kindest and most impersonal man I ever knew," speechwriter Peggy Noonan quotes James Baker, his chief of staff, as saying. Not even Edmund Morris, Reagan's authorized biographer, could penetrate his shell.[1]

Nonetheless, critics and supporters have never stopped trying to explain him. His opponents variously portrayed him as an accidental president, an actor and illusionist who fooled the voters; a product of California's eccentric politics who believed in ruinous economic theories; a manipulator of the myths Americans want to believe about themselves; or simply a befuddled old man, controlled by his wife and unable to cope with the responsibilities of his job. He has been blamed for whatever problems, real or imagined, have bothered Americans since 1981. To his supporters, by contrast, Reagan is a demigod who saved the United States from economic disaster; a visionary who inspired the country; and a warm and thoughtful man who, instead of becoming bogged down in self-doubt, remained faithful to an ideal of national greatness. In their view, Reagan restored national pride and prosperity. These conflicting interpretations sometimes lead to public controversies, as in November 2003 when CBS had to cancel a biographical miniseries on Reagan that his supporters protested was a hatchet job. The clashes stem from a complexity in Reagan's character that neither side, seeking a single explanation for the man and his record, wants to acknowledge. Reagan was in many ways an extraordinary man, one who rose from small-town obscurity to fame, wealth, and the presidency. But he was, at the same time, in many ways a typical American. His experiences—personal and political—were largely the same as those of tens of millions of other Americans. The best way to look at Ronald Reagan, and to begin to understand the decade that revolved around him, therefore, is to look at what made him both exceptional and a common American.[2]

Reagan's early life was ordinary. He was born on February 6, 1911, in Tampico, Illinois, a town of about eight hundred in the northwestern part of the state. His father, Jack, was a shoe salesman with a drinking problem. Jack apparently was an extraordinary salesman when he was sober, but his drinking kept him from success; he moved from job to job and the family often was on the brink of poverty. Ronald's mother, Nelle, was the major influence on her son, and he later claimed that it was from her that he got his indefatigable optimism. Nelle was also a religious woman, active in the Disciples of Christ and charity work. The Disciples did much to shape Reagan's views, for they emphasized the virtues of patriotism and free enterprise, had an optimistic view of progress, and were reluctant to involve the government in the private sphere. The Disciples were not a strict church, however, and they did not insist on temperance or forbid modern entertainments, such as movies. In 1920, the Reagans finally settled in Dixon, a town of eight thousand on the Rock River near Tampico that Reagan considered his hometown. In Dixon, Nelle kept Ronald involved in church activities, including acting in church productions, and encouraged his enjoyment of reading.[3]

Reagan described growing up in Dixon in idyllic terms—"as close as I could imagine for a young boy to the world created by Mark Twain in *The Adventures of Tom Sawyer.*" He was a bright young man, quiet and responsible, but not overly bookish and always interested in sports and outdoor activities; his description of his childhood and youth focuses on swimming, fishing, skating, canoe trips, and minor pranks. In high school he played football, acted in school plays, and was elected president of the student body his senior year. Reagan went on to Eureka College, a small school run by the Disciples, where he continued to play football and act, while his remarkable memory enabled him to get by with minimal studying. Meanwhile, each summer he returned to Dixon, where he worked as a lifeguard at a riverfront beach and, over the course of six summers, saved seventy-seven people from drowning. He graduated from Eureka in June 1932.[4]

Radio was the major mass medium during the 1920s and 1930s, bringing Americans their news, entertainment, and daily contact with the rest of the world. "Radio was magic," Reagan later wrote. "You'd sit in your living room and be transported to glamorous locales around the world." His ambition was to become a radio sports announcer, thereby combining his enjoyment of athletics and theater, and soon after graduation he began hunting for a job. He had no luck in Chicago, but in the fall of 1932 he was hired by WOC, a small station in Davenport, Iowa, to broadcast four college football games. When a full-time announcer's job became available in early 1933, Reagan was hired for a salary of one hundred dollars per month. His voice and delivery were well suited to radio and he turned out to have a talent for announcing baseball games, which he did by embellishing wire service reports as he sat in a studio hundreds of miles from the game. WOC soon was consolidated with WHO, a more powerful station in Des Moines, and Reagan moved to the Iowa capital, then a city of 145,000. His salary rose to seventy-five dollars per week, and thanks to WHO's transmitter he became a celebrity in a large section of the Midwest, supplementing his station salary with frequent speaking engagements. Beginning in 1935, WHO sent Reagan to cover the Chicago Cubs during spring training in southern California, which brought him "tantalizingly close to Hollywood," as he later wrote. Hoping to break into the movies, Reagan used his spring-training trip in 1937 to meet an agent who, in turn, arranged a screen test with Warner Brothers. The studio signed Reagan to a contract for two hundred dollars a week.[5]

Reagan rose quickly in Hollywood. Initially he was cast in B movies, the forgettable films that Warner Brothers and other major studios made on an assembly-line system to round out double features. Reagan worked hard to learn his new trade and proved to be a competent actor. He memorized his lines with ease, obeyed his directors, and projected a straightforward, wholesome image. He gained good reviews and worked steadily, making thirteen movies in his first year. In 1940, the year he married actress Jane Wyman, Reagan waged a successful campaign to break into A pictures, winning the part of Notre Dame football player George Gipp in *Knute Rockne—All American*. The success of the movie brought him more starring roles, including the lead in *Kings Row* (1941), which usually is cited as his finest film. Reagan was making a thousand dollars per week, and seemed to be on the brink of becoming a major star, when the Japanese attacked Pearl Harbor. Several years earlier, while living in Des Moines, Reagan had joined the army reserve as a cavalry officer because it gave him the chance to ride horses; he was called to active duty in April 1942 and spent most of the war making training films at a studio taken over by the army. While Reagan was in the army, his agent negotiated a million-dollar, seven-year contract for him with Warner Brothers, but unfortunately the moviegoing public forgot about him while he was offscreen. After he returned from active duty the studio was unsure how to use him and, as a result, badly miscast him in several films. Reagan's movie career faded, and by the mid-1950s it was over.

The late 1940s and early 1950s were a time of transition for Reagan in other ways as well. Jane Wyman's film career had gone well during the war and she continued to prosper afterward, winning an Academy Award in 1948. The contrast between her success and Reagan's professional troubles strained their marriage, and they were divorced in 1949. Reagan was lonely and unhappy until he met Nancy Davis, a young actress. They were married in March 1952 and, by all accounts, were a happy and devoted couple. Reagan also became politically active during this period. He had followed politics and current events for many years, had been a strong supporter of Franklin Roosevelt and the New Deal (Jack Reagan, thrown out of work during the Great Depression, had remained unemployed until he was hired as a New Deal administrator), and had joined the Screen Actors Guild—the main union for movie actors—in 1938. Reagan was an enthusiastic union man—"I spoke to some of the older career actors I met at Warners and discovered how much they'd been exploited in the past," he later wrote. Reagan became increasingly involved in the guild's activities in postwar Hollywood, which was troubled by rising competition from television as well as by strikes and political struggles caused by the attempts of pro-Communist leaders of rival Hollywood unions and Communist front organizations to expand their influence. Eventually, Reagan served five terms as the guild's president, and he not only gained valuable political skills from his union experience but also became a strong anti-Communist. At first, he wrote in 1990, "I'd shared the orthodox liberal view that Communists—if there *were* any— were liberals who were temporarily off track," but his union experience had convinced him that Communists would use any tactic they felt necessary to advance the cause of Soviet expansionism. He also served as an informer for the Federal Bureau of Investigation, telling the FBI of Communist activities in Hollywood.[6]

Reagan gradually shifted from anti-Communist liberalism to conservatism during the 1950s. In 1954, General Electric hired him to host a new weekly television show, *General Electric Theater*. For $125,000 per year, Reagan introduced each week's show, acted in some, and spent ten weeks on the road speaking for GE and appearing at the company's plants. Reagan's acting career was reborn. *General Electric Theater* became the top-rated Sunday night show, making Reagan a nationally known figure. Meanwhile, he appeared at every GE plant in the United States and spoke to hundreds of other groups on behalf of the company. This, like his union experience, proved to be excellent training for politics; Reagan became an accomplished and popular speaker, learning how to please a live audience and conserve his strength during long speaking tours. But the experience also propelled Reagan steadily toward the right. His rising income led to high taxes (he paid the top marginal rate of 94 percent) and an increasing dislike for the growth of the federal government. Reagan's exposure to businessmen and their concerns, moreover, led him to oppose government regulation of private enterprise. His speeches began to focus on what he and his audiences viewed as the loss of individual freedom, growing bureaucratic regulation, and wasteful federal spending; they were warnings "about the threat of government," he recalled. Reagan was still a registered Democrat when he campaigned for Richard Nixon in 1960, but by the time *General Electric Theater* was canceled in 1962 he usually was identified as a leading conservative spokesman and was a hugely popular figure among Republicans. In the fall of 1962, while campaigning on behalf of Nixon's candidacy for governor of California, Reagan formally changed his party registration to Republican.[7]

Reagan began his next career, as a professional politician, in 1964. That year, he served as co-chairman of Republican presidential candidate Barry Goldwater's California campaign. Reagan spoke throughout the state for Goldwater, using the basic speech he had developed when he was working for General Electric. Goldwater was known for his strident conservative rhetoric, but Reagan projected a calm, reassuring presence that appealed to voters. When the Goldwater campaign televised Reagan's speech nationally on October 27, it turned out to be a surprising success, bringing in more than a million dollars in contributions—an astonishing sum for the time. President Lyndon Johnson crushed Goldwater in the election, but Reagan emerged from the defeat as the new leader of the Republican right. In California, a small group of conservative businessmen saw him as the man who could lead a revival of the moribund state Republican Party. They quickly convinced Reagan to run for governor of California in 1966 against the Democratic incumbent, Edmund G. "Pat" Brown.

During the campaign Reagan portrayed himself as a citizen running because he had become convinced that government had grown too large and taxes were too high. His opponents claimed that he was uninformed, somewhat dim, a right-wing fanatic, and the puppet of a campaign staff that fed him information on index cards. Reagan "would damage the state" if he won, predicted one observer in the *New Republic,* because he would not use the government to address California's numerous problems, and the far right would immediately begin working to make him the Republican presidential nominee in 1968. For his part, Brown underestimated Reagan's abilities and appeal, as well as his own disadvantages. Brown, who was from San Francisco, did not realize the extent to which population shifts had made southern

California, where Reagan lived, the politically more important part of the state. The growing unrest of the mid-1960s, and especially the Watts riot of 1965 and student protests in the University of California system, meanwhile, created grave doubts among voters about Brown's style of liberalism. The riots, protests, and escalation of the Vietnam War also created serious divisions within the California Democratic Party. In addition, Brown's campaign was poorly run, and in desperation the governor tried to liken Reagan to John Wilkes Booth, the actor who had assassinated Abraham Lincoln. In contrast, Reagan was a strong, disciplined campaigner. He was a quick study, mastered the issues, and distanced himself from the more extreme figures on the California right. His mild manner and well-polished skills at playing to audiences made him a formidable presence in front of crowds and on television. Consequently, he was able to overcome perceptions that he was an extremist or lacked the intellect to be governor. On election day, Reagan beat Brown by 3.7 million votes to 2.7 million.[8]

After taking office in January 1967, Reagan used an operating style that he never changed, either in Sacramento or later in Washington. He was a hard worker, but he paced himself by not putting in excessive hours. Reagan immersed himself in the details of issues that he cared deeply about, but on matters of less importance to him he left the fine points of policy development and execution to his staff. Reagan had an aversion to confrontation—he never got involved in disputes among his staff, nor did he fire poor performers himself, a task he always left to others. The advantage of this approach was that he seldom got bogged down in the morass of administrative and technical details; instead, he was able to keep his eye on achieving his major goals. The disadvantage was that his style made him dependent on his staff and sometimes left him in the dark about what was going on around him.[9]

Reagan's early performance as governor was uneven. When he arrived in Sacramento, Reagan knew little about administering or financing a state government, few on his staff had experience in government, and his chief of staff, Philip Battaglia, often was absent and turned out to be inept. The first problem Reagan faced was a cash-flow crisis and mounting deficit—caused by Pat Brown's use of an accounting trick to avoid having to raise taxes in 1966—that he was constitutionally required to close. Reagan's finance director, Gordon Smith, was as inexperienced as the governor and suggested the simple approach of cutting all state expenditures by 10 percent. Reagan agreed, only to find that the method failed when it faced the reality of competing budgetary priorities and the need to make realistic spending decisions. Eventually, the new governor had to agree to large increases in sales, corporate, and personal income taxes, which he pitched to Californians through a set of cleverly conceived television advertisements that portrayed them as a regrettable necessity caused by Brown's spending sprees. Reagan also managed to ease the pain of the tax hikes, passed by the legislature in late July 1967, by using them to reform California's regressive tax system.

Reagan faced another problem after the tax hike, this time in his own staff. In the summer of 1967, a group of Reagan's aides worked in secret to verify rumors that Battaglia was a homosexual. Once satisfied that the rumors were true, they went to Reagan in August to demand Battaglia's removal. Reagan was taken completely by surprise—he had no idea of the maneuvering that had been going on for weeks within his staff. The governor realized his chief of staff had to go—Reagan was not homophobic, but homosexuality then was unacceptable in public figures—and he sent a friend to obtain Battaglia's resignation. Although a brief scandal ensued when the affair became public knowledge, the departure of the hapless Battaglia was a stroke of luck for Reagan. He hired a new chief of staff, William Clark, who revamped the staff system serving Reagan. Clark and his successor, Edwin Meese III, paid close attention to the details of policy development and legislation. Any issue requiring a decision by the governor was outlined in a one-page memo that gave the facts, differing views and arguments, and a recommendation for action; the memos then served as the basis for discussion at cabinet meetings during which Reagan made his decisions. This system forced his staff to define and discuss issues carefully, gave Reagan the information he needed in an easily digested format, and was the model for his staff until he left the White House. (It was only when Reagan later had a poor chief of staff—Donald Regan, in 1985 and 1986—that this system failed him.) Finally, Clark replaced the hapless Gordon Smith with a moderate Republican, Caspar Weinberger, giving Reagan a strong and competent finance director.[10]

Reagan's governorship now ran smoothly. The budget struggle showed that Reagan learned quickly and could turn mistakes to his advantage—by December 1967, reported the *New York Times Magazine*, Reagan enjoyed a reputation as a decisive governor, had a 70 percent approval rating, and could "win an Oscar for the most surprising performance of the year." Reagan further boosted his popularity by taking advantage of the student protests that continued to plague the University of California system during the late 1960s. Like many Californians, he was justly proud of the state's system of higher education and was angered by what he saw as "violent anarchy" at the schools. Reagan engineered the firing of Clark Kerr, the chancellor of the university system, whom many blamed for not controlling the disturbances. He also took a strong public stand against students who disrupted or tried to shut down campuses and, on several occasions, used police and National Guard troops to keep the universities open. At the same time, however, Reagan resisted the political temptation to punish the universities' administrators and faculty. Instead, state spending on higher education rose steadily during Reagan's tenure. This approach was politically rewarding: by maintaining state support for the schools while denouncing the protesters, Reagan emerged as a moderate who was committed to maintaining California's high-quality university system. This, combined with the state's improved financial condition, paid off handsomely in 1970 when Reagan ran for reelection against Jesse Unruh, the speaker of the State Assembly. Reagan won easily, by 3.4 million votes to 2.9 million.[11]

Reagan made welfare reform the centerpiece of his second term. His goal was to reduce the growing costs of Aid to Families with Dependent Children (AFDC), which was funded jointly by the state and federal governments. Although California had not increased AFDC payments since 1957, the number of recipients had grown from 375,000 in 1963 to 1.5 million at the time of Reagan's reelection, and the caseload was rising by 40,000 per month. To prevent a renewed budgetary disaster, Reagan proposed requiring able-bodied AFDC recipients to find work or enroll in job training; at the same time, he wanted to increase assistance to those unable to work. The package, not surprisingly, was controversial and the legislation soon bogged down as Reagan and the Democratic-controlled assembly argued over the reforms. Eventually, the California Welfare Reform Act was hammered out in a long process of detailed face-to-face negotiations between Reagan and Robert Moretti, the new assembly speaker. The law tightened eligibility, contained stringent antifraud provisions and work requirements, and granted a one-third increase in AFDC payments. Although the job and training requirements failed to put many people to work, the AFDC caseload fell from 1.6 million to 1.3 million in three years. In addition, Reagan and Moretti agreed on a sales tax increase that, when added to federal revenue-sharing funds, enabled California to provide property tax relief and increase spending on elementary and secondary schools.

Reagan's achievements as governor were mixed from an ideological point of view. He signed a liberal abortion law in 1967, and taxes, spending, and the number of state employees all increased during his two terms, despite his continued anti-government rhetoric. Nonetheless, conservatives were thrilled by welfare reform and his handling of student protesters. Liberals, although usually disapproving of Reagan's ideas and rhetoric, found that his policies had neither brought the disasters they had predicted nor precluded progress in such key areas as education. Indeed, rather than dismantling California's government, Reagan turned out to be a competent governor who ran an efficient administration, preferred to reach deals rather than achieve nothing, and left the state running better than when he had arrived. Reagan appealed to voters across the spectrum and, as he neared the end of his term in 1974, a poll found that for every Californian who viewed him as a poor governor, two saw him as a good chief executive.[12]

After Reagan retired as governor, speculation soon began about whether he would run for president. His backers had considered him a possible presidential candidate as early as 1966 and, despite his later denials, Reagan was receptive to the idea. He made a run for the Republican nomination in 1968, but his campaign began too late and was too poorly run to have any hope of stopping Richard Nixon's drive to the White House. But by 1975 a Reagan candidacy was attractive to many Republicans. In the aftermath of Watergate and Nixon's resignation the party was desperate for new leaders, and Reagan's popularity made him a natural candidate. Nixon's successor, Gerald Ford, moreover, had angered many conservative Republicans by selecting Nelson Rockefeller, the former governor of New York and the leader of the party's liberal wing, as his vice president instead of Reagan, as well as by pursuing a foreign policy that they considered too accommodating to the Soviet Union. For his part, Reagan was disappointed that Ford had not offered him the vice presidency, shared the conservatives' policy views and belief that Ford was a weak leader, and was personally offended by what he viewed as Ford's attempts to buy his loyalty by offering him second-string jobs in the administration. Reagan began to view the president with contempt and considered Ford's policy problems—such as the economic troubles and expanding budget deficit inherited from Nixon—to be of his own making. In the summer of 1975, backers of the former governor formed a committee called Citizens for Reagan to begin organizing support for a presidential campaign. Reagan formally declared his candidacy on November 20, 1975.[13]

Reagan narrowly lost the nomination to Ford. Although polls before the New Hampshire primary showed Reagan ahead of the president in the state, Ford won a slender victory, 54,824 votes to 53,507. Ford then won in Florida and Illinois, and Reagan's cause seemed doomed. Hoping to gain an advantage, he began emphasizing his charge that the president was soft on the Soviets, had let America's military superiority decline, and was preparing to give away the Panama Canal. The theme caught on and helped him win the North Carolina primary, which restored his credibility as a candidate. Reagan went on to win in Texas, Nebraska, California, and several other southern and western states. Ford, however, won in the big states of Michigan, Ohio, and New Jersey. When the primaries ended in early June, Ford was only about thirty-seven delegates short of the majority required for the nomination, with Reagan still needing a hundred. Reagan made a last-ditch attempt to sway undecided delegates by announcing in July that he had chosen Richard Schweiker, a senator from Pennsylvania who had a liberal record on labor issues but opposed abortion and gun control, as his running mate. It was not enough, however, to overcome the president's advantages as an incumbent, and Ford won the nomination on the first ballot.

Even though Reagan lost, the 1976 campaign was an important step toward his victory in 1980. Reagan's performance in the primaries showed that his brand of conservatism, which combined a message of patriotic strength with his customary optimism, could attract close to a majority of Republicans from all parts of the country. The fact that he had come close to denying an incumbent president his party's nomination was further testimony to Reagan's appeal and solidified his position as conservatism's undisputed national leader. Finally, Ford's loss to the Democratic candidate, Jimmy Carter, in November, demonstrated that moderate and liberal Republicans could not win in a national race. Reagan, by all accounts, realized how strongly he had run and viewed his defeat as only a temporary setback—quoting the English poet John Dryden, he told the Republican convention, "I shall rise and fight again." Before 1976 was over, he and his staff had begun planning his 1980 campaign.[14]

When Jimmy Carter became president in January 1977, Ronald Reagan had been in public life for almost forty-four years. Looking over those years, several characteristics stand out to define him. Reagan was a man of great ability and ambition, one who set his goals and then worked carefully and hard to achieve them. Whether he was trying to break into radio, land a career-advancing movie role, or succeed in politics, he always seemed to know what he wanted and to have a plan for attaining it. He matched his ambition with patience. He was careful to master one set of goals or skills before trying to advance to the next level, as when he labored as a B-movie player before going after the part of George Gipp, or by stumping for General Electric and Republican candidates for a decade before running for office himself. He seems always to have waited until he was prepared and the moment was right and, as a result, he seldom overreached; the withering of his movie career in the late 1940s stands out as his only major setback. These factors help explain another of Reagan's most frequently noted traits, his optimism. While he and his biographers correctly point out that Reagan inherited his sunny disposition from his mother and his religion, it was also the outlook of a self-confident man who knew that he had achieved much.

In another sense, however, Reagan's life was not unusual. His journey from a small town in the Midwest to a city in California was a common one for his generation. In 1910, the year before he was born, the census found that 54 percent of the population lived in rural areas; by 1950, when Reagan was settled comfortably in Los Angeles, 64 percent of Americans lived in urban areas. California—especially Los Angeles—was a popular destination for midwesterners, and the state's population rose from 5.6 million in 1930 to 10.6 million in 1950; it stood at 20 million when Reagan finished his first term as governor in 1970. Although Reagan was much wealthier than most Californians, his prosperity reflected the state's booming economy. In 1940, California accounted for 6.4 percent of the nation's income, but by 1970 the Golden State's portion had increased to 11.1 percent. From the early years of the Republic, moreover, observers of American culture have noted that Americans are forward-looking and inclined to ignore the past. Reagan certainly fits in this mold. For him, the small-town life of his childhood had meant hardship, and he left as soon as he could, ultimately heading for the most modern city and industry in America. Nor did Reagan ever show any desire to return to his origins—"there never was a politician less interested in the past," wrote Edmund Morris. His conservatism did not embrace the conservative veneration of origins and modest, traditional living.[15]

Reagan was like his countrymen in other important ways. Although neither an intellectual nor a man given to deep reflection, Reagan was perfectly capable of thinking through complex issues and making up his mind, as the handwritten drafts of his letters and speeches show. His writings, moreover, show that Reagan had a simple model of the world that defined minimal government and liberal democracy as unquestionably good, Communism as absolutely evil, and success as available to anyone who worked hard; it was his version of what he later referred to as "that unique sense of destiny and optimism that had always made America different from any other country in the world," and he never lost his faith in it. The roots of these views go back to the settling of America, and when he celebrated private enterprise and individualism and warned about government, Reagan was giving voice to Americans' deepest ideals and beliefs about themselves.[16]

Reagan's views, however, were flexible and left room for expediency and compromise. In this, too, he was rooted in America's political traditions, which place little value on ideological consistency and instead reward compromise and deal making. In concrete terms this meant that he could campaign against the cost of government but still raise taxes without stumbling over the contradiction, or denounce welfare dependency while still raising benefits for the needy. In short, by not insisting on ideological coherence, Reagan could hold inconsistent views and thereby navigate the complexities of politics, policy, and compromise without losing his popularity.

1

PAVING THE WAY, 1945–1980

Ronald Reagan's sweeping victory in the presidential election on November 4, 1980, came as a surprise to many observers. Liberalism had dominated American politics for decades and shaped its institutions and assumptions, especially the belief that no politician who advocated reducing the size and role of the federal government could be elected president. Jimmy Carter, moreover, for all his economic and political troubles, had been running a close race. Through the fall of 1980, voters remained uncertain about Reagan's conservatism and lack of experience at the national level; as late as October 28, just a week before the election, a quarter of the electorate still had not made up their minds. On election day, however, Reagan buried Carter. The Republican took 43.9 million votes, or 51 percent of the total, and won forty-four states with 489 electoral votes, to Carter's 35.5 million, or 41 percent (independent John Anderson took 5.7 million votes). Reagan's strength carried over to the congressional races, where the Republicans gained thirteen Senate seats and took control of the chamber for the first time since 1954. The Democrats kept control of the House but suffered a net loss of thirty-three seats. Delighted conservatives and worried liberals alike described the results in terms generally reserved for upheavals abroad. To the editors of *National Review*, conservatism's leading intellectual and media platform, Reagan's election had been an "anti-liberal revolution," while in more understated terms the *Washington Post* described a "major shift of power to the GOP."[1]

As surprising as it may have seemed at the time, however, Reagan's election was not a bolt from the blue. For all its achievements, by 1980 liberalism had been in decline for almost fifteen years. Part of the reason for liberalism's fall was its internal decay, but it was hurt as well by demographic and economic forces that had been at work since 1945. Simultaneously, new conservative ideas had appeared and gained strength, gradually becoming credible political alternatives to liberal orthodoxies. This process unfolded slowly, and at times its implications were barely noticed. But in 1980 it led to the election of the most conservative president of the modern era.

Modern liberalism emerged in the late 1940s shaped by hard experiences. Liberals had had high hopes during World War II—they expected the suffering of war to be redeemed afterward by a resumption of the reform efforts of the New Deal, and eagerly awaited the chance to expand the government's economic role, achieve full employment, institute a range of social and civil rights reforms, and work with the Soviet Union to maintain international stability. None of these hopes were realized; at home, after almost two decades of upheaval and war, the American people proved uninterested in more large-scale change, while abroad relations with Moscow quickly turned hostile. In the roughly three years between the end of the war and President Harry Truman's victory in the 1948 election, liberals went through a bitter struggle as they decided how to respond to these realities. When it was over, Truman's moderate liberal supporters triumphed over the left-wing liberals—known as the Progressives—to establish the liberal mainstream as a cautiously reformist, strongly anti-Communist movement. Liberals still held to their ideals of achieving social and economic justice, but they understood that progress had to be gradual and made through compromises.[2]

In spite of these setbacks, postwar liberalism was marked by self-confidence and a belief in its own strength. Historian Arthur M. Schlesinger, Jr., defined and named this style of liberalism in his book *The Vital Center* (1949), describing it as a "fighting faith" that understood the realities of the world, was strengthened by struggle, rejected impractical idealism and dramatic posturing, and was unafraid to face and attack large problems. Schlesinger's view reflected those of his colleagues. Many liberal intellectuals of this generation—the writers and academics who generated and debated the ideas that informed political debates—had grown up poor, been involved with radical politics as young adults during the prewar years, and had served in the military or government during the war before fighting against the Progressives and Communists in the late 1940s. Like Schlesinger, they viewed themselves as toughened and stripped of illusions by their experiences. Their political battles against the totalitarianisms of both left and right, moreover, now led them to reject any politics based on a rigid ideology; instead, they viewed flexible democratic institutions as the key to a successful political order.[3]

During the almost two decades that it dominated American political life, vital center liberalism produced a rich intellectual legacy. The liberal intellectuals of this generation were among the most talented and perceptive historians, political scientists, and sociologists of the twentieth century. Although university based, they were not cloistered—many continued the activism of their youths, now working in liberal organizations and the Democratic Party and administrations. They also wrote for a general audience, publishing much of their best work in popular magazines and easily accessible books. In doing this, the vital center intellectuals drew on their experiences, as well as their research, to supply an explanation of how American politics and society work. The basic point of their interpretation was that from the beginning of the Republic, Americans had rejected ideological dispute in favor of broad agreement about major political questions. Richard Hofstadter, one of the most insightful and influential of the postwar historians, provided an early statement of this idea in his introduction to *The American Political Tradition* (1948). "However much at odds on specific issues, the major political traditions have shared a belief in the rights of property . . . economic individualism . . . competition . . . [and] capitalist culture as necessary qualities of man," he wrote. Most recently, they concluded, the consensus had evolved to support liberal views, creating broad national support for the modern welfare state and other changes that had grown out of the New Deal. Indeed, vital center liberals viewed this consensus as so broad that it left little room for dissenting views; they portrayed conservative and progressive critics alike as suffering from psychological disorders. Although their attacks on dissidents showed that they sometimes overstated the case, the vital center intellectuals' basic point was correct—American politics is governed by a centrist consensus that operates by compromise and evolves slowly to accommodate change—and their works still are valuable reading for understanding politics in the United States.[4]

Vital center liberalism unraveled with surprising speed after the mid-1960s, however. Signs of trouble first appeared in the late 1950s, as some liberal intellectuals began to complain of the boredom of their moderate role. The emergence of the civil rights movement, with its strong moral claims, excited them but also undermined support for political gradualism and compromise. This manifested itself during the early 1960s with liberals' frequent impatience with President Kennedy's cautious civil rights policies. Once Lyndon Johnson became president, however, liberal hopes for rapid social and economic progress soared—he secured passage of the Civil Rights Act of 1964, started the War on Poverty, crushed his conservative Republican challenger, Arizona senator Barry Goldwater, in 1964, and then secured passage of the Great Society legislation in 1965.[5]

Disillusion came swiftly. Johnson's programs had been enacted and implemented in haste and soon faced serious problems of cost and administration. Poor management led to large wastes of money, and liberals soon found that social problems proved to be more complicated and harder to solve than they had expected. At the same time, rising racial troubles, urban rioting, campus disorders, the growth of the anti-liberal New Left, and the war in Vietnam reduced popular support for liberal political proposals, leaving many vital center intellectuals feeling disoriented. Observing a conference of prominent liberals, including Schlesinger, in late 1968, one journalist noted that liberals "seemed at loose ends" and were more comfortable reviewing their past achievements than they were contemplating an uncertain future.[6]

Liberal intellectuals were unable to pick up the pieces of their movement. The intellectual community had expanded greatly since 1945—a consequence of the growth of colleges and universities—which meant that debates no longer could be shaped by a few dominant figures like Schlesinger or Hofstadter. Scores of writers, few of whom had the experience or analytical talents of their predecessors, vied for attention on every issue. Simultaneously, the civil rights movement and growing self-consciousness among minorities led the rising generation of historians, political scientists, and sociologists to shift the focus of their fields to examinations of small groups. The works of the 1950s that sought to provide a broad analytical framework for interpreting the past and present were replaced by narrowly focused studies that made increasing use of specialized quantitative methodologies and emphasized differences among groups rather than their similarities. Many leading intellectuals ceased writing for popular audiences and began to confine themselves to specialized academic journals, and the work of younger intellectuals, especially those on the left or following radical trends, often lacked rigor or offered glib conclusions that did not stand up to later critical scrutiny. Consequently, a vacuum began to develop at the center of liberal thought, and with neither a dominant analytical framework nor a desire to present readers with understandable conclusions that could be connected to current events, intellectuals gradually withdrew from their role of providing useful ideas to inform politics.[7]

The decades of the vital center's ascendancy and decline coincided with the suburbanization of American life. This was a set of great demographic, geographical, and economic shifts that, taken together, did much to pave the way for Reagan's election. In 1940, only 15 percent of Americans lived in suburbs, but the prosperity that followed World War II made it possible for masses of urban Americans to leave the cities. By 1950, 23 percent of the population lived in suburbs, and in 1970, 37 percent of Americans were suburbanites. In absolute numbers, this meant that the population of the suburbs had grown from 20 million people in 1940 to more than 75 million thirty years later, and that more people lived in suburbia than in either the cities or rural areas. Suburbanites had gone from being the smallest category of residential population to the largest, and were well on the way to becoming a majority of the population (see Table 1).[8]

The suburbanization of American life was part of a transformation and expansion of the middle class. The huge increase in college enrollments after World War II—one of liberalism's greatest achievements—meant that the people moving to the suburbs were better educated than any previous generation of Americans. Only 10 percent of adult Americans had been to college in 1940, and fewer than half of those actually had graduated, but the proportion of the adult population with one or more years of college reached 16 percent by 1960, and 21 percent a decade after that.

This led to a steady expansion of the number of people whose education enabled them to hold well-paying jobs—executives, managers, professionals, academics and teachers, engineers, administrators and government employees, technicians and, later, computer programmers and operators, to name some. By the mid-1970s, people in these and similar occupational categories outnumbered union members in the labor force and, by 1980, formed the largest segment of the workforce. They were smart, sophisticated, comfortable with complexity and new ideas—these were the people who formed the audience for the major intellectuals of the postwar era—and they flocked to the suburbs. "When the doors were thrown open in 1948," wrote *Fortune*'s William Whyte of the new Chicago suburb of Park Forest, the "first wave of colonists was heavy with academic and professional people." Urban-based critics soon began to attack the suburbs as sterile, discriminatory, conformist places that revolved around a culture of shopping and consumption, but they missed the point. The millions of Americans who left the cities in the years after World War II made the suburbs into vibrant communities where, in most cases, they happily raised families in comfortable surroundings.[9]

Suburbanization made middle-class politics increasingly complicated. Many political scientists at first expected the new suburbanites, who had grown up as Democrats in the cities, to vote Republican when they relocated, reflecting their new affluence and property interests. This appeared to be borne out by the suburban majorities for Eisenhower in 1952 and 1956. On closer examination, however, these votes appeared to be driven more by Ike's personal popularity than by changing party identifications. As political scientists gathered more data, they saw that voting patterns varied greatly from one suburb to another, and in many cases voters had retained their urban Democratic preferences. By the 1960s, it was becoming evident that no blanket statement could be made about suburban political preferences.[10]

The confusion about suburban politics gradually was resolved as it became evident that suburbanites had few fixed political loyalties. It was true, for example, that many of their characteristics pointed toward liberalism and continuing to vote Democratic. The Democrats were the traditional party of white ethnics—especially Jews—who were leaving the cities. They had warm memories of the New Deal, union struggles, and the benefits bestowed by urban machines. New suburbanites furthermore understood that it was Democratic programs that had made home mortgages easily available to the masses, and many of those with college degrees had been educated in the ideas of the vital center while the GI Bill paid their tuition. Their liberalism persisted long after they arrived in suburbia—Levittown, New Jersey, became desegregated in the early 1960s without trouble, for example—and public opinion research found that suburbanites supported liberalism well into the 1970s, backing the civil rights movement, the Great Society, and expansions of individual rights.[11]

These liberal tendencies coexisted with newly developed conservative traits, however. The educated middle class and professionals of the suburbs had said their farewells to the cities, and they soon lost interest in urban problems and, just as important, the plight of those who were unable to leave. Once in suburbia, their expectations for government competence rose, and their demand to receive good value for their tax dollars made them impatient with public programs that did not deliver promised results. The suburban landscape made a contribution of its own to the growth of conservative attitudes. The detached homes, large yards, and dependence on cars to get around increased privacy but also reduced contacts among people and the sense of a shared space. Paradoxically, then, suburbanites had grown comfortable with the wider world while at the same time becoming more inward-looking at home.[12]

The full effects of these contradictory tendencies were not felt until much later, but political scientists first glimpsed some of their implications as early as the mid-1950s. Simply put, educated people living in low-density suburbs became more independent in their voting than urban voters who still responded to the directions of political machines. One researcher in Philadelphia, who doubled as a Democratic ward leader, wrote in 1955 that suburbanites were independent thinkers who rejected any sort of political control. Indeed, the growing suburban population felt far more free than their parents to pick and choose among candidates and parties rather than vote a straight ticket. In practical terms, this meant that by the early 1970s the votes of educated suburbanites were up for grabs, as they continued to hold liberal views on social and personal issues while becoming ever more skeptical of ambitious programs like the Great Society or proposed government solutions to economic problems.[13]

The pace of suburbanization slowed in the 1970s, but forecasters predicted another wave in the near future that would further complicate middle-class politics. By 1975, sociologists were projecting that the next stage of expansion would take place in the undeveloped land on the fringes of the suburbs, which would be connected first by the interstate highways and then by new communications technologies that would make it easy to transfer information over long distances. As part of this trend, sociologist Daniel Bell, in his prophetic *The Coming of Post-Industrial Society* (1973), predicted the economy increasingly would be based on the creation and manipulation of information; in such an environment, professionals and managers who were comfortable working with constantly expanding knowledge and rapidly changing technologies would be the dominant class.[14]

But even as suburbanites became connected to the wider world, they were expected to remain inward-looking in important ways. Soon, most would be born in the suburbs, spend their lives with other suburbanites, and have little experience of or interest in the cities. Although liberal in many of their beliefs, they would not have much concern for addressing broader social issues. Such forecasts underscored the political impact of three decades of suburbanization. The suburban middle and professional classes had developed into a dynamic and confident group, one whose members were comfortable with social change and new technologies, and had few doubts about their abilities to cope with complexity and decide for themselves what was in their best interests. In line with American political traditions, they judged politics and politicians by results, not ideological consistency. As their confidence indicated, they did not hesitate to try new ideas if they promised to work better than the old.[15]

Postwar liberalism owed much of its political success to its economic achievements. With the new orthodoxy of Keynesian economics guiding government policy, gross national product (GNP) grew at an average rate of 2.8 percent per year from 1945 to 1960, and living standards—as the mass migration to the suburbs indicated—rose dramatically for almost all Americans. From 1960 to 1965, as liberalism's power and prestige reached their peaks, a combination of tax cuts and increased government spending brought GNP growth to an annual average of 4.8 percent. At the close of

1965 unemployment stood at just 4.2 percent of the labor force, while the consumer price index (CPI) had risen only 1.7 percent for the year. Liberals celebrated, as *Time* put it, the skill with which government economists had been able to "prod, goad, and inspire a rich and free nation to climb to nearly full employment and unprecedented prosperity."[16]

Events during the next decade, however, steadily discredited the idea that the government could manage the economy successfully. By the second half of 1965, spending had begun for the Great Society and, at the same time, the Vietnam War brought a sharp increase in defense expenditures. Driven by the increase in aggregate demand, the boom continued but inflation began to rise—the CPI increased by 2.9 percent in 1966, 3.1 percent in 1967, and 4.2 percent in 1968. From then through the mid-1970s the combination of oil price increases, popular expectations of more inflation, and poor economic management in Washington—including Richard Nixon's ill-advised wage and price controls—led to worsening inflation even as GNP growth slowed and unemployment gradually rose. In another troubling development, it started to become apparent that productivity growth had slowed dramatically since 1973, suggesting a lower long-term growth rate for living standards.[17]

The middle and professional classes detested inflation. They often had been the first in their families to go to college and, while grateful for the government programs that had helped them, they were determined to guard their material achievements. Rising inflation, however, directly threatened their financial security—it eroded the value of their assets, raised the prices of the items that mattered most to them, such as mortgages and college tuition, and threatened to reduce their real incomes. Unlike unionized workers, professionals did not have contracts that gave them automatic raises to match rising prices; in the 1970s, many professionals' incomes barely kept up with inflation—college professors, for example, saw their incomes fall by 15 percent. Those who did receive salary increases, moreover, often found themselves pushed into higher income-tax brackets where much of their gain was lost; indeed, the combination of inflation and "bracket creep" often meant that real returns on savings and investments were negative. Newspaper and magazine articles reflected middle-class concerns, debating the causes and cures of inflation, reporting on how ordinary Americans were affected by it, and

offering tips on how to invest in an inflationary environment. Of equal
concern to the middle and professional classes, as *Newsweek* reported in
a fourteen-page supplement in May 1978, was that inflation took "a toll
in national morality," as the importance of planning for the future was
overtaken by the need to make short-term gains, while simultaneously
creating growing incentives to cheat on taxes.[18]

Another consequence of rising inflation was that it undermined a long-
held orthodoxy of liberal economics, that government regulation of industries and markets enabled experts to protect the public from abusive
practices or other, unintended, malfunctions in a market economy. Regulation had begun in the late 1800s, in response to predatory behavior
by railroads, and then grew slowly during the early twentieth century
before expanding rapidly during the New Deal. By the 1940s, regulators
had gained enormous authority over major industries—the Interstate
Commerce Commission regulated trucking to protect railroads; the Civil
Aeronautics Authority (later the Civil Aeronautics Board), controlled
entry into the airline industry, fares, and routes; and AT&T controlled
the nation's telephone system while the Federal Communications Commission and the states oversaw its rates. But the justification for such extensive control started to crack in the 1960s and 1970s. Economists began
a rigorous examination of regulation and found it responsible for creating large inefficiencies and inflated costs, even as it failed to prevent col-
lusion among firms—or promoted price fixing—and encouraged large
misallocations of capital. In *The Economics of Regulation* (1971), a two-
volume study that has became a classic, Cornell University economist
Alfred Kahn summarized the economists' findings. "Regulation," he
wrote, "tends inherently to be protective of monopoly, passive, negative,
and unimaginative."[19]

These costs remained hidden, and therefore acceptable, until inflation
and slower growth made clear regulation's effects on the lives of the middle and professional classes. The problem first became an issue as a result
of inflation's damage to middle-class savings. Depression-era laws gave
the Federal Reserve authority to regulate the rate of interest banks paid
for savings deposits, and under its Regulation Q the Fed kept rates low to
provide banks with a source of cheap funds for loans. By 1970, however,
with Regulation Q capping interest at 4.5 percent even while inflation

reached almost 6 percent, money in savings accounts was losing value. To protect banks from withdrawals, the Treasury made it more difficult for individual savers to buy Treasury bills, which paid market rates, and thereby left many middle-class depositors with no way to protect their savings. Soon, however, financial entrepreneurs began seeking a way to get around the rules. Two investment managers in New York saw the potential business in helping small savers by creating a new type of mutual fund to buy T-bills, certificates of deposit, and other interest-bearing securities whose yields stayed ahead of inflation; shares would pay dividends based on the yields of the underlying securities. The Securities and Exchange Commission, not quite knowing what to make of the new device, took about two years to approve it, but once it did in late 1972 the money market fund was born. As inflation accelerated, the funds became more popular. In 1976, money market funds held $3 billion; two years later, the total reached $10 billion; by 1980, money market funds held more than $75 billion, and their high yields were crucial to middle-class savers seeking to protect their assets.[20]

Removing federal regulations went from subterfuge to a formal process in the mid-1970s, as first Wall Street brokerage commissions and then airlines were deregulated. The New York Stock Exchange had operated as a cartel since its founding in 1792, with brokers' commissions set according to a fixed schedule. The exchange and the brokerage industry had fended off past efforts to end the system, claiming that negotiated commissions would lead to ruinous competition and destroy their business. Under intense pressure from the government, however, the stock exchange agreed to abolish fixed commissions starting on May 1, 1975, a date known ever since on Wall Street as May Day. Within a month, commissions on large trades by institutions had dropped by as much as 60 percent, and discount brokerage houses appeared soon after, providing individual retail customers with cut-rate service. Airline deregulation came next, stimulated in large part by an investigation sponsored by Senator Edward M. Kennedy (D-Mass.) that revealed the high fares and gross inefficiencies promoted by the Civil Aeronautics Board's rules. Additional studies found that deregulating fares could save customers some $2 billion per year. Against strong protests and predictions of disaster by the major airlines—the the board had neither licensed a new airline since 1948 nor allowed any to go broke—the Ford administration decided to back deregulation. The board began easing its restrictions on fares, and by the fall of 1977 a nationwide price war was under way. Meanwhile, in early 1977, Alfred Kahn became chairman of the Civil Aeronautics Board. Under Kahn, the board encouraged and quickly approved applications for new routes and fare cuts of up to 50 percent as the airlines battled for passengers—"that's a good afternoon's work," said Kahn when an aide told him he had destroyed the fare structure for the North Atlantic routes.[21]

Deregulation had far-reaching benefits for both consumers and companies forced to respond to competition. To attract deposits and help customers maintain the value of their funds, banks began introducing new products, such as interest-bearing checking accounts, and discussion arose of abolishing Regulation Q altogether. On Wall Street, with commissions reflecting the real costs of trades and services, brokerages began providing customers with choices among service levels and new products. As part of this trend, Merrill Lynch, the largest retail brokerage house, in 1977 began offering the Cash Management Account, which paid interest on the cash in customers' accounts and provided checking and credit card privileges—features that were astonishing at the time but now are standard at almost all brokerages. Lower commissions quickly brought a surge in trading and, instead of ruin, Wall Street soon enjoyed a boom. The story was the same for the airlines. By late 1977, about one-third of passengers were traveling on discounted tickets, and the proportion reached 50 percent in mid-1978; the airlines filled more of their seats and doubled their profits in the same period. In late 1978, Congress passed the Airline Deregulation Act, which formally ended the old regulatory structure and revolutionized air travel—new airlines began operation, while established airlines dropped unprofitable routes, added flights where they saw greater demand, began expanding their use of hubs to gain greater efficiencies, and started frequent flier programs to build customer loyalty. Success also led to demands for deregulation in other industries. Trucking was deregulated in 1980—that industry, too, resisted deregulation, but once it happened shipping rates quickly plunged as thousands of new firms appeared—and pressure began building to end AT&T's monopoly on telephone service.[22]

At the same time that inflation and deregulation had been undermining the rationales for long-established policies, conservative economic ideas had been gaining popular acceptance. Conservatives had long denounced Keynesian economics as a fraud that undermined both economic and political freedom, but their spokesmen were generally dismissed as cranks during the long period of postwar prosperity. It was not until the 1960s, as liberalism's troubles began to mount, that a conservative emerged who could combine strong economic credentials with skill at publicizing free-market ideas. This was Milton Friedman, who in his academic work had developed a strong, coherent critique of Keynesian theory that won the grudging respect of his liberal opponents. Friedman also was a cheerful, irrepressible man who argued that, because it gave free rein to the abilities of individuals, free-market capitalism had the power to liberate people and bring prosperity to whole societies by allowing them to pursue their ideas and creativity. In Friedman's view—and here his argument was the same as almost all other conservatives'—capitalism's benefits would be greatest if the state's regulatory role were restricted to providing a basic legal framework in which free markets could operate with minimal government interference.[23]

Friedman made free-market ideas available and acceptable for a mass audience. He tirelessly publicized his arguments for economic and personal freedom in campus lectures, popular books, and, starting in 1966, as a columnist for *Newsweek*. His views remained anathema to liberals—when he received the Nobel Prize for economics in 1976, the *New Republic* described him as a "hyperactive extremist of the right"—but by the end of the 1970s Friedman's critiques of Keynes, his early predictions of worsening inflation, and the success of deregulation made his arguments impossible to dismiss. Indeed, in 1980 his book *Free to Choose,* a summary of his views for general audiences, was a best-seller and the basis for a series on public television.[24]

Inflation, deregulation, and Friedman's efforts combined, in turn, to create the atmosphere in which supply-side economic theory was able to became politically strong in a relatively short time. Supply-side theory was a blend of classical economics and modern libertarianism that its advocates claimed would be able to solve the problems of inflation, unemployment, and slow growth through the power of free markets.

The core of supply-side economics was the work of relatively obscure academic economists, but was popularized by Jude Wanniski, an editorial writer for the *Wall Street Journal* who had no training in economics. The supply-side view, as Wanniski first explained it in 1975, held that the "incentives and motivations of the individual producer and consumer and merchant are . . . the keystone of economic policy." The resultant policy prescription, laid out in the op-ed pages of the *Journal* and in the conservative policy magazine *Public Interest,* was presented as simple and painless. The reduction of artificial barriers and disincentives to production—that is, lowering taxes and eliminating regulations—and the use of monetary restraint, preferably through a return to the gold standard to maintain the value of money, would stimulate the production of goods and end inflation. This, in turn, would lead employers to hire more workers, thus lowering unemployment; the resulting economic expansion soon would generate enough tax revenues to more than pay for the original tax cuts. Wanniski provided a full explanation of supply-side theory in his book *The Way the World Works* (1978), but it was George Gilder, another noneconomist and supply-side publicist, who summarized the theory's promise most succinctly: "By altering the pattern of rewards to favor work over leisure . . . government can directly and powerfully foster the expansion of real demand and income."[25]

Supply-siders admitted that these ideas largely restated existing free-market theories. The supply side's original contribution, however, was to add a moral strand to free-market economics. Wanniski and Gilder viewed Keynesian economics and state interference with free markets as causing the moral degradation of society. Excessive taxation and regulation, Wanniski claimed, drove women to prostitution, fed all manner of criminal enterprises, and even was responsible for the outbreak of World War II. Gilder believed that capitalism would thrive only by embracing risk and uncertainty, gathering courage from faith in God and the future; the secular state, said Gilder, because it is terrified of the unknown, institutes planning rather than allowing the faithful to "accept the risk of failure and death" in pursuit of their dreams. Embracing supply-side policies, Wanniski and Gilder concluded, would reverse moral decline and, along with prosperity, bring people closer to God. The supply side's moral streak made it attractive for people seeking ideological fulfillment—for them, it was something to believe in passionately. David Stockman, a young Republican congressman from Michigan and a disillusioned veteran of 1960s radicalism, captured their feelings when he later wrote that with his discovery of the supply side, "I began to feel as if I were part of a movement. My revolutionary fires had been rekindled once again."[26]

Mainstream economists were dismissive of the supply side. To liberals, the theory was based on a misreading of both economics and history, while its claims of simple solutions to complicated problems seemed to promise a free lunch. Conservative economists looking at it frequently were unimpressed or even suspicious, despite the debt the supply side owed to their ideas. Friedman never lent his support to the supply-side economists, even though their goals for reduced regulation and taxation were the same as his, and Herbert Stein—a prominent conservative who had been chairman of Nixon's Council of Economic Advisers—was especially dismissive. He gave little credence to the supply side's claim that it could quickly and easily solve all economic and moral problems. "There is little evidence that gains will be as large, as prompt, and as free of costs as the public is being promised," he wrote in late 1979.[27]

Whatever the misgivings of professional economists, tax-cutting proposals proved their political potency in June 1978, when California voters passed Proposition 13. Inflation had been rapidly increasing real estate values and hence taxes; many Golden State homeowners, even as their incomes lagged behind inflation, had seen their property tax bills double since 1975. Proposition 13 called for limiting property taxes to 1 percent of market value, rolling back assessments, and limiting future increases—all together, an estimated $7 billion tax cut. The battle over Proposition 13 was eerily similar to those over airline and brokerage deregulation, as a broad coalition of opponents warned that cutting taxes would bring disaster. Liberals claimed that schools and other services would be devastated, the speaker of the State Assembly talked of laying off 150,000 state employees, and a UCLA economist forecast a statewide loss of 450,000 jobs. On June 6, however, the voters ignored the warnings and passed Proposition 13 with 65 percent of the vote.[28]

The voters were right. With Proposition 13 taking effect on July 1, localities began preparing for massive service cuts and firings—Los

Angeles County, for example, made plans to lay off half its 73,000 employees, including 40 percent of its firefighters. But the axe never fell. The State of California had a multibillion-dollar surplus in 1978, and Sacramento quickly allocated $4.2 billion to help local governments cope with the sudden loss of revenue. California's economy was booming, moreover, and in the year following the passage of Proposition 13, the state gained 500,000 jobs with an attendant boost in tax revenues. Most government job cuts that were necessary often were made simply by not hiring replacements as workers quit or retired, although actual layoffs reached 20,000. Budget cuts were greatest for libraries, recreation, and cultural programs but, according to a state report issued in February 1979, almost no public school teachers had been laid off. It was evident, as the *New York Times* reported a year after the vote, that opponents of Proposition 13 had "exaggerated the problems they would face." (California, of course, eventually faced a fiscal crisis, but it did not come until 2002, and Proposition 13 by then was only one of many factors that helped cause it.)[29]

Proposition 13 demonstrated the political force of the supply-side idea, and conservative politicians quickly realized that it was a powerful weapon against liberalism. But the supply side in 1980 was not as revolutionary as some of its promoters claimed. In part, this was a matter of familiarity—Friedman's ideas for reducing government had become well enough known to make people comfortable with their supply-side cousins. In addition, because of the failure of successive administrations' anti-inflation policies, it was harder to dismiss unorthodox economic thinking. Meanwhile, the supply side's two major tenets—deregulation and tax cuts—had been tried on a limited basis and found to bring benefits without drastic upheaval, and were starting to become mainstream ideas. Politicians were quick to see the implications. Soon after Proposition 13 passed, talk of more tax revolts spread around the country. The Republican Party endorsed a long-standing proposal by Congressman Jack Kemp of New York and Senator William Roth of Delaware for a 30 percent federal income tax reduction (Kemp had been one of the first politicians to become a supply-side believer), and presidential candidate Ronald Reagan began to receive supply-side briefings.[30]

As conservatives united around supply-side ideas, the Democrats remained badly divided. The troubles of the Great Society, combined with continuing factional battles spurred by the reforms that followed the 1968 election and the disastrous showing of George McGovern in the 1972 campaign—as well as the need to develop credible policies for dealing with inflation and social issues—led to bitter arguments in the party. On the left, some were moving toward democratic socialism, advocating the nationalization of major industries and large corporations, heavy taxation, and increased spending on housing, health care, and transportation. In the middle, moderate liberals were paralyzed by uncertainty, hoping to protect and improve the programs of the Great Society but also well aware of the public's skepticism of such policies. The conservative wing of the party, for its part, had lost almost all influence; many of its figures joined the Republicans in the early 1980s. In a stark illustration of the party's problems, liberal Democrats met in Chicago in March 1975 to consider their strategy for 1976, but after two days of discussions they could not agree on an agenda or which candidates to support. Political analyst Richard Reeves summarized the situation a few months later when he noted that "there is no such thing as the Democratic Party, at least nothing that can be identified any more as a functioning . . . political organization."[31]

Jimmy Carter shrewdly exploited these divisions when he ran for president in 1976. Born in 1924, and elected governor of Georgia in 1970, Carter was a hard worker who mastered the complex details of legislation and administration. His policies were moderately reformist and technocratic—reforming the structure of the state government was Carter's major effort as governor, and he also instituted new services for the handicapped and backed tax reform, environmental protection, and the development of new budgetary procedures. In the 1976 Democratic primaries, while his rivals for the nomination based their campaigns on appeals to particular party blocs, Carter used his background to portray himself as a moderate who could reach out across factional lines while, at the same time, stressing his personal integrity. Carter continued this strategy in the fall campaign, speaking to his audiences with vague promises and comforting language that avoided alienating any bloc and enabled each group of listeners to assume that he agreed with them.[32]

As president, Carter tried to apply this noncommittal approach to economic policy but wound up in a muddle. He began by working to stimulate growth through tax cuts, public works spending, and jobs programs, and by the end of 1977 he could boast of creating several hundred thousand new jobs. But inflation began to pick up, too, and Carter soon faced a hard choice between continuing to encourage growth and lower unemployment, or cutting spending and accepting higher jobless rates to fight inflation. Whichever he chose, Carter would anger either the middle and professional classes or liberals, labor, and blacks. In response, Carter tried to steer a middle course by reducing and delaying a planned tax cut, and urging voluntary wage and price restraints. His measures accomplished nothing, and by the fall of 1978 inflation was steadily accelerating. In early November, the administration was forced to raise interest rates sharply and begin planning budget cuts to show that it was serious about fighting inflation. Things became even worse in 1979, when the revolution in Iran led to fuel shortages and dramatic increases in oil prices—by midsummer, inflation had risen to about 1 percent per month and showed no sign of slowing.[33]

In July 1979, Carter appointed a new Federal Reserve chairman, Paul Volcker, who finally took strong action. Volcker quickly slowed monetary growth and let interest rates skyrocket—the prime rate was more than 18 percent by April 1980. At the same time, however, Carter continued to avoid taking painful steps of his own. In January 1980, with inflation still running at more than 1 percent a month, he submitted a budget calculated to appease congressional liberals by raising spending on jobs and social programs. Few people, especially in the financial community, viewed the budget as a serious commitment to fighting inflation, and interest rates continued to rise. In March, Carter tried to recoup by submitting a revised budget that included more spending cuts and tax increases, and also announcing restrictions on the use of credit. But it was too late. Just six months before the 1980 presidential election, the economy slipped into a recession even as inflation continued at a double-digit rate. Moreover, congressional Democrats and liberals, infuriated by his budget cuts and willingness to sacrifice employment to combat inflation, began to desert Carter.

As Carter's troubles mounted, liberal intellectuals began to express a deep pessimism about the capabilities of America's democratic institutions. "Our political institutions do not match the scales of economic and social reality," said Daniel Bell. "The national state has become too small for the big problems of life and too big for the small problems." Intellectuals viewed the government's apparent ineffectiveness as the result of political changes since the late 1960s, and especially of the weakening of the parties and fragmentation of power in Washington that followed. They wrote frequently of how organized interest groups blocked sensible policymaking, crippled political leaders, and predicted that the problems only would worsen during the 1980s.[34]

Growing despair about America's governability led liberal intellectuals down an unfortunate analytical path. They began by deciding that America's ruling institutions needed a complete overhaul, one borrowing from foreign models. The most prominent and influential advocate of this view was Harvard sociologist Ezra Vogel, an East Asia specialist and the author of *Japan as Number 1* (1979). Vogel contrasted the United States, whose political system had been established in 1789, with Japan, which since 1945 had created more modern democratic institutions. As he surveyed the structures of Japanese politics, business, and society, Vogel concluded that the United States had much to learn from the Japanese, who he believed had found a way for elites, business, government, and the general population to identify and solve problems through study and consensus rather than American-style competition. Japanese economic policy, Vogel pointed out, was especially successful because all parties "knew that no single group's interests would be placed ahead of the others'," and he advocated adopting this system of centralized, technocratic, consensus-based policymaking. Japan was not the only source of ideas for government reform. Others pointed out, for example, how the division of power between the president and Congress often prevented the chief executive from achieving his political goals and proposed overhauling the Constitution to adopt a European parliamentary model, in which the president could dissolve Congress and call for new legislative elections. This, it was claimed, would ensure the effectiveness of government by granting the same party control of both the White House and Congress.[35]

Such proposals said much about the state of liberal thinking. They showed a growing anxiety about foreigners—which became a hallmark of liberalism during the 1980s—and an assumption that others had figured out something about how to run a society that eluded Americans. Tellingly, these proposals assumed that foreign ways could be transplanted easily to America, and so their authors gave no consideration to the uncomfortable questions of what disadvantages might be inherent in adopting systems developed in different cultures, or that gave far more power to the central government than Americans ever had allowed. Indeed, they betrayed a desire to avoid politics—either by placing authority in the hands of technocrats or by reducing the power of the president's opponents—that helped spare the intellectuals from having to explain how their ideas would work, gain popular support, and be put into action.

Another group of intellectuals questioning the implications of the declining effectiveness of American government was the popular economists. These figures generally were not the most influential among academic economists, but by virtue of their talents as publicists they did much to shape the views of broader audiences. The best example is MIT professor Lester Thurow, who, in his best-selling book *The Zero-Sum Society* (1980), produced a compelling catalog of the country's economic ills, including slow growth, inflation, regulation, and environmental problems. He pointed out that, although solutions existed for all of these problems, each required large sacrifices from individuals and groups before society realized widespread benefits. Taking advantage of the fragmentation of power to protect their interests, said Thurow in one example, potential losers used the political process to block agreement, and "as a consequence, none of the possible solutions can be adopted." But Thurow had no solutions to offer. He advanced a few familiar policy proposals to address the country's ills—including new public works programs, tax reform, and jobs programs—but his belief that politics precluded their adoption made them appear half-hearted. As a result, Thurow was only able to call for vaguely defined political reforms to end the paralysis, but without providing any useful description of what the reforms would be or how they would operate.[36]

This style of political thinking, which recalled the empty posturing Schlesinger had condemned in *The Vital Center*, had serious consequences for the Democrats. Carter, who was badly in need not only of good policy advice but also of an intellectual framework in which to make his decisions, was the first casualty. In the spring of 1979, with his popularity falling as he groped for policies to deal with inflation and the fuel shortages, Carter began paying attention to the argument that the United States was undergoing a psychological and political crisis. As he prepared a major address on energy policy, Carter mulled over the nation's mood and consulted with politicians, intellectuals, and ordinary citizens. The result, on July 15, was one of the strangest speeches ever given by an American president. Carter introduced his energy initiatives with a long discussion of his administration's and the country's problems, and a description of the crisis of confidence he said afflicted the country. It was, he said, a "crisis that strikes at the very heart and soul and spirit of our national will," and that had caused a loss of faith in government and the ability of "citizens to serve as the ultimate rulers and shapers of our democracy." Reflecting his own deep spirituality, Carter also took Americans to task for being self-indulgent. "We've learned that piling up material goods cannot fill the emptiness of lives which have no confidence or purpose," he said.[37]

The speech was politically suicidal. Carter had taken the very real worries of ordinary Americans and described them as selfish and short-sighted. Polls taken immediately after the speech showed widespread agreement with Carter's diagnosis of the nation's ills, but once the country realized that he was blaming the people for these failings his popularity resumed its decline. As the *New Republic* noted in early August, "the past two weeks will be remembered as the period when President Jimmy Carter packed it in, put the finishing touches on a failed presidency."[38]

Carter's troubles appeared to present the Democrats' liberal wing with a historic opportunity. As they grew increasingly angry with Carter in 1979, liberals turned to Ted Kennedy, believing that if he ran for president the people would rally to the liberal cause. Polls of Democrats showed Kennedy with a substantial lead over Carter, and with his own dislike of the president growing steadily, Kennedy decided at the end of the summer that he would run in 1980. He announced his candidacy in Boston on November 7, denouncing Carter for not providing leadership while claiming that "the country . . . is ready to advance . . . and so am I."[39]

Kennedy's campaign soon ran into trouble. Not all the problems were his fault. Just before his announcement, Iranian mobs had overrun the U.S. embassy in Tehran and taken the staff hostage, and in December the Soviet Union invaded Afghanistan. The resulting atmosphere of crisis boosted Carter's popularity as Americans rallied around the president. But Kennedy's biggest difficulties were of his own making and revealed the extent of liberalism's deterioration. Most of Kennedy's major campaign advisers and high-ranking staff either were veterans of John F. Kennedy's administration, Robert Kennedy's 1968 campaign, or were Kennedy family retainers. They clung to the hopes of 1960s liberalism but had not played serious political roles for twelve years. It soon became clear that neither they nor Kennedy himself had a clear idea of how to deal with the country's problems or even why—except for a dislike of Carter—he was running. In an interview broadcast on CBS on November 4, correspondent Roger Mudd asked Kennedy why he wanted to be president, and the senator's reply to this elementary question was so rambling and incoherent that the *Washington Post* said, "Even the fiercest Kennedy partisan would have to concede the inadequacy of the senator's answer."[40]

Kennedy's main campaign theme was his criticism of Carter's inflation policies. Day after day, he denounced budget austerity as too harsh on the poor and the working class. "We must not fight the battle of inflation on the backs of the poor and black and Hispanic and inner-city youth," he told a crowd in Chicago in a typical speech. Kennedy instead proposed wage and price controls, fuel rationing, and expanding social programs without regard for balancing the budget. None of this was new or credible in 1980, especially to middle-class professionals, but liberal intellectuals had nothing else to propose. The results were predictable. In the winter and spring of 1980, Carter, with the advantages of incumbency and popular support during a time of crisis, pounded Kennedy in almost every caucus or primary, and the senator's challenge collapsed in May.[41]

Liberals marked their defeat by throwing a tantrum, albeit one that had been building for some time. Writing in the *New Republic* in April 1980, Schlesinger recited the president's failings at home and abroad, quoted Carter's statement in 1978 that "government cannot solve our problems," and thundered, "Can anyone imagine Franklin D. Roosevelt talking this way?" Schlesinger went on to praise the Democratic Party of Truman, John Kennedy, and Lyndon Johnson, but for the present he offered no idea of what to do other than get rid of Jimmy Carter. Thirty years after the author of *The Vital Center* had given it direction, postwar liberalism had run out of ideas.[42]

Ronald Reagan began the 1980 race as the favorite for the Republican nomination. His experience in a presidential campaign, the loyalty of his supporters, and his familiarity to voters gave him important advantages going into the primaries, where he was part of a crowded field. Although the Republican Party had been moving to the right during the 1970s, the competition for the nomination also included several moderate Republicans, the liberal congressman John Anderson, and another well-known conservative, Representative Philip Crane. Reagan's major disadvantage was that supply-side economics remained untried at the national level and suspect in the eyes of many Republicans—George Bush, one of the moderate candidates, called it "voodoo economics," a label that has stuck to this day. But Reagan's preparation and organization enabled him to prevail quickly. Except for Bush, who hung on until May 26 and subsequently accepted the vice-presidential nomination, Reagan had defeated his rivals by the end of March.

Reagan followed a simple strategy for the fall campaign against Carter. He focused relentlessly on the president's economic record, always reinforcing the voters' perception that conditions had become steadily worse during Carter's term. "Interest rates and inflation have become unconscionably high . . . two million Americans have lost their jobs this year alone," he said in Chicago on September 9. "There is only one phrase to describe the last three years and eight months. It has been an American tragedy." Reagan's proposed solutions were unadorned conservative ideas that avoided the expansive promises of the supply side—tax cuts, reduced government spending and regulation, and a predictable monetary policy.[43]

Reagan also was careful to moderate his statements and tone. His campaign aides worked to undercut charges that Reagan was a conservative extremist by building a public image of a warm, caring man. Reagan's public pronouncements were sunny and optimistic, reflecting his personal belief that the United States was a land of opportunity filled with honest, hard-working people for whom anything was possible. "It is impossible to capture in words the splendor of this vast continent which God has granted as our portion of His creation," he told the Republican convention. "There are no words to express the extraordinary strength and character of this breed of people we call Americans." In keeping with this strategy, Reagan did not provide too many details of his policy proposals but instead continually assured voters that cutting government spending would not affect Social Security, and that his commitment to strength also included a passionate desire for peace. In addition, he was careful not to appear to be a rigid supply-side ideologue, telling *Washington Post* interviewers that the plan to cut taxes by 30 percent was a flexible target, subject to economic and budgetary conditions. The strategy spared Reagan hostile media treatment. The *Washington Post* noted in October, for example, that Reagan was not one to let principles override flexibility, and that everyone who knew him had "concluded that he is a nice guy, a happy secure person who likes himself and most other people."[44]

Well aware of his slipping support and hardly able to run on a record of success, Carter fell back on a strategy of portraying Reagan as an inexperienced and dangerous reactionary. Beginning with his acceptance speech at the Democratic convention in August, Carter denounced Reagan's economic proposals as promising "rebates to the rich, deprivation for the poor, and fierce inflation for all of us." Carter kept up the criticism during the fall, labeling Reagan a warmonger and a racist who would pit Americans against one another along racial, religious, and sectional lines. Carter portrayed himself, in contrast, as a tested leader who understood the responsibilities of office. He could offer, he told the convention, "no easy answers," and said that his "heart is burdened for . . . the poor, the jobless, and the afflicted."[45]

Carter's attacks kept him in the race until close to the end, setting up a moment of high drama when he and Reagan met to debate on October 28.

The two men faced each other on the stage, each using his answers to repeat campaign themes and promises. But more important, their personal qualities were on display. Carter showed his detailed knowledge of issues and continued to attack Reagan as a dangerous man, but also showed an unappealing streak of self-pity—"it's a lonely job," he said of the presidency. Reagan good-naturedly deflected Carter's thrusts and came across as a relaxed, friendly, and optimistic figure who was hardly the demon portrayed by Carter. But Reagan's best moment came at the end, during his closing statement, as he famously asked viewers, "Are you better off than you were four years ago?" In that moment he summarized everything that had gone wrong under Carter in terms that any American could relate to, and effectively ended the campaign. Within hours, both campaigns' polls showed undecided voters turning heavily toward Reagan, giving him a margin over Carter that grew steadily each day until November 4.[46]

The belief that Reagan's victory represented the start of a revolution overstated the case, however. Polling data available soon after the election showed that the voters had repudiated Carter without giving Reagan their complete support. Carter was rejected because of his poor economic record, according to polls taken on election day and during the following week, and the voters' sense that it was time for a change. Many who voted for Reagan, moreover, indicated that these were their only reasons for voting Republican, and that they did not identify themselves as conservatives or members of the GOP. Beyond agreeing with Reagan's most basic and general point, that the government was mismanaging the economy, the polls showed no increase in voter support for conservative positions on social issues, such as restricting legalized abortion or drastically cutting social welfare programs, findings repeatedly confirmed by studies conducted since 1980. Indeed, analyses of public opinion after the 1980 election have found virtually no changes in Americans' beliefs, let alone a significant shift to the right. One study, for example, found that some 40 percent of voters in 1980 did not think of where they sat on the liberal-conservative spectrum, while many of those who did think about their views claimed to be in the middle. This phenomenon even extended to evangelical Christians, who had been widely perceived during the campaign as the vanguard of a new movement for social conservatism but, in reality, proved to be only slightly more conservative than Protestants in general and voted Republican largely on economic grounds. It was a situation that the intellectuals of the 1950s would have recognized instantly. Indeed, as one political scientist summarized the election in 1981, the American electorate remained where it had been for decades, "in the middle, at once attracted to and put off by central features of each party's appeals."[47]

In spite of Reagan's victory, American politics still had no guiding idea that could claim to be politically dominant. On the surface, it appeared at the end of 1980 that the politics of the previous thirty-five years had been reversed. The strong, confident liberalism of the late 1940s and 1950s was gone, and many believed it had been replaced by a conservatism as vigorous as the vital center had been at its peak. But this was only half true. Liberalism certainly had collapsed as a governing ideology, but it was by no means clear that a majority of the population now embraced conservatism as its replacement. Reagan, in truth, had been elected on a trial basis, and if he did no better than Carter on the critical issue of inflation, the voters had made it clear that he too would be tossed aside in four years, along with his conservative views.

2

FIRST TERM: TAXES, DEFICITS, AND POLITICS, 1981–1984

Reagan prepared to take office amid the greatest sense of political and economic uncertainty since Franklin Roosevelt had arrived
in Washington almost fifty years earlier. On the political side, the greatest question was what Reagan's brand of conservatism—Reaganism, as
it inevitably became known—would look like in practice. Reagan had
promised change, and many people, either in hope or in fear, believed he
would lead an ideologically driven revolution. But moderating forces
were at work as well. The administration was staffed by figures with a
range of views, which guaranteed that different factions would compete
to influence Reagan, and his record in California suggested that he was
willing to adjust his course if he had to. At the same time, economic
problems dominated public discussions and it was by no means clear that
any policies could be implemented that would cope with them effectively.
This, combined with the political uncertainty, made it an open question
whether Reagan would be able to govern effectively and see his ideas take
root, or whether he would be a failed and quickly forgotten president.

The incoming team was not yet in a position to answer any of these
questions. Reagan's top aides were consumed with the enormous job of
staffing the administration and preparing economic policy and other legislative proposals to send to Congress. The hard questions of how they
would make deals or cope with unexpected events—which would do as
much to define the substance of Reaganism as any philosophical statements or campaign promises—lay in the future and still were unanswerable.

Eventually, however, all of these factors came together as Reagan's legislation was enacted, events refused to follow the administration's plans,
and the various factions struggled to shape the president's responses. As
it turned out, taxes were the ground on which these events unfolded and
the factions met, and where Reagan made the decisions that defined conservatism for the 1980s.

As he had in California, Reagan depended on his senior staff to
develop specific proposals, provide him with the information he needed
to make decisions, and undertake the complex and painstaking work
required to carry them out. In an unusual arrangement, he placed
responsibility for running the administration in the hands of three men.
The most important was his chief of staff, James A. Baker III. Baker came
from a wealthy and prominent Texas Democratic family, but he had not
become involved in politics until 1970, when he worked on his friend
George Bush's unsuccessful senatorial campaign. Baker served in the
Ford administration, ran the delegate operation that secured the last few
dozen votes Ford needed for the nomination in 1976, and then managed
Ford's fall campaign. Next, he managed Bush's 1980 presidential run,
and then joined the Reagan campaign when Bush became the vice-
presidential nominee. Although his moderate background made many of
Reagan's supply-side supporters suspicious, Baker was a clever strategist—it was he who oversaw the preparations for the debate with Carter.
Baker's campaign performance won him the job of chief of staff, surprising many observers who had assumed that Edwin Meese would get the
job he had held in California.

Baker proved to be an extraordinarily effective chief of staff. Whatever
his private beliefs, he quickly dedicated himself to implementing Reagan's goals—"the ideology of this president is what got him elected,
so taking action that's consistent with that ideology is quite often the
political course to follow," he told the *New York Times* in early 1982.
Journalists writing during Reagan's first term, other senior Reagan appointees, and later scholarly evaluations all agree that he ran a tightly disciplined and organized operation, even as he maintained strict control
over details and priorities. White House memos and papers, moreover,
show that he and his equally able deputy, Richard Darman, ensured that

internal debates remained open and collegial, differing views were heard and presented to Reagan, mistakes were corrected, and that the president was kept informed on all issues. Just as important, Baker also excelled at maintaining good relations with Congress, and he was largely responsible for Reagan's legislative successes in 1981 and 1982.[1]

The second most important figure in the new administration was Michael Deaver. Deaver had been working for Reagan since the gubernatorial years, was absolutely devoted to Ronald and Nancy Reagan, and was their closest confidant. In Washington, he had no policy responsibilities but served as the president's scheduler and handled many of his and Nancy's personal tasks. Deaver's White House papers, in addition, show that he handled hundreds of small but sensitive administrative duties, such as maintaining good relations with prominent Republicans and conservatives, and screening résumés and applicants for administration posts. But Deaver's greatest contribution—in fact, his true genius—was in running a media and public relations strategy of unprecedented sophistication. Working with David Gergen, the White House director of communications, Deaver refined practices used during Reagan's governorship and also by presidents since the 1950s. Deaver and his staff planned media campaigns months in advance, considering what themes to follow and what types of events would work best. Each day, after coordinating with Baker, Deaver and Gergen formulated a "line of the day"— all statements and activities open to coverage revolved around the message—that was designed to support policy efforts. Events were timed and staged to make them irresistible to television news broadcasts, thus giving the administration easy access to the dominant media platform; Gergen used daily tracking studies and polls to monitor how the efforts were working.[2]

As part of his efforts, Deaver scripted Reagan's public appearances and statements to present the president and his policies in the most favorable light possible. The settings, Reagan's movements, and the placing of the audience and the lighting all were chosen and choreographed with care. With his radio, film, and television backgrounds, Reagan instinctively knew how to use these stages, and traditional American visual symbols like the flag or battlefields, to communicate with the public. "Ronald Reagan did more than star" in his appearances, Deaver later wrote. "He glowed." This disciplined approach also enabled the Reagan White House to project an image of strength and control—rarely would confusion be on public display, as it had been so often in the Carter years. In April 1982 the administration added another innovation, Reagan's Saturday morning radio addresses. These brief speeches were instituted as a way to sidestep skeptical media coverage during the recession, and Reagan used them to great effect in presenting his policies directly to the public, along with his customary message of optimism and patriotism.[3]

The media strategy was plainly manipulative, as many in the press complained, but it was not as controlling as many charged. Critics commonly complained, for example, that Reagan's staff controlled the news and provided the people with comforting illusions to build support. These accusations greatly overstated the case, however. By the 1980s, Americans had some thirty years of experience with television advertising and were easily able to separate false claims from reality. In this context, Reagan's use of the media is best understood not as a devilishly crafty plot, but rather as analogous to hiring an attorney. Like skilled lawyers pleading a client's case, Deaver and Gergen presented the most compelling arguments they could, but still could deal only with the facts at hand and, ultimately, were at the mercy of the public's judgment.[4]

The third member of the triumvirate was Ed Meese. A former prosecutor, Meese was, unlike Baker and Deaver, a firm conservative. In the White House, Meese had authority over the domestic policy staff and relations with cabinet departments and agencies. He was famously disorganized, however, and soon gained a reputation for being unable to manage his wide range of responsibilities. Meese gradually lost his authority, and Baker usurped many of his powers.[5]

Just below Baker, Deaver, and Meese were a number of players who further represented a broad ideological mixture. As head of the Office of Management and Budget, David Stockman had authority over tax and budget priorities and was the public face of the supply side. Born to a conservative Republican farm family in Michigan, Stockman was intense and intellectually impressive, but also was a political pilgrim, someone who always sought ideological certainty in his life. In college he had drifted into the New Left, but by the late 1970s, after years as a congressional staffer and then a representative from Michigan, he had become a fervent critic of big government and a dedicated supply-sider. In 1980, Stockman came to Reagan's attention when he was enlisted to play the roles of Anderson and Carter in practice debates; after the election, Stockman's supply-side conservatism, energy, and deep knowledge of the federal budget—he studied federal spending closely and knew its intricacies far better than most other congressmen—helped secure his appointment to the Office of Management and Budget. His meteoric rise, obvious intelligence, bachelor status, and charm and good looks made Stockman the new administration's first media star; by mid-March 1981 he had been on the cover of *Newsweek* and had been the subject of long articles in the *New York Times* and *Washington Post* magazines. But the exposure reinforced his unattractive traits. Stockman, journalists and colleagues often noted, was self-absorbed and manipulative, and now he came to believe that the coming revolution depended entirely on him. "It would be up to me to design the Reagan Revolution," he later wrote, and if "others weren't going to get his administration's act together, I would."[6]

The new secretary of the treasury was Donald Regan, who had been chairman of Merrill Lynch. A maverick on Wall Street, Regan had advocated ending fixed commissions and then guided the brokerage through the changes that followed the May Day deregulation. Regan was a supporter of free markets and entrepreneurial innovation, but he did not have the strong ideological inclinations of the supply-siders. "He spoke the language of the chief executive officer but not that of the supply-sider," noted one magazine profile, but nonetheless was ready to do all he could for Ronald Reagan. "I decided," he later wrote, "that my job as secretary of the treasury was to find ways to carry out the president's promises." Regan, furthermore, made the Treasury a bastion of supply-side crusaders. Paul Craig Roberts, who had helped draft the original Kemp-Roth legislation, became assistant secretary for economic policy, and supply-side consultant Norman Ture was appointed undersecretary for tax and economic affairs. Like Stockman, they saw themselves as capitalist revolutionaries, battling to advance liberty and roll back a bloated state so that individuals would again be free to reap the rewards of their efforts—Roberts, tellingly, later wrote a memoir called *The Supply-Side Revolution*. Meanwhile, Paul Volcker remained chairman of the Federal

Reserve, where he continued to use monetary policy in the fight against inflation. In the House of Representatives, finally, a bloc of forty-seven conservative Southern Democrats—known as the Boll Weevils and terrified that they would be the next Democrats to fall—voted with the Republicans and gave Reagan an effective majority in the House.[7]

The new administration moved quickly to translate Reagan's campaign promises into concrete legislative proposals. Starting in the second half of December 1980, Stockman and his staff began working frantically, reviewing the details of the federal budget, economic forecasts, and tax revenue projections, to develop a new budget that would be consistent with supply-side theory and fulfill Reagan's promise to roll back the growth of government. Much of their work, it turned out, was based on flawed assumptions, inaccurate data, wishful thinking, and outright manipulation, but the resulting problems lay in the future. In the meantime, Stockman produced a tax and budget package for Reagan to unveil in a nationally televised address to Congress on February 18, 1981.

Reagan asked Congress for a basket of tax and spending cuts. He proposed reducing income tax rates 10 percent per year for three years, or by a total of about 27 percent, and accelerating depreciation allowances for business; the income tax reductions would be worth an estimated $44 billion in the first year alone and, cumulatively, some $500 billion by 1986, while the depreciation breaks would be worth $59 billion per year by 1986. On the spending side, Reagan asked for $47 billion in cuts or reductions in planned spending increases, including eliminating job training programs, tightening eligibility for food stamps, ending subsidies for synthetic fuel programs, and reducing corporate export subsidies by one-third. He also pledged to eliminate regulations that were "unnecessary and unproductive or counterproductive." Only the defense budget, set to increase dramatically, was spared. The resulting economic growth, the administration predicted, would transform the projected $55 billion deficit for 1981 into a surplus in 1984 and after.[8]

The next six months saw an intricate political struggle—the complicated details of which need not be recounted—as the administration, various factions in Congress, and outside interest groups competed to shape the legislation. At the White House, Baker formed a small group of senior aides—the Legislative Strategy Group, which included Stockman and

Deaver—to review and coordinate the administration's efforts and dealings with Congress. White House records show that, following the group's recommendations, Reagan made dozens of phone calls to congressmen and senators to ask for their support, and then informed the group of the responses so Baker could plan the next move. Reagan also used his powerful communications skills to rally public support—"no news item, no speech, no trip, no photo-op whatsoever was put on the President's schedule during 1981 unless it contributed to the President's economic program," recalled his spokesman, Larry Speakes. The teamwork paid off. After a final televised appeal to the country for support— and with forty-eight Democratic votes in the House—Reagan got almost all of what he wanted and signed the Economic Recovery Tax Act (ERTA) on August 13. Income taxes were to be cut 5 percent on October 1, and 10 percent each of the next two years; taxes were cut on capital gains by 40 percent and on investment income by 28 percent; and tax rates and exemptions were indexed to inflation starting in 1985, thereby ending bracket creep. On the same day, Reagan signed the Omnibus Budget Reconciliation Act, cutting spending for the next fiscal year by some $35 billion.[9]

It was the largest tax cut in American history and no one, least of all the delighted supply-siders, missed its significance. The *Wall Street Journal* editorialized about the "spectacular tax victory" that gave hope for a brighter economic future, and most press accounts concluded that Reagan had ended fifty years of liberal government. Reagan, moreover, was hailed as a master politician. In January the Democrats, led by Speaker of the House Thomas P. "Tip" O'Neill, had viewed Reagan as a Washington amateur who would be outclassed by the professionals. Now, noted the *Washington Post*, Reagan had shown a sophisticated grasp of the issues and the legislative process, and had shrewdly used his television and bargaining skills to reshape national politics. Indeed, liberals now feared that Reagan would use his mastery of Congress and ability to deliver on his promises to create an enduring Republican domination of government, much as FDR had laid the foundation for the long era of Democratic control in national politics.[10]

At the same time that Reagan was pushing his economic plan through Congress, Volcker had renewed the Federal Reserve's monetarist experiment. When the economy fell into recession in early 1980, the Fed eased monetary policy and allowed interest rates to fall; but the recession turned out to be brief, ending by midsummer, and inflation continued unabated. On November 4, 1980, election day, Volcker again began slowing monetary growth. Interest rates began climbing and, starting in July 1981, the economy was again in recession. Now, however, Volcker continued the tight money policy with a brutal remorselessness that had been lacking in the efforts of the previous decade. The recession was, and still remains, the worst since the 1930s—unemployment peaked at 10.8 percent in the fall of 1982, and more banks failed that year than in the entire decade of the 1950s. Not surprisingly, Volcker and Reagan came under a great deal of political pressure to ease up, but the president, recalled his second chairman of the Council of Economic Advisers, Martin Feldstein, staunchly supported the Fed. "The president listened politely to [a] plea to lean on the Fed to achieve an easier monetary policy, but then explained that would be wrong because it would jeopardize the progress on inflation," Feldstein later wrote. Their persistence paid off, and the 1981–82 recession broke inflation's back (see Table 2).[11]

Well before the severity of the recession was recognized, however, it became apparent that Stockman had miscalculated badly. Stockman's expectations for tax receipts, on which Reagan's February budget package had been based, assumed strong economic growth and moderate inflation, but the economic slowdown and greater than anticipated decline in inflation meant that projected revenues never appeared. The February budget further assumed that billions of dollars in additional budget cuts would be identified later, with the future reductions marked by what Stockman called "magic asterisks." In August 1981, the administration realized that the deficit would grow far beyond previous expectations, and Stockman then tried desperately to find his expected budget cuts. Secretary of Defense Caspar Weinberger's refusal to consider slowing the growth of defense spending, and strong resistance from other cabinet secretaries to further cuts in their programs, meant that his efforts were doomed. "I would spend the next two months learning that all the doors were shut," Stockman later wrote. Thus, instead of the federal budget moving into balance, the deficit appeared to be on the verge of quadrupling. If nothing was done, Stockman's revised estimates now showed, the deficit would climb from $74 billion in 1980 to $300 billion per year by mid-decade.[12]

By the end of 1981, the combination of recession, rising interest rates, and exploding deficits seemed to threaten Reagan with a political disaster. Financial markets were not providing the vote of confidence that the supply-siders had expected would greet the tax and budget cuts—the stock market began a sickening slide immediately after Reagan signed ERTA, and bonds also dropped sharply. The growing deficit, moreover, was widely viewed as inflationary and thus causing interest rates to rise still further. The media, reflecting the popular mood, reported on a growing sense of panic caused by fears of ever increasing interest rates, inflation, and economic turmoil. Reagan's popularity began a steady slide, falling from 60 percent in August 1981 to 42 percent the following May—with especially poor ratings for his economic policies—which prompted unfavorable comparisons to Jimmy Carter's polls. Pressure to reduce the deficit began increasing. Reagan's congressional support eroded as members from both parties worried about the deficits, and discussion of the need to take back some of ERTA's tax cuts became widespread in Congress and the media.[13]

Reagan stubbornly resisted the pressure to modify his program. "I will seek no tax increases this year," he told Congress in his January 1982 State of the Union speech, arguing that tax increases only would slow growth and cost still more jobs. But Stockman, frightened and chastened by the scale of his errors, had concluded that a tax increase was the only choice. He and Baker began working to convince Reagan of its political necessity and, in March 1982, Reagan gave in and authorized Baker to begin negotiations with congressional Democrats. As in 1981, Baker and the Legislative Strategy Group managed the long and complex process for the administration and—after Reagan made another last-minute television appeal to the country—Congress passed the Tax Equity and Fiscal Responsibility Act (TEFRA) in late August. The new law was expected to raise about $98 billion during the next three years, making it the largest tax increase to date in American history. It operated largely by rolling back some of ERTA's breaks for depreciation—some two-thirds of the tax increase came from taxes on business—but also by adding new excise taxes on airports, communications, and tobacco, and by making a large number of small and less visible increases in the nooks and crannies of the tax code, where they were less likely to be noticed by voters. The previous year's reductions in tax rates and the commitment to indexing—which directly affected individual taxpayers—were not touched, however.[14]

TEFRA was the first of several tax increases Reagan ultimately approved. In 1983, as part of the reform of Social Security, a payroll tax increase scheduled for 1990 was accelerated and benefits were taxed; these moves were producing some $70 billion per year in revenues by 1988. Next, Reagan agreed to the Deficit Reduction Act of 1984, which closed a number of loopholes and, by 1988, was generating an estimated $25 billion per year in revenues. In each case, however, Reagan was able to minimize the political impact. He argued, plausibly, that the Social Security tax rise was merely a speedup, and took credit for helping to keep the politically popular system solvent. The 1984 tax increase, which again focused on smaller, technical issues, had little impact on most people and was accompanied, moreover, by $13 billion in spending cuts (see Table 3).[15]

The question of whether to seek a tax increase had set off a vicious civil war among conservatives. The supply-siders bitterly opposed any consideration of reducing the tax cuts for which they had fought since the mid-1970s, and as early as the fall of 1981 they advanced several arguments for standing firm. First, the supply-siders at the Treasury and their allies in the conservative press claimed that the large deficits were a temporary phenomenon and would begin to shrink as soon as recovery began. Great concern also was unwarranted, they pointed out, because the levels of future deficits could not be predicted accurately; Stockman's previous projections, after all, had been wrong and now, they claimed, he was deliberately overestimating the size of the deficits to support his tax-hike argument. The *Wall Street Journal* summarized this view by editorializing, "We have nothing to panic about except panic itself." In addition, the supply-siders argued that the tax cuts were not responsible for the deficits, so it made no sense to use a tax increase to close the revenue gap. Not only had the cuts not yet taken effect, but more important, they claimed, the decline in revenues actually was the Fed's fault, because Volcker's tight money policy had caused the recession and subsequent decline in tax receipts. Moreover, in their view, instead of establishing and maintaining a steady rate of monetary growth, the Fed had allowed it to fluctuate violently, thus making conditions too uncertain for the economy to function properly—Paul Craig Roberts charged that no one could tell what monetary policy was or what it was going to be. Instead of talking about increasing taxes, Representative Jack Kemp claimed that the best policy would be a return to the gold standard, which he believed would ensure a stable monetary policy, bring inflation down, and ultimately restore growth.[16]

Even as they were digging in to defend the tax cuts, the supply-siders received stunning news. Since January 1981, it turned out, Stockman had been having regular breakfast meetings with *Washington Post* reporter William Greider. Stockman had seen their discussions as providing him with a sounding board for his ideas as well as a way to explain the administration's policies through an influential newspaper. Inadvertently, however, he had provided Greider with a running narrative of how policy had been made and his gradual realization that, in practice, supply-side policies did not work as expected. Now, in November 1981, advance copies of Greider's resulting article for the *Atlantic Monthly*, "The Education of David Stockman," were circulating in Washington. Greider provided a long and nuanced description of budgetary politics and Stockman's idealism and subsequent disillusion, but journalists and politicians focused on a handful of striking quotes. The federal budget was enormously complicated, said Stockman, and "none of us really understands what is going on with all these numbers." Echoing long-standing liberal charges, Stockman admitted that the supply-side program was a "trickle-down" theory and the tax cuts were simply a maneuver to reduce taxes on high incomes. Stockman also realized that the structure of American politics made it virtually impossible to create the revolution that the supply-siders had dreamed of. "The system has an enormous amount of inertia," he told Greider, and "you can only do so much."[17]

Greider's article sent the supply-siders into a fury. Stockman was a traitor, they now decided, and was to blame for the administration's ideological wavering and every other unfavorable event. He had never been a true believer, said Alan Reynolds, a close associate of Jude Wanniski, who reminded readers of *National Review* that Stockman first had supported former Texas governor John Connally, not Reagan, for the Republican nomination in 1980. For his part, Roberts later accused Stockman of trying to discredit the supply side and substitute policies of his own that would make him appear to be the man who had rescued the country. The supply-siders demanded Stockman's dismissal but Baker decided to keep him—no one else could match his detailed knowledge of the budget— and Reagan agreed, although the budget director lost his authority and glamour. This only further infuriated the supply-side faithful, who now concluded not only that disloyalty to their side carried no penalty but also that the ideologically suspect Baker was in control. Roberts made his disgust public and resigned as of February 1, 1982; he quickly published an article in *Fortune* blaming the recession on Stockman's perfidy, became a strong critic of the administration's failure to hold to supply-side policies, and wrote a bitter memoir. Most other prominent supply-siders soon left as well.[18]

The supply-siders used Stockman to create a myth to explain their loss of influence in 1982. In their version, Reagan was a man of principle, chosen by the voters because of his compelling supply-side message. Now, as he tried to stand firm in defense of the supply side, moderate Republicans, led by Baker and the turncoat Stockman, worked to manipulate him into accepting the tax increase. The Baker-Stockman faction allegedly kept Reagan from seeing memos and papers supporting the supply-siders' arguments for resisting tax increases while constantly pressuring him with pro-tax messages. Roberts claimed that Baker and Stockman had undermined the president with impunity, and the *Wall Street Journal* editorialized that Reagan needed dedicated supporters who would fight to save his programs. This view enabled the supply-siders to overlook the inconvenient political realities of late 1981 and early 1982 and, instead, convince themselves that if only Reagan had heard the truth from loyal followers he would have held to a pure supply-side position and rallied the country behind him. Like Henry Wallace's Progressives— and, for that matter, Barry Goldwater's and George McGovern's supporters—the supply-siders truly believed that the people shared their ideals and, if they only heard the unadulterated message, would flock to the cause.[19]

The supply-siders, of course, had it wrong. A brief look at Reagan's past would have shown them that he was behaving as he had in California. His reluctant acceptance of the need to raise taxes, efforts to shape the tax increase to minimize the damage to his overall program, and use of television to rally support at the critical moment made the TEFRA saga a virtual replay of the 1967 tax increase. The charges of treacherous manipulation also were nonsense. Those who had been with Reagan since the 1960s and who knew him best, as well as those who worked closely with him in the White House, are unanimous in their description of his decision making—he was fully engaged in the debates, reviewed the situation and his options, considered the political possibilities, and then issued his instructions. To say otherwise, in Ed Meese's words, is "totally false." Reagan, for his part, looked at the issues from a broad perspective. His handwritten notes on papers and memos from this period—from his entire tenure, for that matter—show him asking questions, hearing a range of different views, catching errors, and sometimes going against his staff's recommendations. As Reagan wrote in a 1987 letter to a friend, the "picture which has been presented to you of my being steered, motivated and manipulated by people around me just isn't true."[20]

As much as the supply-siders may not have liked it, Reagan was satisfied to take incremental gains when he could not get all he wanted. Reagan made this plain both in public and in private. In a 1985 interview, for example, he said: "Die-hard conservatives thought that if I couldn't get everything I asked for, I should jump off the cliff with the flag flying—go down in flames. No, if I can get 70 or 80 percent of what it is I'm trying to get, yes I'll take that and then continue to try to get the rest in the future." Similarly, in a letter written in 1988 he described reluctantly signing a bill when a veto was hopeless as a "compromise between reality and my personal distaste." The newcomers to Reagan—men like Roberts—had pinned their highest hopes on him and could understand retreat only as a betrayal rather than as a tactical move in a long struggle, and they quickly marginalized themselves in the political arena.[21]

The tax saga also provides a basic model for understanding Reagan's conservatism. Most important, Reaganism emphasized the long view. In this respect, Reagan followed the method used by cold war liberals in their heyday—keeping his eye firmly fixed on principles and ultimate goals but, in the short term, remaining willing to use flexible tactics and accept incremental progress. Like cold war liberalism, Reagan's conservatism questioned the status quo, but seldom went so far ahead of public opinion or out of the mainstream as to risk a disastrous defeat. The irony is that, in their pique, the supply-siders and other aggressive conservatives did not see how much the Reagan approach could accomplish. The 1981 cuts brought individual taxes down dramatically; the pre-ERTA top marginal rate of 70 percent today seems unimaginable. The slowing of revenue growth through indexing and the leap in the deficit also served supply-side purposes. Greider made it clear that Stockman viewed the ERTA as placing a "tightening noose around the size of government" that would have effects for many years to come. He was right. For the next decade, economic policy debates would revolve around deficit reduction. Democrats refused to consider more spending cuts, Republicans fought moves to increase taxes, and the standoff made it impossible to consider any major spending initiatives. It remains a simple fact—and a significant supply-side victory—that from the time Ronald Reagan took office until the passage of Medicare reform in 2003, the federal government did not institute any large new social or welfare programs.

The first signs of economic recovery appeared during the summer of 1982. In early July, the Federal Reserve began injecting funds into the banking system, leading to a rise in the price of Treasury bonds as traders anticipated interest rate cuts. The Fed soon began to loosen its restrictions on the growth of the money supply and, in the second half of the month, cut interest rates. Interest rates on commercial and Treasury bonds continued to fall, but the stock market was slower to react. Reflecting the continuing gloom about the economic outlook, stock prices still fell during the first half of August, with the Dow Jones Industrial Average closing at 777 on August 12, close to its post-inauguration low. On Tuesday, August 17, Henry Kaufman, an influential credit analyst, predicted that interest rates would continue to fall. Suddenly, Wall Street's pessimism evaporated as traders and investors realized that declining rates could herald better times ahead; the Dow Jones average rose 38.81 points that day, a new one-day record. "Some are saying that this is the start of the

1980s boom," one broker told the *Wall Street Journal*, while another cautiously speculated that the Dow might someday rise as high as 1,200. By the end of the month bankers and economists were confidently predicting further drops in interest rates with little danger of renewed inflation. Their optimism turned out to be justified. Unemployment started to decline early the next year, GNP soon was growing rapidly, and the recovery that began in the second half of 1982 lasted through the remainder of Reagan's presidency. During those six years, as Reagan's supporters always were quick to point out, real GNP increased by more than 25 percent, the economy added more than 15 million jobs, incomes rose steadily, and inflation remained low.[22]

The same supply-side critics who had attacked Reagan's policies when things were going badly also claimed credit for his eventual success. Few economists supported their claims, however. Martin Feldstein, more sympathetic to the supply side than most, noted in 1986 that supply-siders had "conveniently forgotten" that actual growth had fallen well below their forecasts. Others, both Keynesians and non-Keynesians, pointed out that the recovery was largely in line with Keynesian predictions, as it was fueled by tax cuts, military spending, and falling interest rates. The strength of the recovery, moreover, could be attributed to underutilized resources being put back to work, rather than the significant structural changes promised by supply-side theory. Supply-siders would—and still do—dispute these conclusions, but the fact remains that anyone looking in economic literature for an independent confirmation that supply-side policies caused the recovery and boom of the 1980s will find little to support that view.[23]

As the recovery began, however, it was far from obvious that it would be so strong and durable. Despite their declines, for example, interest rates and unemployment remained high by historical standards, income inequality was increasing dramatically, and studies suggested that the tax cuts had mostly benefited upper-income Americans. These trends also appeared linked to one another. In large part because the rise in interest rates and the need for foreign investment to finance the deficit had driven up the value of the dollar, American exports were hurt and imports became less expensive. This, in turn, contributed to the slow pace of recovery in the manufacturing sector, and many of the jobs lost in 1981 and 1982 never returned. Altogether some 2 million industrial jobs disappeared during the 1980s—employment in the steel industry, for example, fell by almost half from 1980 to 1988, a quarter of mining jobs disappeared, and automotive employment stagnated. The industrial states of the Midwest were hit especially hard. Illinois, which in 1980 had ranked seventh among the states in income, fell to eleventh place in 1988, and Michigan dropped from fifteenth to seventeenth place. The expansion did little to improve the poverty rate; although it fell steadily from its peak of 15.2 percent in 1983, it was well above the rate of 11 to 12 percent that had prevailed for most of the 1970s. In one of the most talked about developments of the 1980s, the top 20 percent of households increased their share of national income during the Reagan years, while the shares of the remaining 80 percent either stagnated or, for those in the bottom two quintiles, fell sharply. In another disturbing development, it soon became evident that even for those with jobs, prosperity was not assured; many manufacturing workers who kept their jobs found their real wages declining during the 1980s.[24]

These worrisome statistics soon gave rise to widespread fears that the American economy was in an irreversible decline. In this view, which built on the perception of foreign socioeconomic superiority that had begun to develop during the Carter years, European and Japanese competition was ruining American manufacturing and causing the "deindustrialization" of the United States. In a special issue in June 1980, *Business Week* reviewed the troubles of the steel, auto, machine tool, and other manufacturing industries and declared that "U.S. industry's loss of competitiveness over the past two decades has been nothing short of an economic disaster," and that the future was grim because American industry's ability to innovate and turn new ideas into commercial successes was declining. As the deindustrialization argument developed during Reagan's first term, it claimed that the economy would no longer be able to provide enough well-paying jobs to ensure a middle-class standard of living for its blue-collar workers or, eventually, white-collar workers. Sociologist Andrew Hacker, for example, wrote in mid-1983 that "our economy will not expand much beyond its present bounds, and . . . a high level of unemployment may be with us for the rest of the century." Other social scientists and popular writers warned that increasing numbers of workers would find only low-quality, dead-end jobs. Media reports frequently appeared to confirm these analyses. In Waterloo, Iowa, a city that depended heavily on farm equipment manufacturing and had been devastated by the recession, the president of the Chamber of Commerce told the *Wall Street Journal:* "For the country, 1983 was a boom year. But for Waterloo, it was the worst."[25]

To the surprise of many observers, the uneven nature of the prosperity did not hurt Reagan politically, largely because anxieties about foreign competition and the focus on those left behind during the recovery obscured important facts about those who did well. The 18 million jobs created between 1980 and 1988 dwarfed the 2 million lost, and the great majority of the new positions were in rapidly growing sectors of the economy, paid well, and provided employees with the potential for advancement. The biggest growth—7 million new positions—came in sales jobs, which included not only retail sales but also real estate, insurance, and securities sales (see Table 4). Another 6 million jobs appeared for professionals and technicians, and employment jumped in a range of lucrative areas, including technology, management consulting, finance, and law. The number of people working in computer-related fields more than doubled, for example, and the number of consultants increased by two-thirds, while the economy added millions of well-paying jobs for managers, scientists, teachers, and skilled craftsmen. For the most part, these people did not have to worry about losing their jobs—even at the depth of the recession, unemployment among professionals remained below 3.5 percent.[26]

These patterns of job growth were closely linked to the rise in income inequality during the Reagan years. Since the early 1970s, the job market had increasingly required the well-developed intellectual and interpersonal skills needed in an economy based on services and information, while demand fell for the physical and motor skills traditionally needed in factory and production work. Because of this, wages had been rising steadily for workers with higher levels of education, skill, and experience, while wages for lower-skill workers fell. The wage gap between the two groups, what economists call the "skill premium," also had been growing since the early 1970s, but increased at a sharply faster pace during the Reagan years as the demand for skilled workers accelerated while industrial jobs disappeared. The increase in demand was greatest for those with the highest levels of skill and education—the United States, noted one economist, had an almost insatiable demand for educated workers who could learn to use new technologies. One measurement of the skill premium, the wage difference between college and high school graduates, in the late 1970s was 38 percent, near its postwar low; by 1989, it had increased to 58 percent, a new record (this trend continued into the 1990s). Similarly, real earnings for professionals grew by 15 to 20 percent during the 1980s, while wages for workers with twelve years of school or less fell by as much as 15 percent. These factors, finally, were in large part responsible for the failure of the poor to benefit from the return of prosperity—those in poverty generally did not have the education, skills, or experience that the job markets now demanded.[27]

As the job market changed, however, so did the labor force. Continuing the trend that had begun early in the twentieth century, American workers during the 1980s became better educated and more skilled than ever before. Over that decade, for example, the proportion of the labor force that had graduated from college rose from 22 percent to 26 percent, while the proportion lacking a high school diploma fell from 21 percent to 13 percent. Meanwhile, the share of high school graduates enrolling in college—a predictor of future labor force education levels—rose from 49 percent in 1980 to 60 percent in 1989. Students also shifted their fields of study to meet the demands of the job market. The number of bachelor's degrees awarded in social sciences dropped between 1980 and 1987, but the number earned in computer sciences nearly tripled, and it rose by almost half in mathematics and by about one-third in business. The new generation of workers and professionals understood that their skills made them more productive and increased their value in the marketplace; they believed that their futures were bright and worried little about the troubles of steelworkers or the inequality of income distribution. Indeed, when polls asked in 1984 if Americans were better off than in 1980, the youngest respondents provided the greatest percentage answering yes. Similarly, in a Gallup Poll taken in April 1984, 36 percent said they were better off than they had been a year earlier—a figure that closely mirrored the proportion of the population that had completed one or more years of college.[28]

Like worries about disappearing jobs, rising budget deficits were another political danger that seemed to threaten Reagan. As Stockman had foreseen, the deficits continued to rise, generating unprecedented statistics. The worst year may have been 1983, when the deficit first exceeded $200 billion and reached its peak proportion of GNP for the Reagan years—more than 6 percent. The national debt, which had been about $900 billion in 1980, reached $1.1 trillion in 1982, and $1.5 trillion two years later. The reaction to the deficit's sudden expansion in 1981 had shown how much fear it could cause, and the deficits frequently were blamed not only for causing high interest rates but also for creating inflationary pressure and reducing the availability of funds for private investment. The debt, it was often stated, was in danger of growing so great that to make the required interest payments the government eventually would have to cut spending drastically, raise taxes to ruinous levels, or simply print enormous quantities of money. "With every passing year," reported *Newsweek* in 1984, "the choices become progressively grimmer." Americans had long disliked the idea of large budget shortfalls and now, not surprisingly, polls showed that 80 percent of Americans believed the deficit was a serious problem for the country and that a large majority favored amending the Constitution to require a balanced budget.[29]

But if the evil of the deficit seemed obvious to almost everyone, little else about it was clear. Economists and political scientists noted that the federal budget was huge and complex, and that even specialists had difficulty understanding it. Writing in academic journals, economists noted that they could not even say precisely what the budget was for any given year. Similarly, noted one prominent economist, inflation, questions about accounting methods, and the difficulty of valuing items for which no market existed meant that "we do not even know what the budget deficit, in any reasonable sense, was in any recent previous year." Others pointed out that the budget was shaped by a large number of factors, beginning with the legacies of assumptions and decisions made decades previously. Much of the government's spending was for programs already long since undertaken—like defense procurement or social welfare—that could not be changed on short notice. On top of that came the conflicting priorities of individual members of Congress, interest group pressures, and bureaucratic politics, as well as the haste in which spending decisions often had to be made. Similarly, the costs of Social Security, Medicare, and interest on the debt were taking increased shares of the budget but were politically impossible to cut. Dispassionate economic research and analysis, moreover, played only a small role in the budget process and often turned out to be wrong; politicians, one political scientist noted, learned that they could safely ignore much of what economists said.[30]

The specialists' uncertainty about the budget was reflected in the popular media. Despite all the frightening articles, anyone looking for a definitive statement about the eventual effects of the deficit would not have found it. In the same article that forecast eventual catastrophe, *Newsweek* reported that the deficit was attracting tens of billions of dollars in foreign investment funds that, in turn, fueled growth and helped keep interest rates down. The *New York Times* also routinely presented contrasting views—it was possible to find, on the same page, one economist arguing that the deficits would lead to disaster and another pointing out that no evidence supported such a prediction. Not surprisingly, internal White House polling information found that the public had only a fuzzy idea of the size of the deficit and public debt, and no firm ideas on how to deal with the issue. With no consensus on the consequences of the deficit or how to reduce it, budget politics became paralyzed. Each year, in what became an annual ritual, Reagan proposed a budget with a high deficit. Republicans then pressed to cut spending on what they viewed as wasteful social programs, while Democrats argued for raising taxes and cutting defense spending; the media, meanwhile, decried the politicians' inability to make hard choices. Each side attacked the other but gained little and, after months of political trench warfare and marginal cuts, the appropriations were made and spending went on as before.[31]

Because of this confusion and stalemate, the deficits turned out to have little political impact. Neither Reagan, the Republicans, nor the Democrats could be clearly blamed, and none suffered any significant damage. For most people, analyses of polling data found, unemployment and inflation remained the most important economic issues, and the ones whose consequences could immediately be felt in daily life. The consequences of the deficit—if anyone knew what they would be—were far off.

Meanwhile, by mid-1984 the economy was doing well and people could be forgiven for not believing that catastrophe was imminent or seeing the need for making difficult choices about taxes and spending. With the *New York Times* unable to say anything more substantial in its editorials than Congress had "better do something," politicians, too, could be forgiven for believing that doing nothing would be the politically safe course.[32]

For Reagan, economic recovery and the easing of worry about the deficit brought enormous political benefits. Reagan's political fortunes and popularity, slightly lagging the recovery, had reached bottom during the winter of 1982–83. The November 1982 election cost the Republicans twenty-six seats in the House, leaving the Democrats just seven seats shy of their pre-1981 total. In January 1983, the New York Times/CBS News Poll found that only 41 percent of Americans approved of Reagan's performance as president. By July, however, Reagan's favorable rating had reached 47 percent and, for the first time since early 1982, more people approved of his performance than disapproved. By January 1984, when he announced his candidacy for reelection, Reagan's approval rating was up to 56 percent, and the improvement was reflected among poll respondents of both sexes and parties, as well as across age groups and educational levels. Reagan's personal recovery reflected more than just the return of prosperity, however. Unlike his immediate predecessors, Reagan was in a position to admit that the country had suffered hard times and still argue that his basic promise—that his policies would fix the economy—was coming true. He had admitted in his State of the Union speech in January 1982 that "the economy will face difficult moments in the months ahead," but promised that conditions "will be better—much better—if we summon the strength to continue on the course that we've charted." A year later, he told Congress that the improvement had "taken more time and a higher toll than any of us wanted," but that "America is on the mend." Given Reagan's determination to stick with his basic approach, Americans were quick to give him the credit when his predictions appeared vindicated.[33]

The growing approval of Reagan was accompanied by a general increase in confidence in the federal government. As early as December 1981, a columnist in the *Washington Post* noted that Reagan's statements and actions had communicated an infectious optimism, and that even though the nation still faced serious problems, they no longer seemed beyond control. By mid-1983, public opinion analysts noticed that levels of trust in the government—measured by the prevalence of the belief that the government would usually do the right thing—had begun to creep upward from their 1980 lows. This and other indicators, such as the percentage of people who told poll takers that they were satisfied with the direction in which the country was moving or said they were proud to be Americans, rose during the Reagan years while articles claiming that the United States was ungovernable or that its institutions required over-hauling largely disappeared. Although levels of confidence would not return to the highs they had achieved before the upheavals of the late 1960s and Watergate, political analysts quickly agreed that the improve-ment was significant and as much a reflection of Reagan's personal opti-mism as it was the result his policy successes. Observers, furthermore, almost unanimously noted how central Reagan—and his self-assurance, sense of humor, and simple faith in the future—was to the revival of con-fidence. In retrospect, it became clear, the belief in the late 1970s that the system was in crisis had reflected the poor political leadership of Jimmy Carter, not any fundamental flaw in American democracy.[34]

The combination of prosperity, growing optimism, Reagan's personal popularity, and a general sense of contentment made 1984 into a remark-able year, marked by a mood of national celebration. The momentum began to build after the invasion of Grenada in October 1983—Reagan's decision to overthrow the island nation's Marxist regime turned out to be enormously popular and the military operation, although flawed in its execution, was an impressive reminder of the potential of American power. Next, in June 1984, Reagan went to Normandy for the fortieth anniversary of the D-Day landing and his appearance at the beaches—which ranks as one of his best rhetorical and visual performances ever—reminded Americans of the great achievements in World War II. But Grenada and Normandy proved to be only a warm-up for the main event of 1984, the summer Olympic Games in Los Angeles.

From the time Los Angeles was named host city in 1978, it was clear that these games would be different. Host cities and governments usu-ally spent heavily to build Olympic facilities and then left the bills to the taxpayers; Montreal was not expected to pay off its $1-billion debt from the 1976 Olympics until the 1990s. When Los Angeles was awarded the games, public pressure forced officials to pledge not to use tax money on the Olympics. To make good on the promise, the Los Angeles Olympic Organizing Committee hired Peter Ueberroth, a self-made millionaire travel agency executive, to run the effort.

Ueberroth proved to be an inspired choice. A hard-charging man who tolerated no obstacles, he was determined to prove that private enterprise could not only stage the games but also turn a profit. To finance an expected operating budget of $500 million, he sold the television rights for a record $280 million, corporate sponsorships for $117 million, and racked up another $117 million in advance ticket sales; by the end of 1983, the interest on these revenues totaled another $57 million. To keep costs down, the Olympics used existing facilities—the athletes would be housed in dormitories at universities in the Los Angeles area, and almost all of the events were to held in stadiums and arenas that were already there. As the games drew near, the media reported breathlessly on his accomplishment—the job of coordinating the preparations, said the *New York Times,* had "no parallel in the nation's peacetime history"—and Ueberroth confidently predicted that the Olympics would produce a $15 million surplus.[35]

As impressive as the preparations were in Los Angeles, they were overshadowed by an unexpected phenomenon, the popular reaction to the Olympic torch relay. Starting in New York on May 8, runners carried the torch to Los Angeles on a nine-thousand-mile route that snaked through thirty-three states and across cities, mountains, prairies, and deserts. To the surprise of almost all everyone, the torch set off a wave of intense patriotic displays and reflection. In the cities, large crowds turned out to cheer, wave flags, and sing patriotic songs as the torch passed by. Even as runners jogged through small towns or along empty rural roads, families and small groups of people came from many miles to watch and cheer, often after midnight. In one small town in southeastern Kentucky, hundreds of people lined the streets, holding candles, as the torch arrived at one o'clock in the morning. The *Los Angeles Times* editorialized on July 4 that the torch, while symbolizing the Olympics, was "also a reminder of continuity and union, of the things that, whatever our disagreements, still bind us together." *Time* probably best expressed the mood, describing the reaction to the torch as deeply rooted in America's image of itself. Spectators, the magazine said, watched runners carry the torch out of the troubled recent past and "into that America where the future was full of endless possibility."[36]

The games themselves turned into an American triumph. Retaliating for the boycott of the 1980 Olympics in Moscow, the Soviet Union and its Eastern European allies refused to come to Los Angeles. Their absence lessened the quality and drama of the competition, but it also precluded the politicized judging that had marred previous games and left the fields to be dominated by the American team. In front of flag-waving crowds chanting "USA! USA!" a new generation of Olympic stars—including Carl Lewis in track and field, Mary Lou Retton in gymnastics, Greg Louganis in diving, and Michael Jordan in basketball—took 174 medals for the United States; West Germany was second, with 59 medals. The patriotic celebration continued after the games ended. In Washington, the medal winners were treated to a parade and reception by Congress, and in New York an estimated 2 million people cheered and waved flags as the athletes marched in a ticker-tape parade. "We can't go anywhere without being mobbed," marveled one medalist. Although many observers complained about commercialization, the games were staged flawlessly and, when the final accounting was in, showed a surplus of $215 million. The profit would be used for the training and development of future Olympians.[37]

Looking at the recovery of 1983 and 1984 tells much about how Americans perceived and reacted to Reagan's version of conservatism. What was easily missed amid the well-publicized worries about inequality, deficits, and the fates of those left behind was that Reagan's growing popularity represented a careful judgment of him by the voters. On economics, voters realized that while Reagan's performance was not perfect it was a vast improvement over what had gone before, especially on the key issues of inflation and unemployment. As for the major flaw in Reagan's performance, the deficit, Americans decided not to worry about unknowable future consequences. When it came to the issues raised by increasing inequality, the predominant response was not to waste time decrying the injustice but, rather, to prepare for the future.

The recovery also showed that many of the views and attitudes that had long marked American political culture remained intact. The celebration of the Olympics—both for its management as well as for the athletes' accomplishments—not only appeared to confirm conservatism's point about the superior capabilities of free enterprise, but also showed how Americans still held business acumen and individual achievement in high regard and were delighted to have an opportunity to showcase them. By the summer of 1984, in other words, Reagan was presiding over a country that was largely content, optimistic about the future, and pleased with his performance in office. How the Democrats planned to cope with this remained an open question.

The Democrats began the Reagan years in a state of shock. Not only had they lost the White House and Senate, but the survivors were left leaderless. In the Senate, minority leader Robert Byrd proved to be ineffectual; Ted Kennedy, the figure liberals instinctively turned to, remained discredited by his performance in the 1980 race and began turning his attention to his 1982 reelection drive. On the other side of the Capitol, Speaker of the House O'Neill was the Democrat retaining the most power, which made him, by default, the party's political leader. O'Neill, unfortunately, was not up to the job. His formative political experiences had been in Boston's bitter ethnic feuds, where what mattered most were personal ties, a willingness to overlook corruption, and unquestioning loyalty to the New Deal. As he climbed the ranks in the House from his arrival in 1953, through becoming speaker in 1977, and until his retirement in 1987, O'Neill always practiced the politics of the ward heeler, dispensing favors and spending money while letting others develop the ideas and programs; he never developed the broad view of politics necessary to dominate at the national level. Now, in 1981, O'Neill remained a committed New Deal liberal and, assuming that the voters soon would return to the faith, failed to develop a strategy for opposing the administration's program. In one noteworthy example, O'Neill was junketing in the Pacific in April 1981 while Reagan and Baker were calling congressmen to round up support to win a budget vote. "Who the hell knew all that was going to happen when I was in New Zealand?" he asked when he got home. Indeed, even though O'Neill improved his performance in 1982 and 1983, blocking Reagan's drive for additional budget cuts, he still did not formulate coherent alternatives to the president's policies.[38]

The confusion, however, provided the Democrats with a priceless opportunity to reshape their party. The defeats of so many prominent figures, like George McGovern, and the weakness of the remaining leaders meant that a new generation of Democrats could begin to move into important party positions without having to follow a predetermined line. For the intellectuals, it was a chance to examine new ideas, to redefine what it meant to be a Democrat and a liberal, and to help the politicians update the party's positions. Understanding that the party needed to develop credible alternatives to Reagan's policies and programs if it was to have any chance of regaining the White House, younger Democrats hurried to generate new ideas. The debates were freewheeling, ranged across every conceivable issue, and involved academics, journalists, informal groups, and think-tank intellectuals. The participants presented their views in books, in articles in the *New Republic,* the *New York Times Magazine,* the *New York Review of Books,* and *Washington Monthly,* and on the op-ed pages of the *New York Times* and the *Washington Post.* Indeed, on the eve of the 1984 Democratic convention, one Democrat remarked, "We have been on an intellectual forced march since 1980."[39]

As open as the debates were, they took place largely among moderate Democrats. By 1981, conservative Democrats had almost entirely disappeared. Battered by ten years of defeats in party battles and deeply angered by Jimmy Carter's foreign policies, many had joined Reagan's coalition or, like the Boll Weevils, were unwilling to resist the Republican tide. For its part, the Democrats' left—itself greatly reduced in numbers and influence by the passing of 1960s radicalism and the defeats of many of its candidates—reacted to Reagan's election and subsequent legislative victories by indulging in dire warnings of disaster, rather than formulating politically realistic alternatives. In the *Nation* they wrote of how the rise of Reagan's Republicans was the result of "economic stagnation, declining international strength, and social anxiety . . . selfishness, resentment, [and] paranoia," that was replacing freedom with a combination of McCarthyism, militarism, and cultural regimentation. This portrait of a miserable, repressed America became the left's standard interpretation of the Reagan era, but it found few takers outside progressive circles.

Indeed, sociologist Andrew Kopkind admitted in 1983 that the "left today is dispersed, fragmented, and isolated."[40]

The departure of the Democrats' left and right wings from the party's debates had important implications for the long term. It showed that the party instinctively was trying to find a middle course that would appeal to the moderate middle-class voters who had been attracted to Reagan. Unlike after Hubert Humphrey's defeat in 1968, the Democrats were responding in a measured way and avoiding the temptation to go to extremes. Instead, they sought ways to accommodate the changing political reality—one in which large-scale liberal solutions no longer found favor and market-based ideas were popular—and try to attract alienated voters without, they hoped, angering the party's liberal loyalists. Doing so would not be easy for a party in which strong blocs remained committed to the approaches of the New Deal and the Great Society, that lacked a powerful central authority, and, in the best of circumstances, was prone to factionalism. But the long and painful process of ideological overhaul at least had begun.[41]

Two strains of moderate thought competed for influence among Democrats during Reagan's first term. The first was neoliberalism. Although the term did not appear until 1981, neoliberalism began to develop during the latter part of Jimmy Carter's term, as several Democratic politicians began questioning the party's traditional dogmas. Such figures as Senator Paul Tsongas of Massachusetts, Senator Gary Hart of Colorado, and Representative Timothy Wirth of Colorado emerged as the leading neoliberal politicians; Charles Peters, editor of the political magazine *Washington Monthly,* was neoliberalism's best-known intellectual and his journal, along with sympathetic coverage provided by the *New York Times,* provided the neoliberals' major platforms. The neoliberals were young—Tsongas turned forty a few weeks after Reagan's inauguration—and tended to represent constituencies with large concentrations of high-technology companies and middle-class suburbs. Thus, they were among the first Democrats to understand the politics of the new professional and middle classes. Wirth noted in early 1981 that, in his district, the traditional Democratic blue-collar voters had been replaced by suburban college-educated technology workers. Tsongas further claimed that, as a result of their economic experiences during the 1970s, these voters now resented the poor and no longer were willing to support liberal social and welfare programs.[42]

The neoliberals' goal was to update liberalism so its ideals would appeal to the new generation of voters. Peters, for example, wrote of the need to continue to protect the helpless and aid the down and out, but he and other neoliberals rejected liberalism's traditional operating assumptions. They believed, for example, that government programs often were ineffectual, and Tsongas in particular noted that much of liberal thinking was outdated and of little interest to younger voters. Peters, for his part, went even further and attacked traditional liberals for having lost the ability to criticize their own ideas and learn from those of their opponents; for caring more about preserving gains already achieved rather than seeking ways to help those still in need; and for allowing political parties and their organizations to become dependent on "special interests," especially unions. Rebuilding support for liberalism, the neoliberals argued, required embracing middle-class values and acknowledging that the widespread skepticism of government programs had a basis in fact. Thus, they argued, it was much more important to provide support to business and investors—"to worry about the health of the goose" rather than the distribution of golden eggs, said Tsongas—and they supported tax breaks for business, incentives for capital formation, and deregulation. Peters added that government bureaucracies could no longer be allowed to be "fat, sloppy, and smug"—public employees would have to be fired if they could not do their jobs correctly.[43]

Neoliberalism eventually had its day—Bill Clinton used many of its ideas in the 1990s—but it did not appeal to Democrats in 1984. The major reason was that neoliberalism was not easily distinguished from Reagan's brand of conservatism. Whether it was Peters or Tsongas speaking, the praise of entrepreneurs, skepticism of government bureaucracies, and wariness of entitlements was too close to Reaganism. Indeed, noted the *New York Times,* "neoliberals risk appearing to be neoconservatives in liberal disguise . . . not only tough-minded but also 'tough hearted,'" while Tsongas said that some of his friends wondered if he had long been a closet conservative. Political writer Richard Reeves was blunt, calling neoliberalism the "survival instincts" of young Democrats surrendering to Reaganism. Nor was it ever clear how the neoliberals' carefully constructed policy ideas would, in the end, achieve liberalism's great goals of social and economic justice. Tsongas and the other neoliberals excelled at producing detailed plans to deal with such problems as inflation and energy shortages, but their writings lacked a clear, unifying theme to counter the redemptive message of Reaganism. Arthur M. Schlesinger, Jr., pointed this out as he savaged Tsongas's and Hart's writings as "vapid" collections of "laundry lists, base-touching, boilerplate rhetoric." Neoliberalism also suffered from its dependence on Peters. He dominated neoliberal writing, but his explanations of it tended to be long-winded and confusing, while his criticism of traditional liberalism could take on a nasty, self-defeating tone—when he observed that public school teachers were more concerned about their job security than about improving the quality of instruction, it could hardly have endeared him to one of the Democrats' largest constituencies. Not until 1985, when the Democratic Leadership Council was formed, did neoliberalism begin to attract a critical mass of intellectuals and organizers who could refine and spread the message. Even then, it took the combined effects of the 1984 and 1988 presidential election disasters to force large numbers of Democrats to begin taking neoliberalism seriously.[44]

The other major idea competing for Democratic loyalties was industrial policy, liberalism's answer to the perceived problem of deindustrialization. Industrial policy received its first major publicity in *Business Week*'s special June 1980 issue, when the magazine concluded that American manufacturing's troubles demonstrated the need for a "total reprogramming of the way in which Americans think about their economy." Borrowing from Ezra Vogel and others who had written admiringly of Japan during the late 1970s, *Business Week* proposed that government, business, and labor overcome their suspicions of one another and work together to plan capital investments, tax and regulatory reform, and worker retraining to ensure strong growth. Such a policy was said to be especially critical for maintaining the American lead in new technologies, which were seen as key to creating new industries and ensuring future prosperity. With only a few modifications, these points would form the core of the industrial policy put forth by liberals—a great irony, in view of their advocacy by a pro-business magazine.[45]

As fears of deindustrialization and economic disaster grew in 1981 and 1982, liberal intellectuals seized on industrial policy and made it the vehicle for their plans. Three men took the lead: Robert Reich, a lawyer who taught government at Harvard's Kennedy School of Government; Ira Magaziner, a business consultant; and Felix Rohatyn, the investment banker who had overseen New York City's financial rescue in the mid-1970s. In their essays, published mainly in the *New Republic* and the *New York Review of Books,* they provided detailed explanations of the need for a national industrial policy and how it would work. Unlike in Western Europe and Japan, they argued, American industrial policy—tariffs, corporate tax breaks and bailouts, research and development subsidies, and job training programs—had developed haphazardly, without central coordination or planning. As a result, wrote Reich and Magaziner, such programs had the effect of "retarding economic adjustment or siphoning resources away from more competitive enterprises."[46]

Instead, Magaziner, Reich, and Rohatyn wanted to rationalize industrial policy along their interpretations of German and Japanese lines. Magaziner and Reich proposed creating a strategy to develop businesses that could compete internationally in which the federal government helped workers displaced from failing industries train for new jobs, directed research and development funding to promising areas, and undertook high-risk investments that private firms avoided. Separately, Rohatyn proposed that federal research and development funding and investments be provided through a revival of the Reconstruction Finance Corporation of the 1930s, to be run jointly—and, somehow, without political interference—by business, labor, and the government. The bank would have $5 billion in government-supplied funds to provide capital, tax adjustments, and trade credits to industries. In their grandest ambition, the industrial policy advocates claimed to have the key not only to saving the United States from economic decline but also to transforming American politics and achieving social justice. Industrial policy, Reich grandly proclaimed, would enable citizens to "transcend the old categories of civic culture and business culture." Working together, Americans would not only restore prosperity but also "harness the energy and ideals of all our citizens" to rebuild civic virtue while "striving for justice and decency."[47]

Industrial policy had serious weaknesses, however. As discussion of it became more widespread, professional economists began to look at industrial policy closely and saw that its advocates had badly misinterpreted or misrepresented the data. Robert Lawrence of the Brookings Institution carefully reviewed figures on industry, trade, and employment and concluded in 1983 that deindustrialization was a myth. Growth indeed had been sluggish during the 1970s, Lawrence found, and some industries certainly had well-publicized troubles, but overall employment and investment in manufacturing had grown and, moreover, at rates greater than in Europe and Japan. American industrial productivity, in addition, remained the highest in the world. Another Brookings economist questioned the claims of industrial policy's success abroad, pointing out in the spring of 1983 that claims of French and German success were overstated and predicting that most American industries would recover as the economy resumed its growth. Herbert Stein also reviewed the history of industrial policy and then ridiculed those who thought they could now succeed where all other economic planners and coordinators had failed. "The American economy would be revitalized by the exploitation of a vast and hitherto unused resource, namely, intelligence," said Stein. "This resource is luckily in the possession of some professors willing to bring it to Washington."[48]

Economically literate and politically sophisticated journalists also had a field day with industrial policy. Critics made important points by wondering if the government could really make better investment decisions than free markets and questioning whether union leaders and corporate chiefs would truly sacrifice their interests for the common good or instead conspire to protect what they had. Robert Samuelson noted that Reich's proposals were a "grab bag of vaguely described schemes," with the "dreamy, never-met-a-payroll flavor of the professional theory-spinner," and another writer ridiculed industrial policy's advocates as a group self-promoters and hustlers. The extravagant social claims of industrial policy made it an easy target, especially with regard to Reich's prediction that it would transform American life or Rohatyn's that his neo–Reconstruction Finance Corporation would be above politics. Taken as a whole, the combination of industrial policy's corporatist arguments and calls for groups to sacrifice their interests for the national good sounded uncomfortably like those of European fascists during the 1930s.[49]

Nonetheless, the Democrats found industrial policy far more attractive than neoliberalism. In early 1983, *Newsweek* described Reich as the "Democrats' new guru," with the party's prospective presidential candidates trooping to Cambridge to see him. Indeed, prominent Democrats saw industrial policy as a powerful idea, if only because it offered something to each of the party's main constituencies. Unlike neoliberalism, it embraced the unions, promised a large and successful role for the federal government, and offered liberals a vision of Americans working in harmony for the common good and achieving social justice as part of the process. Almost all of the Democrats competing for the party's 1984 nomination claimed to support industrial policy—Walter Mondale, as he finished Reich's book *The Next American Frontier,* reportedly told his wife, "This should do it for the Democrats in 1984." Politicians also liked industrial policy because it was flexible. Magaziner, Reich, and Rohatyn presented so many proposals that Mondale and the other candidates were easily able to pick some and reject others—depending on what audiences they wanted to address—and still claim to be faithful to the overall idea.[50]

The true political strength of industrial policy became clear in June 1984 when, in a unique case, it was placed in front of voters. Working with the governor of Rhode Island's Strategic Development Commission, in the fall of 1983 Magaziner presented a thousand-page report outlining a proposed industrial strategy for the state. Passed by the legislature on the condition that the voters approve it in a referendum, Magaziner's plan promised to create sixty thousand jobs in high technology by making Rhode Island a leader in the emerging industries of robotics, medical technologies, computer materials, and services for the elderly. To do this, the state would spend $250 million to finance research and development, job creation, and new product development, as well as provide aid to older, ailing industries, such as textiles. All of this would be paid for with new bonds, general tax revenues, and contributions from pension funds, businesses, and local governments. To promote the Greenhouse Compact—named after the proposed research centers—the plan's political, union, and corporate backers blanketed the state with brochures, phone calls, and television advertisements. Opponents, however, soon mobilized. They were led by Brown University's economics department, which the *Washington Post* reported "denounces the plan as an elitist scheme that would aid a handful of favored companies and investors," and labeled the Greenhouse proposals "crackpot economics." Critics also asked pointed questions about who in the notoriously corrupt state would be in charge of allocating the money and how Magaziner could promise the sixty thousand new jobs—a number, one Brown economist pointed out, that was no more than a guess. On June 12, the voters rejected the Greenhouse Compact by a resounding four to one.[51]

Like the Olympic torch relay, which was under way at the same time, the defeat of the Greenhouse Compact revealed much about politics in Reagan's America. If Reagan conservatism drew much of its strength from its roots in American political culture, then it benefited just as much from the weakness and demoralization of its opponents. Despite more than three years of debate and discussion, the Democrats were no closer to finding a new, appealing idea than they had been on the day Jimmy Carter was defeated; industrial policy had been their greatest hope but flopped when put in front of real live voters. Indeed, the intellectual forced march had clearly gone down the road to nowhere, leaving Walter Mondale, the Democratic presidential nominee, without the new, broadly appealing ideas his party knew it needed.

For Democrats seeking a candidate to take on Reagan in 1984, Walter Mondale in many ways represented the best of the party's traditions. Born in January 1928, he grew up in rural Minnesota. Mondale became politically active in college and worked on Hubert Humphrey's successful senatorial campaign in 1948; after the army and law school, he practiced law and worked in Minnesota Democratic politics. In mid-1960, the state attorney general retired and Mondale was appointed to replace him, winning the office in his own right that November. He was a popular attorney general, crusading on consumer protection and standing up for civil rights, and was easily reelected in 1962. When Humphrey was elected vice president in 1964, Mondale was appointed to fill out his term in the Senate, where he proved to be a solid Johnson liberal, supporting the Great Society and civil rights legislation. In 1976, Jimmy Carter chose Mondale—by then a leading Senate Democrat—as his running mate and, during the disastrous four years that followed, he served Carter loyally.

But liberalism's troubles led Mondale to rethink his assumptions, and he realized that government programs and interest group politics could hurt progress as much as help it. By the time of the 1980 election Mondale, like many Democrats, was searching for new political ideas and strategies. Mondale himself admitted that after leaving the vice presidency he was glad to have time for "intellectual replenishment."[52]

But Mondale also reflected the party's inability to find useful concepts. At times he seemed to flirt with neoliberalism, supporting some tax cuts, agreeing with some of Reagan's reductions in unsuccessful social programs, and talking of the importance of restoring low-inflation growth. "The starting point for progressive economic and social policies is the provision of a proper framework for promoting sustainable economic growth and price stability," he wrote in late 1982. As the favored candidate for the nomination, however, Mondale decided to run a conservative campaign, which undermined his ability to adopt new ideas. Mondale's strategy was to stress his years of experience in Washington while at the same time securing the support of major Democratic blocs and contributors to build an organization that would overwhelm his rivals and gain a quick victory in the primaries. By the end of 1983, Mondale had been endorsed by the AFL-CIO, National Organization of Women, National Education Association, and scores of prominent national, state, and local Democrats. This support, however, came at the price of tying him to the views and demands of those Democrats most resistant to change in the party. It also meant that, instead of putting forth imaginative proposals or new ideas, his rhetoric consisted mainly of denunciations of Reagan, standard Democratic promises to expand social and jobs programs, and platitudes like "As we respond to new challenges, we must remain true to our history."[53]

Mondale's strategy quickly fell apart once the primaries began. For all his organizational preparation, he lacked critical experience in campaigning for office from scratch—each time Mondale had moved up a rung on the political ladder it was when he had been appointed by party insiders, and his election victories all had come when he had the advantages of incumbency. In contrast, Gary Hart ran under the neoliberal banner and aimed his appeal at those Democrats seeking innovation, portraying himself as a more independent voice. Hart taunted Mondale, calling him the "candidate of the establishment past" and challenging him in a debate to name an issue on which the former vice president differed with organized labor (Mondale could not). Mondale's plan for a quick victory collapsed when Hart finished an unexpected second in the Iowa caucuses and then won the New Hampshire primary. Mondale was forced to fight Hart all the way through the final primaries in California and New Jersey before winning enough delegates to secure the nomination. By then it was June, and Mondale was weary, bloodied, and tagged in the popular view as the candidate of unions and other old-line Democratic interest groups.[54]

Mondale did no better after becoming the nominee. His main domestic theme was the need to reduce the budget deficit and restore many of Reagan's spending cuts. In September, Mondale proposed a combination of tax increases—some of which would fall on middle-class families—cuts in defense spending, and projected savings on interest payments that he claimed would cut the deficit by two-thirds by 1989. He also proposed shifting funds from defense and agriculture spending to pay for $30 billion in new education, environment, and social welfare programs. But Mondale's proposal was a weak foundation for a campaign strategy, because it assumed that the deficit was uppermost in the voters' minds when, in fact, it was not; in any case, his deficit and budget projections were no more credible than Reagan's. Beyond his statements on taxes and spending, Mondale concentrated on a message that was, in the true sense of the word, reactionary: he claimed that all the changes Reagan had brought about were wrongheaded and had to be reversed. Day after day, moreover, Mondale assailed Reagan as a dangerous right-wing extremist, ready to impoverish the helpless, pack the Supreme Court with fanatically anti-abortion religious conservatives, and roll back civil rights gains. Reagan would deliver a "scary, intolerant, and dangerous future," Mondale said in late September. The remark was typical of Mondale's rhetoric, which consisted mostly of gloomy predictions and scoldings without any guarantee that his alternatives would be better.[55]

The voters quickly concluded that Mondale's description of Reagan-era America did not match their daily observations. A *New York Times* poll in early August found that Mondale had not received the bounce in popularity that challengers usually enjoyed after their conventions and, in addition, that two-thirds of the electorate rejected his claim that Reagan had divided society into the greedy haves and suffering have-nots. Fear of the deficit failed as a rallying call for, as the *Washington Post* reported in early September, most voters seemed contented instead of worried. People soon stopped paying attention to Mondale. "When I see him on TV, I just don't want to keep watching," one Michigan voter told the *Post*. By October, the Democrats were dispirited. "I have yet to meet anyone who is really inspired by the thought of Walter Mondale in the White House," wrote a *New Republic* columnist, who further noted that at least Goldwater and McGovern had been able to generate great passion among their outnumbered supporters, something Mondale seemed unable to accomplish.[56]

Reagan's year was the complete opposite of Mondale's. With no opponent in the primaries, he cruised effortlessly through the spring and summer, greeting the Olympic torchbearers at the White House, speaking to D-Day veterans in Normandy, and opening the games in Los Angeles. As usual, Baker's attention to detail and Deaver's careful planning ensured that the campaign went smoothly and that Reagan's events were perfectly staged and dominated network news coverage. For Reagan's Normandy appearance, Deaver strong-armed the French into changing the schedule so Reagan could make his speech just as the morning news shows were starting in the eastern United States; not coincidentally, the live broadcast of the speech knocked the results of the previous day's California and New Jersey primaries off the news. All the while, of course, Reagan basked in the continuing recovery and his strong popularity ratings.[57]

Reagan's campaign message also was the opposite of Mondale's. Pointing to the return of prosperity and the rise in national morale, Reagan simply promised more of the same. Just as he had from the start of his political career, Reagan spoke broadly of a sunny future of individual freedom, limited government, advancing technology, and in which all things were possible. "Every promise, every opportunity is still golden in this land," he said in his acceptance speech at the Republican convention. "Our children can walk into tomorrow with the knowledge that no one can be denied the promise that is America." During the fall he recited the statistics of lower inflation, restored growth, and job creation, often to enthusiastic crowds repeating the Olympic chant of "USA! USA!" He told his listeners that the "centerpiece of our administration is one word:

freedom," and that his administration was dedicated to maintaining America as a land of dreams and opportunities. The message was classically Reagan and American and, in the context of the economic recovery and resurgent national spirit, it was remarkably strong and led voters to forgive the hard times. In October, a woman in Ohio whose husband had been unemployed just nine months earlier told the *Wall Street Journal* that she was "100% for Reagan"—her husband had found work, as had she and their son. In Waterloo, Iowa, which still was experiencing fresh rounds of job losses, the *Washington Post* found in October that Reagan was enormously popular. "I liked what he did to hold down inflation," said an unemployed Democratic precinct captain. "Although it was painful, he took the proper measures to keep it down." Even Waterloo's Democratic chairman admitted that Reagan was a solid leader.[58]

The contrasts were equally great in the candidates' use of television. Mondale's media campaign was a flop from the start, in large part because he had never become comfortable as a television performer—one newspaper analysis in October noted that he appeared harsh, shrill, and even menacing—and still did not completely understand the importance of television in a modern campaign. On Labor Day, hoping to squeeze in as many campaign events as possible, Mondale's managers asked that the start of New York City's traditional parade be advanced to 9:30 a.m. News coverage that evening showed the candidate walking up empty streets as New Yorkers, who turned out in large numbers for the later parts of the parade, slept late. Reagan's campaign events—not surprisingly, given the more than three years the White House had had to perfect its techniques—were carefully planned and beautifully staged with news coverage always in mind. In his Labor Day rally, Reagan appeared before an enthusiastic crowd with Hollywood stars as warm-up entertainment, high school bands playing patriotic music, and, after his usual speech, the release of thousands of red, white, and blue balloons into the sky. Throughout the fall, Reagan's campaign events sparkled while Mondale's remained dreary; by late October, Mondale had to bear the additional burden of the evening news every night showing the visual contrast as pundits told viewers that his cause was hopeless.[59]

The same differences marked the candidates' paid television advertising. Mondale tried to discuss policy issues in his advertisements, but critics usually noted that the spots were complicated, confusing, or even disturbing; one ad tried to instill feelings of guilt in Democrats who were planning to vote for Reagan while another, meant to emphasize Mondale's commitment to arms control, dissolved from shots of innocent children to nuclear missiles being launched from their silos. Mondale often did not appear in his ads because of his advisers' belief that he came across so poorly on television. Reagan's advertising, best exemplified by the classic "Morning in America" spot, presented his broad, simple themes by using shots of people going to work, getting married, and flags waving in the wind—a set of symbols that worked well in thirty seconds. The *Washington Post* showed a selection of the two candidates' ads to a test audience in Illinois and reported that, for Mondale, the viewers "know he has a plan, but they are not sure what it is," while with Reagan, the president's "soft-sell, feel-good ads about how inflation is down and employment is up were well-remembered."[60]

All of these factors combined on November 6 to give Reagan a stunning victory. He received 54.4 million popular votes—a record that stood until 2004—and 525 electoral votes to Mondale's 37.6 million and 13; only Mondale's 3,700-vote margin in Minnesota, out of more than 2 million votes cast, saved him from the humiliation of losing every state. In the congressional races, the Republicans held on to the Senate and won back many of the House seats they had lost in 1982. The breakdown of the vote also was grim for the Democrats. With 59 percent of the popular vote, Reagan carried virtually every major demographic and income group except blacks and Jews. He did exceptionally well among the young, professionals and white-collar workers, and a new category of voters—those using computers in their jobs—who gave him 62 percent of their votes. In almost every category, Reagan increased his share of the vote compared with 1980 while, overall, Mondale's 41 percent was the same that Jimmy Carter had received. Indeed, it turned out that nothing Mondale had done during the campaign had made much of a difference. Throughout 1984, polls had shown Reagan leading Mondale by roughly 54 percent to 40 percent, and November's results were close to the results from polls taken the previous winter. Most voters, clearly, had made up their minds early in the year.[61]

Nonetheless, for Reagan's critics the scale of Mondale's defeat in the 1984 presidential election was barely comprehensible. To rationalize it, they quickly developed an explanation that portrayed the campaign as devoid of serious ideas and policy debates but marked instead by empty rhetoric and media manipulation that lulled voters into ignoring the country's problems. Reagan's success, argued one journalist the weekend after the election, came because the president was a strong performer who looked good on television as he made meaningless statements. Other political journalists lamented that the emptiness of the campaign had allowed Reagan to escape having to defend his record and positions. Instead, they argued, Reagan had "buried Walter Mondale under a mountain of votes evoked by feel-good television commercials." The results, Mondale's supporters concluded, showed that American democracy was in peril. The success of the "victory of smoke and mirrors," warned a Mondale adviser, meant that "simplification and falsification" would play a large role in politics and produce candidates who were skilled at marketing but poor at governing.[62]

These arguments showed only that the Democrats misunderstood what had happened in 1984. Reagan's victory was not a triumph of slick and empty showmanship but, rather, a confirmation of the victory in 1980 of new political ideas and strategies. Reagan had shown that he could create and maintain a coalition of the educated middle class and technologically sophisticated younger voters, supplemented by blue-collar workers whose pride in the country had been restored. These voters had responded to the emphasis on personal freedom, regulatory restraint, and technological innovation that Reagan promised would bring continued prosperity. Mondale, for his part, had assumed that the old Democratic combination of labor, minority, ethnic, and women voters, combined with a traditional Democratic platform calling for increased social spending, could defeat Reagan. The electorate, carefully measuring what the two candidates offered, chose the new policies over the old. Mondale, after all, proposed little that had not been tried and found wanting during the 1970s, while Reagan's policies, despite the pain of the recession, seemed finally to be delivering better times. "The more I look at it," one Michigan man told the *Washington Post*, "the less

Mondale impresses me and the more Reagan does. . . . His policies have not been as disastrous as I thought four years ago." Newspaper reports from around the country showed that people made it clear that they were willing to continue with the Reagan experiment. "People here are pretty sophisticated," said one politician in Waterloo. "They like the steps [Reagan has] taken on the national level even if we have yet to see the results here."[63]

By the end of 1984, the questions about the nature of Reaganism had been answered. Above all, it was not the revolutionary creed that some had hoped for and that others had feared. It was run by practical politicians—not least, Reagan himself—who were careful not to go beyond the boundaries of popular support. They pursued conservative goals, especially in the areas of taxation and spending, but would not fight to the death over matters of principle, as the supply-siders had come to realize. Instead, Reagan was willing to take incremental gains where he could, and accept stalemate where he had to, secure in the knowledge that he was progressing toward his long-term goals. All the while, Reagan played to Americans' conception of themselves, his efforts made all the more successful because they were sincere. It was no accident that this strategy was reminiscent of postwar liberalism at its most successful. Indeed, the American political consensus allows only a few strategies, and Reagan used the most basic and successful one.

At the same time, Reagan had brought important changes to national politics. He had shown that conservatism was a viable alternative, that a president could govern from the right and push the country in that direction without being labeled as an extremist or destroying his electoral chances. This, in turn, forced the Democrats to begin a systematic reconsideration of their beliefs and strategies—a process that continues more than two decades later. Reagan also changed the rules for presidential use of the media, integrating it with policy and exploiting it to an unheard-of degree. With not only his success in mind, but also with the example of the hapless Walter Mondale, every president since Reagan has sought to use his methods. Finally, Reagan restored the country's confidence in itself and its institutions. His rhetoric about America's possibilities was not just empty symbolism; he backed it up with concrete successes and showed that a determined president could deal with problems that had seemed intractable not long before. Reagan, in short, had done Americans a great service by again giving them reason to believe in the capabilities and legitimacy of their democratic ways.

3

WORK AND LIFE, 1981–1989

What was daily life like for ordinary Americans during the 1980s? Answering this question means speaking in generalities, and this has to be viewed with caution—the experiences of some 240 million Americans are so varied that any broad statements quickly collapse under detailed examination. Nonetheless, some large trends were at work during the Reagan years that produced many common experiences and, in turn, allow some general conclusions to be drawn. The Reagan years were a time when the workplace—responding to deregulation, expanding competition, and new technologies—began a process of transformation and reorganization that continues today. Some people gained dramatically from these developments, and others paid a heavy price, but—and, again, with the perils of generalization in mind—the changes brought important improvements to the majority of Americans' lives.

Guided by supply-side theory, conservatives believed that high taxes were the main cause of America's economic problems, but they never gave up their conviction that excessive government economic regulation also was to blame. Regulation, they believed, wasted billions of dollars per year, penalized successful companies, and stifled innovation and competition. Supply-side adherents viewed the deregulatory experience of the 1970s as confirming this view and, as a result, they were as determined to cut regulations and expand competition as they were to reduce taxes—deregulation was a "pillar of the supply-side platform," said Stockman. Regulation, however, fell into several broad categories—social, trade, industrial, and the market for corporate control—each of which had its own dynamics. In each case, too, politics dictated how regulation was reduced and competition expanded. Consequently, deregulation during the 1980s was a varied process and, ironically, one in which the Reagan administration achieved the most when it did the least.[1]

Reagan began with a well-publicized attack on social regulation, the network of environmental, health, consumer protection, and safety rules that had developed since the late 1960s. He placed Vice President Bush in charge of a task force on regulatory relief and, on January 29, 1981, ordered a sixty-day freeze on all new regulations, pending reviews to ensure that they were needed. On February 17, in Executive Order 12291, Reagan issued requirements to be followed in creating new regulations. Specifically, he directed, cost-benefit analysis would be used to ensure that the costs of new regulations did not outweigh their benefits, while regulators were to consider the state of the economy and the condition of affected industries before issuing new rules. During the months that followed, in what the press dubbed a "war on regulation," new regulations were stopped or cut back, and the staffs and activities of such agencies as the Consumer Product Safety Commission, Occupational Health and Safety Administration, and Environmental Protection Agency were reduced. In just a few months, Martin Anderson later claimed, these efforts produced savings of $18 billion, and in the years that followed the Reagan administration undertook no new large-scale social regulatory initiatives.[2]

The drive against social regulation soon lost its momentum, however. As easy as it was for conservative politicians to score points by complaining about excessive antipollution or safety regulations, such rules actually had a wide base of support, especially among the middle and professional classes. Indeed, polling data and other research shows that, by the early 1980s, such regulations had become part of the American political consensus; politicians could act against them only at their peril. This became clear in early 1983, when a scandal broke out at the Environmental Protection Agency. Since early 1981, the agency had absorbed severe budget and staff cuts—about 25 percent and 20 percent, respectively—its enforcement actions had declined drastically, and, reflecting the administration's

dismissive attitude, many of its senior positions had been filled with political appointees lacking management skills and experience with environmental issues. In March 1983 the head of the agency, Anne Burford,
was forced to resign after an uproar caused by a series of revelations
describing how widespread mismanagement had brought some of the
agency's most important work nearly to a halt. Burford was replaced
by William Ruckelshaus, who had been the agency's head when it was
established in 1970. Ruckelshaus quickly cleaned up the administrative
mess and began working to restore the budget and staff, both of which
returned to close to their Carter-era levels by 1985. The story was
repeated at other agencies as well, where budgets, staffing, and enforcement activity recovered during the mid-1980s and, *National Review*
noted glumly in 1988, reached record levels by the end of Reagan's second term.[3]

Reagan's minimalist regulatory approach failed as well in international
trade. The superiority of free trade was not only a core belief for both
mainstream academic economists and supply-side theorists, but also had
been central to American economic policy since 1945. Reagan, too,
embraced free trade—"my own government is committed to policies of
free trade, unrestricted investment, and open capital markets," he said in
September 1981—as the best path to prosperity and development. But
powerful forces emerged in the 1980s to undermine free trade policies.
The automobile and steel industries, already in decline because of years
of underinvestment in new products, technologies, and quality control
methods, and now suffering from the effects of the strong dollar, by 1981
were in deep trouble. Japan held 19 percent of the American car market
in 1980 and, in that year and the next, American automakers lost a total
of $5.2 billion. Steel imports grew from 16 percent of the market in 1980
to 26 percent in 1984, as the steel industry ran multibillion-dollar losses
and shed half of its employees. Protectionist pressures began to build and
some economists began developing arguments, known as strategic or
managed trade theory, that were similar to those underpinning industrial
policy and purported to justify government intervention to manipulate
international commerce.[4]

The administration retreated whenever it was faced with a major trade
battle. This was especially the case whenever Japanese competitors were

involved. The pattern was set in May 1981, as the tax and spending bills were working their way through Congress and Reagan could ill afford a costly fight on another economic issue. Responding to pressure from Congress, the automobile industry, and unions to give Detroit time to develop improved models that could compete with the Japanese, the administration forced Tokyo to agree to "voluntary" export restraints. Under the terms of the deal, Japan agreed to limit its auto exports to the United States to 1.68 million cars per year, a drop of about 140,000 from 1980; the quota was increased in 1984 to 1.85 million and then 2.3 million in 1985 and afterward. In the next major case, in September 1984—less than two months before the election—Reagan responded to the steel industry's charges of unfair foreign competition by imposing import quotas to reduce foreign producers' market share to 20 percent. In the third important trade case of the Reagan years, the administration reacted in July 1986 to complaints by the semiconductor industry that Japanese firms were selling computer chips at below-cost prices. Once again, Tokyo was pressured into signing an agreement, this time to establish minimum prices for semiconductors and stating an "expectation" that foreign firms would gain a 20 percent share of the Japanese market within five years.[5]

The results of these trade agreements were exactly what economic theory predicted. To maintain their profits, the Japanese auto producers added new, high-margin features to their cars; because of this and the shortage created by the quotas, consumers paid up to $2,500 extra per Japanese car, according to some estimates, while Chrysler, Ford, and General Motors also inflated their prices. Economists calculated that by 1990 the quotas may have provided Detroit with as much as $10 billion in additional profits while transferring billions more to the Japanese. Ironically, this did not help the Big Three in the long run. Detroit improved its quality and productivity, but so did Japan, which left the Americans still chasing the Japanese. Moreover, to evade the quotas and maintain their market share, the Japanese began building production plants in the United States. In another strategic move, in 1985 and 1986 the major Japanese auto companies launched new luxury brands—Acura, Infiniti, and Lexus—that competed directly with Cadillac and Lincoln, and ultimately took much of their lucrative market. When the quotas loosened in the mid-1980s, the Japanese again began to expand their market share, which rose to about 25 percent by the time Reagan left office. The steel quotas, similarly, transferred money from steel consumers to protected producers, but brought no compensating capital investments or improvements in productivity or quality, and failed to stop the continued disappearance of steel companies and jobs. In the semiconductor case, higher chip prices and collusive behavior among producers were the most notable results. Even economists sympathetic to Reagan wrote sadly of how protection was weakening American industries when they badly needed international competition to force them to improve their performances.[6]

Given the tentative nature of its approach, the Reagan administration enjoyed much greater success in expanding competition when it had a foundation of previous achievements on which to build. Transportation, as a result of pre-Reagan deregulation, was a particularly dynamic sector of the economy. During the 1980s airlines continually appeared, went bankrupt, and merged or disappeared entirely. As a result of the competition, fares continued to drop, especially for those who received big discounts in return for booking far in advance of their travel. Lower fares led to increasing passenger traffic, which rose more than 50 percent during the Reagan years, and kept airplanes more full than ever (albeit at the price of coach passengers' comfort). The case was similar for the railroads, which had been in chronic financial difficulty before they were deregulated in 1980. As competition forced them to overhaul their procedures and pricing practices, the railroads cut their labor forces, improved service, and dropped their rates; the industry quickly returned to profitability.[7]

The best-known regulatory change of the 1980s, the breakup of AT&T, also had its roots in pre-Reagan developments. AT&T had held a monopoly on telephone service in the United States since the 1920s, providing all long distance and almost all local service, and manufacturing and owning almost all of the nation's telephone equipment, down to the phones in customers' homes, and its long-distance profits subsidized local service and such benefits as free directory and operator service. But technological advances after World War II, especially in microwave communications, made competition in long-distance service feasible. In 1969, the Federal Communications Commission allowed MCI to begin offering long-distance service; more competitors appeared during the 1970s, and the Justice Department filed an antitrust suit against AT&T in 1974. With the company's regulatory and legal problems mushrooming, in 1981 it settled with the government: starting on January 1, 1984, in return for the freedom to compete in the long-distance market, AT&T would divest itself of its local operations, which would be taken over by seven new regional telephone companies—soon known as the "Baby Bells." AT&T would not be completely deregulated, however. To ensure that AT&T would not be able to take advantage of its still-commanding position in long distance, the Federal Communications Commission retained authority over its rates, and the states still regulated local rates and service. Nonetheless, the breakup of AT&T provided the telephone industry with a level of competition that would have been unimaginable just a few years before, even as defenders of the old system, like Felix Rohatyn, predicted "higher costs and poorer service for the customer."[8]

The results of the breakup were similar to those in industries where competition previously had been introduced. During the five years following the breakup, local rates rose by about one-third, reflecting their true costs, and the Baby Bells unbundled their services and began charging fees for information, repairs, and other benefits that customers previously had received for free. But even as local rates rose, hundreds of companies began offering long-distance service, and growing capacity and competition forced rates down—by 1989 rates had fallen by about 50 percent, and they continued to decline into the 1990s. The long-distance companies rushed to build new, technologically advanced networks with digital switches and fiber optic cable, and AT&T, now facing competition for equipment sales to the Baby Bells and retail customers, accelerated its research and the pace at which it rolled out new products and services. Competition also wrought drastic change in the lives of AT&T's employees. The company, which for decades had virtually guaranteed lifetime employment, cut ninety thousand jobs by 1990 as it worked to lower costs and increase efficiency; the remaining employees, reported *Fortune,* went through a wrenching cultural shift as they learned to sell their goods in a competitive market.[9]

In retrospect, it is clear that these changes helped lay the foundations of the telecommunications boom of the 1990s. Fiber optics made possible such things as the rapid transmission of large amounts of data, and Alfred Kahn predicted that "telecommunications services to business, like high-speed data transmission, teleports, etc. will continue to grow strongly." Indeed, it is hard to imagine how the explosive growth of the Internet in the 1990s could have occurred with AT&T still in control of the nation's telephones, telecommunications infrastructure, and prices.[10]

The Reagan administration's greatest, and most far-reaching, success was in the deregulation of the market for corporate control—the actual ownership of large corporations. Here, too, the success of the 1980s had its roots in developments that had taken place long before. Since World War II, the federal government had followed strict antitrust policies— codified in the Celler-Kefauver Act of 1950—to prevent industrial concentration by stopping horizontal and vertical mergers. To expand, many corporations found that they could acquire only firms unrelated to their main businesses. Thus, during the 1960s, large conglomerates developed as corporations sought to grow by taking over companies in other industries. Unfortunately, the conglomerates' executives often were unable to manage such diverse businesses very well and, by the late 1970s, their poor financial performances frequently were causing their stock prices to fall. At the same time, stock prices in general had been taking a beating from inflation and—depending on the cases—poor management and industry overcapacity. "For the last decade or so, shares of the average U.S. public company have traded for about two-thirds to three-quarters of the value of the share's underlying assets," reported *Business Week* in March 1985.[11]

Economists had long foreseen the opportunity that now existed. If poor management or other factors caused a stock price to fall, they pointed out, new managers could buy the firm at a substantial discount. The control of a corporation, therefore, was itself an asset for which a market existed and, explained one economist in 1965, the "return from the successful takeover and revitalization of a poorly run company can be enormous." Before this market could operate freely, however, the government had to become more relaxed about allowing mergers within industries. As it happened, during the 1970s a new generation of economists and lawyers had become established in the Justice Department's antitrust division, bringing with them free-market views. During the 1980s, they provided important bureaucratic support for the views of the Reagan administration, and updated antitrust guidelines issued in June 1982—the first since 1968—and June 1984 clearly indicated that the government now took a lenient view of mergers. The new rules alone were not enough to enable the market for corporate control to take off, how-ever—new methods of financing were needed to support an expansion of the number and size of mergers. This was provided mainly by Michael Milken, a revolutionary figure in American financial history. A bond trader and salesman, Milken realized in the late 1970s that low-rated, high-yield corporate debt, so-called "junk bonds," which had long been seen as disreputable and were traded only on the fringes of the financial system, could be marketed on a large scale. By 1984, Milken and the firm he worked for, Drexel Burnham Lambert, had almost single-handedly created a multibillion-dollar market for junk bonds and had begun using them to finance takeovers. Other Wall Street firms soon began under-writing junk bonds, providing additional funds to finance takeovers.[12]

Merger activity quickly took off. In 1980, some 1,500 mergers, worth $32 billion, had taken place. The figures then climbed through the Reagan years, with the number of deals peaking at almost 4,400 in 1987, and their value topping off at $226.6 billion the next year. The scale of the deals grew as well, from a few tens of millions of dollars each to a then-record $24.88 billion for Kohlberg Kravis Roberts' buyout of RJR-Nabisco in December 1988. In general, an investor or corporation would spot a company whose shares were undervalued and then, often financed by Milken's junk bonds and other borrowed funds, bid for control of the target firm's stock at a premium to the current market price. Most such takeovers were uneventful and the sale was wrapped up quickly. In other cases, the target company fought back, often in court or sometimes by ransoming its shares from the would-be acquirer, or finding a third party to make a counteroffer.

Many of the disputed takeovers turned into dramatic battles, chroni-cled on the front pages and evening news. Milken and the other men prominent in the takeovers—and it was an all-male enterprise—became household names. In the aftermath of a successful takeover, the new owners frequently sold off parts of the company to pay down the takeover debt. In many cases, breakups not only paid for the takeover but also generated substantial profits—in an extreme case, after Beatrice Foods was taken over in 1986 for $6.3 billion, its divisions gradually were sold off at a total profit of $1.8 billion, and the company disappeared. In other cases, the new owners worked to improve the company's performance, often by replacing managers, overhauling operations, closing loss-making plants, and dismissing excess employees; often, they sold the company back to the public a few years later at a substantial profit. Milken and other takeover figures amassed enormous fortunes, and the armies of investment bankers, lawyers, and brokers that worked with them raked in astonishing fees—some $800 million in the RJR-Nabisco deal alone.[13]

The frenzied activity generated substantial debates as to whether the takeovers made economic sense or were motivated solely by the greed of raiders, investment bankers, and corporate managers. Economist and lawyer Benjamin Stein wrote in *Barron's* that deals often shortchanged ordinary shareholders, and investment bankers' behavior was "characteristic of an age of self-obsession and self-promotion." Other critics compared takeover specialists with pirates and condemned them as greedy and rapacious. Concern that uncontrolled takeover-related lending was creating dangerously high levels of corporate debt also grew. "The tactics used in corporate takeovers . . . often result in weaker companies," wrote Rohatyn in mid-1984, and he and others wondered if highly leveraged companies would be able to survive a recession. For his part, Robert Reich argued that takeovers moved assets around but did little that was truly productive or that generated new wealth. Indeed, the critics often complained that takeover-generated speculation was turning the financial markets into casinos, destroying the structure of the antitrust laws, and would lead to a disastrous 1929-style crash or even the end of American capitalism.[14]

To a limited extent, the critics were correct. Investors and speculators became carried away by visions of huge profits to be made in takeovers, and the market overheated in the latter part of the decade. In 1987, *Fortune* published an analysis showing that the quality of new junk bonds was deteriorating—the *Wall Street Journal* later said that the junk had become "junkier"—and one study later confirmed that, compared with deals earlier in the decade, takeovers in the late 1980s tended to be both overpriced and more risky in their financing. In other words, buyers of corporations were paying more than the companies were worth or they could afford to repay. Simultaneously, it came to light that Milken had been using his dominance of the junk bond market to engage in a gigan-

tic fraud. To maintain the value of the bonds, he engaged in insider trading, market manipulation, and self-dealing on a colossal scale; with federal prosecutors closing in, Milken was forced to resign from Drexel in
late 1988 (in 1990 he received a ten-year prison sentence and was fined
$600 million, and several prominent investment bankers also went to
jail). The reckoning came in the second half of 1989. During the summer
and early fall several major junk bond issues defaulted and, with Milken
no longer available to prop up prices, the junk bond market collapsed
in mid-October. Drexel filed for bankruptcy the following February.
Merger activity declined sharply and did not recover until the mid-
1990s.[15]

Overall, however, freeing the market for corporate control had important benefits for the American economy. It was no secret in the early
1980s, as *Business Week* noted correctly, that "tremendous pressures"
existed to "shrink and streamline the bloated bureaucracy of big business." At Gulf Oil, reported the *Wall Street Journal,* executives had large
personal staffs to see to their needs even as the company's financial performance steadily deteriorated. After it was taken over by Chevron in
1984, Gulf's managers were shocked by their new owner's modest offices,
shared secretaries, and strict financial controls; Chevron soon announced
that eight thousand to twelve thousand jobs would be cut. Other companies took less draconian, but still dramatic, steps to improve their operations. Scott, a poorly-performing fertilizer and seed division of the
conglomerate ITT, was spun off in a leveraged buyout in 1986. The newly
independent management cut inventories and prices to raise cash, negotiated new terms with its suppliers, made more aggressive use of its sales
force, and used its workers more flexibly. Scott's profits increased sharply,
and the company quickly lightened its debt load. Scott's moves were by
no means unusual. In the aftermath of a takeover or buyout, companies
frequently sought new efficiencies wherever they could—including forcing their suppliers to give better deals and therefore begin overhauling
their own operations—and competed more aggressively for sales.[16]

These examples were representative of general developments caused by
the takeover wave. Perhaps most important, the conglomerates were broken up, reversing the mistakes of the 1960s. Corporations no longer
viewed diversification as a viable strategy and they returned to specializa-

tion, concentrated on their primary businesses, and cut bloated payrolls. Spin-offs and breakups aided this process—most businesses that were sold by conglomerates went to buyers in the same industry—and the post-takeover managers generally brought sharp increases in productivity, as the Scott experience demonstrated. Because the increased buying power provided by junk bonds enabled smaller companies, or even individuals, to make plausible takeover threats, corporate managers became less likely to follow risk-averse strategies that hurt shareholder returns. In fact, the knowledge that lagging performance could now cost a company its independence and its managers their jobs proved to be beneficial to companies and shareholders alike. Simply put, since the deregulation of the 1980s, if a corporation is too slow to restructure, replace managers, or respond to changing demand, the market for corporate control has been free to make the necessary moves. During the Reagan years the process often was messy and sometimes was brutal, but Milken, Kohlberg Kravis Roberts, and the other takeover players did much to move capital and jobs to areas where they could be used more efficiently. No wonder critics like Rohatyn and Reich were aghast—they could only watch from the sidelines as the deregulated market for corporate control did what they had dreamed of doing themselves.[17]

For all the setbacks and inconsistencies, Reagan-era deregulation was remarkably successful. Just as free-market theory had predicted, whenever regulations were cut and competition expanded, companies were forced to make their plants and processes more efficient, cut excess capacity and personnel, and develop new and improved products. *Business Week* noted in 1987, for example, that industries had been forced to "become innovators in product development, marketing, and distribution—constantly discovering ways to do the job better and cheaper." Indeed, competition expanded and became more intense throughout the 1980s and, by one estimate, deregulation added $40 billion per year to the GNP. Eventually, every sector of the economy was affected and, in turn, the lives of millions of ordinary workers were changed.[18]

More than 100 million Americans went to work on an average day during the 1980s. In many respects, changes in their work lives were governed by trends that had begun decades earlier—the proportion of

workers employed in the service sector continued to increase, their education levels rose, women constituted a larger share of the workforce than
ever before, and unions remained caught in a decline that had started in
the 1950s. But deregulation, increased competition, and the adoption of
new technologies brought new developments. The results were complex
changes in the workplace—changes that previously might have taken
twenty years were compressed into seven or eight, by one estimate. The
results of these changes, moreover, were unevenly distributed. Some
workers lost ground, some gained, and many had both gains and losses.[19]

Deregulation and expanding competition caused rapid changes in the
workplace. Whether facing competition from abroad, feeling the effects of
deregulation in their industries, or fearing a takeover, corporate managers
realized that they had to look hard at all their processes and do whatever
they could to cut costs and increase productivity. As a result, companies
made enormous capital investments in technology during the decade,
especially in computers and information processing. Most notably, the
prices of personal computers, which had been expensive rarities in 1980,
dropped steadily during the decade and the machines became standard
equipment by the end of the Reagan years—some 14 million were operating in the workplace by 1989, and businesses were starting to connect
them in local area networks. Personal and other computers increasingly
took over routine tasks—operating machinery and moving materials in
factories, tracking sales, or sorting, filing, and retrieving data in offices.
The increasing use of advanced technology in the workplace, finally, made
jobs generally more complex and intellectually demanding. This, combined with the rising education levels of workers, led to the steady replacement of less-skilled workers by employees with the skills needed to
operate computers and advanced production machinery.[20]

The combination of increased competition, the spread of computers,
and the growing skills of employees led companies to begin searching for
new ways to organize work. Early in the Reagan years it had become apparent that new information technologies—if put to work correctly—made it
possible to achieve new efficiencies by cutting product development time,
quickly switching production lines from one item to another, cutting
waste, reducing inventories and backlogs, and improving the quality of finished goods. Companies began a wave of organizational experiments—one

that continued through the 1990s and into the twenty-first century—as they sought the best ways to reduce costs and take advantage of improving skills and technology. Most often, companies sought to capitalize on the flexibility inherent in well-educated workers. What this meant, in practice, was that job classifications were consolidated so individual employees could do a wider range of tasks. Workers often were reorganized into teams, given greater responsibility for product quality, and paid according to new incentive systems. They then were expected to be more productive, take more initiatives, make more decisions, and keep their skills up-to-date. Firms also sought flexibility by making more use of temporary and contract workers. Such workers, noted *Fortune,* enabled a company to "replace a vacationing clerk, [or] augment an assembly line for a seasonal peak," and could, of course, be let go quickly and without severance costs if business slowed.[21]

Information technology and reorganized work processes, when combined successfully, brought great payoffs. Business and management publications soon filled with examples of successful reorganizations. At a General Electric circuit breaker plant, for example, computers and revamped work processes increased productivity 20 percent and cut manufacturing costs by almost one-third; Xerox cut in half both the number of people and the amount of time required to design a new product; and at one industrial controls manufacturer, computerization of assembly lines enabled it to customize and improve the quality of its products as well as undercut competitors' prices. These were not isolated examples—statistics from the 1980s showed improvements in the rate of productivity growth for manufacturing and retailing, another sector that invested heavily in information technology. Later research by economists, moreover, found that these productivity figures had greatly underestimated actual progress—the measurements in use at the time failed to capture many of the contributions of computers and new ways of working. This research, in turn, has made it clear that the sharp takeoff in productivity growth that began in the mid-1990s was in large part rooted in the workplace innovations of the 1980s.[22]

The reorganization of work and rising productivity do much to explain the accelerating growth of income inequality during the 1980s. Change and innovation in the workplace often worked to the benefit of the most skilled and educated employees, as the decline in demand and wages for lower-skill workers suggests. In addition, labor economists found, the gains for high-skill workers often were self-reinforcing. The spread of computers, for example, made it possible to store and retrieve huge amounts of data, which fed demand for educated, high-wage workers who could manipulate such information. They, in turn, found new uses for the information that created still more high-skill jobs. Similarly, the greater flexibility of high-skill workers—both white and blue collar—raised demand for their services, and this, combined with their greater productivity, brought them higher wages. Despite these gains, however, the reorganization of work had some negative consequences for high-skill workers. Some, especially at the highest education levels, found themselves working longer hours than before. Many professionals accustomed to a high degree of independence—such as physicians and attorneys—saw their autonomy erode as managers and outside parties, like insurance companies, gained the ability to watch their costs and performances more closely. Finally, in some cases conflicts broke out between permanent and temporary workers.[23]

The geography of work changed as well. Just as predicted during the 1970s, the movement of business and industry to the outer suburbs accelerated during the 1980s. High urban rents gave companies incentive to move out, and declining telecommunications and computing costs made it possible for them to spread their operations across wide areas and then link their people and computers by phone. In regions as varied as San Francisco, Dallas, Atlanta, northern New Jersey, and Washington, D.C., large office and industrial parks sprang up at the outer edges of the suburbs, often at highway intersections or strung along the interstates. These complexes—writers variously labeled them as urban villages, technoburbs, constellations, and edge cities—quickly became so large that they had more square feet of work space than the downtowns of many midsize cities. They were occupied by technology companies and their manufacturing facilities, corporate "back office" operations that did not need to be in the high-rent areas near headquarters, financial services companies, and a large range of other professional services. "The finished product" of the edge cities, reported journalist Joel Garreau in 1991, "is cleverness . . . everything from decisions to buy and sell, to designs and

redesigns, to software, to reports, to legal opinions, to television advertising." By the end of the 1980s, millions of Americans lived and worked
in technoburbs, commuting from one to another by car, and hardly ever
venturing into the cities.[24]

Many of the workers who gained the most during the 1980s worked in
the complexes of the edge cities. The office and industrial parks were
filled with engineers, computer programmers, scientists, managers, lawyers, doctors, and other professionals whose earnings were at the high
end of the national pay scales; the edge cities also created millions of jobs
in teaching, government, finance, real estate, and other specialized, well-
paid service fields. But the success of the technoburbs and their workers
should not obscure the complexity of developments in the overall American labor force. Looking at the major subgroups of American workers
provides a more complete and nuanced picture of who gained and lost
from the changes in the workplace during the 1980s.[25]

The largest group to be hurt was the displaced workers, defined as
workers who had been in a job for at least three years and then lost it
because of a plant closing or cutbacks. Labor Department statistics
showed that 5.1 million workers were displaced from 1979 to 1984, and an
additional 4.3 million from 1985 to 1989. Most eventually found new jobs,
especially once the economy strengthened, but the effects of displacement mirrored the broader changes in the labor market. Displaced workers in the early 1980s tended to be from industrial and manufacturing
firms, younger, and with fewer skills and lower levels of education and
experience; their searches for new jobs usually took longer than those of
older, experienced displaced workers, although some of the older workers retired rather than seek new employment. Displaced workers' new
jobs often paid less than the ones they had lost, or were only part-time,
and many never regained their previous income levels.[26]

Job displacement hit white-collar workers as well. Starting in mid-
decade, and reflecting the drive to increase corporate competitiveness
as well as the dominance of the service sector, older, skilled, and white-
collar workers began to suffer displacement at much greater rates than
before—especially among middle managers and financial industry
employees. The fates of these displaced workers were not much better

than their blue-collar predecessors'—fewer than half of displaced managers and executives found similar jobs and many displaced white-collar workers had to settle for lower salaries.[27]

Job displacement had a terrible impact on black men, another group that lost heavily in the 1980s. Blacks had made tremendous economic progress from the 1940s until the mid-1970s, as improving education and declining discrimination enabled them to narrow the economic gap with whites. The average wage of a black man grew from only 43 percent of that of an average white man in 1940 to 73 percent in 1980, a trend that was strengthened in part by the start of affirmative action in the late 1960s and early 1970s, which increased demand—and thus wages—for skilled blacks. The majority of black families, moreover, moved into the middle class during this time. But starting in the late 1970s, the trend reversed and black men actually lost ground. The poor economy of the late 1970s and the early 1980s hit black manufacturing workers—many of whom had only a high school education or less—especially hard. Large numbers were displaced from jobs in midwestern cities and, reflecting the legacy of poor schooling, they typically took far longer than displaced white workers to find new jobs; many simply dropped out of the labor force. Black men who had been to college also did relatively poorly, in part because they were concentrated in occupations, like teaching, that did not pay as well as the managerial and professional fields in which white college graduates worked, and also because the boost from the start of affirmative action had leveled off. They did not gain as much from the rising skill premium as whites did and, perhaps in part because of this, black male college enrollments dipped during the first half of the 1980s before recovering later in the decade. Some evidence indicates as well that reduced pressure from the Reagan administration to enforce affirmative action regulations also contributed to the stall in black men's progress, as did the increasing difficulty of winning discrimination suits.[28]

Job displacement widened a divide that already existed among black Americans. The decline in industrial jobs meant that blacks in the cities had few prospects, and social writers began to speak of a growing black underclass—poor, unemployed, uneducated, and trapped in urban poverty. Meanwhile, blacks who escaped the effects of displacement pulled further away from the underclass. Part of the pressure on black men's earnings eased after the mid-1980s as the displacement burden shifted from manufacturing to management and white-collar jobs; employed black men now were no more likely than whites to see their jobs disappear. Black men again began narrowing the gap with white men's earnings after the mid-1980s, while black men with the requisite skills and education continued to move up to better-paying jobs (some black workers also gained access to better jobs as deregulation and the decline of unions reduced discrimination in hiring). Census information indicates that the proportion of employed blacks working in professional and middle-class jobs reached 50 percent by 1988—up from about 40 percent in 1980. Contemporary reporting from around the country reflected this progress—the number of upper-income black families grew, and those blacks who could left the cities for the suburbs, where decreasing housing segregation enabled them to gain higher standards of living and access to better schools. Similarly, the growing number of black professionals gave rise to a new generation of black entrepreneurs.[29]

Organized labor also went through a series of painful adjustments during the 1980s. Troubles for unions were not new—the proportion of workers in unions had been declining slowly since 1953—but the decline accelerated during the Reagan years. Membership had fallen from about 27 percent of workers in 1953 to about 20 percent in 1980, but then tumbled to 16 percent during the next ten years. The growth of government unions kept this situation from becoming even worse, for in the private sector only 12 percent of workers were unionized by 1990. Unions compiled a dismal organizing record, consistently failing to win certification elections—in 1983, they organized only ninety-one thousand new workers, or 0.1 percent of the workforce. Unions also were forced to make large concessions to employers, accepting wage and benefit cuts as well as lower salaries for less experienced workers ("two-tier" wages), and they went on strike far less frequently than in previous decades, even after the recovery began. Labor officials looked desperately for explanations of their decline and ways to reverse the trend, but they issued only empty statements such as "unions are leaner and meaner now than they have

been," and a recommendation that labor "demonstrate that union representation is the best available means for working people to express their
individuality on their job and their desire to control their own working
lives."[30]

Because they were subject to the same forces that altered corporate
behavior, the unions could not stem their declines. Their biggest problem was that deregulation and the expansion of competition had destroyed the conditions that had made it possible for them to win large
gains for their members and thereby attract new adherents. Under regulation, unions had to deal with only a few companies in each industry,
which made it easy to organize and negotiate industry-wide agreements,
while the firms were able to pass rising labor costs along to consumers.
But with new companies appearing in deregulated industries—often with
nonunion workers, lower wages, and more flexible work rules—the
older, unionized firms came under heavy pressure to cut their labor costs.
In these industries, union wages began to drop closer to nonunion levels—in trucking, for example, the gap closed completely, and it also narrowed for airline and railroad workers. The process was quickly repeated
when AT&T broke up and the number of phone companies mush-
roomed. The Baby Bells were "competing with highly entrepreneurial
phone-equipment and computer suppliers in a booming information
industry that, in many cases, keeps labor costs down by employing
nonunion workers," reported the *Wall Street Journal* in March 1984.
Wage advantages for union workers in the telecommunications industry
began to erode—soon after the breakup, Southwestern Bell Telecom, for
example, was paying sales representatives $188 per week for work that had
previously carried a unionized weekly wage of $300.[31]

While displaced workers, black men, and union members lost ground,
two other groups stand out as big winners in the 1980s—immigrants and
women. The 1980s saw a sharp rise in immigration—7.3 million legal
immigrants arrived in the United States (and millions more came
illegally), the most since the first decade of the century. The immigrants
of the 1980s were different from their predecessors, however. Because of
changes in the immigration laws, the proportion of new arrivals from
Europe plummeted and about 85 percent now came from Asia and Latin

America. The immigrants were a varied lot, including educated professionals from Taiwan seeking political security, small businessmen from India escaping a stifling socialist system, and poor Hispanics fleeing war and oppression. Probably all that they had in common was that they provided a pool of highly mobile people willing to work hard and that life in the United States, no matter how difficult, offered opportunities that did not exist for them in their native lands.[32]

The experiences of the immigrants were as varied as their origins. Because of the heavy representation of Latin Americans and refugees, most of whom were unskilled and spoke English poorly, economists concluded that the immigrants of the 1980s were of "lower quality" and unlikely to enjoy as much success as earlier arrivals. The prediction turned out to be correct, but it also hid as much as it revealed. It was true, for example, that Latin Americans with poor educations and English ended up in low-wage jobs, but those who were able to attend school after arriving increased their earnings. It was equally true, moreover, that Asians—especially Chinese, Indians, Japanese, and Koreans—who had been educated before arriving in the United States saw their incomes quickly rise to native levels. Similarly, immigrants arriving later in the decade generally were better educated than those who had come in the early 1980s and thus earned higher wages. Finally, Asian-American and Asian-born women no longer encountered significant racial discrimination in the workplace, and successful immigrants of all backgrounds transformed city neighborhoods and found themselves welcome in the suburbs. In other words, as for everyone else, education and skill were the keys to immigrant success.[33]

For women, the 1980s was a time of tremendous progress. American women had been moving steadily into the workforce for decades, but had lagged far behind men in earnings and were largely confined to traditional jobs such as teachers, nurses, and office clerks. Now, however, declining sex discrimination combined with the demand for experience and skill enabled them to break out of these confines. More than half of all women now held jobs and, because they were not heavily employed in the manufacturing sector, escaped the displacements of the early 1980s and continued gaining work experience. During the 1970s, moreover, women college students had begun shifting the focus of their majors from teaching and the social services to business, engineering, and other well-paying, traditionally male-dominated fields; now they were in the work-force and beginning to move up in their professions. Female enrollment in business, law, and medical schools also shot up during the 1980s, and the proportion of working women classed as professionals increased by half. The spread of computers favored female workers, both because they could substitute mastery of technology for physical strength and also because they increasingly rewarded the skills of educated women. The result was that women as a whole, whose average earnings had been 58 percent of those of men in 1979, earned 68 percent ten years later. Breaking down these figures reveals that women of all ages gained on men, but that women in their twenties—those coming out of college and graduate school in the 1980s and who became senior professionals and managers in the 1990s—were the best off, earning 80 percent as much as men by 1989. Nor were these gains exclusive to white women. Black women, whose earnings in the 1970s had virtually caught up with those of white women, were able to build on their gains in the 1980s, and Hispanic women began moving into professional and managerial positions.[34]

Progress toward earnings parity did not solve all of women's problems, of course. Poorly educated women suffered declining earnings just as their male counterparts did, and households headed by low-skill women often were stuck in poverty. Much of this was caused by social changes, especially increased divorce and illegitimacy rates, that were unrelated to the workplace or lingering sex discrimination, but that was of little comfort to these women. Professional women, too, often interrupted their careers to have children and then faced the problem of how to combine work with family life and motherhood. This, more than any other factor, kept all but the most determined women from completely closing the earnings gap with men (although, on the bright side, some evidence indicates that working wives were able to get their husbands to help with the housework). Indeed, women understood these problems and made it clear in surveys that they felt torn between the needs of home and work. But as their educations brought new hopes, openings, and higher earnings, the opportunity cost of not working also increased, so women continued to go to work, make progress, and make whatever compromises they felt were best.[35]

As this brief survey indicates, the 1980s was a decade of transition in the world of work. Although the wide range of experience among workers makes generalization difficult, it appears that the workplace almost always treated most people more fairly than in the past. Indeed, the workplace of the 1980s was far less discriminatory—by race, sex, or national background—than at any previous time in American history. While no one would go so far as to suggest that all discrimination had ended, it is clear that increasing competition and the need for skilled workers imposed ever higher costs on employers who did not hire and promote on the basis of training and demonstrated capability; by the mid-1980s, significant evidence already existed to show that deregulation and competition had reduced racial and sexual bias in the workplace and created many new opportunities for qualified women and minorities, especially in management positions. Wages, too, reflected changes in the value of skills more quickly than ever before. Sometimes the results of change were harsh. Competition and new technology eliminated millions of jobs and permanently reduced the wages of millions of workers. At the same time, however, growing opportunities and rising earnings elsewhere sent unmistakable signals to workers and accelerated the shift from older industries to the service and technology-based industries that would drive growth in the 1990s and beyond. The combination of these factors, moreover, ensured that gender- and racially-based earnings gaps continued to narrow during the 1990s. Finally, as industries restructured and workers adjusted, the capital markets underwent a revolution of their own, one that changed the way people saved and invested.[36]

The 1980s are remembered as a great time on Wall Street, and the statistics of the bull market remain impressive. From its 1982 low of 776.92 on August 12, the Dow Jones Industrial Average rose—albeit with some harrowing moments—to a high of 2,722.42 on August 25, 1987, a gain of more than 250 percent. From 1981 to 1988, trading volume on the New York Stock Exchange rose from 12 billion shares per year to 41 billion, and the market value of NYSE stocks increased from $1.1 trillion to $2.4 trillion. The rising market attracted millions of investors, and hundreds of billions of their dollars. The number of mutual fund accounts—which became the favored investment of the middle class—tripled, from 18 million to 54 million; the number of funds themselves quadrupled, from 665 in 1981 to 2,718; and the funds' assets rose from $241 billion to $810 billion.

It was by no means clear before 1983 that times would be so good, however. The 1970s had been a dismal era for investors in equities. The Dow Jones average had closed above 1,000 for the first time in November 1972, but it did not rise permanently above that level again until 1983. In the meantime, stocks went through several cycles of fall and recovery—the 1973–74 bear market was one of the most gruesome on record—but, overall, drifted sideways. Some shrewd investors were able to make money, but most either watched as inflation reduced the real values of their shares by more than half or, as millions did, gave up and walked away from stocks. Equity mutual funds, for example, had $45 billion in assets in 1970, but only $41 billion in 1981; money market funds, which did not exist in the early 1970s, held $182 billion in 1981.[37]

Given this experience, the middle class needed a good reason to return to Wall Street. Several factors brought them back during the Reagan years, starting with the provisions of the 1981 tax act that changed the rules for individual retirement accounts (IRAs). IRAs had been introduced in the mid-1970s as a way for workers without pension plans to build savings for retirement—such workers could make tax-deductible contributions of up to $1,500 per year in an account where the money would grow, tax free, until withdrawals began after retirement. As part of the 1981 tax bill, Congress extended IRA eligibility to all workers, raised the annual ceiling to $2,000, and allowed an additional contribution of $250 to cover a nonworking spouse. The new rules took effect on January 1, 1982, with each tax year's deposit to be made by April 15 of the following year. The Treasury expected that contributions for 1982 would total about $9 billion.[38]

The Treasury's estimate was wildly off the mark. Soon after IRA eligibility was expanded, newspapers and magazines began publishing countless articles explaining the immediate tax savings of starting an account, detailing different investment options, and demonstrating how, for a younger worker earning moderate returns, an IRA could accumulate hundreds of thousands of dollars. In response, people rushed to establish accounts. They contributed about $30 billion by April 15,

1983—more than the value of all IRA accounts at the end of 1981—and the stampede was repeated each year thereafter. Every spring, as people prepared their taxes, another $30 to $40 billion flowed into the accounts, almost all of it money that would not have been saved otherwise; by 1986, about one-third of households had IRAs, including about half of those in the middle income brackets. Contributions slowed after the 1986 tax act placed limits on their deductibility, but by the end of 1988, IRAs held $393 billion.[39]

At first, IRA contributors stayed away from equities. In 1981, more than 90 percent of IRA funds were held by banks, insurance companies, and other savings institutions, which offered high-interest certificates of deposit and security for the accounts. The improving economy changed investors' calculations, however. The recovery and lessening of inflation made stocks more valuable while, at the same time, declining interest rates cut the return from bank deposits, certificates of deposit, and other fixed-income investments. The growing belief that the bull market would not end quickly, as several had during the 1970s, also led investors to become more bold. By early 1985, people were moving their IRA funds to equity mutual funds and brokerages; by 1988, 40 percent of IRA money was in funds or accounts managed by investors themselves, which offered a wide range of investment options.[40]

Structural change in the financial industry also brought investors back to the stock market. This, too, was largely the result of the continuing effects of deregulation. Since the end of fixed commissions on May Day 1975, discount brokers had continued to take retail business from the full-service firms while institutional customers demanded ever lower commissions. As a result, the traditional brokerage houses watched their trading profits decline. Simultaneously, a surge of innovation swept the world of finance as new types of financial instruments—including zero coupon bonds, various types of options and other derivatives, creative futures instruments, and securities—appeared in the markets, in addition to junk bonds. Competition among Wall Street firms for trades and underwriting became fierce. Investment banks and brokerages that had grown fat and complacent serving the same clients for decades now found that their customers were shopping around for new services and better terms. Consequently, the firms had to fix their chronically poor

management, overhaul their internal processes, and become more efficient. No longer could an old, prestigious firm like Lehman Brothers
continue to work without internal budgets or spending controls while,
reported journalist Ken Auletta, its "partners spoke of 'my clients,' as if
they would remain so forever."[41]

In such an environment, firms had to be large, innovative, and aggressive to survive. They needed access to large amounts of capital to propose
and underwrite deals, build and cover the risks of large trading operations, and create the computer and communications systems such operations required. Smaller, old-line firms could not compete and merged
or were bought by larger investment houses or corporations. Lehman
Brothers was taken over by Shearson/American Express, and Kidder, Pea-
body found itself too small to compete for shares of major deals—even
though it had $900 million in assets and $465 million in capital—and
was purchased by General Electric.[42]

The survivors made relentless efforts to expand. This, in turn, led them
to the middle-class market, where they sought the deposits of ordinary
savers and young people just starting to accumulate assets. This was
a pool of customers that Wall Street previously had ignored but now
realized had a great deal of potential to generate lucrative business.
Prudential-Bache, reported *Barron's*, "sees its clients as the $40,000-a-
year young professional on the fast track." To attract them, retail brokers
and insurance and mutual fund companies copied Merrill Lynch and
began offering cash management accounts as well as stock trading, credit
cards, insurance, and other financial services. Boston-based Fidelity Investments created numerous specialized funds to attract investors, spent
millions on advertising, set up branch offices around the country, offered
discount brokerage services, and became the country's largest mutual
fund company. Banks, too, began offering mutual funds and discount
brokerage services, and even Sears, the venerable retailer, provided real
estate, stock, and insurance brokers in its department stores. Known as
"financial supermarkets," by 1982 these firms were pitching their services
to customers with incomes as low as $25,000 per year.[43]

The strategy worked and brought in money that helped fuel the bull
market through the mid-1980s. Many individual investors, unsure of their
stock-picking abilities, turned to the funds and advisory services as a way

to invest in equities at low cost and earn better returns than they could on their own. Stock ownership became increasingly indirect and the funds continued to grow, reported the *New York Times* in March 1986, "reflecting many investors' beliefs that the stock market is too sophisticated and professionally dominated to navigate on one's own." As the market continued to advance and tales spread of the profits that others had made, more individuals became willing to go it alone but still hedged their bets, often picking a few individual stocks while still placing most of their money in funds. Given the uncertainty inherent in stock markets, this cautious behavior indicates that investors were carefully seeking to balance risk and profit; indeed, the burgeoning sales of investment newsletters and magazines such as *Money* also indicates that individual investors had been educating themselves about the workings of investments, markets, and risk.[44]

The rise of the huge financial firms altered the behavior of the stock markets, however. With money pouring in, commissions at rock bottom, and computers to automate the record keeping, the funds and other large institutions traded in far greater volumes than in the past. Seeking to pounce on every possible chance for a profit, they also started to use computerized systems to identify brief price discrepancies in the markets and—with speeds that had been impossible just a few years before—move huge amounts of money to capitalize on these arbitrage opportunities. "You push a button and, bam, it goes," said one trader. "There's absolutely no regard for values, just strategy." This contributed to the increase in market volatility during the 1980s, as stocks took sudden, frightening falls or rose sharply for no apparent reason. "Sure, this could get out of hand and disrupt the market," the chairman of the New York Stock Exchange admitted in June 1986. Investors, however, appear to have adjusted. From newspaper and magazine articles they learned about options, arbitrage, program trading, the "triple witching hour," and—as months went by with no catastrophe—learned to take their effects on the markets in stride.[45]

The catastrophe finally arrived in October 1987. In retrospect, it became clear that the stock market had given in to a wave of reckless speculation—from the start of 1987 to August 25, the Dow Jones average rose more than 40 percent. But nervousness had been growing, too, about the economic effects of the budget and trade deficits as well as stocks' high valuations. In early September, Alan Greenspan, the new chairman of the Federal Reserve, raised interest rates, and stocks began to decline. Then, in a day that still ranks as Wall Street's worst in percentage terms, the Dow fell 508 points on October 19, ending at 1,738. The magnitude of the crash inevitably led to comparisons with 1929 and widespread fear that a new Depression was imminent. October 19 proved to be the low point, however. The Fed ensured that the markets had enough liquidity to avoid a repeat of the forced selling that followed the 1929 crash and, although trading remained volatile through the rest of the year, the Dow ended 1987 slightly above where it had started. By late 1989, the average had regained its pre-crash high.[46]

The aftermath of the crash showed how shrewd middle-class investors had become. Equity fund redemptions rose but most investors seem to have held on to their stock funds; most of those who sold generally put their cash into money market funds and waited for better times to return, but others began snapping up bargains within days of the crash. Middle-class investors did not have the sense that their losses in October mattered much in the near term, if only because the money had not been for immediate use. The funds in IRAs were not easily accessible and, economists found, people spent only about 4 percent of their other stock profits. As *Fortune* noted a year after the crash, 1987's "wondrous rise in stock prices came and went too quickly for that rich feeling to sink in among investors." Instead, they simply went on with their lives and remained mindful of the long term. "You buy stocks to build long-term capital," one woman told the *Wall Street Journal* at the end of the year. This view turned out to be correct or, perhaps, self-fulfilling. The economy did not collapse and 1988 turned out to be a good year for stocks; by 1989, fund sales again were strong.[47]

The movement of middle-class savers into stocks during the 1980s had several additional effects that went beyond placing more money into their hands. In the immediate term, the hundreds of billions of dollars invested in equity funds became an important source of funds for the capital markets. This money, supplemented by investors' direct purchases of stock, provided corporations with access to much more investment capital than before. Mutual funds also became large purchasers of the shares of young companies going public, thus providing smaller or less creditworthy firms with access to capital. For the longer term, the experience of the 1980s prepared the middle class to participate in the bull market of the 1990s. Starting in late 1994, the Dow Jones average began a 7,000-point rise that continued until early 2000. The Clinton-era market was marked by the excitement of takeovers, initial public offerings, soaring options values, and unprecedented returns, as well as high volatility and nerve-wracking drops. Educated during the 1980s, however, the middle class was in this market from its beginning and most investors managed their money sensibly, earned substantial sums, rode out the storms, and held on to much of their gains when the stock market bubble burst early in the next century.[48]

Other results of the stock market boom were more ambiguous. Middle-income families certainly enjoyed a substantial increase in their net worths but, as with so much else in the 1980s, those at the top received the lion's share. In 1989, the Federal Reserve's triennial Survey of Consumer Finances found that not only did the proportion of families with various financial assets rise as incomes increased, but so did the value of their holdings. About 21 percent of families with incomes between $30,000 and $50,000 owned stocks in 1989, for example, but the figure was 45 percent for families making above $50,000, and the latter's holdings tended to be far larger. The net result, the Fed and other studies found, was that during the 1980s stock market wealth became more concentrated. (Few of the wealthy made their money in the stock market, however. Federal Reserve studies found that the wealthy of the 1980s tended to make their money in business and entrepreneurship and then move into stocks. In fact, during the decade stocks became proportionately smaller parts of their portfolios.)[49]

Separately, the growth of IRAs and other new retirement savings vehicles started a shift in the structure of pension plans. Under a traditional defined-benefit plan an employee contributes to a pension fund for many years and then receives a monthly, predetermined payment after retiring. Under this system, the employer owned the pension assets and assumed the risks of market fluctuations and of employees living a long time. IRAs and, later, 401(k)s reversed the system—employees contributed a defined amount and owned the assets, but also assumed all of the risks. Defined-contribution plans make sense for workers when their job mobility or insecurity increases, as they did during the 1980s; workers take the assets with them when they change jobs, and employers can reduce their costs and shed a major liability. But younger workers often fail to establish such plans, and it is by no means clear that people with defined-contribution plans will save enough to last their lifetimes.[50]

One unqualified financial disaster took place during the 1980s, the collapse of the savings and loans (S&Ls). The S&L business had long been simple and dull—thrifts, as they were known, took in deposits and loaned the money for home mortgages. This system had critical weaknesses, however. The interest the thrifts could pay on deposits was limited by Regulation Q; in the 1970s, as interest rates rose above what the S&Ls could pay, depositors began moving to money market funds. At the same time, the thrifts' income—the interest on the mortgages, most of them low-interest loans made years before—was fixed, so that even if they were allowed to offer market rates of interest to their depositors, the thrifts would not have the income to pay. By the early 1980s, the S&Ls were running enormous losses and hundreds of them went under. To resolve the problem, Congress passed the Depository Institutions Deregulation and Monetary Control Act in 1980 and the Garn–St. German Depository Institutions Act in 1982. These acts, and changes in state laws, allowed the thrifts to pay market rates of interest, expanded the types of loans and investments they could make, lowered capital requirements, and raised the insurance ceiling on accounts to $100,000. (Regulation Q also was to be abolished by March 1986.)[51]

The new rules unintentionally created a volatile situation. The S&Ls needed more income to cover the higher interest rates, but they still were stuck with their portfolios of old mortgages. To increase their incomes, the thrifts began making risky, high-interest loans. Perversely, their incentives to do this had been increased by the new insurance guarantees. The S&L's insurance premiums were fixed as a proportion of deposits, with no adjustment for the riskiness of a particular institution's loans. Moreover, if its loans went bad and an S&L failed, the government would take the loss, but if the loans paid off, the thrift would keep the profits. Crucially, oversight of thrifts also weakened during this time—the number of examiners and audits fell, especially in the Southwest. At first, however, all seemed well. By 1983, the S&Ls were making a broad range of new investments and loans, particularly in commercial real estate, and had returned to profitability. The Tax Reform Act of 1986, however, changed the rules on real estate depreciation at the same time that oil prices slumped. As a result, commercial real estate investments, particularly in the Southwest, lost much of their value. As loans went bad, hundreds of thrifts became insolvent, leaving taxpayers with a bill that ultimately amounted to several hundred billion dollars.[52]

The spectacular nature of their implosion obscures the fact that in many ways the S&Ls were a typical case of deregulation. Once turned loose, the thrifts quickly expanded their activities and services, much as the airlines and brokers had. As in those cases, companies that were badly managed or made poor decisions came to grief (much would be made about thrift operators who looted their S&Ls, but they were responsible for only a small proportion of the collapses). The major difference between the thrifts and other deregulated industries was that Congress had waited until 1980 and 1982, when the thrifts already were in financial trouble, before taking action. After that, moreover, neither Congress nor the executive branch kept in mind the need for deregulated institutions still to maintain adequate capital nor the requirement for continued supervision and enforcement of remaining regulations. The result was a badly botched case of deregulation and the cautionary lesson that delay and haphazard procedures can destroy an otherwise sensible policy. Sadly, however, it was a lesson that went largely unlearned as, by the late 1990s, Congress and executive-branch regulators again turned a blind eye toward questionable corporate behavior. The result was several spectacular bankruptcies shortly after the turn of the century—Enron's is the best known—that exposed large-scale frauds and also cost thousands of people their jobs and savings.[53]

As the Reagan years came to a close, the media frequently sought to measure his success by turning his question from the 1980 debate—"are you better off than you were four years ago?"—back at him. The answer most frequently reported in newspapers and magazines, provided both by Reagan's critics and many economists, was no. They based their con-

clusion on what, by the late 1980s, was a familiar list of economic statistics and problems. As inequality grew, for example, census data showed a
decline in the proportion of the population in the middle income ranges.
The scale of the decline varied according to how the middle was defined
and the statistics were presented, but it certainly had taken place.
Government statistics further showed that mean annual household
income had risen from about $25,400 to $27,200 during the Reagan
years, an increase of only 7 percent, and critics pointed out that this
masked real declines in the incomes of many workers in the lower seg-
ments of income distribution. The loss of well-paying manufacturing jobs
also figured in the evaluations, as critics argued that most new service-
sector jobs offered little opportunity for advancement or high wages.
This often led, in turn, to predictions that in the future the average
American's standard of living could only decline because of the continuing effects of apparent slow productivity growth, high budget deficits,
and increasing inequality. Many who so far had managed to hold on to a
middle-class life, so the forecasts went, probably would not be able to do
so for much longer. Americans, wrote social critic Barbara Ehrenreich in
a prediction typical of these views, were heading toward a split between
an "affluent minority and a horde of the desperately poor."[54]

The view that life for most Americans was becoming more difficult
gained additional strength from long-standing anxieties and flaws in government statistics. By 1988, fears of foreign economic competition and
deindustrialization were a decade old. For observers like Robert Reich, it
was by now axiomatic that the United States was caught in a long-term
economic decline—he compared America's situation to that of Great
Britain—and the statistics seemed only to confirm their arguments. But
the figures supporting the critics' points were flawed and made conditions appear to be worse than they actually were. Many patterns of household consumption changed rapidly during the 1980s, but government
data were slow to catch up. Consequently, the effects of the introduction
of new or improved goods, new services, and new technologies into the
marketplace—and dramatic falls in their prices—often were not captured,
and official statistics on real income and purchasing power became
increasingly distorted. Economists were forced to address this problem in
the 1990s, when the pace of such changes became even more frenetic,

and they found that real incomes may have been rising during the Reagan years almost twice as fast as originally believed. Similarly, consumption may have been increasing as much as one-third faster.[55]

Although Reagan's critics were not responsible for mistaken conclusions drawn from flawed data, they still were guilty of sloppy research. It was clear in the late 1980s that their analyses of declining living standards could not be reconciled with other easily obtained statistics. Had they looked carefully, they would have seen that their claim that the middle class was sinking into poverty—potentially the most serious criticism of Reagan's policies—simply was not true. The critics were right when they noted that the proportion of people in the middle income ranges decreased during the 1980s, but so did the proportion at the bottom, and the proportion in the upper income ranges grew by almost 5 percent. In other words, the middle class shrank not because people were moving down but because, on balance, they were moving up (see Table 5). This explanation was well understood during the 1980s—Labor Department studies from the time noted it—but it often was overlooked or distorted by writers like Ehrenreich or Reich who wanted to pursue different policies or, simply, criticize Reagan.[56]

Other observations should have given the critics pause as well. If incomes were stagnant, people were falling down the income ladder, and the middle class's standard of living was eroding, the effects should have appeared in a wide range of other economic statistics. But home ownership rates, for example, did not slip and for married couples the rate actually rose by 4 percent. Consumer debt increased, but the rise was concentrated in the top income groups, suggesting that the middle class was not going into debt to maintain its living standards. The share of income spent on recreation and leisure activities rose. Moreover, if the standard of living for most Americans was stagnant or slipping, Reagan's popularity should have suffered. To explain why it had not, some commentators suggested that inflation fooled people into believing that their incomes were rising faster than they truly were, while others asserted that people simply did not understand how badly the economy was performing. If such explanations were accurate, however, it meant that millions of intelligent, educated Americans could not understand what was happening in their own lives, even as they read about it in the newspapers. This presumption of widespread ignorance simply makes no sense.[57]

In fact, for most Americans the 1980s was a time of rising living standards, the human side of which is sometimes obscured by debates about economic statistics. Americans went on a shopping spree in the 1980s as retail sales, adjusted for inflation, rose by a third from 1980 to 1988, compared with only a 12 percent increase during the preceding eight years (see Table 6). Several factors fueled the urge to spend. Some probably was the result of pent-up demand from the sluggish 1970s. Part of it probably was a result of the feelings of relief at the end of the recession and then, especially in 1984 and after, of people being swept up in the celebration of the return of good times. Americans in their twenties and thirties proved to be especially enthusiastic consumers. Young, well-paid professionals—the so-called yuppies—became famous for their self-indulgence and free spending on upscale goods. One advertising study found that yuppies made large purchases of "stocks, bonds, and other investment instruments; expensive cameras; ice cream; chocolate; Japanese cars and sports cars." Similarly, children of blue-collar workers who were the first in their families to go to college and become professionals consumed at a level that their parents could barely understand. Indeed, they told interviewers that they would not forgo the material goods that their parents never had. Women and working couples had larger incomes to spend and, in families where the mother worked, many household services now were purchased from outsiders. These consumers sought greater variety in their choices, embraced new products, and demanded higher quality in the goods they purchased. Not only was the growth of these expectations by itself an indicator of a rising standard of living, but it also led to a push by producers to increase the variety and quality of mass-market consumer goods—a trend that continues today.[58]

The spending began at home, where people purchased more comfort and convenience. Declining interest rates made mortgages more affordable, and many more new single-family homes were built in 1988 than in 1980. Although their average cost had risen by about 75 percent, the new houses were more comfortable than older homes—they were larger, had more bedrooms and bathrooms, and three-quarters had central air conditioning. Homes also were better equipped. Annual shipments of microwave ovens more than doubled during the 1980s, and by the end of the decade about two-thirds of homes had one. Similarly, home furniture sales about doubled. The percentage of households hiring housekeepers—like extra bathrooms, often viewed as a necessity for two-earner families—increased, as did the proportion hiring gardeners or lawn care services.[59]

Consumption outside the house increased as well. The number of car models from which consumers could choose expanded sharply during the 1980s. A good rough indicator of increasing automotive choice is the number of models listed by *Consumer Reports*—a critical resource for middle-class car shoppers—in its annual April car review issue. From 1980 to 1988, the number of models reviewed increased by half. The increase resulted in part from the growing demand for luxury vehicles, as the introduction of Japanese brands like Acura and Lexus had shown, but also for cars that responded to specific consumer needs. The best-known example is the minivan, introduced by Chrysler for the 1984 model year. Its large seating and cargo capacities made it an immediate favorite of suburban families, and by 1988 minivans accounted for some 10 percent of car sales and were well on their way to devastating the market for station wagons. The middle class's use of its cars for vacations declined, however. The Labor Department found that, by taking advantage of lower air fares and discount packages, families flew to their vacation destinations more often than in the past. These destinations were not just in the United States—the number of people flying overseas rose by 40 percent during the 1980s.[60]

The middle class drove off to shop, eat, and drink. Many of the goods people bought, such as VCRs and computers, had been too expensive in 1980 for the mass market, but falling prices made them fixtures in American homes by the end of the Reagan years. Other items, such as cell phones and compact disc players, had not been available at any price in 1980, but had multibillion-dollar sales by 1988. After a day of work or shopping, people went out to eat—especially two-income couples who had little time to cook. The percentage of people eating out rose, as did the share of food spending on meals outside the home; in response, the number of restaurants rose by a third and their sales nearly doubled. The variety and quality of restaurant food increased as well. "It's clear that the number of gourmet restaurants has grown sharply in the past decade as eating out has become an adventure," reported the *Wall Street*

Journal in 1986, while the *New York Times* found that restaurant patrons had become "more demanding and knowledgeable," leading chefs to "offer a wide variety of dishes prepared in imaginative ways." This phenomenon even extended to the beer industry, as small breweries appeared around the country, offering high-quality, expensive brews with distinctive flavors.[61]

Much of this, of course, was charged to credit cards. Credit cards were easily obtained—issuers, for example, offered cards to students with little income as a way of signing up customers who later would generate lucrative fees and interest payments. Card spending almost doubled, and credit card debt more than doubled, but consumers managed their debt well. Most of the increase in debt was driven by higher-income households that could pay their bills. Cardholders in other income groups who ran up large debt-to-income ratios generally paid them down successfully, and the default rate on credit cards actually fell during the 1980s.[62]

The demand for quality and variety caused a major change in how goods were developed and sold to the mass market. Reflecting not only consumer demands but also the pressure of expanded competition, corporations poured billions of dollars into research. They pushed their scientists to improve old products and to pay more attention to potential commercial applications in their research—after stagnating during the 1970s, the number of annual patent applications rose by one-third from 1981 to 1988, and new products ranged from more absorbent disposable diapers to new types of pots and pans to new birth control pills. In 1988, for example, one-third of the 3M corporation's sales came from products introduced during the previous five years. Many of the consumable goods were shipped to supermarkets, which in 1984 offered double the number of goods as they had a decade before; to handle the products, supermarkets grew larger and added in-store bakeries, delis, pharmacies, and other specialty areas.[63]

Previously, the middle class had done much of its shopping for durable goods in large department stores that carried a full range of items— clothes, jewelry, appliances, cookware, and electronics—at full price. Now, however, specialty chain stores—The Gap, The Limited, Polo, Banana Republic, Victoria's Secret—that offered goods aimed at a particular type of customer and could quickly adjust to new trends began to dominate retailing. "There's a tendency for customers to identify their needs with a particular shop instead of a department store," said one retailing executive. Specialty stores also emphasized higher-quality service. Nordstrom, a West Coast–based clothing and shoe retailer famous for its extraordinary customer service, expanded from fifteen to forty-two stores during the 1980s; its first eastern store, opened in Virginia in 1988, set a record for first-year sales by a new department store, selling $100 million worth of goods. Specialized and high-quality catalog retailers, such as Land's End, also prospered as they speeded service by taking orders by phone; it was also during the Reagan years that Michael Dell, a college dropout from Texas, began selling customized computers over the phone for delivery by mail.[64]

Middle-class shoppers did not spend their money foolishly, however. For everyday discounts, they flocked to Wal-Mart, whose annual sales rose from $1.6 billion in 1980 to $20.6 billion in 1988. For commodity goods, such as major appliances, CDs and videos, VCRs and televisions, or hardware, they went to "category killers"—specialty discount stores like Tower Records, Circuit City, and Home Depot—that carried immense inventories, covering all brands of a major type of good. What these stores had in common was a combination of immense buying power, aggressive marketing, sophisticated technology, and knowledgeable sales help. Wal-Mart was the leader in implementing these methods. The discount chain used its huge purchasing clout to wring rock-bottom prices from suppliers, then tracked deliveries, inventories, and sales with sophisticated computer and communications networks, and used the data it collected to refine further its purchasing and marketing strategies. The category killers, for their part, "suck up market share like crazy," said one analyst speaking in mid-1986, and profited on the resulting sales volumes. (The discount stores also were important to lower-income consumers and workers losing ground in the 1980s.) In addition, shoppers soon learned that bargains were to be had even at full-price specialty stores, which often stocked too many goods that looked alike and, as a result, had to cut prices. Traditional retailers, meanwhile, were forced to adapt or die. Losing customers to Wal-Mart and the category killers, Sears turned itself into a discount store, while other department stores opened specialty boutiques within their walls. Nonetheless, by the end of the 1980s many old-line, full-price retailers were in deep trouble, and stores such as Woodward & Lothrop, Bonwit Teller, Garfinckel's, and Gimbels either were gone or would soon disappear.[65]

The changes in housing and consumption took place against a landscape that was being transformed. As in the world of work, much of the action in these areas took place in the edge cities and repeated what had taken place in the inner suburbs after World War II. As businesses moved in and housing developments sprouted, some edge cities grew to cover up to two or three thousand square miles—in the most extreme example, expanding technoburbs brought the Los Angeles area to more than four thousand square miles. Their populations soared as people moved outward, wanting to live near their jobs or seeking better housing at a lower cost—census data shows that the growth rates of the outer suburbs were as great, or greater, than those of the older suburbs had been in the 1950s. In the mid-1980s, Gwinnett County, Georgia, on the eastern fringes of the Atlanta area, was the fastest growing suburban area in the country; its population more than doubled between 1980 and 1989 and, in early 1987, its schools were adding ninety pupils per week.[66]

The stores soon followed. The number of malls and shopping centers in the United States increased by two-thirds—from twenty-two thousand to thirty-six thousand—during the 1980s. Like their tenants, the malls became more specialized—some served upper-income customers with higher-priced stores, while others attracted bargain hunters with concentrations of outlet or discount stores. Increased locations and specialized marketing paid off; by the end of the decade, suburban stores accounted for more than half of all retail sales. Small wonder that, as the *Wall Street Journal* reported about Gwinnett County, people arriving "from older, stodgier suburbs often feel at the edge of a dynamic new future."[67]

The growth of the technoburbs stimulated a debate that had begun in the mid-1970s—should they be viewed as a new type of city, with all that implied about diversity of population and experiences? One housing analyst described an "urban civilization without cities," where residents had comfortable homes with access to high-quality schools, jobs, and recreational facilities. Others suggested that—fulfilling predictions made in the early 1960s—the malls were becoming the new downtowns where, as in traditional cities, people could spend time in a shared public space. Some observers, however, pointed to the negatives. The chain stores and category killers often destroyed local independent and "mom and pop" stores, which not only reduced the diversity of suburban life but also set off bitter fights when established merchants tried to block large stores from opening in new territories. "Wal-Mart really craters a little town's downtown," said one Oklahoma merchant who was forced to close his shop. Popular writers and social scientists often harshly criticized malls, which they portrayed as artificial, manipulative, and celebrating false values. Critics of suburban life in general launched additional broadsides charging that the new cities were ecologically disastrous, sterile refuges for the white middle class that existed mostly to entice people to consume. As for consumption itself, one economist compared it to habit-forming drugs that provided only short-lived pleasure but that left people ever more discontented as they searched for a greater high.[68]

The critics missed the point. The rise in consumption during the 1980s brought real benefits to real people. Sometimes the benefits appeared to be minor, like the ability to watch an old movie at any time; sometimes the benefits were temporary, like being able to take a vacation abroad because of a reduced air fare; and sometimes the benefits were tangible and permanent, like leaving a declining neighborhood for a new, comfortable house in an area with good schools. But in each case, they brought more enjoyment and comfort into people's lives, something they easily understood and appreciated. The accusation that the new housing developments and malls were conformist and dominated by consumption, furthermore, was an empty charge. It assumed that people did not understand their own needs, could be easily manipulated into decisions contrary to their interests—a belief that flies in the face of easily observed reality—and would be unable to create new communities and satisfying lives as their parents had when they moved to the suburbs three decades earlier. Indeed, the fact that millions of people willingly moved to the technoburbs and urban villages suggests that not only did they like where they were going but, like their parents had before them, they sent word back to friends and family that life there was good and they, too, should come to the outer suburbs.[69]

The 1980s was a decade of change in how people worked and lived. The changes often were disorienting—jobs with long-term security in industries that ran according to established patterns disappeared, to be replaced by jobs with less security that required adapting to new ways of working, saving, and living. It is not surprising, therefore, that as the old, familiar ways vanished people often believed that conditions were worsening. But it is clear in retrospect that these changes were overwhelmingly for the good. The increased competition of the 1980s brought renewed innovation, rising productivity, and, most important, an adjustment in how people were rewarded for their labors. That some benefited more than others should not obscure the major result, which for most people was greater fairness, more choices, and an improved standard of living.

It is also clear that the changes of the 1980s laid the foundations for much of what would happen during the 1990s. The hypercompetitive, fast-paced, technology-based economy of the 1990s would not have been possible without the restructurings of the preceding decade. Indeed, the 1980s were in many ways a rehearsal, and much of what happened during the Reagan years was repeated, on a grander scale, in the Clinton era. Takeovers grew to a scale that dwarfed even the largest deals of the 1980s; computers at work and home were linked to the Internet, transforming it from a limited academic network to a major engine for commerce; and the stock market rose to new heights that not only brought great gains to ordinary investors but also created colossal fortunes for the founders of Dell, Microsoft, and other technology companies that first gained notice in the 1980s. All the while, the middle class prospered, the edge cities expanded, and inequality increased.

No one knew in 1989, of course, what the next decade would bring. But people understood that the 1980s had been good to them. As the 1988 election approached, the *New York Times* lamented that voters seemed not to be concerned about too many issues. Because of peace and prosperity, the *Times*'s editorialists concluded, "bread and butter concerns . . . have lost their fire." Considering the state of bread and butter concerns in 1980, this would seem to be as favorable a judgment of the Reagan years as any.[70]

4

SECOND TERM: TRIUMPH, DISASTER,
AND RECOVERY, 1985–1989

Ronald Reagan took his presidential oath for the second time, in January 1985, under conditions far different from those of just four years earlier. Gone was the sense of uncertainty and worry that no president could cope with the nation's troubles. Instead, for the first time in almost thirty years, a president was starting his second term with a combination of enormous popularity, prosperity, and national optimism. In the new context, Reagan turned his attention to fresh tasks. His main priority was to deal with the unfinished budget and tax issues from his first term. Simultaneously, Reagan worked was to ensure that conservatism would have the political and ideological strength to carry on after he left office. Reagan's efforts were not entirely successful—his term was marked by some spectacular self-inflicted failures—but by the time of the 1988 presidential election, it was clear that his brand of conservatism was the most vigorous force in American politics.

As always, Reagan's success or failure depended on the skills of his top staff. The team was changing, however. James Baker was exhausted after almost four years as chief of staff and, in November 1984, he and Treasury secretary Donald Regan began discussing a job swap. They approached Reagan in early January, and he quickly agreed—Baker would take over the Treasury and Regan would become chief of staff. Ed Meese, meanwhile, had been nominated in early 1984 to become attorney general, and Michael Deaver would depart in May to start his own lobbying firm. Simultaneously, numerous high-ranking aides from the first term left, reducing both the administration's experience level and the ranks of those most devoted to Reagan.[1]

Donald Regan was the wrong man to be White House chief of staff, a job that demands sophisticated political, bureaucratic, and management skills. Determined and strong-willed, Regan had attended Harvard on a scholarship, seen combat as a Marine Corps officer in World War II, and then risen from trainee to chairman at Merrill Lynch. But in contrast to Baker, who was a natural politician, tolerant of factions and able to sooth ruffled feathers, Regan saw himself as an outsider and a fighter. "Do you know why I'm hated?" he asked a *Washington Post* interviewer in 1985, as he proudly recalled the reaction of other brokerages to his pre–May Day opposition to fixed commissions. "I broke up their cozy little club." Now, Regan was determined to fix what he viewed as Baker's loose management system—the memos he requested to help him plan the reorganization of the White House staff emphasized the damage allegedly done by fragmentation and turf battles—and replace it with a corporate-style hierarchy. Regan was determined "to bring a semblance of managerial order to the affairs of the Presidency," he later wrote, and see that the president's orders were executed without question. He gathered the functions of Baker, Deaver, and Meese into his own hands, established himself as the unquestioned boss, tolerated no dissent, and did not present dissenting views to Reagan. Unfortunately, as Ed Meese later noted, this made the job of chief of staff too big for anyone to handle alone. In addition, by ensuring that Reagan's orders were carried out without discussion, Regan abandoned a primary responsibility of the chief of staff— to tell his boss when he was making a mistake and try to steer him in another direction.[2]

Doubts about Regan surfaced almost immediately. He was a self-promoter who focused attention on himself rather than the president and had a disdainful attitude toward Congress. Newspaper articles soon began to speculate as to whether Regan had the political skills to run the White House and maintain good relations with Capitol Hill. By the fall of 1985, the papers frequently were reporting on growing unhappiness among the White House staff, a decline in the quality of staff work, that his brusque manner had irritated important legislators, and that Nancy

Reagan was upset with his performance. These were not simply rumors or grumbling. Scholarly surveys and research have since confirmed that the autocratic Regan's poor understanding of how to build coalitions and prod and coordinate the activities of numerous government institutions, combined with poor administrative skills, made him an ineffective chief of staff.[3]

Regan's biggest problems lay in the future, however, and for the next two years politics were shaped by the same two issues that had dominated Reagan's first term—the deficit and taxes. As the new Congress assembled and Reagan prepared for his second inauguration, the deficit remained the prevailing issue in Washington. On January 3, Stockman reported that it again was growing faster than had been expected and that the administration would have to seek new spending cuts. Politicians from both parties were glum. Senator Thad Cochran (R-Miss.) admitted that it was a "little depressing" to think about the budget votes ahead, and Speaker O'Neill talked of how the people would judge Congress by whether it proved willing to make difficult spending decisions. The politicians, however, still were operating without any clear sense of what Americans expected or would accept to reduce the deficit. On the eve of Reagan's inauguration, a *Washington Post* poll found substantial majorities opposed to increasing taxes, cutting domestic spending, or reducing the defense budget. Not surprisingly, in this difficult and uncertain environment, both parties sought an escape. The result was the Balanced Budget and Emergency Deficit Control Act of 1985, one of the most disgraceful and irresponsible laws ever passed.[4]

The law was born of fear. Through the spring, summer, and fall of 1985, Democrats and Republicans wrangled over the budget but accomplished little. Separately, as the result of their 1980 victory, the Republicans knew they would have to defend twenty-two Senate seats in 1986, making the GOP increasingly worried about the electoral effects of failing to control the deficit. On September 25, Senator Phil Gramm (R-Texas) offered an amendment to the bill raising the national debt limit, which was critical for allowing further borrowing to keep the government running. Gramm's amendment proposed a simple solution to the deficit problem. It established a series of declining annual limits for the deficit, with a deadline for eliminating it completely in 1991; should the deficit begin rising above the limit in any year, the amendment created a mechanism by which the comptroller general—a presidential appointee who, however, works for Congress—was to identify and implement the cuts required to bring the deficit down to the allowable level. Because of the importance of the debt ceiling bill, the amendment—popularly known as Gramm-Rudman, after Gramm and his co-sponsor, Senator Warren Rudman (R-N.H.)—was never subjected to hearings or committee action. Instead, the Senate approved the amendment on October 10 and the bill went to a House-Senate conference committee the next day. After weeks of frantic work, debate, and votes, Congress approved the increased debt ceiling and Gramm-Rudman by lopsided majorities on December 11. On December 12, with no fanfare, Reagan signed the bill.[5]

The cynicism behind Gramm-Rudman was in the open for all to see. The law was passed not because congressmen and senators believed in it, but because they saw it as a way to relieve themselves of their responsibilities for making fiscal decisions. For the immediate term, members of Congress from both parties saw it as an easy way to do what they could not build enough support to accomplish in budget votes. Conservatives viewed Gramm-Rudman as paving the way for cuts in social spending, while liberals viewed it as a way to reduce defense spending and, as it inflicted pain, pave the way for tax increases. For the longer term, Gramm-Rudman set a dangerous precedent as Congress and the White House abandoned their political responsibility for making fiscal decisions, and rushed instead to hand power to automatic, technical mechanisms; this is hardly how republican institutions are intended to function. Moreover, despite Gramm-Rudman's quick and overwhelming approval, it was difficult to find anyone who had a good word to say about it. Congressmen, senators, and outside observers took turns denouncing Congress's irresponsibility. In early October, Senator Bill Bradley (D-N.J.) called Gramm-Rudman a "mindless pursuit of a dubious economic objective," and conservative writer Irving Kristol said it was "stupid." The White House accepted it, internal memos suggest, only to avoid battles that might doom legislation that was more important to the administration. Finally, because it was obvious that Congress would always have the freedom to revise Gramm-Rudman in later years, adjusting deficit goals and schedules as it saw fit, no one believed that it would ultimately succeed in its stated purpose. "I doubt that the things that are set out here will ever happen," Rudman said in October.[6]

Rudman was right. Two hours after Reagan signed Gramm-Rudman, Representative Mike Synar (D-Okla.) filed a suit challenging its constitutionality. In July 1986, the Supreme Court ruled in his favor, finding that when Gramm-Rudman placed responsibility for identifying and making spending cuts—an executive-branch function—in the hands of the comptroller general, Congress had violated the separation of powers. Congress soon passed legislation to affirm $11.7 billion in automatic cuts that had been made in March, and amended the statute in the late summer of 1987 to make it conform to the Court's ruling, but otherwise it was dead. By then, too, the growth of the deficit had eased, although economists noted that numerous factors—including a slowing of military spending—other than Gramm-Rudman were at work. As a result, the sense of urgency behind the bill dissipated, even as the deficits continued, the administration and Congress manipulated budget figures to give the appearance of progress, Congress ignored the law's deadlines, and each side blamed the other. Thus, a year after Gramm introduced his amendment, economist Benjamin Friedman accurately called the law a "sham," and wrote that "there are no real plans—more importantly, there is no political will—to make [deficit reduction] happen."[7]

The deficit issue briefly regained its urgency after the stock market crash in 1987. In the frightening days after October 19, many were quick to blame the deficit for the collapse. A Chrysler executive told the *Wall Street Journal* that "we are finally paying the piper for seven years of profligacy by this administration," and his views frequently were echoed by economists, who cited the anxieties created by the deficits as a major cause of the crash. (Given that Reagan had signed the revised Gramm-Rudman bill on September 29, such comments were additional strong evidence that no one believed the automatic cuts would work.) Nonetheless, the crash forced the White House and Congress to begin a fresh round of budget negotiations and, in late November, they announced a plan that combined spending cuts mandated by the repaired Gramm-Rudman Act, new reductions, and tax increases to reduce the projected 1988 fiscal year deficit by $30 billion. In the event, however, the plan did not work. When the Treasury totaled up revenues and spending in October 1988, the deficit exceeded the agreement's level by about $20 billion, leaving observers to note that Congress continued to find ways to avoid cutting spending and that no law could force it to do otherwise, especially if the people were not forcing it to.[8]

In contrast to the Gramm-Rudman fiasco, Congress and the administration worked together closely in 1985 and 1986 to reform the income tax system. By the early 1980s, the income tax was badly in need of a thorough overhaul. For decades, Congress had shifted rates, added scores of preferential credits, deductions, exemptions, and loopholes (subsidies, actually), and tried to use income taxes to promote all manner of economic and social goals. The result was a set of laws and regulations that had grown with no coherence and, consequently, made the income tax hideously complex, unfair, and reliant on a shrinking base. It also had become a major source of economic inefficiency, as investment decisions often were made for tax reasons, not because they made good business sense. Economists had long recognized these problems and had been making reform proposals for years. Now, in the 1980s, popular dismay was spreading, fueled not only by the complexity of the system but also by well-publicized cases of wealthy individuals and major corporations paying less in taxes than ordinary middle-income people, or even no taxes at all. The income tax system, Regan later wrote, "had become a burden on the economy and an affront to economic and social justice." Unfortunately, the outlook for reform appeared bleak. Previous attempts had failed—Jimmy Carter had made the most recent effort—and it was universally assumed that lobbyists, congressmen, and senators would fight any threats to tax breaks of interest to them, thereby gutting any effort at comprehensive reform.[9]

Spurred by his secretary of the treasury, Reagan made tax reform the top domestic priority for his second term. In his State of the Union address in January 1984, he told Congress that he was directing Regan to develop a "plan for action to simplify the entire tax code, so all taxpayers, big and small, are treated more fairly." Regan presented his plan, developed by Treasury tax specialists working under his careful supervision, in late November. Incorporating the thinking of economists and drawing on a 1982 reform proposal by Bill Bradley and Representative Richard Gephardt (D-Mo.), the Treasury plan was a radical proposal to reduce the number of tax brackets from fourteen to three, cut tax rates for individuals, and pay for it by raising taxes for corporations, eliminating many shelters and deductions, and broadening the tax base by including previously untouched sources of income. Baker, taking over the Treasury in early 1985, realized that the plan was an economist's dream but believed it went too far to be politically viable, and in detailed memos to Reagan he recommended a series of changes that the president considered carefully and approved. He modified, for example, the plan's proposed increase in the capital gains tax, eliminated proposals to tax employee fringe benefits, and restored preferences for the oil industry. Nonetheless, Regan's package remained the basis for the plan that Reagan submitted to Congress in late May 1985—"we're reducing tax rates by simplifying the complex system of special provisions that favor some at the expense of others," he told the country in a televised address.[10]

Tax reform worked its way through Congress during the next sixteen months, supported by an unlikely coalition. For its Democratic supporters, reform offered an opportunity to make the system fairer by ensuring that corporations and the wealthy paid taxes; for Reagan and the Republicans, it was a chance again to reduce tax rates as well as simplify taxes; both sides agreed that it had to be "revenue neutral," neither raising nor lowering overall tax revenues. Opposition, however, was fierce as interests of all types mobilized to protect their tax breaks. The White House received hundreds of letters from businessmen and industry groups pleading their cases—the president of the Houston Rockets basketball team, for example, wrote to Reagan warning of the dire consequences if businesses no longer could deduct the costs of their tickets. Politicians worked, too, to protect their constituents and themselves. Governor Mario Cuomo of New York and the state's congressional delegation, for example, defeated the proposal to eliminate the deduction for state and local taxes, claiming it would unduly penalize the Empire State's highly taxed citizens.[11]

On several occasions, opponents came close to killing reform, but it was saved by the efforts of a few determined men. The chairman of the House Ways and Means Committee, Dan Rostenkowski (D-Ill.), shepherded the bill through the House, and Senate Finance Committee chairman Bob Packwood (R-Ore.) saw it through the Senate. Working from the Treasury, Baker oversaw the administration's side of the effort and made crucial deals, while the White House staff geared up the biggest effort since 1981 to monitor progress in Congress, maintain good relations with Rostenkowski, and arrange presidential phone calls to persuade lawmakers to support the bill. The House and Senate reached agreement on the bill in August, and Reagan signed the Tax Reform Act of 1986 on October 22, in the largest signing ceremony of his presidency. In its final form, it collapsed the previous fourteen tax brackets to four, with a top marginal rate of 33 percent, raised the personal exemption enough so that several million low-income people would no longer pay income tax, increased corporate taxes, and eliminated numerous loopholes, shelters, credits, and special breaks—including some instituted in the administration's 1981 tax package.[12]

Compromises had been necessary during the political process, but the Tax Reform Act still was hailed as a remarkable political and economic achievement, comparable to the passage of the 1981 tax and budget acts. The chief drafter of the original Treasury plan pointed out that the act made great strides in taxing all income equitably, and Regan later called its passage an "outstanding accomplishment." Almost all outside observers agreed. For conservatives, claimed *National Review,* the rate reductions were proof that the tax revolt of the 1970s still lived. With so many investment-distorting tax breaks gone, the *Wall Street Journal* predicted that investment decisions would now reflect economic, not tax, considerations, while liberal newspapers and magazines praised the bill's fairness and Congress's achievement. Similarly, legal scholars praised the law as a great step toward making the tax system more fair, and economists believed it would create new work and savings incentives, as well as help the growth of the computer, biomedicine, and other high-technology industries.[13]

In reality, however, tax reform did not quite live up to these high hopes. Looking back during the 1990s, economists found that the Tax Reform Act brought important gains by stimulating business investments in technology, broadening the tax base, and improving fairness. Hoped-for increases in the labor supply and savings did not materialize, however, and the tax laws still remained complex. The reform's impact also seems to have been limited by its revenue neutrality, which led many of its provisions to balance one another. Overall, however, the consensus appears to be that the law improved the tax system and, as a bonus, provided economists with valuable data on the effects of large-scale tax changes on business and individual behavior for use in future research and reform efforts.[14]

The stories of Gramm-Rudman and tax reform are good examples of how American politics were working during the later Reagan years. In the aftermath of Gramm-Rudman, some of the Carter-era doubts about the ability of the federal government to address serious questions surfaced again. Complaints of presidential-congressional indecision and deadlock, as well as about the power of interest groups to stop legislation, were common—one commentator likened the paralysis on the deficit to doctors' failing to treat a cancer—and arguments from the late 1970s about the need for constitutional changes resurfaced. Because of this, the success of tax reform was unexpected—Congress had responded with laughter to Reagan's original call for tax reform—and political scientists later acknowledged that their theories had predicted that interest groups would mobilize to kill such a fundamental change.[15]

The successful passage of a tax reform bill even as budget politics stalemated shows, however, that when politicians acted seriously, the political system was able to deal with complex issues quite well. In this case, it had become evident that an important public policy problem had developed as the tax system deteriorated. Interested politicians and government experts drew on ideas provided by the academic community as well as lessons from recent tax and economic changes—that economic efficiency could be enhanced and everyone helped by reducing subsidies and legal complexity—and worked together to draft a reform plan. The politicians then formed coalitions, made compromises, and otherwise used the tools of their trade to translate the ideas into law. None of those involved in the process rose above party or personal interests—Rostenkowski backed reform to ensure that the Republicans would not be able to claim all the credit, Packwood joined in to repair his reputation as the best friend of special interest breaks, and Baker ensured that Reagan's desire for reform was fulfilled while protecting Texas oil interests. Their motives may have been selfish, but they responded to strong incentives—the *New Republic,* which had called Packwood "Hackwood," in May 1986, found kind words the following month for his role in crafting the bill. All of this took a long time and the final law, moreover, was an incremental improvement of the tax system, not a complete replacement. In this, too, the political system worked as it had for generations.[16]

In contrast, Gramm-Rudman was the product of panic and a desire to circumvent politics. Gramm offered his amendment because Republicans feared that voters would hold them responsible for the deficits. His colleagues in both parties shared his fear, and passed the legislation quickly and without much consideration for its fiscal impact, constitutionality, or their own responsibilities. Rather than use the same time, care, and bargaining that went into tax reform to address the deficit, they sought to transfer responsibility for complex budget and spending decisions to an automatic, nonpolitical process. By setting a schedule, furthermore, they tried to solve the deficit problem quickly and finally. Not surprisingly, in a system geared toward deal making and gradual change, the attempt failed. Its failure, however, was a blessing; had Gramm-Rudman succeeded, it would have become a precedent for turning over major issues in the future to automatic systems, allowing elected officials to duck their responsibilities as well as their accountability to the people.

Attitudes toward politics and incrementalism have shaped many of the attempts to measure the economic legacy of the Reagan years. Those who see problems largely in technical, nonpolitical terms tend to be harsher in their judgments, often seeing the deficit as evidence of systemic breakdown and portending an inevitable disaster. Economist Franco Modigliani, a winner of the Nobel Prize, believed the deficit would inevitably create serious problems in the future, and that the gains of the 1980s eventually would be lost completely. Other economists with similar views argued that Reagan's deficit-fueled prosperity was an illusion that was based on borrowed time. But economists who took a longer and broader view were not as certain about the future. They generally noted that the Reagan years had been a time of major change in American economic policy and understood that during the 1980s the structures of many industries had been transformed. To them, worries about the deficit often were simply hand-wringing, and they pointed out that none of the dire predictions of the era yet had come to pass. Recognizing the difficulty of prediction in a dynamic system, these analysts avoided alarming judgments and were willing to give matters time to be sorted out by the political process.[17]

For a brief moment in the fall of 1986, Reagan basked in the glow of remarkable success. At about 65 percent, his approval ratings not only had remained consistently high since his second inauguration but were at a level that was extraordinary by the standards of recent presidencies. During the summer, when Reagan appeared at the centennial celebration of the Statue of Liberty—another perfectly staged White House show— *Time* gushed about his "easy and sometimes mysterious communion with the American people." In September, the press was filled with praise for tax reform and his role in achieving it. In the cover story of its September 15 issue, *Fortune* noted that Reagan had achieved almost every goal he had set for his presidency and held him up as a managerial example for chief executives to follow. Conservatives were optimistic. With tax reform achieved, they still had ambitious goals for appointing conservative judges, aiding Nicaraguan rebels fighting the country's Marxist regime, and cutting budgets. The next two years, however, turned out to be a time of near disaster for Reagan and disappointment for conservatives. The fault lay squarely with the president and his management style, which, *Fortune*'s remarks notwithstanding, had serious flaws.[18]

The truth is that while Reagan paid close attention to matters that he cared about, in many other areas he was an indifferent manager. He never changed his style of trusting his subordinates to tell him what he needed to know and assuming that they gave him full, accurate accounts. His ideal was to "surround yourself with the best people you can find, delegate authority, and don't interfere," he told *Fortune*. He chose well in those areas that mattered most to him, appointing such capable men as Caspar Weinberger and George Shultz as his secretaries of defense and state, as well as Baker and, to a lesser degree, Stockman. But his record was spotty in those areas he cared about less, and many of Reagan's appointees proved to be poor managers or worse. Rita Lavelle, the head of the Environmental Protection Agency's toxic waste cleanup program, was convicted of perjury and obstructing a Congressional inquiry. Another serious scandal, at the Department of Housing and Urban Development, broke shortly after Reagan left office. Secretary Samuel Pierce was personally honest but an incompetent administrator and, because of chronic disagreements with the White House about filling high-level jobs, many of the department's senior positions remained vacant or turned over frequently. Taking advantage of lax supervision, numerous department officials, including Pierce's executive assistant, ran wild, accepting bribes and payoffs and overlooking billions of dollars in fraud. The resulting investigations took more than five years and ended with several former department officials in jail.[19]

Problems with ethics, judgment, and money also affected Reagan's inner circle, especially during the first half of his second term, when he lacked a strong chief of staff. After leaving the administration to start his lobbying business, Michael Deaver attracted corporate and foreign government clients willing to pay more than a million dollars each for the high-level access he could provide. Unfortunately, Deaver soon ran afoul of the Ethics in Government Act of 1978, which restricted lobbying by former federal officials. An independent counsel was appointed to investigate and, in December 1987, Deaver was convicted of three counts of perjury and sentenced to three years' probation. Lyn Nofziger, another close Reagan friend and White House political director in 1981–82, also was investigated by an independent counsel and convicted for illegal lobbying (his conviction was later overturned). Similarly, Ed Meese's confirmation as attorney general was held up for a year while an independent counsel investigated and cleared him of allegations of financial wrongdoing and favoritism. As attorney general, however, Meese did not learn to keep away from friends seeking favors and, by mid-1987, was under investigation by yet another independent counsel. The prosecutor reported in July 1988 that Meese's "conduct probably violated the criminal law, but that no prosecution is warranted," and the attorney general, unconvincingly, claimed vindication and resigned. Taken together, these scandals created a sense of chronic wrongdoing around the Reagan administration. Commenting to the *Wall Street Journal* in July 1987, one law professor noted that it was by no means unusual for public officials to be in trouble, "but it seems to me to happen a whole lot more in this administration."[20]

All of these episodes paled, of course, in comparison with the Iran-Contra scandal, which began on November 4, 1986, election day. Iran-Contra was a confusing tale whose details came to light over a period of several months. In brief, the story began in mid-1985, when Robert McFarlane, then Reagan's national security adviser, proposed selling arms to Iran as a way of establishing relations with purported moderates in Tehran's revolutionary regime. At the same time, Reagan, for his part, desperately wanted to secure the release of American hostages held by pro-Iranian terrorists in Lebanon. The sales, predictably enough, soon degenerated into a straight arms-for-hostages deal, coordinated by Lieutenant Colonel Oliver North, a marine serving on the staff of the National Security Council. Not only did the scheme violate the administration's publicly stated policies regarding Iran and refusing to deal with terrorists, but it turned out to be an abysmal failure. The Iranians soon realized that the United States could be easily manipulated, and by the time the sales came to light in November 1986, the number of hostages had actually increased. Then, as the story unfolded during the next few weeks, North was revealed to have been using profits from the arms sales—the Iranians had paid inflated prices—to finance Nicaraguan rebels, the Contras. Taken together, McFarlane, North, McFarlane's successor Vice Admiral John Poindexter, and others involved in the schemes had violated numerous laws governing arms sales, banning aid to the Contras, and handling public funds, not to mention basic principles of diplomacy and sensible policymaking.[21]

The investigations began immediately. Meese was the first to look into the affair, but he made a slow, fumbling start that gave North time to destroy crucial documents. On December 1, Reagan appointed a special commission headed by former senator John Tower (R-Texas) to review the matter and the National Security Council's role, and an independent prosecutor, Lawrence Walsh, was appointed on December 19. The House and Senate each formed an investigatory committee and held televised hearings in mid-1987. In the meantime, the White House struggled to explain it all. Reagan gave false and contradictory accounts in his public statements and interviews with the Tower commission, giving the impression that he was confused and did not understand what was going on in his own White House—indeed, his private correspondence from this period shows that he had not known about North's use of the Iranian revenues to fund the Contras. The public, of course, was appalled by what it learned of the affair itself, Reagan's violation of his no-negotiations pledge, and the president's apparent confusion. By early December, his approval ratings had plunged to 46 percent, near the same level as at the depth of the recession, and only about 40 percent of those polled believed Reagan was telling the truth about the affair. To make things worse, the Tower commission report, released in late February 1987, was harsh in its criticism. Because Reagan had failed in his responsibility to manage the National Security Council, said the report in its understated tone, "established procedures for making national security decisions were ignored," and "applicable legal constraints were not adequately addressed." On March 4, 1987, Reagan went on television to apologize to the country. His approval ratings rose, but he never regained the levels of popularity and trust he had enjoyed just six months before.[22]

Along with Reagan's credibility, the White House's administrative system was devastated by the scandal. The blame for all of this lay clearly with Donald Regan. Regan had been present for the early discussions of the arms sales to Iran but lacked the political sense to tell the president to quash the idea. The Tower report, moreover, later would point out that Regan had centralized control over White House operations in his own hands, been present for almost all of the discussions regarding Iran, and should have ensured that an orderly decision-making process was followed and that contingency plans were made in case the scheme became public. Regan, the report found, had "primary responsibility for the chaos that descended upon the White House" when the disclosure came.[23]

Well before the report's release, however, Regan was in deep trouble. He was inexplicably slow to respond to the crisis—it was not until mid-December that he set up a group in the White House to manage the issue—and his papers from the winter show that he was trying desperately to find a way to shift media attention to other subjects. Meanwhile, in December, the newspapers were filled with stories based on anti-Regan leaks and describing Nancy Reagan's efforts to have him fired—"Don Regan would never have got in this trouble if he hadn't gone around telling everyone that he ran everything and knew everything," one anonymous source told the *New York Times*. Several of Regan's top aides resigned during the winter, and more stories appeared in the media detailing paralysis in the White House and efforts to circumvent or remove the chief of staff. Finally, on the eve of the Tower report's release, Regan resigned in a fury after learning from CNN that his successor, former senator Howard Baker (R-Tenn.), had already been named.[24]

Howard Baker was the right man for the job of fixing the White House staff. He was a moderate Republican who had achieved national prominence during the Watergate hearings, when he famously asked, "What did the president know, and when did he know it?" Baker had been Senate majority leader during Reagan's first term and, like James Baker, he brought to the job political experience, strong administrative skills, and an ability to forge compromise. He quickly overhauled White House staff operations and helped the badly shaken Reagan recover his self-confidence and more of his lost popularity.

At the same time, however, it soon became clear that Baker would not fight to regain the political initiative, let alone advance conservative policies. Reagan's power was much diminished—he now faced not only a Democratic Senate but also, as a result of Iran-Contra, public skepticism of his trustworthiness and ability to pass his legislation—and the White House scaled back its ambitions, focusing on maintaining the achievements of the previous six years rather than seeking new programs. Conservatives saw themselves as once again displaced by a moderate who would not support conservative policies—"Mr. Baker's political strategy has been to cooperate with his Democratic opponents in Congress, conciliate any differences, and then declare victory," wrote columnist Paul Gigot. Experienced officials, especially those dealing in policy development, began to leave the administration in 1987, both because they understood the poor prospects for their ideas and because they needed to find new jobs as the end of the Reagan era approached. For his part, Baker resigned in the summer of 1988 because his wife was ill, and his deputy, Kenneth Duberstein, took his place. Duberstein, too, proved to be an able, moderate chief of staff and guided the administration through its final months. But the truth remained that the Iran-Contra affair had turned Reagan into a caretaker president.[25]

The common thread linking the scandals of Reagan's second term is that they originated in his lack of attention to the details of his administration. While no president can be expected to know all that goes on, Reagan never developed a system to ensure that important positions, even at agencies of secondary interest like the Environmental Protection Agency, would be consistently filled with capable people. The public appeared willing to overlook this as long as turnover and ineptitude affected specialized agencies or individual programs, but the Iran-Contra affair revealed that this sloppiness reached top levels and national security policy as well. McFarlane and Poindexter were Reagan's third and fourth national security advisers, respectively, and neither was effective at his job. That Oliver North—well known within the National Security Council as an unreliable man who had trouble distinguishing truth from fantasy— could establish and run his extensive operations with virtually no supervision is a telling example not only of how poorly McFarlane and Poindexter ran the council but also of the price that Reagan eventually paid for tolerating such substandard work.[26]

The impact of Reagan's managerial lapses still reverberates in American politics. The first instance of this was the battle over the nomination to the Supreme Court of Judge Robert Bork. Liberals and conservatives both viewed control of the Court as vital to their interests—liberals for protecting the civil and abortion rights rulings of the 1960s and 1970s, and conservatives for reversing them and ending what they viewed as unacceptable judicial activism. In 1981, Reagan's first appointee to the Court, moderate conservative Sandra Day O'Connor, had been easily confirmed, both because the Senate was in Republican hands and because she was the first woman named to the Court. In June 1986, when Chief Justice Warren Burger retired, Reagan nominated Associate Justice William Rehnquist, a conservative Nixon appointee, to take his place and Antonin Scalia to fill the resulting vacancy. This was a clever tactical move. Rehnquist drew fire from liberal groups, and in September thirty-three senators voted against his confirmation, but he deflected attention from the more conservative Scalia, who was unanimously confirmed. The Court had four conservative justices when the moderate Lewis Powell announced his retirement in June 1987, giving conservatives their chance to gain a majority. On July 7, Reagan nominated Bork, who had long been the right's leading choice for a Court seat.[27]

At first glance, Bork seemed to be an outstanding choice and most observers expected an easy confirmation. He had been a distinguished legal scholar and law professor at Yale—his book *The Antitrust Paradox* (1978) made an important contribution to the change in thinking on mergers—served as solicitor general under Nixon and Ford, and had been appointed to the United States Court of Appeals for the District of Columbia circuit by Reagan in 1982. Bork was a staunch social and free-market conservative, but what made him the favorite of conservatives was his unyielding belief that the Constitution had to be interpreted according to the original intent of the Framers. In numerous articles and speeches he had rejected the idea that new rights could be uncovered, and he thus stood firmly against the liberal belief that the Constitution contained such unenumerated rights as those to privacy or abortion. "Bork's ideology is only the conviction that judges must obey the Constitution rather than rewriting it," explained *National Review* shortly after he was nominated.[28]

To liberals, the idea of Bork on the Supreme Court was horrific. They saw his constitutional views as anathema and had never forgotten that, in 1973, he carried out Nixon's order to fire Watergate special prosecutor Archibald Cox. Expecting that Bork would be the next Court nominee, they had been preparing to oppose his nomination since Scalia's confirmation. Minutes after his nomination was announced, Ted Kennedy denounced Bork on the floor of the Senate. "Robert Bork's America is a land in which women would be forced into back alley abortions, blacks would sit at segregated lunch counters, rogue police could break down citizens' doors," with the federal courts unable to protect citizens from an abusive state, he declared in a speech as memorable for its passion as for its exaggerations and deliberate mischaracterization of Bork. Liberal groups, working closely with Kennedy, immediately mobilized to prevent confirmation.[29]

The battle was fierce and liberals—desperate for a political victory against Reagan—were united, determined, and unusually well organized. Bork's opponents spent the summer of 1987 rallying their forces. Alarmed by his writings on civil rights—as a professor, for example, Bork had questioned the Supreme Court's reasoning in several civil rights cases— the NAACP and other black groups placed heavy pressure on southern Democrats to oppose the nomination. Other groups raised funds for advertisements—People for the American Way, formed in 1980 by television producer Norman Lear to provide a liberal counter to the media efforts of conservative organizations, collected $2 million—warning of dreadful consequences if Bork was confirmed. Legal scholars circulated letters and wrote op-ed pieces and other articles. In addition to these efforts, some of Bork's opponents carried on a simultaneous campaign of name calling and outright character assassination. Bork, wrote liberal legal scholar Ronald Dworkin, was a reactionary "constitutional radical" whose views rested on a "meager and shabby . . . intellectual base." Anthony Lewis of the *New York Times* stoked fears that Bork would contemptuously wipe away Court precedents he disliked.[30]

The administration put up a poor fight. White House papers make it clear that Howard Baker was unenthusiastic about Bork. He made few efforts on Bork's behalf during August and the first half of September, when the storm was growing, and took no steps to set up the kind of coordinated efforts that James Baker had used when he was determined to win a major battle. The lack of coordination, in turn, led to a strategic muddle. Meese and conservative hard-liners at the Justice Department wanted to take a confrontational stand and emphasize Bork's conservatism, while moderates at the White House wanted to play down his views in hopes of attracting support from conservative southern Democrats and moderate Republicans. Without a strong figure like James Baker to decide which course to follow, the result was confusion and fatal delays. The White House also did a poor job of rehearsing Bork for his confirmation hearing. When he testified in mid-September, Bork came across as pedantic and passionless, seeming to confirm his opponents' caricature of him as someone who could bloodlessly roll back the rights of Americans. Finally, the administration overlooked a crucial factor—not only had the Republicans lost the Senate in the 1986 election but, because the Democrats owed their victory to black votes in the South, southern Democrats now could not be counted upon to support the administration as they had in the past. In a striking example, Reagan's phone call notes show that the reliably conservative John Stennis of Mississippi refused to commit himself, even after a presidential conversation. On October 6, the Senate Judiciary Committee voted against Bork's confirmation. Bork, the committee reported, read the Constitution "in a mechanical way, as if it were a rigid legal code," and on October 23 the full Senate rejected him by a vote of 58–42.[31]

The Bork nomination was a major loss for conservatives. In Bork's place, Reagan nominated another conservative judge, Douglas Ginsburg, but Ginsburg had to withdraw after media revelations of his marijuana use in the past. On the third try, Anthony Kennedy, a judge almost as conservative as Bork, was nominated and confirmed. But Kennedy's success was small consolation to furious conservatives. "No senior White House official," complained conservative writer Suzanne Garment, "showed notable zest for the Bork fight." *National Review* complained that Baker had taken no actions to defend the nomination, even as the left mobilized its national anti-Bork campaign. What probably angered conservatives the most, however, was the realization that the battle had shown that the nomination of Bork had gone beyond what the American political and constitutional consensus would support. Bork's opponents, to be sure, twisted his words and mischaracterized his views—even Dworkin admitted afterward that some of the anti-Bork advertisements had been misleading—but, in the end, it was the southern Democrats' fear that his confirmation could lead to reversals of civil rights decisions and the reopening of old, painful conflicts that sank Bork. "We've already fought those fights, and we're happy with the outcome," said Senator Lloyd Bentsen (D-Texas), and no groundswell of popular support for Bork emerged to contradict him. Indeed, even as the Supreme Court has remained conservative since the Reagan years, it has consistently declined to reverse key rulings on abortion and affirmative action, suggesting that the justices believe that dramatic changes would be worse than living with the current, albeit uneasy, compromises.[32]

The White House's mishandling of Bork left a poisonous political legacy that still affects American politics. The success of the attack against Bork legitimized sensational personal attack strategies against nominees for senior offices, and led angry conservatives to swear revenge. Thus, since 1987, congressional Democrats and Republicans both have posed searching ideological questions to nominees, distorted candidates' views and smeared their characters in advertising campaigns, filibustered to prevent final confirmation votes, or simply taken no action on nominations and left judgeships vacant. Presidents, in response, have started to use recess appointments to go around the confirmation process. The problems in the confirmation process have spread beyond judicial nominees, as the experiences of several of President Clinton's nominees—most notably law professor Lani Guinier's nomination to head the Justice Department's civil rights division—showed. Not only do these maneuvers undermine the smooth running of the judicial and executive branches, but they gradually erode respect for constitutional procedures.[33]

The other major long-term effect of Reagan's poor management was the increasing use of independent counsels, or special prosecutors. This practice was a result of Watergate, in which special prosecutors played a critical role in the investigations of Richard Nixon. The Ethics in Government Act of 1978, passed because Congress did not believe that the Justice Department could be trusted to police the executive branch, institutionalized independent counsels and specified the conditions for their appointment and operation. In brief, if the attorney general received credible information of misconduct by a high official, the act required him to investigate the charges and notify a three-judge panel of the United States Court of Appeals for the District of Columbia circuit of his findings. If the matter warranted further investigation, the judges would then appoint a prosecutor who would have complete autonomy to continue the investigation and, if necessary, prosecution.

The act raised serious questions from the start. On the constitutional side, the appointment of a powerful prosecutor—a function of the executive branch—by a court struck many legal scholars as a violation of the separation of powers. On the practical side, the terms for appointing a prosecutor took away all discretion from career Justice Department attorneys for determining the credibility of an allegation, whether it merited prosecution, and the ability to protect a subject's privacy—political pressures alone could determine whether a prosecutor would be appointed. As for the prosecutor himself, he was accountable to no one and had no limits on time, budget, or manpower. Even before Reagan became president, these issues had moved from theoretical to real. A special prosecutor was appointed after President Carter's chief of staff, Hamilton Jordan, was accused in 1979 of using cocaine. The charges were baseless and Jordan was cleared, but not before being subjected to extensive publicity and running up a six-figure legal bill.[34]

The situation steadily became worse in the 1980s. As Reagan's poor supervision led to one scandal after another, each brought another independent counsel and the investigations became longer and more politically charged. Inevitably, the constitutional issues came before the courts. In *Morrison v. Olson,* a case growing out of a political dispute between Congress and the White House during the EPA scandal, the Supreme Court ruled seven to one in June 1988 that the independent counsel system did not violate the separation of powers. The decision surprised many legal analysts—the Court used strained constitutional reasoning to allow the courts to appoint prosecutors—and meant that special prosecutors no longer had to fear any restraints on their activities. Justice Scalia wrote a stinging dissent, not only attacking the erosion of executive-branch authority but warning that the law had created a political tool that was just waiting to be abused. A political opponent of the president could easily "trigger a debilitating criminal investigation," he wrote, and partisan judges could "select a prosecutor antagonistic to the administration, or even to the particular individual" under investigation. Answerable to no one, Scalia argued, such a prosecutor could then take his time to search for a crime to pin on a helpless target.[35]

Iran-Contra proved Scalia to be prophetic. Lawrence Walsh took seven years and spent tens of millions of dollars before completing his work. As if to confirm Scalia's warning about politicized investigations, Walsh indicted Caspar Weinberger just four days before the 1992 presidential election, a move that no professional prosecutor likely would have considered. Also, as if determined to prove Scalia's points, Walsh in his final report accused George Shultz of perjury, even though Shultz had never been charged, let alone convicted. At the same time, however, Walsh's prosecutions had mixed success, largely because they were hampered by grants of immunity given by Congress in its parallel investigation. Walsh obtained convictions against North and Poindexter, but they were overturned on appeal and only one person—a minor figure in the affair—

actually went to jail. It was a sad irony that the system set up to police the executive branch had, in its first major test, proved unable to cope with a serious scandal. The length and politicization of Walsh's investigation, finally, turned out to be another way in which the 1980s were a preview of the 1990s. President Clinton, dogged by accusations of financial wrongdoing even before he was elected, became the subject of seemingly never-ending, ever-widening, hopelessly politicized inquiries for almost his entire time in office.[36]

The disappointments of Reagan's final two years in office had surprisingly little effect on conservatives' confidence in their ideas, however. A small number of conservatives gave in to despair, believing that Reagan's post-1986 weakness had cost them the opportunity to reshape American politics permanently. "I feel we're back to 1977," lamented Norman Podhoretz, the neoconservative editor of *Commentary*, in August 1988. Others agreed and blamed several factors, including Reagan's lack of attention to personnel matters, what they viewed as his personal laziness, and their belief that conservatives had failed to build a strong grassroots movement during the 1980s. Other conservatives, like *American Spectator* editor R. Emmett Tyrell, lamented the movement's failure to prepare for the post-Reagan era, when they would need new ideas to enable them to face new problems and issues.[37]

The majority of conservatives viewed matters differently, however. They accepted the incremental nature of American politics and change and understood that the system could not be overhauled completely in just eight years. In this light, they realized that the Reagan years, as Ed Meese later put it, had been a tremendously successful time. As the end of Reagan's term drew near, these conservatives listed the numerous accomplishments of his years—tax reduction, restricting opportunities for government expansion, economic recovery, continued deregulation, the appointment of conservative judges, and stronger defense and foreign policies. Bork provided the best summary of this view. Writing in August 1988, he acknowledged that Reagan had had his share of failures but emphasized that a "realistic assessment would stress how much the nation's condition has improved since 1980 and how much Reagan has done."[38]

Consequently, most conservatives saw no need to reevaluate their thinking. Indeed, this period stands out for the lack of ideological debate on the right, an indication that concerns about the weakness of the movement were misplaced. In the pages of the *Wall Street Journal, National Review, American Spectator,* and *Commentary,* conservatives expressed regret about Reagan's tactical errors but consistently reaffirmed their positions on taxes, the economy, social issues, judicial appointments, and national security. Most saw their prospects as bright and believed that whoever succeeded Reagan would carry on his work. Irving Kristol argued that Reagan had provided the "first critical stage in the evolution of a conservative majority in American politics." As for the times to come, said Secretary of Education William Bennett, "American conservatism is the party of the future, because it is the party of spirit, the party of energy and enterprise, the party of ideas." Others pointed to rising stars in a new generation, including Representative Newt Gingrich, Bennett's chief of staff, Bill Kristol, and the thousands of young activists working at the state and local levels. Instead of showing uncertainty and dismay, the conservative movement of the late 1980s was strong, vigorous, and embraced the chance to continue working for its ideas. The same, however, could not be said for liberals and Democrats.[39]

In the wake of Mondale's defeat, the Democrats again faced the agonizing process of figuring out where they had gone wrong and how to prepare for the next election. They began as they had in 1981, trying to soften the party's liberal image and, they hoped, thereby increase its appeal to middle-class and centrist voters. In late January 1985, the Democratic National Committee met in Washington and elected a new chairman, party treasurer Paul Kirk. Kirk was a cautious man and suspicious of the party's many groups and caucuses, which he viewed as responsible for the Democrats' chronic squabbling and image as a collection of narrow interests. Consequently, he saw his task not in terms of encouraging open debate of the party's ideas and future but, rather, as ending the discussions as quickly as possible and presenting a unified front to the public. "Today marks the end of the soul-searching and the end of the identity crisis of the Democratic Party," he said at the close of the January meetings. Liberal Democrats at the meeting, however, were disgusted. "One more meeting like this and I'm going home and hang myself," said one.[40]

Kirk acted quickly to prevent public discord. In 1984, the convention had voted to allot a seat on each of the party's major committees to each of the seven recognized caucuses, which included those representing blacks, women, gays, and progressives; to reduce the opportunities for public displays of factionalism, Kirk had the rule changed and the seats taken away. Next, Kirk canceled the midterm convention scheduled for 1986, noting that each of the previous such gatherings had been little more than "a place for mischief," and served only to publicize party divisions and the power of special interests. Kirk's moves pleased the neoliberals—the *Washington Monthly* had been savage in its criticisms of the caucuses—but still could not hide the party's divisions. Robert Kuttner, for example, published a steady stream of articles denouncing what he viewed as the Democrats' abandonment of their principles, while other activists fought against any move to the right. Thus, as Kirk chaired a meeting of the Democratic National Committee in Atlanta in May 1986 and proclaimed that the party no longer was the "brokered sum of countless demands of competing factions," liberal groups and union leaders met in Washington to protest that "one Republican Party is more than enough." That both meetings were prominently reported on the same page of the *Washington Post* could hardly have pleased Kirk.[41]

Even as Kirk was trying to force unity upon the party, Democratic intellectuals undertook their own debates. For them, too, the task was the same as in 1981—to define the ideas that liberals should believe in and could serve as a basis for Democratic policies. But the debate was different this time. Unlike during 1981–84, the discussions during Reagan's second term lacked energy; the pages of the *New Republic*, the *New York Review of Books, Washington Monthly,* and the op-eds of the major liberal newspapers showed none of the excitement or willingness to experiment that had marked the previous four years. Some liberals who had been prominent voices during Reagan's first term, like Ira Magaziner, retreated into private pursuits and silence. Others lamented that policy debates were dominated by conservative intellectuals and think tanks, perhaps as a way to justify their relative silence. As for those who continued to debate, much of the material in their arguments was recycled and they often complained of their inability to generate interesting ideas. "Obviously, there's a crisis of morale among liberals," said *New Republic* editor Hendrik Hertzberg in March 1985, and journalists covering the Democrats noted that party loyalists had little enthusiasm for ideas they realized were badly out of date.[42]

Hertzberg was correct. Liberal intellectuals showed themselves still beset with economic anxieties and unable to break free from past perspectives, fear of foreigners, or unproductive abstractions. The first to demonstrate this was Lester Thurow, who updated his Carter-era economic arguments in *The Zero-Sum Solution* (1985). Thurow painted a bleak picture of the American economy and its prospects. In his telling, productivity continued to stagnate, American-made goods were inferior and uncompetitive in world markets, and the middle class was falling into poverty. The causes, according to Thurow, were the deficit, pointless mergers, inadequate savings, and tax-induced investment distortions, among other structural faults. A financial crisis, inflation, and another severe recession were not far off, he warned. To prevent disaster, Thurow presented a detailed plan for a comprehensive Democratic industrial policy, complete with—once again—Japanese-style institutions for policy planning and coordination, a nonpolitical federal investment bank, and government identification of industries to be promoted, restructured, or phased out. His argument gave no hint that his proposals already had been under discussion for four years or, more important, had fallen flat in 1984. Indeed, the most realistic point in the book was Thurow's concession in his closing pages that none of his ideas were likely to be adopted. This, however, simply led him to give in to hopelessness. "I describe myself as an intellectual pessimist," he wrote, because "there are few examples of nations rebuilding their economies and consciously accelerating their rate of growth of productivity without the sting of a military defeat."[43]

Another book that showed the problems liberals had in developing coherent political ideas was Robert Reich's *Tales of a New America* (1987). This was a confused work, one that mixed a few perceptive observations with abstract cultural theorizing. Reich began by reviewing what he described as the major American cultural myths, especially those of the triumph of the rugged individualist and the supremacy of the free market. He pointed out that popular acceptance of these myths shaped public discussions and helped define what policies would be acceptable, but that continued adherence to these tales was damaging Americans' abilities to identify and solve their problems—"the stories may begin to mask reality rather than illuminate it," he wrote. Reich correctly identified some of the issues and understood their impacts—he saw, for example, that technology was forcing changes in the organization of work and increasing the importance of skill—but more often his observations descended into complaints that had been repeated frequently since 1981. Mergers and leveraged buyouts only destroyed value, American corporations remained hopelessly outclassed by their Japanese competitors, and suburban life was empty, claimed Reich. Overall, moreover, *Tales* had an abstract quality. Reich's emphasis on myths and descriptions of unhappy suburbanites left it unclear how well grounded he was in the realities of people's beliefs and lives. His major recommendation, that Americans update their myths so they could begin to develop a "political culture that engenders an ongoing search for possibilities of joint gain and continued vigilance against the likelihood of mutual loss," was vague and confusing, to say the least. In the end, however, this mattered hardly at all—Reich provided no particular recommendations on which liberals could act.[44]

Other prominent liberals proved no more able to provide workable political suggestions. Arthur M. Schlesinger, Jr., in the title essay of his book *The Cycles of American History* (1985), took refuge in an optimistic fatalism. Reviewing his father's observation that American politics regularly alternate between periods of liberalism and conservatism, Schlesinger noted that the Reagan era had arrived right on schedule—like the 1920s and 1950s, the 1980s was a time of disenchantment that followed two decades of activism and reform. Even though Reagan seemed invincible, Schlesinger argued that the timing of American political cycles soon would catch up with conservatism—"the 1980s will witness the burnout of the most recent conservative ascendancy, and the age of Reagan . . . will fade into historical memory." Schlesinger further comforted his readers by telling them that they only had to prepare and wait patiently, and soon the people would turn to liberals for leadership.[45]

In contrast to Schlesinger, however, Felix Rohatyn fell into a deep pessimism. Because of deficits and foolish spending priorities, he wrote in June 1987, the "United States today is headed for a financial and economic crisis . . . the only real questions are when and how." Six months later, Rohatyn took the stock market crash as confirming his predictions; catastrophe could only be averted, he claimed, if governments developed and coordinated new policies with the advice of experts like himself. Within a few months, however, Rohatyn saw even that option as fading. Deficits and debt had left the United States at the mercy of foreign capital, he wrote in February 1988, and the country had fallen into the "classic model of a failing economic power," marked by high debt, a depreciating currency, and increasing foreign ownership of its assets. The United States soon would be so dependent on foreign financing, Rohatyn predicted, that it would lose its ability to act independently in the world and protect vital national interests. Rohatyn's recommendations, which he admitted were desperate measures, included painful tax increases, restricting the freedom of overseas investors in the United States to purchase major corporations, and providing large credits to aid the modernization of the Soviet Union to avoid losing future Russian trade to European and Japanese companies.[46]

The fear of foreign competition had been growing since the mid-1970s, but in 1985 it gained a new label—declining international competitiveness. If American firms did not improve their ability to compete with foreign rivals, so the argument went, the United States would lose its leading economic position and, like Great Britain, decline into relative poverty and social strife. Trade deficits and the loss of manufacturing jobs were the most frequently cited evidence that American firms could not compete against their foreign rivals, with the blame usually placed on the low rate of productivity growth and the budget deficit, but competitiveness quickly became a catch-all phrase for everything that was perceived to be wrong with America. "What kind of Invisible Hand is it that creates 46 brands of breakfast food?" asked Robert Kuttner as he condemned corporations for providing too much consumer choice. Writers on competitiveness would cite any number of problems as causing it and then advance their favorite programs—or boosts to their own interests— as solutions. Harvard Business School professor Michael Porter, who became a leading writer on competitiveness, argued that the United States had to address problems in labor relations and quality control, which in turn required the government to make large investments in public schools, universities, and advanced research institutes. Finally, the editors of *Business Week,* as if to certify that competitiveness had become an important issue, in April 1987 published another of their special reports proclaiming the need to overhaul government, business, and society.[47]

Promoting competitiveness as an issue, however, did not help liberals define a politically attractive agenda. Because it was so broad, the term meant little. As Reich put it in one of his more perceptive observations, competitiveness had become a Rorschach test—"an ink blot in which we discern our highest hopes and worst fears." In fact, except for the long-standing issues of deficits and productivity, little evidence existed to suggest that the United States was losing its leading economic role. Regardless of evidence, moreover, the need to improve competitiveness quickly became a point of near universal agreement. Democrats, Republicans, unions, and business groups all rushed to proclaim that they would never accept second-rate status for the United States and each offered its solutions. It also was clear that much of what was going on was a rehash of the industrial policy debate but, as one economist commented, no one wanted to use the term because it had been discredited in 1984. As a result, the competitiveness debate became a sterile repeat of what had already been under discussion—how to deal with the deficit and what, if anything, should be done to aid manufacturing and boost productivity.[48]

In another way, the competitiveness issue probably hurt liberals. The debate had always been gloomy—predicting economic decline and lower standards of living was hardly a cheerful business. But in late 1987, with the publication of Paul Kennedy's *The Rise and Fall of the Great Powers,* the liberals' gloom became even thicker. Kennedy was a prominent British-born historian at Yale and his best-known previous work, *The Rise and Fall of British Naval Mastery* (1976), had demonstrated how England's economic troubles caused the decline of the Royal Navy. Now, in a sweeping, detailed, and elegantly written work, he traced the connection "between an individual Great Power's economic rise and fall and its growth and decline as an important military power." Looking at the fates of the great European states, Kennedy concluded that Great Powers and empires must maintain healthy economies and not waste their resources if they are to maintain their strength. Few people questioned this point—it was by no means original—but controversy arose when Kennedy applied the lesson to the United States. In the American case, he argued, the economic base supporting the nation's power was deteriorating as manufacturing shrank, debts rose, and trade balances worsened. The task now, he wrote, was to adjust to this loss of global leadership—to "recognize that broad trends are under way, and that there is a need to 'manage' affairs so that the relative erosion of the United States' position takes place slowly and smoothly."[49]

Kennedy's conclusion became the focus of a vigorous debate. He was not the only academic making this argument about American strategic decline, but his book appeared at the height of the competitiveness discussion. It became a best-seller and the focal point of a combined discussion of competitiveness, national decline, and historical methods. Conservatives were respectful of Kennedy's command of historical detail, but they viewed the book as an extended criticism of Reagan's defense and budget policies, and dismissed his suggestion that the United States was fated to decline. "Our 'problem' is loss of national will," said Norman Podhoretz, not overspending on defense. America's ultimate fate "depends on what we do" in response to the problems Kennedy had outlined, argued another prominent strategist. Liberals had criticisms of their own but, overall, were receptive to Kennedy's argument, if only because it matched their criticisms of Reagan. "Thanks to this extraordinary compendium, we are much the wiser," commented one economic historian. The result was that liberals' concerns about the economy became popularly identified with predictions of an inevitable national decline, something that was unlikely to help them win political support.[50]

The consequences of liberals' continuing ideological problems first became apparent in the 1986 elections. On the surface, it was a Democratic victory—they took back the Senate with fifty-five seats, and added six seats to their majority in the House. The voters, however, had not repudiated Reagan. Most successful Democratic candidates had avoided attacking the president, declared their support for controlling federal spending, and emphasized local issues in their campaigns. In states where Reagan had campaigned for Republicans behind in the polls, the GOP candidates often narrowed the gap. In Nevada, for example, the Republican candidate for the Senate was behind by 13 percentage points before Reagan came to the state twice in the last week of the race; he lost by 6 points. The Republicans also picked up eight governorships, including those of Florida, Texas, and California. Political analysts across the spectrum agreed on the implications for the Democrats. One said the Democrats had shown little faith in their own arguments, and another pointed out that the election resembled the Democratic victory in 1926—"a small uptick for the out party in the era of Calvin Coolidge, quickly forgotten" in just a few years.[51]

The Democrats' problems were further complicated by the change in leadership that followed the election. Tip O'Neill had engineered a remarkable personal and political change after the disasters of 1981. He never changed his beliefs or sought new ideas—the speaker remained a true believer in New Deal and Great Society liberalism, was an outspoken defender of Social Security, and celebrated Democrats' leading role in building a strong middle class while creating programs to care "for those who cannot take care of themselves." But with the help of young, media-savvy aides, the speaker lost weight, bought new suits, and learned how to use television to his advantage. As a result, O'Neill transformed himself from a symbol of failed liberalism into a national grandfather figure. He seemed to embody Democratic opposition to Republican budget cutting, and his popularity ratings were as high as Reagan's in 1986. O'Neill retired after the 1986 election, however, and was succeeded as speaker by Majority Leader Jim Wright of Texas. Wright had none of O'Neill's liberal instincts. Instead, he was a staunch defender of Texas business and pork-barrel interests—federal water projects were among his favorites and, when social programs faced deep cuts in 1981, Wright fought desperately to save billions of dollars in subsidies for corporate synthetic fuel development programs. Unlike the plainspoken O'Neill, Wright talked in convoluted, flowery language that made him a miserable performer on television—*Newsweek* reported that even his admirers admitted he sounded like a snake-oil salesman.[52]

Wright's term as speaker turned out to be short and sad. He long had been dogged by accusations that he was too close to Texas business interests who had, in turn, helped him become rich from questionable oil and gas investments. In September 1987, only eight months after he became speaker, news broke that Wright had been receiving a 55 percent royalty—

some five times the standard rate—for a book published for him by a friend's printing company. The House Ethics Committee began an investigation and, during the months that followed, more questionable deals came to light. Under heavy political pressure, Wright resigned from the House in June 1989.[53]

Wright's problems helped illuminate the corrosive effects that money was having on the Democrats. Money and politics were by no means strangers before the 1980s, but by 1981 the Democrats were having serious money problems. The party had allowed its grassroots fund-raising to decline during the 1970s and labor unions, with their own troubles, could not increase their contributions. Meanwhile, the increasing importance of expensive media campaigns and competition from lavishly funded Republicans greatly increased the Democrats' need for cash during the Reagan years. Mike Synar, for example, said that his campaign costs had risen from $52,000 in 1978 to more than $400,000 ten years later. Similarly, Federal Election Commission figures show that spending by the Democratic Party increased from $35 million in 1979–80 to $122 million in 1987–88, but that in both periods the Republicans still outspent them by more than $100 million.[54]

The need for money greatly increased the importance of individual Democratic fund-raisers, the most effective of whom was Representative Tony Coelho of California. Born in 1942 to a farm family in California, Coelho would later say that President Kennedy had inspired him to try to help people. Rejected for the priesthood after he was diagnosed with epilepsy, Coelho went to work in 1965 for a California congressman. When the congressman retired in 1978, Coelho won the seat. Coelho proved to be hard working and intensely ambitious, but his politics remained undefined. Although Kennedy had inspired him, Coelho admitted that he had little idea what the president had stood for, and California reporters covering him found themselves unable to say what he believed in. One Democratic congressman charitably remarked, "I don't think Tony has a fully thought-out notion of where we should be going."[55]

But Coelho had a fully thought-out notion of how to raise cash. Placed in charge of the nearly broke Democratic Congressional Campaign Committee in 1981, and with small contributors and labor unproductive,

Coelho went after corporate political action committees. He bluntly reminded them that the Democrats still played a large role in Washington and would someday return to power. "We're going to be involved in your business," *Fortune* quoted him as telling business lobbyists, "so it doesn't make sense for you not to get involved in our business." Coelho raised tens of millions of badly needed dollars for the party and its candidates, and he rose to become the majority whip. But stories about him frequently used the words "extortion" and "protection racket" to describe his operations.[56]

Some Democrats understood the damage Coelho's operation could do to the party. Rather than using money in a nourishing role, to build support for candidates and Democratic proposals, Coelho had reversed the priority and made money the dominant goal. Seeing his operations unguided by any sense of idealism, liberals had begun to worry if Coelho was selling the party's soul for corporate money. "Our butts are being peddled around town, one dollar at a time," one congressman complained in 1983. In 1986, Tip O'Neill—who despised Coelho and his methods—publicly rebuked him for promising contributors that the tax reform bill would be amended to protect their loopholes. The next year, Kuttner reported a Democratic congressman's charge that roll-call votes had been delayed at Coelho's request when they coincided with fund-raising events, to avoid placing members in the awkward position of voting on business interests that Coelho simultaneously was tapping for cash. Coelho, concluded one journalist, was a "hustler who made an art of shaking down businessmen to finance the reelection of Democratic congressmen."[57]

The problem was worse than Coelho's critics realized. In April 1989, the *Washington Post* reported that in 1986 Coelho had purchased $100,000 worth of Drexel junk bonds—"normally available only to institutional investors and regular Drexel customers"—that had been issued to finance the Beatrice Foods takeover. The next day, he admitted to having made a $6,900 profit on the bonds. Drexel, not surprisingly, had been a large donor to the Democratic Congressional Campaign Committee and Coelho's own campaigns, and Coelho had publicly praised "my very good friend" Michael Milken. Coelho, with little personal commitment to politics, did not endure a long investigation but, rather, simply resigned from the House in June 1989. He soon took a job as an investment banker and became wealthy.[58]

On the eve of the 1988 presidential election, Democrats had good reason to be anxious. On the intellectual side, the party remained exhausted and unable to generate ideas that could unify it or attract voters. Indeed, Democratic intellectuals offered only visions of despair and no real suggestions for what to do. The organizational and political sides of the party also were in deep trouble—despite Kirk's efforts to give the Democrats the image of harmony, they remained deeply divided, had replaced a popular spokesman with an oily, corrupt pol, and their fundraising was dogged by accusations of ideological sellouts and extortion. These desperate circumstances explain how Michael Dukakis, a mediocre politician from a small state, could win the presidential nomination.

Michael Dukakis was a doomed presidential candidate from the start. Although personally a smart and decent man, he had no experience beyond the small stage of Massachusetts politics, no coherent ideas of his own to present to the voters, and, because the Democrats had failed to come up with an appealing idea, could not adopt one from his party. Dukakis also had an unfortunate tendency toward brooding and indecision when things went badly. As a result, he ran a confused and incompetent campaign. The voters understood this and, quite sensibly, rejected him.

Born in 1933, Dukakis was the son of a Greek-born doctor and a teacher. He grew up in the suburb of Brookline, Massachusetts, graduated Phi Beta Kappa from Swarthmore and, after a tour in the army, went to Harvard Law School. After Harvard, he practiced law in a Boston firm, became active in Brookline politics, and was elected to the Massachusetts House of Representatives, where he served from 1962 to 1970. Brookline was an upper-middle-class liberal bastion, and Dukakis represented it perfectly—he established himself as a maverick liberal, backing reform and immersing himself in the details of legislation while rejecting the patronage-driven, go-along-get-along traditions of the State House. Dukakis gained a well-deserved reputation as a man who was scrupulously honest but uncompromising, humorless, and cerebral. Friends and opponents alike noted that he could quickly understand complex problems, never doubted that his conclusions were correct, and rarely listened to contrary arguments; reporters later wrote that Dukakis reminded them of Jimmy Carter. These qualities led him to disaster after he was elected governor in 1974. Massachusetts was suffering from high unemployment and a large budget deficit, and candidate Dukakis pledged not to raise taxes. In office, he first tried to balance the budget by cutting social programs but, when that failed, he was forced to raise taxes. Separately, throughout his term he battled the Democrats' patronage system and, as a bonus, tried to ban smoking in the State House. As a result, he managed to alienate both liberals and businessmen, while earning the scorn of Democratic politicians. In the 1978 primary, Dukakis was defeated by a conservative Democrat, Ed King.[59]

While King's governorship became marked by corruption and cronyism, Dukakis taught at Harvard's Kennedy School of Government and thought about his experiences. He returned to politics chastened and somewhat more willing to make deals. With the help of a new campaign manager, John Sasso, Dukakis defeated King and regained the governorship in 1982. At this point, Dukakis turned into one of the luckiest politicians in the country. Massachusetts had cut taxes during the King years and, with its concentrations of universities, financial companies, and defense and high-technology industries, was in an ideal position to benefit from the 1980s boom. By 1986, Massachusetts had the lowest unemployment rate in the country and Dukakis was able to cut taxes, increase spending, reform welfare, hand out patronage jobs, and still run a budget surplus. The governor, naturally, claimed the credit for the "Massachusetts Miracle." Sasso and friendly journalists, especially at the *Washington Post,* began promoting Dukakis as a potential president even before he was reelected in November 1986 with 69 percent of the vote.[60]

It is not clear that Dukakis really wanted to be president. Contemporary reports and later accounts of the election all agree that it was Sasso's idea. "Dukakis-for-president sentiment is running most strongly in the fevered imagination of his chief secretary, John Sasso," reported the *Boston Globe* in February 1986. Sasso had managed Geraldine Ferraro's vice-presidential campaign in 1984 and the experience convinced him that voters would not elect a Democrat until they believed he could be trusted with the economy. In Sasso's view, Dukakis had met this test during the prosperous years of his second term, and he convinced the governor that he could run and win. Sasso built a national Dukakis field organization that, by the spring of 1988, was more effective than those of the other Democrats running for the nomination. By then, too, Sasso's fund-raising operation had taken in more than twice as much money as any other Democratic contender.[61]

In his excitement about Dukakis's economic record, Sasso overlooked the candidate's serious flaws. Dukakis was a cautious man, not motivated by any particular idea. He described himself not as a liberal but as a manager, someone who could run the government and solve problems. He had the "experience to manage," he said as he announced his candidacy on March 16, 1987, and he talked in terms that owed much to Robert Reich. Dukakis spoke of government "investments" instead of spending, called for government-business "partnerships," and told an audience in New Hampshire to "ask more than whether we have new ideas; ask whether we have already made new ideas work." The uninspiring language hinted at another problem: Dukakis remained eccentric and hard to like. Some of his habits—buying discounted clothes at Filene's, doing the family grocery shopping himself to ensure that no money was wasted, clearing the snow with his twenty-five-year-old snowblower—could have been turned into symbols of thrift and folksiness by a more skilled politician. Dukakis, however, came across as a dour cheapskate, especially after his financial disclosure report showed him to be modestly wealthy. Another revelation, that his wife had been addicted to diet pills for nineteen years without his knowledge, made him seem remote and obtuse.[62]

Dukakis also had an unfortunate tendency toward self-defeating moralism. The most telling example came in September 1987. Sasso learned that Senator Joseph Biden of Delaware, one of Dukakis's rivals for the nomination, had plagiarized a speech by British Labour Party leader Neil Kinnock. Sasso obtained videos of the two speeches, edited them into one that showed Biden copying Kinnock's words, and—without telling Dukakis—gave the tape to NBC News and the *New York Times.* The *Times* printed the story on its front page, and Biden was forced to withdraw from the race. Dukakis, still in the dark, denied initial reports that his campaign had been the source of the tape. After Sasso told him the full story, Dukakis agonized for a day about what to do, then fired Sasso and publicly apologized to Biden. Political professionals were troubled by Dukakis's indecision and surprised by the firing. In their view, Sasso's move had been a legitimate part of the game and certainly not a firing offense. To Dukakis, however, Sasso had committed a serious ethical offense, undermined what the *Globe* called his vision of "good, clean, issue-based politics," and had to go, even if it meant the loss of the strategic mastermind behind his candidacy.[63]

Sasso's organization was strong enough to see Dukakis through the primaries, but without him the governor was unable to prepare his campaign for the general election. Dukakis replaced Sasso with Susan Estrich, a Harvard law professor and veteran of the Mondale campaign. Estrich proved to be a disaster—by numerous accounts imperious, condescending, and a poor strategist. Dukakis stumbled in several late primaries and lost faith in her advice but could not rouse himself to fire her. By midsummer, his campaign was adrift—Estrich had no strategy, did not supply the candidate with themes for his campaign, and allowed media planning to fall apart—and was beset by infighting caused by Estrich's difficult personality and tendency to alienate senior campaign workers. Dukakis brought Sasso back at Labor Day, but by then it was too late.[64]

George Bush, unlike Dukakis, knew that he wanted to be president. Born in 1924 to a wealthy New England family that believed deeply in public service, he attended Andover and then served as a navy pilot during World War II, flying fifty-eight combat missions against the Japanese. After the war, he went to Yale and was elected to Phi Beta Kappa. He moved to Texas, where he became moderately wealthy in the oil business before entering politics. Bush lost a race for the Senate in 1964, but was elected to the House from Houston in 1966. After losing another Senate race in 1970, he was appointed by President Nixon to be ambassador to the United Nations and, subsequently, chairman of the Republican National Committee, where he defended the president until close to the end of the Watergate saga. Gerald Ford considered appointing Bush as his vice president but, after choosing Nelson Rockefeller instead, made Bush his envoy to China and then director of central intelligence. In all of these jobs, Bush proved himself to be a skilled political operator, loyal to his superiors, and also a man of great personal decency and integrity. Apparently it was after Ford's defeat in 1976 that Bush made the presidency his goal. He returned to Houston and began laying the groundwork for his campaign in 1980, which ultimately resulted in his selection as Reagan's vice president.[65]

In spite of his experience and qualifications, Bush had to overcome serious problems in running for the presidency. The first was ideological. He had an uneasy relationship with much of the conservative movement, which was suspicious of his elite, moderate background and had not forgotten his attacks on supply-side economics in 1980. "These qualities give many conservatives the willies" about Bush, editorialized *National Review* in early 1986. Bush understood the conservatives' distrust of him and moved early to build support on the right. In April 1985, *National Review* reported that he already had gained substantial backing among conservative activists and the religious right. He also obtained the endorsements of prominent conservatives. Congressman Robert Dornan of California, for example, declared in November 1987 that Bush was an "intelligent, decisive, indefatigable, committed . . . conservative," and the "best hope for keeping that Reagan coalition together." Taking nothing for granted, Bush continued to cultivate conservatives, particularly by embracing additional tax cuts. This strategy, combined with careful organizing and the advantages of being Reagan's vice president, enabled Bush to defeat his two main rivals, Jack Kemp and Senate Minority Leader Bob Dole, with relative ease.[66]

Another problem for Bush was that he was not a strong retail politician. He had a distaste for rough politics, his record in elections was not encouraging—two defeats in two statewide elections—and all of his political positions since 1970 had come as the result of appointments. Bush had spent almost all of this period, moreover, in the shadows of others. In addition, his mannerisms and speech patterns had given him an effete, almost prissy, public image. The newspapers described aides' concerns about Bush's "sometimes squeaky voice, his tendency for stepping on his speechwriters' best lines," and his understandable propensity to come across as a representative of traditional eastern Republican elites rather than as a common man. Bush worked hard in 1988 to reduce these disadvantages. With the help of his staff, he became a disciplined campaigner, a better public speaker, and a politician able to turn nasty—as he did to defeat Dole in New Hampshire—when he had to. James Baker left the Treasury at the end of the summer to run the campaign, which also helped Bush. Nonetheless, the vice president's strongest campaign assets were peace and prosperity, his willingness to embrace conservative ideas, and his promise that he would carry on Reagan's work.[67]

The differences between Bush and Dukakis became clear during the summer of 1988. All seemed well for Dukakis through July—he came out of the Democratic convention with a seventeen-point lead in the polls. But Bush wanted the presidency and was willing to fight hard for it. With his consent, the Republicans began to wage the nastiest campaign since Lyndon Johnson had tarred Barry Goldwater as a right-wing lunatic in 1964. Dukakis had vetoed a bill requiring Massachusetts teachers to lead their students in the Pledge of Allegiance after the state attorney general and supreme court had advised him it was unconstitutional. The Bush campaign seized on the veto—"this may be hard for you to believe," Bush told an audience as he described Dukakis's action—and presented it as evidence that the governor was unpatriotic. Willie Horton, a black prisoner in Massachusetts serving time for murder, had raped a woman in Maryland while on a furlough from prison. Bush used this as evidence that Dukakis was soft on crime—a "generous vacation to prisoners" was how he described the furloughs—and his supporters used Horton to make not-too-subtle appeals to racial fears. Bush used Dukakis's membership in the American Civil Liberties Union to claim that he was hopelessly out of touch with the values of the majority of Americans. Combining these themes, Bush's speeches and advertisements caricatured Dukakis and liberalism as something threatening and un-American. By Labor Day, Bush had a slight lead in the polls that he never lost.[68]

Dukakis proved to be helpless against this attack. Massachusetts, for all the roughness of its politics, was a one-party liberal state, and Dukakis never before had faced a determined, ruthless opponent. Now, in the national campaign, he was out of his depth—"I ran a lousy campaign," he admitted fifteen years later. Believing that voters supported his desire for a high-minded debate about issues—the politics of Brookline and Harvard—he did not understand that Bush's attacks could be effective and so he tried to ignore them. As his lead evaporated, Dukakis withdrew into himself, brooding and unsure of what to do, but unwilling to listen to his advisers. When he finally tried to answer the Republicans, it was with legalistic arguments—he was duty-bound to veto the unconstitutional

Pledge law, the furlough system had been established by his predecessor—that fell flat in the heat of the campaign. Dukakis's advertising was deeply flawed as well, showing no understanding of how to use symbols and communicate a message in thirty seconds. "Dukakis ads are full of facts and figures," said the *Washington Post*, and analysts noted that they were confusing and unfocused, while Bush's aimed for "passion and poetry." The campaign also suffered from embarrassingly poor organization—in one instance, Dukakis spoke to an audience of workers on the danger of growing foreign ownership of American companies only to learn afterward that the site of his speech, an auto parts plant in Missouri, was owned by an Italian company. "Even his partisans wonder why he's so inept," said a *Boston Globe* columnist in October.[69]

Dukakis also paid a heavy price for liberals' failure to understand the new world of the 1980s. The governor continued to put forward the Reich-Thurow themes of economic stagnation, declining competitiveness, and the disappearing middle class. He used these, in turn, to try to attract middle-class suburban voters with promises of help and competent economic management—on the stump Dukakis promised them a "new era of economic greatness" that would end the "middle-class squeeze." But Dukakis had problems convincing voters to accept these claims. For one, his target audience, the educated residents of the technoburbs, had little reason to feel miserable. With the failure of his descriptions of unhappy middle-class lives to match easily observed reality, Dukakis created another problem: voters were left to focus on his managerial talents, which turned out to be poor. The newspapers frequently reported on the chaos in his campaign, leading to the obvious question of how he could run the country if he could not run his candidacy. At the same time, the Massachusetts Miracle came crashing down. Slowing growth led to lower than expected tax revenues—by July 1988, the Bay State had a $450 million deficit—and, despite Dukakis's use of Washington-style optimistic forecasts, borrowing, and accounting tricks, the gap was growing quickly.[70]

Finally, Dukakis found that, having long claimed that the election was about who had the competence to govern, he could not easily fall back on an appeal to traditional Democratic liberalism. Indeed, it was not until the last, desperate days of October that Dukakis claimed to be a liberal.

Even then, however, he was careful to say that his was the liberalism of Franklin Roosevelt, Harry Truman, and John Kennedy, not of the modern Democratic Party. This did not help him at all, if only because all of his statements until then had been those of gloomy late 1980s liberalism, not the vigorous and optimistic rhetoric of the New Deal or the New Frontier. The result, concluded the *Globe* shortly after the election, was that Dukakis "seldom gave voters a reason to choose him."[71]

No one was surprised by the outcome. When the ballots were counted on November 8, Bush received 48.8 million votes, 53 percent of the popular vote, and Dukakis took 41.8 million and 46 percent; in the Electoral College, the count was 426 to 111. Dukakis could take comfort in knowing that he had done better than Mondale—with the popular Reagan no longer on the ballot, he attracted almost half of the Democrats who had voted Republican in 1984 (see Table 7). Beyond that, however, the news was bad for the party. Dukakis had won only ten states and Washington, D.C., while losing the South and West—the fastest growing parts of the country. The election also demonstrated the electoral effects of the changes in the middle class. Reflecting the tendency of those in the middle income ranges to move up during the Reagan years—and the fact that affluent people vote more than the poor—the proportion of voters from the top three income categories grew from 52 percent in 1984 to 59 percent in 1988. The share of the electorate made up of people who had been to college grew as well, from 59 percent to 65 percent. These voters did not give Bush as overwhelming a majority as they had given Reagan, but their margins for him still were greater than those of the general population. Combined with the growing numbers of these voters in the technoburbs of the South and West, the result showed that the Republicans could win without the votes of the blue-collar Reagan Democrats.

Liberals blamed Dukakis's loss on the Republican attack strategy. In a typical comment, historian C. Vann Woodward asserted in December 1988 that the Bush campaign had used "cynicism and unscrupulous methods," and "McCarthyite character assassination," which "gulled and deceived" the electorate. This view, based on the flawed assumption that well-educated voters could be easily duped, simply was wrong. Contemporary reporting strongly suggested that it was Dukakis's amazingly inept responses to Bush's charges—even as he claimed to be a strong manager—not the accusations themselves, that led voters to question whether he could be an effective president. Furthermore, subsequent research has shown that voters demonstrated a sophisticated ability to sort issues and evaluate Bush and Dukakis. In particular, the Republicans' use of Willie Horton, the Pledge of Allegiance, and other so-called hot-button issues had little impact on voters, who instead based their decisions on how they viewed the economy and the personal characteristics of the two candidates. Here, too, Dukakis did himself in. Throughout the campaign, he struggled to get the voters to warm to him, but failed. His impatience with others, reported the *Washington Post* in October, "creates a kind of puritan smugness and an aura of superiority" that was evident on television as well as in his live appearances. Political journalists further noted that Dukakis's arrogance and lack of humor led voters to wonder if he could succeed as president. Journalists' comparisons of him to Jimmy Carter suggest that the public probably understood that the governor's personality was similar to those of unsuccessful presidents. This, combined with his lack of realistic campaign ideas, led the voters to the obvious decision not to elect him.[72]

The voters' wisdom soon was confirmed. After the election, Dukakis turned his attention to the Bay State's mounting fiscal problems. In a surprise move, he announced in early January 1989 that he would not run for reelection the following year so he could provide the leadership to "face our fiscal problems squarely and courageously." Unfortunately, Dukakis succeeded only in turning himself into a lame duck with no political leverage and, hence, declining power. By April, reported the *Globe,* the legislature was ignoring his budget requests, his approval rating was at 19 percent, and 79 percent of Massachusetts voters believed Dukakis had "not been candid about the state's deteriorating financial condition" when he had touted the Massachusetts Miracle in 1988. In November, with Massachusetts essentially leaderless, the deficit for the coming year was projected to be $720 million and the state's bond rating fell to last in the nation. Dukakis's popularity from 1983 to 1987 turned out to be a fluke in his career, made possible by riding a wave of prosperity, and now, as in his first term, he had shown himself to be an inept politician. Around the country prominent Democrats did their best to forget Dukakis had ever existed. "He's an asterisk," said one on the anniversary of his nomination.[73]

Deficits, Iran-Contra, and Bork notwithstanding, Reagan's second term was a success. He had achieved a major legislative goal in tax reform, put conservatives in a strong position on the Supreme Court, and then handed over the presidency to his chosen successor. He maintained his high popularity ratings for most of his term and, among conservatives, became a venerated figure. Indeed, a comparison of the political land-scapes of 1980 and 1988 shows how much of an imprint he had made. The federal budget was discussed almost entirely in terms of cuts, not spend-ing increases; tax increases were considered, but at rates far below those before Reagan took office; for the courts, the question was not whether conservatives would be appointed, but which ones; and in Republican politics, the issue was not Reagan's ideas, but who would continue to implement them. In all of these cases, and many more, Reagan and the conservatives set the terms.

Nonetheless, Reagan's two terms showed that conservative political power had been restrained by an important internal factor. From the start, Reagan had depended on forming coalitions with moderate Republicans and conservative Democrats because the pool of conservative Republicans was not yet large enough to staff an administration completely. This need constituted an important check on conservatives' power, as Robert Bork's fate showed. Ironically, however, during the 1980s it was the much-maligned moderate Republicans who did the most for Reagan—James Baker brought the administration most of its successes, and Howard Baker rescued Reagan from Iran-Contra. In the decade after Reagan's departure, however, conservatives would fill many of the gaps in their personnel ros-ter. The Republican takeover of Congress in the 1994 elections gave con-servatives valuable experience—and some harsh lessons—in running the legislative branch and setting a national agenda. As a result, when George W. Bush became president in 2001, his administration would function smoothly even though it relied little on nonconservative allies.

Less surprising was the condition of American liberalism. The deterio-ration that had begun in the mid-1960s continued through the 1980s, leaving liberalism badly weakened. The search for new guiding ideas had proved fruitless, as had the efforts to win back the votes of the middle class. In Washington, the Democrats could stop Reagan only when his budget proposals touched on programs that had become sacred to the middle class or when he blundered, as with Bork. Michael Dukakis's lethargic, uncertain campaign—a dramatic contrast of tone and style with those of almost all previous Democrats—was a clear demonstration of how bad things had become for the party. Indeed, by the end of the 1980s, the idea that liberalism had any hope of reversing Reagan's changes without first changing itself dramatically was simply unreal.

Conservatives could not translate Reaganism's dominance into the type of national consensus that liberalism had forged after World War II, however. Even as much of political liberalism was discredited and unpopular, many of the cultural changes it had brought about had become part of the national consensus. Conservatives tried to attack both during the 1980s, but liberals had much better luck defending the cultural front than they had had in traditional politics. The result, the so-called culture wars, was a series of bitter battles inside and out of the political arena, many of which continue today.

5

IF THINGS ARE SO GOOD, WHY DO I FEEL
SO BAD? 1981–1989

American social and cultural life could not escape the effects of the political and economic changes of the Reagan years. As was the case with politics and economics, much of what happened in the sociocultural sphere during the 1980s was rooted in the events of the preceding decades. The 1960s and 1970s had been a time of broad liberalization of American social and moral behaviors—it had been the era of desegregation, the expansion of individual rights, and the sexual revolution, to name just some of the changes. Many of these had been controversial or even violently resisted but, by the start of the 1980s, gradually were finding acceptance and their places in the American consensus.

In spite of this slow move toward consensus, the social and cultural spheres were not stable. Social conservatives—those on the right who emphasized the importance of traditional moral and religious values— were by no means reconciled to such changes as legalized abortion, the changing roles of women, or the growing acceptance of equal rights for homosexuals. They still hoped to roll back many of these developments and saw Reagan's election as an opportunity do so. In race relations, the growth of immigration from Asia and Latin America was changing the ethnic mix of the population and, as a result, upsetting carefully worked out affirmative action balances. In the academic world, the changing demands for technical skill in the workplace devalued the skills and prestige of the humanities and social sciences, which infuriated many intellectuals and led to bitter conflicts on campuses. Indeed, the common thread connecting these cases is that the changes of the 1980s created uncertainties as well as winners and losers, while at the same time raising questions about the futures of emotional issues or privileged groups. It is perhaps the greatest irony of the 1980s that, because of such concerns, a time of prosperity and progress ended with many people in a nasty mood.

Like lower taxes and deregulation, reversing what they viewed as America's moral decay was a vital goal for social conservatives during the 1980s. These conservatives deeply disapproved of many of the legal and cultural developments of the 1960s and 1970s, especially those involving family, sexual, or religious questions. The most prominent of these changes was the legalization of abortion by the Supreme Court in *Roe v. Wade* in January 1973, but social conservatives' grievances also included the growth of the gay rights movement and increasing tolerance of homosexuality, the more open availability of pornography, and the abolition of prayer in the public schools. Some of their goals, such as overturning *Roe* or teaching creationism and restoring prayer to the schools, were easily defined, but it was not always clear what social conservatives believed they could do about other developments they disliked, such as the changing roles of women. Nonetheless, social conservatives perceived that they had widespread sympathy for their positions on these issues. The adoption of supply-side economics, with its incorporation of George Gilder's and Jude Wanniski's claims that it would improve America's spiritual well-being, brought conservative morals to discussions of public policy. Other social issues, such as school busing and crime, helped move voters toward conservative positions. In addition, a significant number of educated suburbanites often appeared to share conservatives' ethical concerns, claiming a desire to restore "traditional" values and strong moral authority to American life.[1]

The social conservatives' confidence was increased further by the rise of the religious right. By 1980, 30 million to 65 million Americans were estimated to be evangelical or fundamentalist Protestants, or theologically conservative members of other religions. Fundamentalist and evangelical Christians traditionally had kept out of secular politics, concentrating their energies instead on spiritual matters. In the 1970s, however, the abortion debate and the growing importance of other family-related social issues caused many to become politically active. Led by such well-known figures as the Reverends Jerry Falwell and Pat Robertson—who, along with other conservative preachers, made effective use of television to spread their messages—and organized in such groups as Falwell's Moral Majority, Christian political activists by 1980 claimed to be mobilizing tens of millions of voters. By then, too, they had claimed credit for defeating liberal candidates in state and local contests and for blocking the ratification of the Equal Rights Amendment to the Constitution, and had begun organizing for Reagan. Reagan, for his part, happily accepted their support and declared that, in return, "I want you to know I endorse you and what you are doing."[2]

Social conservatives, both secular and religious, stated their goals in words that reflected the strength of their convictions. Hard rhetoric was not new to conservatism—too-threatening language had, after all, been part of the reason for Barry Goldwater's loss in 1964—but the combination of deep moral belief and post-election confidence generated tough, determined language. "Our nation's internal problems are direct results of her spiritual condition," wrote Falwell in 1980. "It is now time that moral Americans awakened to the fact that our future depends upon how we stand on moral issues." Other conservatives backed this view, writing of the need to draw a firm line against further moral decay and supporting what they expected to be Reagan's radicalism in support of conservative morals. In addition, during the Reagan years social and religious conservatives worked tirelessly to advance their views and, through their allies in Congress, were able to introduce bills seeking, for example, to restrict the Supreme Court's jurisdiction and amend the Constitution to permit prayer in the schools.[3]

The social conservatives failed to accomplish their goals, however. When the 1980s ended, abortion still was legal, religion had not returned to the public schools, and the women's and gay rights movements were as strong as ever. The social conservatives' failure had several causes, the most important of which was that the number of the Christian conservatives—their critical base of support—was never as great as Falwell and others had claimed. The assertion of 30 million to 65 million potential supporters was suspect from the start, as its lack of precision suggested. Even if this had been a good approximation of the number of theologically conservative

Americans, it did not follow that all of them would join conservative groups. Indeed, researchers looking carefully at polling and other data soon found that the Moral Majority and other conservative Christian organizations' claims of how many followers they had were greatly inflated— the true numbers, while still uncertain, may have been only 5 million to 10 million.[4]

Christians proved to be more difficult to mobilize than the leaders of the religious right had expected. Like Americans in general, Christians were a diverse population with conflicting interests, and often had complex views that could not easily be categorized or directed. One 1988 study, for example, noted that sympathy for the Moral Majority's social views did not translate into automatic support for its policy positions— only a tiny segment of the population agreed with all of its policy proposals, for example. Later studies confirmed, moreover, that theological conservatives were divided on many issues and, indeed, that a significant number of conservative Christians were put off by preachers who mixed politics and spiritual affairs. In addition, some evangelical and fundamentalist Christians were not conservatives at all, especially among blacks, and in some cases Christians followed their theology to arrive at liberal social views. It is not surprising, then, that in the mid-1980s Christian conservative organizations went into a decline. Several, including the Moral Majority, closed down as members lost their zeal or tired of constant appeals for donations. The credibility of Christian conservative leaders' was eroded, moreover, by scandals involving sex and money. Jim Bakker, a prominent television preacher, had to resign as the head of his ministry, PTL, in May 1987 after revelations that he had paid hush money to a young woman employee with whom he had had an affair; he was convicted of fraud in 1989. In early 1988, another television evangelist, Jimmy Swaggart, left his ministry after he admitted hiring prostitutes.[5]

The social conservatives' ambitions were hindered further by the moderate tendencies of American society and politics. Abortion, gay rights, the women's movement, and other social changes had generated major controversies in their early years but, during the 1980s, began to find their places in the national consensus. Studies of public opinion data, for example, found that although significant moral opposition to abortion still existed, acceptance of its legality was growing. Similarly, most

Americans continued to believe that homosexuality was morally wrong, but during the 1980s they increasingly opposed discrimination against gays. The same attitude of increasing acceptance characterized popular views of the changing roles of women. These more tolerant—and, it is worth noting, ideologically inconsistent—views were not limited to any specific sector of society. Americans in general were less willing to judge one another than they had been a generation earlier—the emphasis on individual rights that had developed during the 1960s and 1970s and loosening of moral standards had given rise to greater individualism and a "live and let live" ethos. Rising tolerance cut across all class, educational, and occupational boundaries and frequently reflected an understanding of the complexity of social issues and a reluctance to maintain that a single view was correct for every situation. Increasing acceptance, moreover, meant that groups once outside the mainstream now became included— annual gay pride parades, for example, became as common in many cities as other ethnic or cultural festivals. Given this combination of ambivalence and tolerance, it is not surprising that the majority of Americans were unwilling to engage in large fights about socio-moral issues or that religious conservatives found only limited support in Congress for their proposals.[6]

The issue of gay rights provides a useful illustration of how the complexity and ambiguity of social and moral questions affected conservative views. The best example of this is in *National Review*'s discussions of homosexuality. Like Americans in general, conservatism's leading magazine could not arrive at a consistent, coherent conclusion and its articles featured both rejections and defenses of gay rights, calls to tolerate individual homosexuals, and overall uncertainty about how to think about the place of gays in society. Some contributors, like columnist Joseph Sobran, maintained a harsh line against homosexuality and gay rights— writing on AIDS in May 1986, he declared that the disease was the result of "promiscuous homosexuality," which was the "behavior gay-rights legislation protects" and "forbids normal citizens to disapprove." In contrast, critic Terry Teachout advanced a muddled argument for tolerating homosexuals if they would remain discreet in their activities—they should drop their "noisy demands for Gay Rights Now" and "keep quiet about their leisure-time activities," he wrote in 1983. Still others, like critic Ralph de Toledano, worried less about homosexuality itself than the effects of its acceptance on society at large. "It is not, moreover, what he practices in the privacy of his closet that is of greatest concern," de Toledano wrote of homosexuals in 1984, "but the lifestyle that he is making more prevalent with every passing day."[7]

The argument was further complicated by occasional unexpected reminders of the presence of gays in the conservative movement. The possibility that prominent conservatives could turn out to be homosexual gave those on the right a good reason to tone down their rhetoric and, later, led them to greater tolerance. In October 1980, for example, conservative representative Robert Bauman (R-Md.) was arrested for soliciting sex from a teenage boy. The resulting scandal cost him his seat and conservative leadership positions, but *National Review* editor William F. Buckley, Jr., wrote that Bauman was "as welcome in my home today, as yesterday." Similarly, in September 1986, *National Review* published a long rejoinder to Sobran's article by a pseudonymous friend of Buckley's. The author admitted his homosexuality, defended the need for gay rights legislation, and condemned Sobran's arguments as vicious homophobic nonsense. Finally, Marvin Liebman, a longtime conservative activist and close friend of Buckley's, came out in an open letter in *National Review* in July 1990, warning that growing homophobia threatened to reverse decades of political progress by conservatives. Buckley, in reply, admitted that he remained unsure how society's heterosexual majority should treat homosexuals, but welcomed gays as "partners in efforts to mint sound public policies" and—perhaps with articles like Sobran's in mind—promised that the magazine would not publish thoughtless gay-bashing writings.[8]

Another factor working against the social conservatives during the 1980s was the combination of technological change and expanding consumer choice, a phenomenon illustrated by the case of pornography. Although the size of the pornography business in the 1980s remains uncertain—one estimate placed it at $7 billion in 1984—it is clear that the industry enjoyed rapid growth during the Reagan years. The main cause was the arrival of cheap video technology. Would-be pornographers no longer needed to pay for expensive cameras, film, processing, and skilled production labor. Instead, they could use inexpensive equipment that

required minimal training. As a result, the cost of producing pornographic movies plummeted, as did the costs of duplication. On the
demand side, people who would not go to seedy pornographic movie
theaters proved eager to buy and rent the videos for private viewing at
home. Pornographic tapes first had become available in 1977 and, until
Hollywood began releasing large numbers of movies on video in the early
1980s, X-rated tapes dominated the sale and rental markets. Even as its
relative share of the rapidly growing video market shrank, pornography
remained a large and growing business. In 1986, the *Wall Street Journal*
reported that three-quarters of the nation's video stores carried pornographic tapes, and the rentals—the majority, according to store owners
and pornography entrepreneurs, to middle-class customers—were worth
about $250 million per year.[9]

Social conservatives tried to fight pornography on two fronts, and
lost on both. The first was in the legal arena, where they formed a surprising alliance with radical feminists. The conservatives opposed pornography because they believed it undermined the family and debased
sexuality; the feminists believed it was a key prop for male supremacy
and the oppression of women. Led by legal scholar and theorist Catharine MacKinnon and writer Andrea Dworkin, feminists worked to pass
local ordinances that would define and outlaw pornography as a form
of discrimination against women. Working with the Moral Majority, they
were successful in Indianapolis, where such a law was passed in April 1984,
only to see the ordinance struck down in federal court the following
November as a violation of the First Amendment. No similar ordinances
have been enacted since.[10]

Attorney General Ed Meese opened the second front in May 1985,
when he appointed a commission to study the effects of pornography and
ways to control it. The commission reported in July 1986 that pornographic depictions of coercive or violent acts—and the report made it
clear that this included most pornography—caused an increase in aggres-
sion toward women and recommended new local, state, and federal laws
to control pornography. The report created a brief controversy as social
scientists debated its methodologies and evidence, and pressure from several commission members led some eight thousand chain convenience
and drug stores to stop selling adult magazines. The Department of

Justice cracked down on pornographers with links to organized crime and indicted some distributors. In the longer term, however, the commission had little effect. Videos, not magazine sales, were driving the growth of the pornography industry, and little support existed for a sustained crackdown on tapes, especially because of the combination of middle-class consumption and individualist morality. Technology, moreover, continued to be more powerful than conservative morals; by the mid-1990s, the Internet had made pornography even cheaper to produce, as well as universally and instantly available to consumers. George Gilder and Jude Wanniski turned out to be wrong—markets were amoral, and unleashing the power of capitalism had not reversed America's moral decline.[11]

For his part, Reagan gave only lukewarm support to the social conservatives. His religious beliefs were not strict enough to move him to insist on taking firm action in these areas, and any such effort would have been politically risky and promised little profit. Even if he had tried, Reagan would have had to take the chance of alienating large numbers of middle-class voters as he challenged the rough consensus of tolerance that had developed on abortion, homosexuality, and other issues. In any event, given the social conservatives' lack of internal agreement and strength in these areas, Reagan likely would have had trouble developing policies that could satisfy his supporters. Instead, the administration walked a careful path. Reagan gave strong verbal support to social conservative activists—every January, for example, he addressed anti-abortion protesters demonstrating in Washington on the anniversary of *Roe v. Wade*—the Justice Department filed amicus briefs in Supreme Court abortion cases, and Meese formed his pornography commission, but otherwise the administration never initiated substantive action in these areas.

Even as these efforts failed, however, social conservatives had high hopes for achieving another goal, to reshape the federal judiciary. Indeed, almost all conservatives believed that *Roe* and many other decisions on race, religion, affirmative action, and individual rights had been the result of judges—including Supreme Court justices—seeking to write, rather than interpret, the law. Reagan agreed with this view and conservatives' determination to replace judges they saw as too liberal or activist. At the start of his administration—and indicating the importance he placed on picking conservative judges—Reagan put in place a system to ensure that judicial appointees would be conservatives. The White House revamped the procedures used by previous administrations that had chosen judges based on a mixture of qualifications, patronage, politics, and—last— ideology, with the Justice Department playing a major role in selection. Now, to ensure that nominees would agree with Reagan's policies, selection was placed in the hands of a White House committee, which carefully reviewed candidates' written records and interviews. Each of those selected for nomination was notified in a personal phone call from Reagan, which probably helped solidify his loyalty. Meese was especially important in this process, particularly after he became attorney general, ensuring that nominees were constitutional conservatives—meaning, in his definition, that they were committed to interpreting the law and would avoid the temptation to rewrite it. Reagan's two terms coincided, moreover, with an expansion of the federal judiciary. As a result of this and normal turnover, he appointed 368 lower-court judges—almost half of the judiciary and more than any other modern president.[12]

As important as these efforts were, the Supreme Court remained the great prize for conservatives, for only it could overturn *Roe* and other rulings they detested. Reagan's four appointments (counting Rehnquist's promotion to chief justice) appeared to build a solid conservative bloc on the Court. As it turned out, however, differences in conservative thought, combined with personal dynamics among the justices, often divided the conservatives on critical rulings. Justice Antonin Scalia turned out to be the key figure in the disagreements. As the Catholic-school-educated son of a linguist, Scalia believes that words have clear meanings. Calling himself an "originalist," Scalia has described in several articles his belief that a law means exactly what it says and that questions of its intent can be answered through careful historical research. If a law's intention no longer fits with modern needs or goals, Scalia argues, then it is the task of the people and their elected representatives—not the courts—to change it. "To say otherwise," he explains, is to "render democratically adopted texts mere springboards for judicial lawmaking." Thus, in Scalia's view, rulings that rely on finding new rights in the Constitution, such as *Roe,* are plainly wrong and should be overturned. He is a pugnacious counterrevolutionary, embarked on a long-term mission to correct what he views as decades of judicial error, and is never afraid to tell his colleagues when he believes they are wrong.[13]

In contrast, Sandra Day O'Connor and Anthony Kennedy, the other two justices Reagan placed on the Court, did not arrive with such strongly fixed ideologies. O'Connor has turned out to represent a cautious conservatism. After graduating from Stanford Law School at the top of her class in 1952, she received only one job offer from a law firm—as a secretary. O'Connor went to work instead as a county attorney and, eventually, served as assistant attorney general in Arizona before being elected to the Arizona Senate, where she rose to majority leader. Conservatives were uneasy about her nomination to the Supreme Court—she had voted against several anti-abortion bills in Arizona—but accepted her because, as *National Review* pointed out, abortion was only one conservative priority among many. They view O'Connor's subsequent behavior, however, as justifying their fears. Her style of conservatism has made her reluctant to overturn precedents, and her experience as an elected politician gives her a keen awareness that rulings going against broad public opinion on politically sensitive issues could damage the Court's legitimacy. O'Connor, moreover, is known for valuing politeness and civility in arguments, which has led to personal clashes with Scalia. Kennedy, for his part, lacked Scalia's ideological zeal and moderated his conservatism during the 1990s. The reasons for this remain unclear, but legal analysts have noted that he shares O'Connor's caution about overturning sensitive precedents and also may have been personally offended by the strident styles and views of Scalia and, later, Bush appointee Clarence Thomas.[14]

Beyond the differences in personality, Reagan's Court appointees soon split ideologically. The most contentious issue—not surprisingly, given its divisive role in American political life—was abortion. In the 1989 case of *Webster v. Reproductive Health Services,* O'Connor denied that *Roe* should be reconsidered; Scalia, in reply, said that her reasoning "cannot be taken seriously," and that decisions about abortion should be returned to the political sphere. Three years later, in the case of *Planned Parenthood v. Casey,* O'Connor and Kennedy (joined by Bush appointee David Souter), argued that to reverse *Roe* would be to "surrender to political pressure," a point that Scalia dismissed with contempt. O'Connor, meanwhile, has been careful to draw fine distinctions between her views and Scalia's, even when they are in overall agreement, probably to avoid falling into an ideological trap that would pressure her to vote with Scalia to overturn *Roe*.[15]

Scalia, in his obvious frustration with his colleagues, spoke for many social conservatives. Like the true believers in the supply side, by the end of the decade they felt they had missed their chance during the 1980s. They did not view themselves as having the comfort of important partial victories, as did the less doctrinaire free-marketers and the advocates of deregulation. In a comment typical of the social conservatives, one contributor to *Commentary* wrote in 1987 that their movement had been helpless before a "revolutionary transformation" in American society. Many social conservatives believed that they had lost every major political and legal battle of the decade and saw themselves as watching helplessly while prosperity and technology further eroded the values they held dear. George Gilder, disappointed in his expectation that supply-side economics would bring people closer to God, lamented instead that the "breakdown of the moral codes of civilized society" had been a major trend during the 1980s.[16]

In their dismay, however, these social conservatives made the same mistake that other despairing conservatives made—overlooking some important progress. Even if it had achieved little of its social agenda, the Christian right had pushed its views into the public debate in a way that had been unimaginable in the 1970s. Reagan had seeded the federal judiciary with conservative judges who were, as Ed Meese later pointed out, more restrained in their rulings than previous liberal appointees. One of these judges, Scalia's friend Alex Kozinski, argues that the justice's presence on the Court forces lawyers and judges to consider originalist views and that, as a result, originalism is slowly gaining influence. Like those on the right who compared Reagan's tax and economic achievements against the situation before he took office rather than against unattainable—if ideal—results, conservatives with reasonable expectations were satisfied with the progress of the 1980s.[17]

The 1980s should have been a time of improving race relations, especially between blacks and whites. Since the 1950s, not only had the legal structures of segregation and institutionalized racism been swept away, but blacks had made tremendous strides toward gaining social and economic equality with whites. No one claimed that equality had been achieved or that all vestiges of prejudice and racism had been eliminated—they certainly had not—but all the evidence pointed to a sea change in white attitudes and drastic, continuing decreases in prejudice throughout American society, particularly within the educated professional and middle classes. The return of prosperity and the further decreases in discrimination during the Reagan years should have stimulated further improvements in black-white relations, if for no other reason than an expanding economy meant gains for blacks were less likely to be seen as coming at the expense of whites.[18]

By the late 1980s, however, many observers believed that race relations in the United States had deteriorated badly during the decade. In early 1988, for example, New York City police commissioner Benjamin Ward declared that civil rights progress had ended at the "time of the election of President Reagan"; stories in the popular media and accounts written by black academics both spoke of a resurgence in racism that enabled bigotry to flourish publicly for the first time in a generation. As was so often the case during the 1980s, the facts were more complicated than these statements suggested. Controversies regarding several issues—including the continuation of affirmative action, growing Asian and Hispanic immigration, and the future of black relations with the Democratic Party—had raised sensitive questions. The questions had not been resolved, however, which resulted in uncertainty and increased anxiety.[19]

Discussions of race during the 1980s revolved first around affirmative action. Having grown out of equal employment policies begun during Franklin Roosevelt's administration, but formally established and expanded by a series of executive orders and laws during the 1960s and 1970s, affirmative action by 1980 covered the great majority of public and private employers. Affirmative action was, foremost, a regulatory system governing the operation of labor markets to ensure that education, hiring, and promotions reflected the racial composition of the general population. But affirmative action had a political importance that transcended its regulatory operations—it served as a symbol of the federal government's commitment to preserving and extending the gains of the civil rights movement. For blacks, affirmative action was especially important because much of the reason for establishing it had been to help them, after they had achieved formal legal equality, gain economic parity with whites.[20]

Affirmative action by 1980 occupied an uneasy position in American politics. When asked, most white Americans said they opposed it, especially because its goal of equality for all and identification of people by race clashed with American political culture's emphasis on individual achievement. But, in fact, white views of affirmative action were more nuanced than such reactions indicated. Sociological and public opinion studies revealed, for example, consistent white disapproval of race-based quota systems but, simultaneously, support for ensuring equality of opportunity for people at a disadvantage because of poverty or poor education. Polls showed that whites' support for affirmative action, moreover, increased if the concept was widened beyond blacks, to include women and other minorities. Blacks, for their part, overwhelmingly supported affirmative action. While understandable, such support became problematic during the 1980s, as careful economic studies found that the bulk of affirmative action's benefits went to the most prosperous segment of the black population—those with more education and skills— and provided little or no help to those on the bottom, who needed it most.[21]

Reagan's election appeared to threaten this delicate stability. He opposed affirmative action, a stand that was well-grounded in conservative theory. Milton Friedman, for example, had long argued that free markets would put an end to discrimination on their own, supply-side theorists saw affirmative action as actually hurting black progress, and neoconservatives hated quotas because they recalled the limits on Jews in the Ivy League and other elite institutions that persisted until after World War II. Reagan's campaign rhetoric added to black unease about conservatives—in July 1980, for example, the Ku Klux Klan endorsed Reagan, citing his opposition to busing and affirmative action as it declared that the Republican platform read "as if it were written by a Klansman." Once Reagan was in office, William Bradford Reynolds, the new assistant attorney general for civil rights, shifted the Justice Department to a policy of protecting individual—not group—rights. Instead of seeking relief for groups that had been the victims of bias in the past, the new policies sought remedies only for individuals who had suffered specific acts of discrimination, and required employers to increase minority recruitment and training but—rather than use goals or quotas—to be color- and gender-neutral in promotions. As it did with other social regulatory agencies, the administration drastically cut the budget and staffing of the Labor Department's Office of Federal Contract Compliance Programs, which oversaw the government's affirmative action enforcement.[22]

The new approach gave rise to fears that the civil rights gains of the previous thirty years would be wiped away. The executive director of the NAACP, Benjamin Hooks, warned that Reagan's policies would "wreak havoc, suffering, pain and despair" on blacks and other minorities. One lawyer who resigned from the Justice Department's civil rights division in 1983 described Reagan's policies as a radical assault on the rule of law, while Reynolds's predecessor charged that the administration had "undermined, if not violated outright, settled law in the field of civil rights." In the end, however, the administration's efforts to change civil rights regulation suffered the same fate as its reform efforts in the environmental, health, and safety arenas. By the early 1980s, affirmative action had become institutionalized and had developed strong and varied supporters, in both the public and private sectors. In the government, the Department of Labor had acquired both resources and prestige because of its oversight role, and so opposed abolishing affirmative action. Secretary of State George Shultz, who as secretary of labor under Nixon had helped establish affirmative action, wanted to maintain it, as did the politically astute James Baker. Finally, the Supreme Court walked a cautious path. Reflecting public opinion, the Court during the 1980s refined the rules for affirmative action on a case-by-case basis but refused to make any definitive ruling on its constitutionality.[23]

Perhaps the most surprising source of support for maintaining the status quo came from large corporations. Corporate affirmative action programs not only provided protection from discrimination suits but, because the programs had been in place for so long and become important to minority employees, corporations feared the consequences of abolishing them; the major government action they wanted was a reduction in the legal complexity and paperwork of affirmative action, not its abolition. In addition, sociologists found, corporate personnel management officers had convinced their superiors that affirmative action had important business benefits. By forcing companies to recruit more widely, it enlarged their talent pools. In hiring and promotion, the clearly defined rules and procedures required by affirmative action gave companies a way to modernize and rationalize their personnel systems, and its statistical collection requirements gave managers a way to measure their progress. As a result, even as enforcement pressure eased, business journalists and legal analysts reported that corporations were expanding their affirmative action programs—albeit often under the less contentious label of diversity. "It has become clear to us that an aggressive affirmative action program makes a lot of sense," the president of the Pillsbury Company told *Fortune* in 1985. As a result of these factors, the 1980s ended with affirmative action in place and almost unchanged. In view of their original fears of the Reagan administration, however, blacks undoubtedly believed that affirmative action's survival had been a close call.[24]

Another major force affecting race relations in the 1980s was immigration. The Immigration Act of 1965 had—because of series of miscalculations—unintentionally revolutionized immigration to the United States. The act set quotas for annual immigration but also instituted a policy of family reunification, which enabled immigrants eventually to bring their relatives to the United States outside the quotas, a phenomenon known as chain immigration. At the time the act was passed, immigration had been projected to be about 300,000 people per year, but immigration to the United States in the 1980s totaled some 7.3 million legal immigrants, another million refugees, and millions of illegal immigrants.[25]

Immigration began to change the face of the population. In the 1980s, almost half of the legal immigrants came from Latin America and the Caribbean, and about 40 percent were from Asia. As a result of this and natural increase, the Census Bureau and demographers reported, the Hispanic population of the United States rose by 34 percent from 1980 to 1988, reaching almost 20 million, and the Asian population doubled, rising to 7 million. At the same time, the black population increased by only 14 percent, to 29 million. (The disparity in black and Latino growth rates continued during the next decade, and by mid-2001 Hispanics had passed blacks to become the largest minority group.)[26]

It was urban blacks without a good education and marketable job skills who saw themselves as most threatened by the arrival of large numbers of immigrants. For the middle and professional classes, both black and white, immigration was not a danger—indeed, it was a benefit in that it could provide either low-cost labor or higher-cost skilled workers to fill jobs when too few natives could be found. But for urban blacks on the bottom of the ladder, hit hard by the loss of manufacturing jobs and their lack of qualifications for new positions, immigrants appeared to be a threat, competing for the limited number of low-wage positions. In truth, this fear likely was groundless. Economists began looking in the mid-1980s at the impact of immigration on native employment and wages. The question had no simple answer, if only because labor markets constantly were changing, the talents and abilities of immigrants varied greatly, and jobs and wages were affected by many factors other than the presence of immigrants. At most, researchers concluded, the impact was hardly noticeable—immigrants probably took no jobs from natives, and when their presence in the job market depressed wages at all, it was by only a fraction of a percent. This conclusion was consistent with separate studies of poverty during the 1980s, which attributed the persistence of higher poverty rates during the era not to immigration but, rather, to the declining demand for low-skill labor and other factors not related to immigration. It was an unfortunate misperception—but one that nonetheless produced real tensions, especially later in the decade and in the early 1990s—that poor blacks often viewed immigrants as far more of a menace than they really were.[27]

Another problem created by immigration was that, by changing the ethnic composition of the population, it upset existing affirmative action arrangements. This issue was especially sensitive in higher education, where it affected admissions to elite universities. Asian students, often immigrants or the children of immigrants, had gained a reputation for hard work and high scholastic achievement and their university enrollments were rising quickly, especially in the sciences. By mid-decade, Asians believed that the Ivy League universities were deliberately holding down their numbers to keep them from becoming "overrepresented," just as once had been the case for Jewish students. The best-publicized case of suspected bias against Asians, however, involved the University of California's most prestigious campus, Berkeley.[28]

In the early 1980s, California's rising population and the increasing costs of private universities had led to a sharp increase in applications to the state's low-tuition university system, making it difficult to accommodate all qualified applicants. At Berkeley, meanwhile, admissions of Asian students were soaring—in 1986, Asians accounted for a quarter of the student population, up from 17 percent a decade before—reflecting the high grades earned by California's growing population of Asian high school students. But, because Berkeley reserved spots for black and Hispanic applicants, it was white applicants who suffered a squeeze—the proportion of white applicants accepted by the school dropped from 70 percent in the 1970s to 48 percent in the early 1980s. With no advance notification, Berkeley changed its admissions criteria and Asian admissions dropped suddenly in 1984, leading to accusations that the university had instituted an informal quota system to hold down their numbers and favor white applicants. Investigations followed and Berkeley's change of admissions criteria was found to have worked to the disadvantage of Asians, although the school was cleared of the charge that it had sought deliberately to hold down Asian admissions. Berkeley's chancellor publicly apologized, but resentment lingered and the basic question—how to balance merit, affirmative action goals, and population change—remained unanswered.[29]

Race relations during the 1980s also suffered because of a missed political opportunity. Despite the tensions with Asians and Hispanics, many blacks still felt a sense of solidarity with other minorities who, they understood, also had suffered from racism and prejudice. Well into the 1980s, for example, blacks in Los Angeles maintained effective political coalitions with Asians, Hispanics, and white liberals. An opening existed, therefore, for a leader who could calm growing fears and reduce suspicions, and build a coalition—one combining different minorities as well as whites left behind in the 1980s—on the national level. Success in this project not only would make its leader a figure of national importance, but also had the potential to give those on the bottom a sense that they had a voice in national politics and bring millions of badly needed votes to the Democrats.[30]

The Reverend Jesse Jackson appeared to be a natural for this role. Born in 1941 to an unwed teenage mother, he grew up in South Carolina. Jackson joined the civil rights movement while a college student, became an aide to Martin Luther King, and was present when King was murdered in 1968. In 1971, he formed his own organization, Operation PUSH (People United to Save Humanity), which emphasized programs for black self-help. In addition, Jackson was an ordained Baptist minister with a rhetorical style and views of social justice deeply rooted in black religious and prophetic traditions. Combining PUSH with his extraordinary skills as a public speaker, tireless activism on behalf of the poor, and a flair for self-promotion, by the early 1980s Jackson had become, as *Ebony* noted, the "most charismatic, most combative, most visible" black leader in the United States. Some aspects of Jackson's efforts promised to complicate any role for him in national politics, however. He supported Palestinian nationalism, which made Jews wary of him, and often was accused of not following through on projects he launched. In addition, Operation PUSH had accepted money from the dictatorial Libyan and Syrian regimes, and Washington had questioned PUSH's accounting for federal grant money.[31]

These contradictory forces all were on display when Jackson ran for president in 1984. Serious talk of a campaign had begun when Jackson led a successful voter registration drive in the South in 1983, signing up several hundred thousand new black voters. Declaring his candidacy for the Democratic nomination in November 1983, Jackson claimed to speak for not only minorities but also the poor and dispossessed of all races—his "Rainbow Coalition"—whom he viewed as abandoned by the Democrats as well as left out of the boom. The party, he said in his announcement, had been "too silent, too long" as the "voiceless and downtrodden" suffered under Reagan. His platform was straightforward progressivism—enormous cuts in defense spending to finance public works and jobs programs, and a tax increase to be followed by tax reforms that would eliminate breaks for the wealthy—and he delivered it with a moral passion that no other candidate could match. Jackson's campaign was haphazardly organized and financed on a shoestring, but he won 3.5 million primary votes and 384 delegates, coming in third behind Mondale and Hart and showing it was possible for a black candidate to run strongly at the national level. Jackson's voter registration work, which he continued in 1984, left an important legacy as well—these new voters not only helped create a record black vote for Mondale, but in 1986 they elected the senators who turned out to be crucial in defeating the Bork nomination.[32]

With these achievements, however, Jackson created problems for the Democrats. The first was the strain his candidacy created between the party and the Jews. This was the result, in part, of his pro-Palestinian stance but also of his failure to apologize quickly in February 1984 after the *Washington Post* revealed that he had casually referred to Jews as "Hymies." Jackson, moreover, refused to disavow his relationship with Nation of Islam minister Louis Farrakhan, who was a race-baiting anti-Semite—"Jackson has turned his rainbow into a violent black thunderhead," editorialized the *New Republic*. The second problem was his demand that the 1984 party platform incorporate his views, which were far to the left of the majority of Democrats'. Mondale walked a middle path, deciding not to add to the party's divisions by denouncing Jackson's connection to Farrakhan, but keeping his views out of the platform and snubbing Jackson by refusing to consider him for the vice-presidential slot. The unfortunate result was that Jackson—always quick to take offense—publicly blamed his isolation on "Jewish leaders." Jewish Democrats were incensed and Mondale was caught in the middle, looking indecisive.[33]

Jackson learned from his mistakes. He worked hard after 1984 to improve his relations with the Jewish community and expand the Rainbow Coalition. His core constituency remained the nation's blacks, but he spoke tirelessly on behalf of other minorities, the working poor, displaced workers, women, and gays. When he ran again in 1988—his campaign was better organized than in 1984, though it still had a comparatively small budget—these voters turned out for him. On Super Tuesday—March 8, 1988, when twenty-one states held primaries or caucuses—Jackson came in second to Dukakis, with 350 delegates to the governor's 372. Next, he won a surprise victory in the Michigan caucuses, with 55 percent of the vote. In the end, Jackson took almost 6.6 million primary votes, or nearly 30 percent of the total—more than all other Democrats, except Dukakis, combined. But, as in 1984, Jackson's success deeply worried Democratic leaders. Party officials feared that embracing Jackson would threaten their efforts to appeal to suburban and moderate voters and win back Democrats who had voted for Reagan. Jackson's progressivism, moreover, ran counter to Dukakis's desire to run a non-ideological campaign. Dukakis kept his distance from Jackson, and Susan Estrich went out of her way to treat Jackson rudely in an effort to show that he would not have undue influence over the Dukakis campaign. This treatment, understandably, angered Jackson and many of his supporters. The resulting well-publicized tensions continued through the fall campaign and, in response, many of Jackson's voters stayed home on election day rather than vote for Dukakis.[34]

Jackson's story sheds light on several aspects of race and politics during the Reagan years. Jackson himself is a tragic figure, a man of potential greatness who was unable to fulfill his promise. Unlike many activists, Jackson not only spoke out but also organized a significant movement and ran for office—he could legitimately claim to have added hundreds of thousands of loyal voters to the Democrats' base and to be the representative of millions more. But Jackson's personal flaws—his blindness to the danger posed by Farrakhan and his sensitivity to perceived insults—left him unable to translate these achievements into deals with other major players in Democratic politics. For the Democrats, Jackson's campaigns were illustrative of how liberalism had worked itself into an impossible position during the 1980s. The Democrats, it was true, needed to update their beliefs and policies so they could again appeal to a broad spectrum of moderate voters. But in this effort, the party's intellectual and political leaders could not find a way to accommodate the leading representative of those at the lower ends of American society—the very people for whom the Democrats claimed to speak. Indeed, they appeared afraid of these people and showed twice that they wanted nothing to do with their leader. Finally, and perhaps most sadly, because of Jackson's failures and the Democrats' confusion, blacks by the end of the 1988 campaign were almost powerless within the Democratic Party.[35]

The Democrats' and Jackson's failures created a leadership vacuum that still affects American racial politics. Jackson's inability to gain a major role for his coalition gave opportunists and hustlers an opening to make bids for their own leadership, claiming that they could more effectively represent poor blacks. Farrakhan, for example, was an obscure fringe character until Jackson's missteps brought him the attention of the media, and he used this experience to make himself a national figure. But the best case of the rise of a shady figure is that of the Reverend Al Sharpton in New York City. Sharpton, born in 1954, was not a religious leader, despite his ordination. He had no congregation but, instead, reportedly survived as a con artist—allegedly raising funds for nonexistent groups, fronting for a Mafia trash-collection racket, and so on. New York, meanwhile, had suffered a series of violent racial incidents during the mid-1980s, and Sharpton began involving himself in these to build a claim to be a community activist and spokesman. He got his big break in November 1987, when a black teenager named Tawana Brawley was seen crawling into a garbage bag in Wappingers Falls, a town south of Poughkeepsie. Police and an ambulance crew were summoned and found her smeared with dog excrement and with racial slurs written on her body. Brawley claimed to have been abducted by several white men, held for four days, and repeatedly raped. The horror of the crime created an instant sensation and, as the investigation began, Sharpton and two black lawyers with histories of exploiting racial incidents, C. Vernon Mason and Alton Maddox, rushed to become advisers to Brawley and her mother, Glenda.[36]

Sharpton, Mason, and Maddox turned the Brawley case into a legal and media circus. Claiming that a racist justice system was protecting Brawley's assailants, they maneuvered Governor Mario Cuomo into appointing a special prosecutor, Robert Abrams. Following the advice of the trio, Glenda and Tawana refused to cooperate with the investigation, and Glenda eventually took sanctuary in a church to avoid a grand jury subpoena. Meanwhile, Sharpton and his two associates made a series of wild accusations—declaring that Brawley's kidnappers were from a cult connected to the Irish Republican Army, naming specific individuals as participants in the rapes, and comparing Abrams to Hitler and claiming that he had masturbated over medical photographs of the girl—with each carefully orchestrated to obtain maximum television coverage. Even as all this was going on, however, Brawley's story fell apart. Tawana, it turned out, had a stormy relationship with Glenda and Glenda's boyfriend—a man who had killed his wife—and, the grand jury found after an exhaustive investigation, she had concocted her story to avoid punishment after being away from home without permission. Painstaking examinations of the physical evidence, moreover, showed conclusively that she had never been assaulted and had smeared the excrement and written the epithets herself. Mason, Maddox, and Sharpton had known this early on but kept the story alive to serve their own ends—"if we win this case, we'll be the biggest niggers in New York," Sharpton reportedly told an associate.[37]

Sharpton was right about the spoils to be had from the Brawley case, but only he was shrewd enough to benefit. Once the truth came out, Mason and Maddox were subject to legal disciplinary proceedings for their conduct in the case—Maddox's law license was suspended and Mason eventually was disbarred for repeated instances of misconduct. Sharpton, however, was subject to no professional or legal discipline and so suffered no repercussions, continued his race-baiting activities, and used his newfound fame to launch a career in politics. He has never made it to a general election, but in 1992 Sharpton took 16 percent of the vote in the New York Democratic Senate primary; he ran again for the Senate in 1994 and took 26 percent in the primary; and in 1997 he received 32 percent of the vote in New York City's Democratic mayoral primary. Although he never has apologized for his actions in the Brawley case, held public office, formed an effective political group, or brought any benefits to his supporters, and continues to be dogged by questions about his finances, Sharpton nonetheless has used his primary showings to make himself a racial power broker in New York. Hillary Clinton was careful to maintain good relations with him when she ran for the Senate in 2000—and, perhaps most disturbingly, he claimed a spot on the national stage as candidate for the Democratic presidential nomination in 2004.[38]

In spite of all these ups and downs, it is by no means clear that race relations were worse at the end of the Reagan years than at the start. The American political and social consensus continued to evolve during the 1980s as it had since World War II, in the direction of greater tolerance and inclusion. The lack of support for ending affirmative action—and, for that matter, the opposition of southern senators to the Bork nomination—is a good indication of the strength of the consensus, as is the infrequency of serious racial incidents during the Reagan era. Indeed, the Tawana

Brawley affair stands out because it was so unusual, was resolved by a thorough investigation, and never led to violence. No evidence supports claims of a return of national or systemic racism during the decade and, in fact, the continued movement of blacks and immigrants up the economic ladder and to the suburbs suggests the opposite.

The real problem in race relations during the 1980s was the uncertainty created by demographic change. Most important was that blacks began to face fundamental questions about their social and political positions. American racial politics long had assumed that blacks were the minority group that mattered the most, but the rise in Hispanic and Asian numbers brought that into question. As the Berkeley case had shown, this raised the issue of how affirmative action would be adjusted and who would gain or lose. The political uncertainties were on display as well in Jesse Jackson's campaigns. Jackson's stand for the dispossessed was admirable, but it was unclear that his positions, both because the Democratic Party now shied away from his progressivism and because changing economic conditions made them unrealistic, would bring any benefits to his constituents. Even worse, the Democratic leadership's ambivalence toward him left him out in the cold. The result was a vacuum in minority leadership that made possible the rise of figures like Farrakhan and Sharpton, who made their livings by stirring up racial resentments.

The 1980s, at first glance, was a good time for American colleges and universities. The numbers of students in undergraduate, graduate, and professional programs all increased to record levels—a total of almost 14 million by 1990. The financial health of the universities improved dramatically after 1982, as the rising stock market and return of prosperity increased endowments and tripled both endowment income and gifts. Some schools were able to run large capital campaigns—Tufts University, whose endowment totaled $60 million in 1983, raised an additional $145 million by 1986—and build new facilities. Faculties benefited, too, as schools hired more professors and salaries recovered some of the ground lost during the 1970s. Despite the prosperity, however, by the end of the Reagan years many campuses were in turmoil. Racial and political conflicts, particularly in the humanities and social sciences, broke into bitter public disputes that soured the tone of the nation's intellectual life.[39]

Underlying much of the turmoil in higher education during the 1980s was a shift in the composition of the campus population. Women, who already were the majority of college and university students in 1980, continued to expand their share of the student body. As more women came out of graduate programs, the number of female faculty—and the proportion of the faculty made up of women—increased sharply. Black, Hispanic, and Asian enrollments grew as well, and among Asians and Hispanics the rise was especially sharp for women. As beneficial as these changes were for women and minorities, however, they soon led to unexpected problems. Universities tended to be poorly managed and, because of tenure, had a lifetime employment system. The result was that senior academic ranks still were dominated by men with long years of seniority, and women faculty, often facing discrimination, advanced slowly. Indeed, this was similar to the situations that professional women had faced in many other industries before deregulation and expanding competition opened new opportunities, but in academia there was no serious discussion of changing the system. Meanwhile, the rise in minority enrollments led to an increase in racial tensions and incidents. A large part of the problem was that, while many schools worked hard to recruit minority students, they provided little support for them after they enrolled; the students often felt lost or excluded. White students at many selective private universities often were wary of minorities who they feared had been admitted as the result of affirmative action, not merit, and whose presence might indicate a lowering of standards and the value of diplomas. The two groups eyed each other with growing suspicion and, for many minority students, growing alienation.[40]

At the same time, the academy was becoming isolated from the mainstream of American life. This problem had been building since academics began withdrawing from public life in the late 1960s. The growth in the number of professors, from 165,000 in 1946 to 688,000 in 1980, had brought increased specialization as academic departments offered more courses and scholars sought to create niches for their work. Specialization had benefits—it enabled scholars to begin exploring new fields and developing new research methods—but had drawbacks as well. Specialization led many researchers to stop communicating across fields and become self-absorbed; prominent historians noted on several occasions during the 1980s, for example, that their colleagues had failed to use the new scholarship to write coherent narratives that appealed to a broad audience. This pattern of specialization and withdrawal was repeated in other disciplines and, as they ceased to inform public debates, professors effectively dropped out of politics. Academics like Arthur M. Schlesinger, Jr.—who had combined scholarship, popular writing, and involvement in Democratic and liberal politics—virtually disappeared.[41]

Another problem for the universities was that, as was so often the case during the 1980s, the benefits of prosperity were unevenly distributed on the campuses. The result was a growth in inequality in the academic world that mirrored that of society in general. Even before Reagan took office, students had begun shifting into fields that they saw as offering better job prospects—"toward courses that help provide a sense of usefulness and toward career and professional education," wrote an engineering dean in the *Chronicle of Higher Education* in October 1980. The pattern held throughout the decade as the numbers of degrees awarded in such fields as business, computer science, engineering, and mathematics soared. These departments and their faculties were the big winners on campus—the University of Arizona, for example, reorganized its research centers and laboratories to make them more competitive for federal grants and, as a result, was able to double its research spending in the sciences. Growing enrollments in business and the sciences also created jobs for more professors and, to attract these teachers, universities had to pay them higher salaries and provide them with more research funding and perks. Professors in these departments, furthermore, often supplemented their salaries with well-paid consulting work.[42]

The liberal arts and social sciences were the losers. The numbers of degrees earned annually in such fields as English, history, and sociology had fallen sharply during the 1970s and continued to drop in the 1980s. New openings for professors were relatively few and, with too many Ph.D.s coming out of graduate schools, competition for jobs was fierce. Except for a handful of superstar professors at wealthy schools, salaries for liberal arts teachers—already lower than those in business, engineering, and the sciences—fell further behind and few professors found opportunities to earn significant outside income. Because many schools had distribution requirements, however, liberal arts professors had to teach basic courses to rising numbers of students, which made for increasing workloads. These were the lucky ones, however. At some schools, administrators turned to "retrenchment"—the academic term for cutting departments and laying off faculty. By the late 1980s, the nation's humanities faculties were seething with resentment.[43]

With intellectuals withdrawing from politics at the same time that many of them were losing resources and prestige, academics became receptive to strange ideas. The problem, not surprisingly, was most acute in the humanities and social sciences, which were swept by illiberal and antidemocratic ideological fads. The best known of these was deconstruction, a French import that had grown out of postmodernism. Building on postmodernism's questioning of rationality and definitions, deconstruction taught that written words never can be assigned fixed meanings and, as a result, that close readings of texts can reveal ambiguities, hidden meanings, contradictions, and indications of repressive political relationships. Deconstruction claimed, furthermore, that because texts are open to innumerable interpretations, no absolute values can be said to exist—all meanings, at bottom, are matters of interpretation by the reader or are the results of social constructions. Consequently, deconstruction argued, no absolute values of right and wrong, universal experiences, or hierarchies of quality can be said to be valid.[44]

Deconstruction may have sounded at first glance like a benign, if eccentric, literary theory, but in practice it was a pernicious idea for both literature and politics. Deconstruction presented itself as emancipatory—it was, as its adherents claimed, an excellent tool for knocking down the claims of ideas and institutions and analyzing hidden sources of power—but did not trouble itself to offer any firm ideas about what was good, or propose alternatives that would be better than existing situations. Indeed, because deconstruction taught that truth and values are unknowable, its believers had an excuse not to respond seriously to political questions. Just as important, because of its denial of absolute values, deconstruction could be used to justify anything—a frightening possibility, given how ideas claiming to bring liberation had been used by dictators during the twentieth century. This problem, in particular, became the subject of widespread discussion after the discovery in late 1987 that Paul de Man—a Belgian-born professor at Yale who had done much to establish deconstruction in the United

States—had collaborated with the Nazis during World War II, writing anti-Semitic articles for the German-controlled press, and then later was involved in a financial fraud and bigamy. For de Man, at least, deconstruction might have been less a literary philosophy than a way to avoid admitting guilt.[45]

Another attractive set of ideas, which became known as identity politics, broke down the common identities of society by emphasizing the differences of ever smaller, ever more particular groups. The best example of the effects of the growth of identity politics on campus was the fragmenting of women's literature, a field that had been started during the 1970s. The establishment of women's literary studies was an important achievement, for it greatly enriched literary studies in general as it enabled scholars to expand the breadth of their subject and to begin to understand the different experiences and views of women writers. During the 1980s, however, studying women's literature went beyond the recovery of a lost heritage and expansion of scholarly boundaries to become, for many feminist professors, a way to attack what they viewed as patriarchal literary traditions and male domination of the campus and society. As an emancipatory movement, moreover, women's literary studies was prone to doctrinal splits—lesbians began to claim a separate literary tradition that rejected what they viewed as heterosexual domination, and black and Hispanic critics soon made similar particularistic claims as did, ultimately, minority lesbians. The overall effect was to split women's literature into competing schools of thought—often sharply critical of each other and, eventually, even of its founding figures—with each using difficult prose or theories to put literature at the service of their politics.[46]

The attractions of deconstruction and particularist theories are easy to understand, as are their failures. Their claims to offer radical, emancipatory politics were attractive to academic leftists, many of whom viewed themselves as carrying on the work of the New Left. In particular, they provided humanities professors with an explanation for their difficulties and a vocabulary for attacking the dominance of the scientific and business departments. "Neo-Marxian, postmodernist, and feminist" theory, wrote one professor of education, enabled an analysis of how those prosperous fields and faculty had been "privileged" during the 1980s. Similarly, feminism's and deconstruction's claims to expose power and oppression were especially attractive to faculty women and minorities who still found themselves with little authority in the academic world. Deconstructionists for their part tended to write in dense, complex prose—often, it was unreadable—that they used to pose as an academic elite and intimidate outsiders. In fact, however, because their work was so abstract and hard to read, it appealed only to a small, inward-looking community of academics; they had, in effect, substituted playing with language for the true, hard political work of building public support for ideas and parties. Intellectuals in the humanities may have flattered themselves into believing that they were politically engaged, but few people outside the academy were fooled by this posturing. The deconstructionists, wrote the president of the American Studies Association in 1989, were "an upper middle-class intelligentsia comfortably entrenched in the university and playing at radicalism." Meanwhile, the national press caught on and began making sport of the pretensions of literary studies.[47]

Ironically, few people outside academia might have cared about any of this had Reagan not, in November 1981, appointed William Bennett as chairman of the National Endowment for the Humanities. Born in 1943, Bennett had earned a Ph.D. in philosophy from the University of Texas and a law degree from Harvard. He was a conservative academic who believed deeply in the importance of the humanities, the values of Western civilization, and the use of schools to inculcate moral values. In particular, Bennett believed that the Western classics—the "canon"—constituted a body of superior work that addressed questions of timeless importance. Reading them, in his view, was a critical part of a liberal education as well as a liberating experience for anyone, regardless of sex or personal background. "Reason, moral excellence, the promise of freedom, principles of honor and justice, and the search for meaning and salvation" were to be learned from the humanities, he wrote in 1983. Bennett believed, however, that a loss of faith in civilized values, reinforced by the "self-isolating vocabularies" of theories like deconstruction, had wrecked the humanities and the abilities of the universities to produce educated graduates—"persons freed from ignorance and callousness." Never afraid of a controversy, from the time he was appointed to the National Endowment for the Humanities in late 1981, Bennett used his position to speak on the plight of the humanities with brutal honesty.

Graduate programs had become "insignificant, lifeless, and pointless," Bennett said in a typical comment in 1984, and he reoriented the endowment's grants to provide support for traditional teaching of the classics, history, literature, and philosophy. Nominated to become secretary of education in the second Reagan administration, Bennett told the senators at his confirmation hearing that he planned to continue this effort, because "there ought to be some common learning experiences, some things, books, ideas, notions," to tie Americans together. His view, of course, ran directly counter to those of the academic left.[48]

Bennett's appointment to the humanities post had coincided with the start of a national debate about education reform, and his arguments went to the core of the discussions. The issue was what would compose the basic humanities reading lists for college students—in other words, how the canon would be defined in practice and what interpretations taught to young citizens. Although feminists and minority students already were pressing for the inclusion of more works by women and non-Western writers, their efforts had gained little public attention. Once Bennett began speaking about the question of who and what should be read, however, the issue became more prominent. Conservatives argued that maintaining the traditional Western canon would preserve high intellectual and academic standards. Jeffrey Hart, an English professor at Dartmouth, accused feminists of trying to add second-rate works by women to the canon for purely political reasons—"the prerequisite for inclusion is not literary quality but resentment," he wrote. For feminist theorists and deconstructionists, however, revision would provide an opening to break the male Eurocentric lock on the canon, add works of their choosing, and, most important, claim that their views had joined the accepted standards. They argued, therefore, that white Western writers had no monopoly on intellectual or artistic merit, and that the conservative argument was merely an excuse for maintaining control of the educational system and society in general—conservative views, said one writer, revealed a "crippling ethnocentrism and almost a contempt for the struggle" of others to be heard.[49]

The curriculum debate quickly polarized and, intersecting with other campus tensions, created an atmosphere that led to bitter quarrels at several prominent schools. The longest-running fight probably was at

Dartmouth, where racial problems combined with curricular arguments. To increase diversity on its campus, Dartmouth had made substantial efforts to recruit minority students, added courses in women's, black, and Native American studies, and dropped the college's official symbol, an Indian. The changes angered conservative students, who feared that affirmative action admissions and courses in "victim classes" would devalue their degrees; they also objected to what they viewed as the loss of Dartmouth's identity. In a series of incidents from January 1986 until the spring of 1989, activists associated with the *Dartmouth Review*—an off-campus newspaper published by conservative students—destroyed a shantytown erected by left-wing students protesting South African apartheid; printed the names of homosexual students; published a brutal criticism of, and then harassed, a black professor they believed to be a poor teacher; and mocked the college's liberal Jewish president in terms that verged on anti-Semitic. Dartmouth, in response to the attack on the professor, suspended two staff members of the *Review* only to have its action overturned in January 1989 on free speech grounds by a New Hampshire court. By then, said one professor, Dartmouth was in a state of "moral and intellectual civil war."[50]

Another civil war broke out at Stanford University. In 1980, Stanford had reinstated a mandatory Western civilization course—the original, established in 1935, had been abolished in 1970—with a reading list that went from Genesis through ancient Greece, the Renaissance, the Enlightenment, and finished with Freud. In 1988, in response to complaints from the school's growing number of black, Asian, and Hispanic students that the list had a "European-Western and male bias," the faculty and administration began considering how to reform the class. The argument quickly escalated and the future of Stanford's course became an issue for debate in newspapers across the country. Supporters of the Western civilization course defended the need for reading traditional works of timeless moral and intellectual value, while reform proponents attacked the list as racist and sexist. In April, Stanford's faculty senate approved a proposal that kept much of the course intact but added a requirement to study a non-European culture and works by women and non-European writers. Two weeks later, William Bennett flew to Stanford and denounced the decision as a "capitulation to a campaign of pressure politics and intimidation."[51]

Officials at several schools tried to restore civility to their campuses, but their efforts only made things worse. One problem was that the arguments about racism and sexism, as well as the rise in racial incidents, had increased sensitivities to behavior that long had been encouraged or tolerated in colleges—asking pointed questions in classes about racial and political issues, challenging professors' statements, or holding parties based on stereotypical ethnic themes. To avoid hurt feelings or worse, some university administrators began to place restrictions on speech. The University of Michigan appears to have been the first school to do this, banning in April 1988 any speech or behavior that "stigmatizes or victimizes an individual on the basis of race, ethnicity, religion, sex, sexual orientation, creed, national origin, ancestry, age, marital status, handicap, or Vietnam-era veteran status." In the spring of 1989 Stanford began debating a speech code, and Tufts followed that fall with an elaborate set of rules classifying different types of speech and designating areas of the campus where each was allowed. The codes quickly met the fates they deserved—Michigan's was dismissed by a federal court, and Tufts rescinded its rules after newspaper coverage made the university look foolish. Unfortunately, some legal scholars continued to insist that the codes were appropriate responses to speech perceived as racist or sexist, and a disturbingly large number of prominent schools—including Brown and the Universities of Pennsylvania, California, and Wisconsin—had established speech restrictions by the early 1990s. On top of all their other problems, academics now were turning against freedom of expression.[52]

The curricular and speech disputes were a dramatic illustration of the unexpected consequences of broader social change. The universities had adjusted before to societal shifts that had changed the campus population, brought representatives of newly arrived groups to positions of authority, and created demands for curricular changes. Indeed, it had not been long since the nation's universities had accommodated influxes of new ethnic groups—the arrival of large numbers of Jews at midcentury was within the memory of many faculty members in the 1980s—without falling into a crisis. In the late 1980s, however, few in academia were in a mood to compromise on issues of change. Liberal and left-wing humanities professors viewed themselves as under siege. To them, opposition to altering the reading lists was part of the same conservative trend that had devalued their departments and jobs, and they viewed Bennett and his allies as right-wing zealots. For their part, conservatives viewed the assault on the canon as the latest in a series of attacks that had undermined the quality of liberal education since the 1960s. Added to that was the conservatives' recent failure to achieve all of their social goals—it is worth noting that they often portrayed suggestions to change the canon as an effort to establish quotas for studying various groups, and so attacked them as a form of affirmative action. The issue of core reading lists, as a result, was where each side was determined to make its stand and, in the colleges and universities, the 1980s ended in an angry stalemate.[53]

As the decade came to a close unresolved disputes about social issues and racial questions, along with the well-publicized campus fights, combined to give the impression that American society was riddled with deep conflicts. The situation seemed to worsen after Reagan left office. The growing academic tendency to research differences among groups and their experiences led to the rise of multiculturalism, which sought to deny the possibility that various ethnic groups should seek a common American identity, let alone try to emulate a superior Western ideal. The campus speech codes evolved into a new phenomenon as well, "political correctness," that sought to limit speech and debate through informal means. By the early 1990s, academics and journalists had begun to speak of "culture wars," which combined all of these disputes into what sociologist James Davison Hunter defined as "political and social hostility rooted in different systems of moral understanding." The participants in the wars were not so dispassionate in their definitions, however. It was a "battle about matters of the spirit," declared neoconservative writer Midge Decter in 1991, and a "war to the death" to control the ideas that, in turn, dominate American politics.[54]

The emergence of social and cultural conflicts during the 1980s is not, in retrospect, suprising. The Reagan years were a time of political, economic, and social change that created distinct groups of winners and losers. The losers of the 1980s tended to be liberals or those to their left who, like supporters of affirmative action or humanities professors, had a large stake in the pre-Reagan status quo. During the decade they not only lost ground because of market developments but also, as the Democrats' troubles worsened, found themselves unable to make any progress in the traditional political arena. Consequently, they began to abandon electoral politics in favor of other means of making political gains, whether it was by challenging the content of university education, limiting free speech, or employing self-serving racial demagoguery. This only furthered their isolation—they made some gains in the universities, where liberal and left-wing views found the most sympathy, but at the cost of revealing themselves as antidemocratic and desperately opposed to the views and culture of the majority of Americans.

In this context, what is striking about the conflicts of the 1980s is how mild they were. That well-organized and articulate groups—literature professors, conservative Christian activists, and supporters of William Bennett—had significant grievances is undeniable. Similarly, others who found themselves losing influence, like the former Justice Department official who accused the Reagan administration of breaking the law on civil rights, often exaggerated issues as a way to call attention to their views. But in practice, grievances almost always were handled through debate, regulatory channels, or the courts—it is difficult to think of a case of violent protest during the 1980s, even in a racially charged case like that of Tawana Brawley.

What this suggests is that the culture wars actually were isolated skirmishes between small groups of antagonists and did not involve issues that most people felt were central to their lives. The impression of extensive conflict came about, in large part, because it was easy for journalists looking for interesting stories to see specific well-publicized incidents—anger about a judicial decision, Al Sharpton's antics, or a curriculum fight—as clashes representing views held by most Americans. In fact, however, the pundits had it wrong. Sociological and public opinion studies from the late 1980s through the mid-1990s confirmed what previous research had found—Americans, especially in the middle and professional classes, continued to move gradually toward greater tolerance or acceptance of racial, sexual, and moral differences, and were less forgiving of those with extremist, nonaccommodationist views. (The only major exception to this was abortion, where attitudes hardened during the 1990s.) Furthermore, no evidence suggests that Americans had become significantly more ideological during the 1980s, or that the cultural conflicts excited much interest beyond a narrow audience—unlike during the civil rights and Vietnam eras, no one marched to keep Plato on a reading list. Instead, most people simply went about their business and, as sociologist Alan Wolfe noted in his perceptive study of middle-class morals, tried to live their lives as best they could "in a world without fixed rules." If they paid any attention to cultural battles, it was probably to wonder why anyone would argue so angrily about obscure questions that had little observable effect on people's daily lives. The attitude was the same on the campuses, where the quarrels were most intense. There, the vast majority of students paid no attention, content to live in a late adolescent culture that emphasized the pursuit of personal pleasure and not worrying too much about what they were told to study.[55]

CONCLUSION: CHANGE AND CONTINUITY

Contrasting the United States in 1980 and 1989 reveals the scope of change during the decade. At the start of the 1980s, conservatism had been the home of the political outsiders. At the end of the decade, it dominated American politics and set the country's agenda, while liberalism searched for a way to confront it effectively. In economics, inflation had been controlled, unemployment cut, and growth restored. Income tax rates, the central issue for Reagan's conservatism, had been lowered dramatically and, it appears, for the long term. Meanwhile, federal budget deficits that once would have been unimaginable had become routine. Extensive social changes marked the 1980s as well, whether in the way people worked, in how they lived, in the ethnic composition of the population, or in their willingness to tolerate differences.

A focus on change, however, should not obscure the continuities of the era. Looking at the Reagan years in the context of the period from the 1940s to the 1990s shows little deviation from established customs and trends. Political change remained gradual and within traditional boundaries. Americans remained nonideological but, consistent with recent trends, society continued to become more open, tolerant, and individualist, while the middle and professional classes continued to make political and social gains. Sorting through this combination of change and continuity provides a final understanding of the 1980s.

The greatest change in the 1980s was the movement of conservatism to the leading position in American politics. In 1980, conservatism still was a strange idea to most Americans, often viewed as an extremist philosophy and tainted by Barry Goldwater's defeat. Liberalism's loss of strength during the 1970s had not led to a corresponding gain for conservatism; those Americans who were disenchanted with the Democrats did not automatically turn into conservatives, and few had given much thought to alternatives to the liberal institutions and assumptions they had grown up with. That so many voters decided in favor of Reagan at the last minute in 1980 simply shows that he was elected not because Americans had become conservatives but, rather, because they decided to hire him on a try-and-see basis.

The conservatism they got proved to be cautious. Reagan himself, like most Americans, was not a man given to extremes, and he was not personally drawn to rigid commitments or inflexible ideology. He was a man of conservative instincts, but above all a practical politician, one who knew the importance of concentrating on a few priorities and who had an instinct for when to take a deal. With the exception of the true believers in the supply side—who quickly left the stage—and the hapless Donald Regan, he surrounded himself with capable men of similar outlooks. The result was that Reaganism turned out to be a moderate conservatism, by instinct one close to the center of American politics, and by necessity one that would not go too far to the right. Reagan delivered lower taxes and somewhat less government regulation of business, and generally tried to leave decisions to individuals and markets. But he never risked his political support by pushing for a fundamental restructuring of the role of government, nor did he try to impose drastic changes on existing social arrangements. Reaganism brought incremental changes, not a revolution.

Reaganism's moderate ways can obscure its more far-reaching achievements, however. In 1980, no one knew whether conservatives could govern the country—they were small in number, and had little experience on the national stage or in managing large governmental institutions. Reagan proved conclusively that conservatives could govern effectively. On his highest-priority issues—reducing taxes, controlling inflation, encouraging growth and innovation, appointing conservative judges, and ensuring that conservatism would carry on its work after he left office—Reagan worked carefully and almost always was successful. His administration had its share of failures—Bork, Iran-Contra, and the setbacks in deregulation—but these were no greater in number or severity than what generally happens in a two-term presidency. Indeed, compared with the records of presidents from Johnson through Clinton—which includes one president driven from office because of a failed war, one who resigned in disgrace, two who failed to be reelected, and one who was impeached—Reagan's ability to manage the complexities of political and governmental affairs is impressive.

In addition to his immediate successes, Reagan shifted some of the basic assumptions of American politics, especially regarding taxes. Reagan first brought taxes to the center of political debate, and then reduced income tax rates in 1981 and again in 1986, added indexing, and reformed the income tax system. In so doing, he showed that previous assumptions—the need for and acceptability of high taxes, and the belief that the system could not be improved—were wrong. His successors have ignored this lesson at their peril. George H. W. Bush agreed to a tax increase in 1990, and lost the support of conservatives and then his reelection bid in 1992; Bill Clinton won a tax increase in 1993, but the Democrats lost Congress the following year; and George W. Bush, no doubt mindful of his father's fate, has insisted on maintaining or expanding tax cuts, even as war has forced increased spending at a time of rising deficits.

The change in outlook on taxes led to a change in assumptions about the possibilities for federal programs. Reagan's belief that federal social programs accomplished little meant that he proposed no significant measures. As the 1980s progressed and the country seemed to be doing well without new programs, support for them gradually eroded. The effects of this became clear in the 1990s—Bill Clinton could not convince a Democratic Congress to pass his health care plan and, even as the government enjoyed huge budget surpluses later in the decade, little support emerged for any major new government programs. In fact, the most important innovation in social programs between 1980 and the Medicare reform of 2003—the reform of welfare in 1996—was a measure designed to reduce the role of government, not increase it.

Another big change in the 1980s was in how Americans viewed their relationship with the marketplace. For the roughly fifty years from the start of the New Deal until Reagan's inauguration, government policy had been to try to protect people from the fluctuations of free markets. The programs, to be sure, did not insulate people from risk entirely, but unemployment insurance, Social Security, Medicare, and the host of industrial and social regulations provided a certain degree of safety. De-regulation, increased competition, and the rise in personal investing each chipped away at that structure, however, by making jobs and retirement funding less secure. With little fanfare, and probably little thought to the long-term risks, Americans accepted greater economic uncertainty in re-turn for the possibility of greater personal prosperity.

These changes help explain another major development during the 1980s, the implosion of the Democratic Party. The party was in trouble before 1981, of course, but that does not explain the duration and sever-ity of its problems—the Republicans, after all, had been written off after the Goldwater debacle in 1964 and were in deep trouble in the mid-1970s after Watergate and Gerald Ford's defeat, but they came back quickly both times. The differences between the Republican and Democratic ex-periences are instructive, however. The Republicans proved to be adapt-able, willing to jettison their old moderate ideology for loyalty to the supply side and Reaganism; they also did a better job than the Demo-crats of maintaining a cohesive party structure and internal discipline. The Democrats, in contrast, proved stubbornly unwilling to adjust to changing times and political conditions. In part this was the price the Democrats paid for representing a broad coalition of liberals, workers, minorities, and white ethnics—each group fought hard to protect its interests. Success in politics, however, requires adapting to changing real-ities. Change, as the neoliberals realized, also presents an opportunity to develop new ideas and policies to accomplish traditional goals. But the Democrats were too fractious to agree on new ways and so failed to com-pete effectively with the Republicans. Indeed, when they did well, as in the 1986 Senate elections, it was because they moved toward Republican positions, not away.

The Democrats' continuing problems have caused other difficulties in national politics. Democrats appear to understand instinctively the need to appeal to the centrist majority but, as Jesse Jackson's campaigns showed, this has led them to lose interest in representing those at the bottom of society. Because of this, in turn, characters like Al Sharpton have been able to stake leadership claims and present themselves as legitimate actors on the national scene. Even as they have moved to the center, the Democrats still have not developed a coherent set of ideas that can attract enough votes to regain control of the government, and their electoral position has continued to erode. Bill Clinton's victories—both with less than 50 percent of the popular vote—look like anomalies that can be attributed to his extraordinary personal talents, but not to a Democratic recovery. This point was driven home in 1994, when the Democrats lost Congress, and again by Al Gore's defeat in 2000—an election in which peace and prosperity should have made him a shoo-in—and by John Kerry's loss in 2004.

Outside of politics, the 1980s were marked by numerous other changes, both big and small. Some were intangible, like the growth of confidence in institutions. Others were measurable, but had consequences that became clear only gradually and ambiguously, like the rise in immigration. Some were significant, but almost hidden from daily view, like the continuing decline in discrimination. Still others became apparent quickly and starkly, like the income gap caused by the sharp decrease in demand for unskilled labor or the growing prosperity of the educated. Finally, many changes were plainly beneficial, like the arrival of computers at work or the increasing availability of high-quality goods at reasonable prices. Taken together, these added up to large changes in how Americans lived, worked, and decided what they expected in life. Except for the displacement of lower-skilled workers, almost all of these changes left Americans better off at the end of the Reagan years than at their beginning.

Looking at these changes from the vantage point of the early twenty-first century shows that the 1980s was above all a time of transition. Whether it was in politics, economics, or the ways people lived, it was a decade when old ways began to disappear and new ones emerge. What was revolutionary in the Reagan years—lower taxes, less job security, rapid technological innovation, takeovers, IRA investing, or ideological quarrels—was routine in the 1990s. Indeed, in some ways the 1990s seemed like an accelerated version of the 1980s—technology changed at a frantic pace, the stock market soared to previously unimaginable levels, inequality continued to grow, and the mood of the country was even more celebratory than it had been in 1984. As a result, the United States has become a different country than it was in 1980, one that is faster paced, hypercompetitive, largely uninterested in using the government to ensure personal economic security, and embracing of technological change. The unattractive aspects of the 1980s, too, have become more prominent. In particular, the ideological struggles over political appointments that started with Bork have become harsher—both Clinton and George W. Bush have had trouble obtaining confirmations of judges and other high-level appointees. Individualism continued to increase, making society more atomized. Cultural battles, too, continued during the 1990s and became more bitter, culminating with Clinton's impeachment and trial. The effect of these developments has been to make national politics into an angry contest in which almost any tactic is legitimate.

If the changes of the 1980s are striking, so too are the continuities. The United States has always been a dynamic society, forward-looking and experimental. To understand this, it is instructive to count the number of events in American history that are labeled as revolutions—the American Revolution, the Jacksonian revolution, the second revolution under Lincoln, the industrial revolution, the New Deal, the civil rights revolution, and the technology revolution. Except for the first, none of these were revolutions in the strictest sense of the word, but they point to Americans' tendency to define themselves in terms of change. Whether they embraced, or just accepted, the changes of the 1980s, Americans were acting as they always had, looking toward the future and trying new ways.

Looking at the 1980s in a more recent context—starting in 1945— shows additional important ways in which the United States did not change during the Reagan years. Most notably, the United States remained a land of political consensus. The consensus evolved and, like society in general, accommodated change and made room for new ideas and developments. Thus, homosexuals gradually gained new rights, women's new roles became accepted, and college reading lists were adjusted to reflect changes in the student population. The process was slow, but opposition generally was not rigid—the great majority of

Americans remained tolerant and accepting. Reagan clearly understood this. Whenever he had a choice about whether to challenge the consensus view—whether it was reducing environmental regulation, fighting to roll back abortion rights, or ending affirmative action—he turned away from confrontation. Indeed, except for the alienation of relatively small groups like hard-core Christian conservatives or angry humanities professors, the absence of discontent during the Reagan years is striking.

Closely related to the consensus is that fact that American politics and society remained open and flexible, renewing themselves by bringing new groups and outsiders into the mainstream. Starting with Reagan himself, the conservatives who came to power in the 1980s had long been outsiders in the political system, distrusted even by a large segment of their own party. Many of those who rose to prominence or prospered the most during the 1980s also once had been on the margins—Michael Milken, who had started selling a disreputable product for a minor firm, was one, as were the millions of women, immigrants, and minorities rising in the business, professional, and academic worlds. Progress, certainly, could be bumpy—as the experiences of women and minorities on the campuses showed—but it was real nonetheless. Another aspect of continuity was the continued expansion of the middle and professional classes, both materially and politically. In this case, not only did a trend that had been in place for decades continue, but the middle and professional classes also showed themselves to be open and flexible as they incorporated newly rising groups.

Americans remained nonideological. Daniel Bell, Richard Hofstadter, and the other consensus writers of the 1950s were correct when they observed that Americans paid little attention to ideology and were, instead, content to live in an inconsistent, contradictory political world. This American trait was on full display during the 1980s. Some of the changes of the Reagan years were conservative, such as accepting the consequences of deregulated markets, or reining in selected federal programs. Other changes went in a liberal direction, like finding ways to maintain affirmative action, or taking no firm steps to reduce the spread of cheap video pornography. Still others pointed to an ideological muddle—most notably, the way in which a dislike of deficits combined with a decision to wait and see if they actually led to problems.

If ideology remained unimportant to Americans, however, ideas did not. All of the changes and continuities of the 1980s were examples of ideas put into action—whether as a commitment to reduce the role of government in the marketplace, to maintain hard-won rights and privileges, or to study a different group of writers in a different way. Conversely, the Democrats' problems largely were the result of not having ideas to put into action. This, perhaps, is the final irony and complexity of American society and politics, that a people who agree on so much and deny the importance of ideology in their actions still need something to believe in.

APPENDIX

Table 1. Changes in Residence, Employment, and Education, 1940–80 (All figures in millions, except percentages)

	1940	1950	1960	1970	1980
Total population	132.6	152.3	180.7	205.1	227.7
Percentage in suburbs	15.3	23.3	30.6	37.2	43.4
Employed civilians	47.5	59.9	66.7	78.6	97.2
Professional, technical, and managerial workers	7.3	10.0	14.5	19.4	26.5
Union members	8.9	15.0	18.1	20.7	22.8
Higher-education enrollment	1.5	2.2	3.6	7.4	12.1
Percentage of adults with one or more years of college	10.0	13.1	16.5	21.2	31.9

Sources: Statistical Abstracts of the United States, 1952, 1962, 1972, 1982–83; Muller, *Everyday Life in Suburbia.*

Table 2. GNP Growth, Inflation, and Unemployment, 1980–88

	GNP Growth (%)	Inflation (CPI, %)	Unemployment (%)
1980	3.4	13.5	7.0
1981	1.9	10.3	7.5
1982	−2.5	6.2	9.5
1983	3.6	3.2	9.5
1984	6.8	4.3	7.4
1985	3.4	3.6	7.1
1986	2.7	1.9	6.9
1987	3.7	3.6	6.1
1988	4.4	4.1	5.4

Source: Statistical Abstract of the United States, 1990

Table 3. Federal Budget Receipts, Outlays, and Deficits, 1980–88 (billion $)

	Receipts	Outlays	Deficit
1980	517.1	590.9	73.8
1981	599.3	678.2	78.9
1982	617.8	745.7	127.9
1983	600.6	808.3	207.7
1984	666.5	851.8	185.3
1985	734.1	946.3	212.2
1986	769.1	990.3	221.2
1987	854.1	1,003.8	149.7
1988	909.0	1,064.0	155.0

Source: Statistical Abstract of the United States, 1990

Table 4. Employment and Occupations, 1980 and 1988 (thousands of workers)

	1980	1988	Change (%)
Total employment	**97,270**	**114,968**	**18.19**
Sales*	6,172	13,747	122.73
Transportation	3,468	4,831	39.30
Professional, technical, managerial	26,532	32,711	23.29
Services	12,958	15,332	18.32
Laborers	4,456	4,866	9.20
Precision production and craftsmen	12,529	13,664	9.06
Clerical and administrative	18,105	18,264	0.88
Agriculture, forestry, fishing	3,529	3,437	−2.61
Machinery operators, production workers, assemblers	10,346	8,117	−21.54

*Includes retail sales, sale representatives, real estate, insurance, and securities sales personnel

Totals do not add correctly because of rounding or inconsistencies in data reporting

Sources: Statistical Abstract of the United States, 1981, 1982–83, and 1990

Table 5. Money Income of Households, 1980 and 1988

Income level (constant 1988 dollars)	Percentage of households	
	1980	1988
0 to 4,999	6.3	6.2
5,000 to 9,999	12.0	10.8
Subtotal, 0 to 9,999	**18.3**	**17.0**
10,000 to 14,999	11.1	10.3
15,000 to 24,999	20.0	18.6
25,000 to 34,999	17.5	16.0
Subtotal, 10,000 to 34,999	**48.6**	**44.9**
35,000 to 49,999	17.5	17.3
50,000 and more	15.8	20.8
Subtotal, 35,000 and up	**33.3**	**38.1**

Totals do not add to 100 because of rounding

Source: Statistical Abstract of the United States, 1990

Table 6. Selected Standard of Living Indicators, 1980 and 1988

	1980	*1988*
Mean household income (1988 dollars)	25,426	27,225
Housing		
Single-family homes built	957,000	1,085,000
Average price	64,600	112,500
Average size (square feet)	1,740	1,995
Central air conditioning (%)	63	75
More than 3 bedrooms (%)	20	26
More than 2 baths (%)	25	42
Transportation		
Automobiles sold (millions)	8.9	10.6
Minivans sold	NA	700,000
Number of models reviewed in *Consumer Reports* annual car issue	95	140
Air travel		
Domestic passengers (millions)	273	419
International passengers (millions)	24	34
Retail Purchases		
Retail sales (billion 1982 dollars)	1,073.3	1,435.4
Wal-Mart sales (billion $)	1.6	20.6
Home computers (millions)	NA	22.4
Cellular telephone spending (billion $)*	NA	2.4
Compact disc sales (billion $)	NA	2.1
Videocassette recorders in homes (millions)	1	51
Food and drink		
Restaurants (thousands)	217	290
Sales (billion $)	80.4	145.8
Breweries	86	183
Credit card spending (billion $)	205.4	397.1
Outstanding credit card debt (billion $)	81.2	180.0
Default rate (%)	2.7	2.2

*1980 and 1987

NA = not available

Sources: Statistical Abstract of the United States, 1990; *Consumer Reports; Wall Street Journal; Journal of Political Economy,* August 2002.

Table 7. Income Levels and Voting, 1984 and 1988

	1984			1988		
	Percentage of voters	Percentage voting for:		Percentage of voters	Percentage voting for:	
Income level		Reagan	Mondale		Bush	Dukakis
$0–$12,499	15	46	53	12	37	62
$12,500–$24,999	27	57	42	20	49	50
$25,000–$34,999	21	59	40	20	56	44
$35,000–$49,999	18	67	32	20	56	42
$50,000 and above	13	68	31	19	62	37
Less than high school education	6	49	50	8	43	56
High school	30	60	39	27	50	49
Some college	30	61	37	30	57	42
College graduate	29	58	41	35	56	43
Democrats	38	24	75	37	17	82
Republicans	35	93	6	35	91	8
Democrats voting for Reagan in 1984			0	9	48	51
All voters		59	41		53	46

Source: New York Times/CBS News Exit Polls, 1984 and 1988

ACKNOWLEDGMENTS

In writing this book, I have been fortunate to have the help, advice, and encouragement of a large number of friends, colleagues, and family members. Several people read parts or all of the manuscript and offered insightful comments and suggestions. They include Ed Berkowitz, Joel Corman, Glen Jeansonne, Bruce Mizrach, Leo Ribuffo, and Mike Warner. Bill Weber listened patiently to my arguments and was always quick to tell me when I should consider other points of view. I presented portions of Chapter 2 at the Organization of American Historians meeting in Boston in March 2004, and I thank Mike Flamm, David Greenberg, and Jonathan Schoenwald for their comments, as well as people in the audience for their observations and suggestions. Finally, an anonymous reviewer for Yale University Press made several good suggestions.

Tim Ray and Ed Berkowitz shared copies of their unpublished research, which filled in some important gaps in Chapters 2 and 4. I have also tried to follow Ed's advice from many years ago to remember that historians are supposed to tell stories. Frank Levy kindly allowed me to cite some of his unpublished research. Former attorney general Edwin Meese generously gave me his time and patiently answered my questions. At George Washington University's Law School, Professor Todd Peterson gave me lessons in constitutional law.

No author can survive without the help of librarians. At George Washington University, Valerie Emerson was always a pleasure to work with. The Ronald Reagan Presidential Library is a wonderful resource for scholars—Meghan Lee, Cate Sewell, Jenny Sternaman, and Ben Pazzillo made me feel at home and made my stay productive. My thanks also to the reference librarians at George Washington's Burns Law Library, the George Mason University Law Library, and the Alexandria and Arlington County Public Libraries.

My agent, Carl Brandt, was always full of encouragement, good ideas, and sound advice. At Yale University Press, Chuck Grench acquired this book when it was still a rough idea. His successor, Lara Heimert, and her assistants, Keith Condon and Molly Egland, have been a pleasure to work with, as has been my manuscript editor Phillip King.

Authors have long-suffering families. My wife, Diane, always made time for me to work and kept us all fed while I was on leave to finish writing. Our children, Ben and Rachelle, tried not to interrupt too often when I was downstairs working on "Daddy's Book."

This book is dedicated to my parents, Leonard and Peggy Ehrman. Since I was a small boy, they have fed my interest in history and writing, and it is long past time that they got something in return.

Finally, this book has been reviewed by the United States government. That review neither constitutes authentication of information nor implies government endorsement of its views.

NOTES

Introduction

1. Since 1980, historians and political scientists have produced a rich literature on the origins and development of the modern American conservative movement. The standard history of the movement remains George Nash, *The Conservative Intellectual Movement in America Since 1945,* updated ed. (Wilmington: Intercollegiate Studies Institute, 1996). For overviews of the literature on conservatism, see Alan Brinkley, "The Problem of American Conservatism," *American Historical Review* 99 (April 1994): 409–29; Leo Ribuffo, "Why Is There So Much Conservatism in the United States and Why Do So Few Historians Know Anything About It?" *American Historical Review* 99 (April 1994): 438–49; Leo Ribuffo, "The Discovery and Rediscovery of American Conservatism Broadly Defined," *OAH Magazine of History* 17 (January 2003): 5–10; and James Hijiya, "The Conservative 1960s," *Journal of American Studies* 37 (August 2003): 201–27. Other general histories of postwar conservatism are Paul Gottfried, *The Conservative Movement,* revised ed. (New York: Twayne, 1993), and Godfrey Hodgson, *The World Turned Right Side Up* (Boston: Houghton Mifflin, 1996).

For histories of pre-1980 conservatism, see Jerome Himmelstein, *To the Right* (Berkeley: University of California Press, 1990); Dan Carter, *The Politics of Rage* (New York: Simon and Schuster, 1995); Robert Goldberg, *Barry Goldwater* (New Haven: Yale University Press, 1995); Mary Brennan, *Turning Right in the Sixties* (Chapel Hill: University of North Carolina Press, 1995); Rick Perlstein, *Before the Storm* (New York: Hill and Wang, 2001); Jonathan Schoenwald, *A Time for Choosing* (New York: Oxford University Press, 2001); and Lisa McGirr, *Suburban Warriors* (Princeton: Princeton University Press, 2001). For conservatism during the Reagan era, see Sidney Blumenthal, *The Rise of the Counter-Establishment* (New York: Times, 1986); J. David Hoeveler, Jr., *Watch on the Right* (Madison: University of Wisconsin Press, 1991); Gary Dorrien, *The Neoconservative Mind* (Philadelphia: Temple

University Press, 1993); and William Berman, *America's Right Turn* (Baltimore: Johns Hopkins University Press, 1994).

Prologue: The American

1. Peggy Noonan, *What I Saw at the Revolution* (New York: Random House, 1990), p. 150.

2. "Hollywood Stumbles at Doorstep of Politics," *New York Times,* November 6, 2003, p. E1; Edmund Morris, "Too Big a Man for the Small Screen," *New York Times,* November 9, 2003, sec. 4, p. 11. No full, satisfactory biography of Reagan has yet been written. The best books on Reagan to date are the three by Lou Cannon, the reporter who covered him as governor and president: Lou Cannon, *Reagan* (New York: G. P. Putnam, 1982); Lou Cannon, *President Reagan* (New York: Simon and Schuster, 1991); and Lou Cannon, *Governor Reagan* (New York: Public Affairs, 2003). Additional perceptive observations of Reagan are in Garry Wills, *Reagan's America* (Garden City: Doubleday, 1987), and Alonzo Hamby, *Liberalism and Its Challengers,* 2d ed. (New York: Oxford University Press, 1992), chap. 8. Reagan's post-presidential memoir, Ronald Reagan, *An American Life* (New York: Simon and Schuster, 1990), is interesting for Reagan's selective view of his past but otherwise is of little value. Edmund Morris, *Dutch* (New York: Random House, 1999), is an unusual literary effort but Morris's insertion of himself as a character in the book makes it an unreliable guide to Reagan's life. The best description of Reagan's personality is in Noonan, *What I Saw,* chap. 8. This biographical sketch draws mostly from Cannon and Wills.

3. For the influence of the Disciples on Reagan, see Stephen Vaughn, "The Moral Inheritance of a President: Reagan and the Disciples of Christ," *Presidential Studies Quarterly* 25 (Winter 1995): 109–25.

4. Reagan, *American Life,* p. 29.

5. Reagan, *American Life,* pp. 59, 77.

6. Reagan, *American Life,* pp. 89, 115 (emphasis in the original).

7. Reagan, *American Life,* p. 129.

8. Robert Goldberg, *Barry Goldwater* (New Haven: Yale University Press, 1995), pp. 236–37; Julius Duscha, "But What If Reagan Becomes the Governor?" *New Republic,* November 5, 1966, p. 13. An excellent account of the 1966 gubernatorial campaign is in Matthew Dallek, *The Right Moment* (New York: Free Press, 2000).

9. Edwin Meese, interview by the author, Washington, D.C., January 7, 2004.

10. For the Battaglia scandal and Clark's appointment, see Cannon, *Governor Reagan,* chap. 18.

11. Meese interview; Julius Duscha, "Not Great, Not Brilliant, but a Good Show," *New York Times Magazine,* December 10, 1967, pp. 29, 122; Reagan, *American Life,* p. 180.

12. "Reagan Nears End of Tenure with Positive Rating, Poll Finds," *Los Angeles Times,* August 27, 1974, sec. 1, p. 3.

13. Wills, *Reagan's America*, p. 365; Cannon, *Reagan*, pp. 194–204. See also "Reagan Future: Which Office to Aim For?" *Los Angeles Times*, August 13, 1974, sec. 1, p. 3.

14. Wills, *Reagan's America*, pp. 393–94; Cannon, *Reagan*, p. 226; "Weakened by Defeat, Party Is Likely to Move Further to the Right," *Wall Street Journal*, November 4, 1976, p. 1; "Reagan Hints at Active Role in Shaping GOP Future," *New York Times*, November 5, 1976, p. 16; "Reagan Urges His Party to Save Itself by Declaring Its Conservative Beliefs," *New York Times*, December 16, 1976, p. 18.

15. Morris, *Dutch*, p. 394. For the political culture that the midwesterners brought to California, see James Q. Wilson, "A Guide to Reagan Country," *Commentary*, May 1967, and Lisa McGirr, *Suburban Warriors* (Princeton: Princeton University Press, 2001). For an early example of the observation that Americans leave their pasts behind them, see J. Hector St. John de Crèvecoeur, *Letters from an American Farmer* (first published 1782; reprint, New York: Penguin, 1986).

16. Reagan, *American Life*, p. 219; Hugh Heclo, "Ronald Reagan and the American Public Philosophy," in *The Reagan Presidency*, ed. W. Elliot Brownlee and Hugh Davis Graham (Lawrence: University Press of Kansas, 2003). For selections of Reagan's handwritten letters and speeches, see Kiron Skinner, Annelise Anderson, and Martin Anderson, eds., *Reagan in His Own Hand* (New York: Free Press, 2001), and Kiron Skinner, Annelise Anderson, and Martin Anderson, eds., *Reagan: A Life in Letters* (New York: Free Press, 2003).

Chapter 1: Paving the Way

1. "The Anti-Liberal Revolution," *National Review*, November 28, 1980, p. 1434; "A Sharp Right Turn," *Washington Post*, November 6, 1980, p. A1. See also Norman Miller, "A New Era?" *Wall Street Journal*, November 6, 1980, p. 32; "The November Surprise," *New York Times*, November 6, 1980, p. A34. See also "Reagan Coast-to-Coast," *Time*, November 17, 1980; Sheldon Wolin, "Reagan Country," *New York Review of Books*, December 18, 1980; and John Kenneth Galbraith, "The Conservative Onslaught," *New York Review of Books*, January 22, 1981.

2. For a sample of liberal postwar plans, see "America and International Organization," *New Republic*, November 29, 1943; "America and a World Economy," *New Republic*, November 29, 1943; "Charter for a New America," *New Republic*, March 22, 1943; "Prosperity After the War," *New Republic*, July 24, 1944. For a detailed review of the fate of liberal policy proposals in 1945 and 1946, see Alonzo Hamby, *Man of the People* (New York: Oxford University Press, 1995), chap. 21.

No comprehensive history of postwar liberalism has been written, but a substantial literature exists on particular periods and issues. Good introductions are Gary Gerstle, "The Protean Character of American Liberalism," *American Historical Review* 99 (October 1994): 1043–73, and Alonzo Hamby, *Liberalism and Its Challengers* (New York: Oxford University Press, 1985). Among the best works on the war and immediate postwar years are Alonzo Hamby, *Beyond the New Deal* (New York: Columbia University Press, 1973); William O'Neill, *A Better World* (New York: Simon and Schuster, 1982); Richard Pells, *The Liberal Mind in a Conservative Age* (New York: Harper and Row, 1985); Diana Trilling, *The Beginning of the Journey* (New York: Harcourt Brace, 1993); and Alan Brinkley, *The End of Reform* (New York: Random House, 1995). For the 1950s, see Kent Beck, "What Was Liberalism in the 1950s?" *Political Science Quarterly* 102 (Summer 1987): 233–58. For liberal politics after the 1950s, see Alan Matusow, *The Unraveling of America* (New York: Harper and Row, 1984); Steve Fraser and Gary Gerstle, eds., *The Rise and Fall of the New Deal Order* (Princeton: Princeton University Press, 1989); John Patrick Diggins, ed., *The Liberal Persuasion* (Princeton: Princeton University Press, 1997); and H. W. Brands, *The Strange Death of American Liberalism* (New Haven: Yale University Press, 2001).

3. Arthur M. Schlesinger, Jr., *The Vital Center: The Politics of Freedom,* Sentry ed. (Boston: Houghton Mifflin, 1962), pp. 243, 256. For the development of Schlesinger's arguments, see Arthur M. Schlesinger, Jr., "Not Left, Not Right, but a Vital Center," *New York Times Magazine,* April 4, 1948, and Arthur M. Schlesinger, Jr., "What Is Loyalty? A Difficult Question," *New York Times Magazine,* November 4, 1947. Few of Schlesinger's points were original; *The Vital Center* and his other works drew heavily on arguments that Protestant theologian and political philosopher Reinhold Niebuhr had been developing since the 1930s. See Reinhold Niebuhr, *Moral Man and Immoral Society,* Touchstone ed. (New York: Simon and Schuster, 1995); Reinhold Niebuhr, *The Children of Light and the Children of Darkness* (New York: Charles Scribner's Sons, 1945); and Richard Fox, *Reinhold Niebuhr* (New York: Pantheon, 1985; reprint, Ithaca: Cornell University Press, 1996). For an example of the personal background of one of the major liberal intellectuals of this era, see Seymour Martin Lipset, "Steady Work: An Academic Memoir," *Annual Review of Sociology* 22 (1996): 1–27.

4. Richard Hofstadter, *The American Political Tradition* (New York: Alfred A. Knopf, 1948; reprint, New York: Vintage, 1989), p. xxxvii. For a sample of vital center attitudes toward dissidents from the consensus, see Thelma McCormack, "The Motivation of Radicals," *American Journal of Sociology* 56 (July 1950): 17–24; Granville Hicks, "The Liberals Who Haven't Learned," *Commentary,* April 1951; Morris Janowitz and Dwaine Marvick, "Authoritarianism and Political Behavior," *Public Opinion Quarterly* 17 (Summer 1953): 185–201; Nathan Glazer, "New Light on 'The Authoritarian Personality,'" *Commentary,* March 1954; Herbert McClosky, "Conservatism and Personality," *American Political Science Review* 52 (March 1958): 27–45; Daniel Bell, ed., *The Radical Right* (Garden City: Doubleday, 1963); and Richard Hofstadter, *The Paranoid Style in American Politics and Other Essays,* chaps. 2, 3 (Chicago: University of Chicago Press, 1979).

For other examples of the consensus interpretation of American history, politics, and society, see Daniel Boorstin, *The Genius of American Politics* (Chicago: University of Chicago Press, 1953); Louis Hartz, *The Liberal Tradition in America,* Harvest/HBJ ed. (New York: Harcourt Brace Jovanovich, 1991); Lionel Trilling, *The Liberal Imagination* (New York: Viking, 1951); Daniel Bell, *The End of Ideology,* reprint ed. (Cambridge: Harvard University Press, 1988); and Richard Hofstadter, introduction to *The Age of Reform* (New York: Vintage, 1955). For scholarly comments on the consensus interpretation, see John Higham, "The Cult of the 'American Consensus,'" *Commentary*, February 1959; John Higham, *History*, updated ed. (Baltimore: Johns Hopkins University Press, 1989); John Patrick Diggins, "Consciousness and Ideology in American History: The Burden of Daniel J. Boorstin," *American Historical Review* 76 (February 1971); Peter Novick, *That Noble Dream* (New York: Cambridge University Press, 1988), chap. 11; and John Patrick Diggins, *On Hallowed Ground* (New Haven: Yale University Press, 2000).

5. For the growing anxiety and boredom of intellectuals in the 1950s, see Irving Howe, "This Age of Conformity," *Partisan Review*, January–February 1954; David Riesman and Nathan Glazer, "The Intellectuals and the Discontented Classes," *Partisan Review*, Winter 1955; Granville Hicks, "Liberalism in the Fifties," *American Scholar*, Winter 1956; Arthur M. Schlesinger, Jr., "The Plight of the American Intellectual," *New Republic*, June 4, 1956; Arthur M. Schlesinger, Jr., "*Time* and the Intellectuals," *New Republic*, July 16, 1956; Arthur M. Schlesinger, Jr., "Highbrow in American Politics," *Partisan Review*, March 1953, p. 165; and Norman Podhoretz, *Breaking Ranks* (New York: Harper and Row, 1979). For developing critiques of vital center liberalism's assumptions, see John Kenneth Galbraith, *The Affluent Society* (Boston: Houghton Mifflin, 1958); Andrew Hacker, "The Rebelling Young Scholars," *Commentary*, November 1960; and "Criticisms of Kennedy," *New Republic*, May 18, 1963.

6. Walter Goodman, "The Liberal Establishment Faces the Blacks, the Young, the New Left," *New York Times Magazine*, December 29, 1968, pp. 21, 30. The literature on the 1960s and the collapse of liberalism is vast. For the urban conflicts and other unintended consequences of Great Society programs, see Daniel Patrick Moynihan, *Maximum Feasible Misunderstanding* (New York: Free Press, 1969); Matusow, *Unraveling of America;* Nicholas Lemann, *The Promised Land* (New York: Alfred A. Knopf, 1991); Fred Siegel, *The Future Once Happened Here* (New York: Free Press, 1997); and Steven Gillon, *That's Not What We Meant to Do* (New York: W. W. Norton, 2000). For a concise history of the New Left, see John Patrick Diggins, *The Rise and Fall of the American Left* (New York: W. W. Norton, 1992), chap. 6. For the impact of the New Left on liberalism, see Jonathan Eisen and David Steinberg, "The Student Revolt Against Liberalism," *Annals of the American Academy of Political and Social Science* 382 (March 1969): 83–92, and Peter Clacek, "'The Movement' and Its Legacy," *Social Research* 48 (Autumn 1981): 521–56.

7. For the retreat of the intellectuals, see Daniel Bell, "The Cultural Wars," *Wilson Quarterly*, Summer 1992, and Thomas Bender, "Politics, Intellect, and the American University, 1945–1995," *Daedalus* 126 (Winter 1997): 1–38.

8. Population statistics for the suburbs are from Sylvia Fava, "Beyond Suburbia," *Annals of the American Academy of Political and Social Science* 421 (September 1975): 11, and Peter Muller, "Everyday Life in Suburbia: A Review of Changing Social and Economic Forces That Shape Daily Rhythms Within the Outer City," *American Quarterly* 34 (1982): 267. The standard history of American suburbs is Kenneth

Jackson, *The Crabgrass Frontier* (New York: Oxford University Press, 1985). The best study of postwar suburban life remains Herbert Gans, *The Levittowners* (New York: Columbia University Press, 1967). Sylvia Fava, "Suburbanism as a Way of Life," *American Sociological Review* 21 (February 1956): 34–37, and Alan Ehrenhalt, *The Lost City* (New York: Basic, 1995), chaps. 9–11, also are valuable for understanding daily life in the postwar suburbs.

9. William Whyte, "The Future, c/o Park Forest," *Fortune,* June 1953, p. 127. For the heterogeneity and sophistication of the new suburbanites, see Robert Faris, "The Middle Class from a Sociological Viewpoint," *Social Forces* 39 (October 1960): 1–5, and Frederick Wirt, "The Political Sociology of American Suburbia: A Reinterpretation," *Journal of Politics* 27 (August 1965): 647–66. See also Herbert Gans, "Park Forest: Birth of a Jewish Community," *Commentary,* April 1951; Herbert Gans, "Progress of a Suburban Jewish Community," *Commentary,* February 1957; and, for criticism of suburban life, John Keats, *The Crack in the Picture Window* (Boston: Houghton Mifflin, 1956).

10. Robert Wood, *Suburbia* (Boston: Houghton Mifflin, 1958), pp. 135–49; Fred Greenstein and Raymond Wolfinger, "The Suburbs and Shifting Party Loyalties," *Public Opinion Quarterly* 22 (Winter 1958–59): 473–82; Wirt, "Political Sociology of American Suburbia," pp. 657, 665–66.

11. Gans, *Levittowners,* pp. 370–84; Tom Smith, "Liberal and Conservative Trends in the United States Since World War II," *Public Opinion Quarterly* 54 (Winter 1990): 479–507.

12. Harry Gersh, "The New Suburbanites of the '50s," *Commentary,* March 1954, p. 216. On the inward-looking nature of the suburbs, see Jackson, *Crabgrass Frontier,* chaps. 13–15.

13. For the contradictions in suburban politics, see G. Edward Janosik, "Suburban Balance of Power," *American Quarterly* 7 (Summer 1955): 123–41; Everett Ladd, Jr., "The Radical Right: The White-Collar Extremists," *South Atlantic Quarterly* 65 (Summer 1965): 314–24; Samuel Huntington, "Postindustrial Politics: How Benign Will It Be?" *Comparative Politics* 6 (January 1974): 163–91; Smith, "Liberal and Conservative Trends," p. 501. See also Fred Greenstein and Raymond Wolfinger, "The Suburbs and Shifting Party Loyalties," *Public Opinion Quarterly* 22 (Winter 1958–59): 473–82; A. James Reichley, "As Go the Suburbs, So Goes U.S. Politics," *Fortune,* September 1970; and Paul Abramson, "Generational Change and the Decline of Party Identification in America: 1952–1974," *American Political Science Review* 70 (June 1976): 469–78.

14. Fava, "Beyond Suburbia," pp. 11, 13; Daniel Bell, *The Coming of Post-Industrial Society* (New York: Basic, 1973; reprint, New York: Basic, 1976), p. 125, chap. 3; David Birch, "From Suburb to Urban Place," *Annals of the American Academy of Political and Social Science* 421 (September 1975): 30.

15. Fava, "Beyond Suburbia," p. 15. On the voters' abilities to sort out complexity in politics and campaigns, see Samuel Popkin, *The Reasoning Voter,* 2d ed. (Chicago: University of Chicago Press, 1994).

16. "We Are All Keynesians Now," *Time,* December 31, 1965, p. 67. See also John Kenneth Galbraith, "Came the Revolution," *New York Times Book Review,* May 16, 1965.

17. For a readable account of economic events and policymaking during the 1960s and 1970s, see Herbert Stein, *Presidential Economics,* 3d ed. (Washington: American Enterprise Institute, 1994), chaps. 4–6. For an early prediction of accelerating inflation, see Milton Friedman, "The Role of Monetary Policy," *American Economic Review* 58 (March 1968): 1–17. Allen Matusow, *Nixon's Economy* (Lawrence: University Press of Kansas, 1998), is the best account of Nixon's economic policies. For the development of the energy crisis, see Daniel Yergin, *The Prize* (New York: Simon and Schuster, 1991), pp. 561–633. John Sloan, "The Ford Presidency: A Conservative Approach to Economic Management," *Presidential Studies Quarterly* 14 (Fall 1984): 526–37, and J. Bradford De Long, "America's Only Peacetime Inflation: The 1970s," http://econ161.berkeley.edu/pdf_files/Peacetime_Inflation.pdf, are useful for understanding the Ford years. For the slowdown in productivity growth, see Paul Krugman, *The Age of Diminished Expectations,* 3d ed. (Cambridge: MIT Press, 1997), chap. 1.

18. Paul Blumberg, "White-Collar Status Panic," *New Republic,* December 1, 1979, pp. 21–23; Scott Kerlin and Diane Dunlap, "For Richer, for Poorer," *Journal of Higher Education* 64 (May–June 1993): 349; Howard Bowen and Jack Schuster, *American Professors* (New York: Oxford University Press, 1986), pp. 84–85; "The Inflation Surge," *Newsweek,* May 29, 1978, p. 68. See also Douglas Hibbs, *The American Political Economy* (Cambridge: Harvard University Press, 1987), pp. 19–26.

19. Alfred Kahn, *The Economics of Regulation,* vol. 2, *Institutional Issues* (New York: John Wiley and Sons, 1971; reprint, Cambridge: MIT Press, 1988), p. 325. Two good general histories of government regulation are Thomas McCraw, *Prophets of Regulation* (Cambridge: Harvard University Press, 1984), and Marc Eisner, *Regulatory Politics in Transition,* 2d ed. (Baltimore: Johns Hopkins University Press, 2000). Richard Vietor, *Contrived Competition* (Cambridge: Harvard University Press, 1994), chaps. 2, 4, has excellent case studies of airline and telephone regulation. For studies that undermined the rationales for regulation, see James Nelson, "Effects of Public Regulation on Railroad Performance," *American Economic Review* 50 (May 1960): 495–525; Harvey Averch and Leland Johnson, "Behavior of the Firm Under Regulatory Constraint," *American Economic Review* 52 (December 1962): 1052–69; Fred Westfield, "Regulation and Conspiracy," *American Economic Review* 55 (June 1965): 424–43; George Stigler, "The Theory of Economic Regulation," *Bell Journal of Economics and Management Science* 2 (Spring 1971): 3–21; and George Hilton, "The Basic Behavior of Regulatory Commissions," *American Economic Review* 62 (May 1972): 47–54.

20. For the difficulties of individual savers as inflation rose, see "Pity the Small Savers," *Wall Street Journal,* February 16, 1970, p. 10; "Short-Term Treasury Bills' Minimum Size Is Boosted to $10,000," *Wall Street Journal,* February 26, 1970, p. 3;

"Overnight Mutual Funds for Surplus Assets," *New York Times,* January 7, 1973, sec. 5, p. 3; William Burke, "Raising Ceilings," Federal Reserve Bank of San Francisco *Business and Financial Letter,* July 13, 1973; Jack Beebe, "Again, Reg Q," Federal Reserve Bank of San Francisco *Business and Financial Letter,* July 9, 1976; and Edward Kane, "Accelerating Inflation, Technological Innovation, and the Decreasing Effectiveness of Banking Regulation," *Journal of Finance* 36 (May 1981): 355–67. For details of the invention of the money market fund, see Joseph Nocera, *A Piece of the Action* (New York: Simon and Schuster, 1994), pp. 74–84, and Thomas Hammond and Jack Knott, "The Deregulatory Snowball: Explaining Deregulation in the Financial Industry," *Journal of Politics* 50 (February 1988): 13–18.

21. For accounts of the ending of fixed commissions, see Chris Welles, *The Last Days of the Club* (New York: E. P. Dutton, 1975), chaps. 4, 5; Robert Sobel, *NYSE* (New York: Weybright and Talley, 1975), pp. 322–29, 334; Donald Regan, *For the Record* (New York: Harcourt Brace Jovanovich, 1988), p. 134; "SEC Orders an End to Fixed Rates of Brokerage Firms by April 30, 1975," *Wall Street Journal,* September 12, 1973, p. 3; "Brokers Prepare for the Day of Reckoning on Rates," *New York Times,* January 5, 1975, sec. 3, p. 5; "Brokers Admit That End of Rate Fixing Isn't End of World," *Wall Street Journal,* April 28, 1975, p. 1. For coverage of May Day and the collapse in commission rates, see Welles, *Last Days,* p. 117; "Cutting of Brokerage Rates on Big Trades Escalates into All-Out War Among Firms," *Wall Street Journal,* May 23, 1975, p. 30; "Rate War Rages Among Brokers," *New York Times,* May 30, 1975, p. 1; "Study Shows Severe Broker Competition Yields Huge Stock Trade Discounts for Banks," *Wall Street Journal,* July 1, 1977, p. 23; "Individual Investors Receiving Discounts at Quick & Reilly," *Wall Street Journal,* June 17, 1975, p. 17; "Discount Brokers Do What They Advertise, Three 'Investors' Find," *Wall Street Journal,* April 5, 1977, p. 1; "Leslie C. Quick Jr., a Pioneer in Discount Stock Brokerage, Dies at 75," *New York Times,* March 9, 2001, p. A16.

On the drive for airline deregulation, see Adam Clymer, *Edward M. Kennedy* (New York: William Morrow, 1999; reprint, New York: Harper Perennial, 2000), pp. 227–31; McCraw, *Prophets,* pp. 266–99; Martha Derthick and Paul Quirk, *The Politics of Deregulation* (Washington: Brookings Institution, 1985), pp. 71–77; "Federal Controls on Airlines Seen Increasing Fares," *New York Times,* February 24, 1977, p. 1. For the start of the fare wars, see "As a Senate Panel Considers Deregulation of Airlines, Rival Lobbyists Press Efforts," *Wall Street Journal,* August 4, 1977, p. 32; "UAL's United Joins TWA in Opposing American Air's Super Saver Fare Plan," *Wall Street Journal,* February 17, 1977, p. 8; "Air Ticket Prices Drop as More Major Carriers Try to Undercut Rivals," *Wall Street Journal,* September 30, 1977, p. 1; Derthick and Quirk, *Politics of Deregulation,* pp. 151–64; "CAB Chairman Kahn Leads Agency Activists Spurring Competition," *Wall Street Journal,* July 3, 1978, p. 1.

22. Jack Beebe, "Checking-Account Interest," Federal Reserve Bank of San Francisco *Business and Financial Letter,* August 26, 1977; "Securities Firms Hit Jackpot Despite End of Fixed Commissions," *Wall Street Journal,* January 23, 1976,

p. 1; "Competition in Securities Industry Brings Increase in Mergers of Brokerage Houses," *Wall Street Journal,* November 3, 1977, p. 44; Richard West, "Brokers' Fortunes Since May Day," *Wall Street Journal,* November 24, 1978, p. 10; Aharon Ofer and Arie Melnik, "Price Deregulation in the Brokerage Industry: An Empirical Analysis," *Bell Journal of Economics* 9 (Autumn 1978): 633–41; Seha Tinic and Richard West, "The Securities Industry Under Negotiated Brokerage Commissions: The Structure and Performance of New York Stock Exchange Firms," *Bell Journal of Economics* 11 (September 1980): 29–41; Gerald Blum and Wilbur Lewellen, "Negotiated Brokerage Commissions and the Individual Investor," *Journal of Financial and Quantitative Analysis* 18 (September 1983): 331–43; Gregg Jarrell, "Change at the Exchange," *Journal of Law and Economics* 27 (October 1984): 273–312; Charles Jones and Paul Seguin, "Transaction Costs and Price Volatility: Evidence from Commission Deregulation," *American Economic Review* 87 (September 1997): 728–37; "Airline Bookings Soar with Supersaver Fare," *New York Times,* May 27, 1978, p. 6; McCraw, *Prophets of Regulation,* pp. 276–77; "Mr. Competition," *Forbes,* October 16, 1978, p. 49; T. A. Heppenheimer, *Turbulent Skies* (New York: John Wiley and Sons, 1995), pp. 319–20; "Airline Deregulation Is Increasing Service, CAB's Study Shows," *Wall Street Journal,* March 23, 1979, p. 2.

23. For an understanding of Friedman and his role in the conservative movement, begin with Milton Friedman, *Capitalism and Freedom* (Chicago: University of Chicago Press, 1962; reprint, 1982); Milton and Rose Friedman, *Free to Choose* (New York: Harcourt Brace Jovanovich, 1980); and Milton and Rose Friedman, *Two Lucky People* (Chicago: University of Chicago Press, 1998). Some of Friedman's major criticisms of Keynes are in Milton Friedman, *A Theory of the Consumption Function* (Princeton: Princeton University Press, 1957); Milton Friedman and Gary Becker, "A Statistical Illusion in Judging Keynesian Models," *Journal of Political Economy* 65 (February 1957): 64–75; and Friedman, "The Role of Monetary Policy." James Tobin, "The Monetary Interpretation of History," *American Economic Review* 55 (June 1965): 464–85, is an example of a respectful review of Friedman by an intellectual opponent. For examples of dismissals of free-market economics and Friedman, see Paul Samuelson, "The Case Against Goldwater's Economics," *New York Times Magazine,* October 25, 1964, and Milton Viorst, "Friedmanism," *New York Times Magazine,* January 25, 1970. Friedman's growing popular acceptability is evident from "The Intellectual Provocateur," *Time,* December 19, 1969, p. 71; Michael Laurence and Geoffrey Norman, "Playboy Interview: Milton Friedman," *Playboy,* February 1973; "The World Tests Friedman's Theories," *Business Week,* November 1, 1976, p. 73; and Arthur Kemp, "The Political Economy of Milton Friedman," *Modern Age,* Winter 1978. For the reception of the *Free to Choose* television series, see "Economics 101, with Milton Friedman," *New York Times,* January 6, 1980, sec. 3, p. 15, and Alfred Malabre, "The Milton Friedman Show," *Wall Street Journal,* January 11, 1980, p. 16. Friedman, of course, was part of a larger conservative movement that had long been advancing arguments against liberalism and in the late 1970s saw many of its ideas become popular. See

George Nash, *The Conservative Intellectual Movement in America Since 1945*, updated ed. (Wilmington: Intercollegiate Studies Institute, 1996).

24. "Friedman's Currency," *New Republic*, November 6, 1976, p. 6.

25. Jude Wanniski, "The Mundell-Laffer Hypothesis—A New View of the World Economy," *Public Interest*, Spring 1975, p. 50; Jude Wanniski, *The Way the World Works*, 4th ed. (Washington: Regnery, 1998), pp. 100, 117; George Gilder, *Wealth and Poverty* (New York: Basic, 1981; reprint, San Francisco: ICS Press, 1993), p. 56. For additional examples of supply-side explanations and claims, see Paul Craig Roberts, "The Economic Case for Kemp-Roth," *Wall Street Journal*, August 1, 1978, p. 16; Paul Craig Roberts, "The Tax Brake," *Wall Street Journal*, January 11, 1979, p. 22; and Paul Craig Roberts, "Supply-Side Economics," *Wall Street Journal*, February 28, 1980, p. 24.

26. Wanniski, *Way the World Works*, pp. 94–95, 155–59; Gilder, *Wealth and Poverty*, pp. 281, 282; George Gilder, "The Need for Growth," *National Review*, February 2, 1979, p. 170; David Stockman, *The Triumph of Politics* (New York: Harper and Row, 1986), pp. 39–40.

27. Walter Heller, "The Kemp-Roth-Laffer Free Lunch," *Wall Street Journal*, July 12, 1978, p. 20; "Mrs. Rivlin Rejects the Supply-Side View," *New York Times*, April 14, 1980, p. D1; Walter Heller, "Supply-Side Tax Reductions," *New York Times*, December 17, 1980, p. D2; Walter Heller, "Supply-Side Moves Assayed," *New York Times*, December 19, 1980, p. D2; Herbert Stein, "The Real Reasons for a Tax Cut," *Wall Street Journal*, July 18, 1978, p. 20; Herbert Stein, "The Never-Never Land of Pain-Free Solutions," *Fortune*, December 31, 1979, p. 74. For a later comprehensive liberal critique of supply-side economics, see Paul Krugman, *Peddling Prosperity* (New York: W. W. Norton, 1994), chap. 3.

28. "Jarvis Riding a Whirlwind and Loving It," *Los Angeles Times*, January 23, 1978, sec. 2, p. 1; "Generals of a Rebellion by California Taxpayers," *New York Times*, June 8, 1978, p. A25; "Jarvis: Master of Crowd Psychology," *Los Angeles Times*, May 17, 1978, sec. 1, p. 3; "Mutiny in California," *New Republic*, June 3, 1978, pp. 5–6; "Sound and Fury over Taxes," *Time*, June 19, 1978, pp. 12–21; Carl Landauer, "California's Losing Proposition," *New Leader*, July 17, 1978, p. 6; "Only the Beginning," *Los Angeles Times*, April 16, 1978, sec. 6, p. 4; "Teacher Tax Initiative Strike Threatened," *Los Angeles Times*, March 10, 1978, sec. 2, p. 3; "Voters Didn't Believe Warnings," *Los Angeles Times*, June 7, 1978, p. 1.

29. "Budget Cuts Begun After Californians Vote to Curb Taxes," *New York Times*, June 8, 1978, p. 1; "Impact of Proposition 13 as It Takes Effect," *New York Times*, July 1, 1978, p. 6; "Little Impact Seen in Coast Tax Slash," *New York Times*, February 11, 1979, p. 33; "Prop. 13: Change, but Not Disaster," *Los Angeles Times*, June 3, 1979, p. 1; "Californians Finding Proposition 13 Less Potent Than Was Predicted," *New York Times*, June 5, 1979, p. 19.

30. "The Economic Wind's Blowing Toward the Right—For Now," *New York Times*, July 16, 1978, sec. 5, p. 1; Walter Adams, "Economic Scene: Competition and

Inflation," *New York Times*, August 1, 1978, p. D2; "Sound and Fury over Taxes," *Time*, June 19, 1978; "Walk on the Supply Side," *Newsweek*, June 2, 1980.

31. Richard Reeves, "Nationally, the Democrats Are a Fiction," *New York Times*, June 1, 1975, sec. 4, p. 2. For various Democratic views during the mid-1970s, see John Kenneth Galbraith, "Tasks for the Democratic Left," *New Republic*, August 16–20, 1975, pp. 19, 20; Walter Dean Burnham, "Jimmy Carter and the Democratic Crisis," *New Republic*, July 3–10, 1976, p. 18; "Liberal Democrats to Meet on 1976," *New York Times*, February 13, 1975, p. 40; "Liberals Search for 1976 Agenda," *New York Times*, March 16, 1975, p. 29; "Democratic Left Urged to Take Radical Posture," *Washington Post*, March 16, 1975, p. 7. For a description of the conservative Democrats, see John Ehrman, *The Rise of Neoconservatism* (New Haven: Yale University Press, 1995), chap. 4. A substantial literature exists on the troubles of the Democrats between 1968 and 1976. For summaries of the post-1968 reform process, see Theodore White, *The Making of the President, 1972* (New York: Athenaeum, 1973), chap. 2, and Judith Center, "1972 Democratic Convention Reforms and Party Democracy," *Political Science Quarterly* 89 (June 1974): 325–41. For reform's effects, see William Cavala, "Changing the Rules Changes the Game: Party Reform and the 1972 California Delegation to the Democratic National Convention," *American Political Science Review* 68 (March 1974), and Arthur Miller, Warren Miller, Alden Raine, and Thad Brown, "A Majority Party in Disarray: Policy Polarization in the 1972 Election," *American Political Science Review* 70 (September 1976): 753–78. For the 1974 midterm conference, see Jeffrey Pressman, Denis Sullivan, and Christopher Arterton, "Cleavages, Decisions, and Legitimation: The Democrats' Mid-Term Conference, 1974," *Political Science Quarterly* 91 (Spring 1976): 89–107.

32. Surprisingly little has been written on Jimmy Carter. The most thorough biography remains Betty Glad, *Jimmy Carter* (New York: W. W. Norton, 1980), and the best treatments of his presidency are Burton Kaufman, *The Presidency of James Earl Carter* (Lawrence: University of Kansas Press, 1997), and Gary Fink and Hugh Graham, eds., *The Carter Presidency* (Lawrence: University Press of Kansas, 1998). Shorter but insightful treatments of Carter's personality and politics are Leo Ribuffo, "Jimmy Carter and the Ironies of American Liberalism," *Gettysburg Review* 1 (Autumn 1988): 738–49; Leo Ribuffo, "God and Jimmy Carter," in *Right, Center, Left* (New Brunswick: Rutgers University Press, 1992); and Leo Ribuffo, "'Malaise' Revisited: Jimmy Carter and the Crisis of Confidence," in *The Liberal Persuasion*, ed. Diggins. For Carter's campaign strategy in 1976, see "Jimmy Carter—Promises . . . Promises," *Washington Post*, March 7, 1976, p. 31; David Broder, "The Status of the Democratic Front-Runner," *Washington Post*, April 14, 1976, p. A13; "How Carter Built His Bandwagon," *Washington Post*, May 9, 1976, p. 1; William Shannon, "Liberalism, Old and New," *New York Times*, October 2, 1976, p. 25; James Ceaser, "Political Parties and Presidential Ambition," *Journal of Politics* 40 (August 1978): 708–39; Gerald Pomper, "New Rules and New Games in Presidential Nominations," *Journal of Politics* 41 (August 1979): 784–805; and Donald Beachler, "The South and

the Democratic Presidential Nomination, 1972–1992," *Presidential Studies Quarterly* 26 (Spring 1996): 402–14.

33. For details of Carter's economic policies, see Kaufman, *Presidency of Carter,* chaps. 8, 12; Bruce Schulman, "Slouching Toward the Supply Side: Jimmy Carter and the New American Political Economy," in *The Carter Presidency,* ed. Fink and Graham; and D. Quinn Mills, "U.S. Incomes Policies in the 1970s—Underlying Assumptions, Objectives, Results," *American Economic Review* 71 (May 1981): 283–87. For the effects of the Iranian revolution on oil prices, see Yergin, *The Prize,* pp. 684–98.

34. "Deep Government Disunity Alarms Many U.S. Leaders," *New York Times,* November 12, 1978, p. 1; James Sundquist, "The Crisis of Competence in Our National Government," *Political Science Quarterly* 95 (Summer 1980): 183; Sheldon Wolin, "The State of the Union," *New York Review of Books,* May 18, 1978, p. 28.

35. Ezra Vogel, *Japan as Number One* (Cambridge: Harvard University Press, 1979; reprint, New York: Harper Colophon, 1980), pp. 5, 36, 42, 43, 51, 52, 124, 216; Lloyd Cutler, "To Form a Government," *Foreign Affairs,* Fall 1980, pp. 132, 139–43. See also Isaac Shapiro, "Second Thoughts About Japan," *Wall Street Journal,* June 5, 1981, p. 24, and Joseph Kraft, "The Post-Imperial Presidency," *New York Times Magazine,* November 2, 1980.

36. Lester Thurow, *The Zero-Sum Society* (New York: Basic, 1980), pp. 11, 42, 93, 210–14.

37. "Energy and National Goals," *Public Papers of the Presidents: Jimmy Carter, 1979,* vol. 2 (Washington: U.S. Government Printing Office, 1980), p. 1237. For the background to Carter's speech and its preparation, see Ribuffo, "Jimmy Carter and the Crisis of Confidence."

38. Ribuffo, "Jimmy Carter and the Crisis of Confidence," pp. 168–75; Ken Bode, "It's Over for Jimmy," *New Republic,* August 4–11, 1979, p. 15.

39. "Kennedy Declares His Candidacy, Vowing New Leadership for Nation," *New York Times,* November 8, 1979, p. 1.

40. Willam Honan, "The Kennedy Network," *New York Times Magazine,* November 11, 1979; Clymer, *Edward M. Kennedy,* pp. 286–87; "As Mr. Kennedy Announces," *Washington Post,* November 7, 1979, p. A18; Morton Kondracke, "Superman Crashes," *New Republic,* December 22, 1979, p. 8.

41. "Kennedy's One-Note Message," *Time,* March 24, 1980, p. 18; "What Makes Teddy Run?" *Time,* April 21, 1980, p. 21; Clymer, *Edward M. Kennedy,* pp. 300–312.

42. Richard Margolis, "Carter's Record at Home," *New Leader,* January 16, 1978, p. 9; Arthur M. Schlesinger, Jr., "The Great Carter Mystery," *New Republic,* April 12, 1980, p. 21.

43. "Transcript of Reagan Speech Outlining Five-Year Economic Program for U.S.," *New York Times,* September 10, 1980, p. B4; "Text of Reagan's Speech Accepting the Republicans' Nomination," *New York Times,* July 18, 1980, p. 8.

44. "Text of Reagan's Speech"; "Candidates Eye Economic Pinch of This, Dash of That," *Washington Post,* September 21, 1980, p. G1; "Reagan Plan Is to Make

Carter the Issue, Stress Large Industrial States," *Wall Street Journal*, July 14, 1980, p. 1; "The Two Reagans: Conflicting Images," *Washington Post*, October 11, 1980, p. 1; "Reagan: A Life Built on Performing," *Washington Post*, October 22, 1980, p. 1; "30% Tax Cut by 1983 Is Simply a Flexible 'Target,' Reagan Says," *Washington Post*, October 26, 1980, p. A6.

45. Jack W. Germond and Jules Witcover, *Blue Smoke: How Reagan Won and Why Carter Lost the Election of 1980* (New York: Viking, 1981), pp. 205–8; "Carter Plans to Win by Depicting Reagan as Shallow, Dangerous," *Wall Street Journal*, August 14, 1980, p. 1; "President, Accepting Nomination, Assails GOP Program as 'Fantasy,'" *New York Times*, August 15, 1980, p. B3; "Reagan and Carter Exchange Charges on Election Fears," *New York Times*, September 24, 1980, p. A1; "Carter Plans Shift in Campaign Tactics," *New York Times*, October 9, 1980, p. B8.

46. Everett Ladd, "The Brittle Mandate: Electoral Dealignment and the 1980 Presidential Election," *Political Science Quarterly* 96 (Spring 1981): 9–11; "Closing Statements," *New York Times*, October 29, 1980, p. A29; Germond and Witcover, *Blue Smoke*, pp. 281–85.

47. "Displeasure with Carter Turned Many to Reagan," *New York Times*, November 9, 1980, p. 28; "Poll Shows Iran and Economy Hurt Carter Among Late-Shifting Voters," *New York Times*, November 16, 1980, p. 1; Kathleen Knight, "Ideology in the 1980 Election: Ideological Sophistication Does Matter," *Journal of Politics* 47 (August 1985): 850; Ladd, "The Brittle Mandate," pp. 17–18, 21. See also Steven Weisman, "What Is a Conservative?" *New York Times Magazine*, August 31, 1980; Jerome Himmelstein and James McRae, "Social Conservatism, New Republicans, and the 1980 Election," *Public Opinion Quarterly* 48 (Fall 1984): 592–605; John A. Fleishman, "Trends in Self-Identified Ideology from 1972 to 1982: No Support for the Salience Hypothesis," *American Journal of Political Science* 30 (August 1986): 517–41; John P. Robinson and John A. Fleishman, "Ideological Identification: Trends and Interpretations of the Liberal-Conservative Balance," *Public Opinion Quarterly* 52 (Spring 1988): 134–45; David Lawrence, "The Collapse of the Democratic Majority: Economics and Vote Choice Since 1952," *Western Political Quarterly* 44 (December 1991): 797–820.

Chapter 2: First Term

1. "Reagan's Staff Is Like-Minded but Not Always of One Mind," *New York Times*, January 17, 1982, p. E5; Edwin Meese, interview by the author, Washington, D.C., January 7, 2004. For the organization of the White House staff under Baker, see "Talking Points for Presentation on White House Office," n.d. (probably December 1980 or January 1981), Richard Darman Files, Box 5–6, folder "WH Budget, Organization & Staffing (2)," Ronald Reagan Library. For examples of procedural improvements made later, see Memo, Richard Darman and Craig Fuller, "Weekly Update for the President," November 30, 1981, Michael Deaver files, Box 3, folder "Miscellaneous Memos and Correspondence, 1," Ronald Reagan Library, and Memo, Richard Darman, "Preparation of Presidential Speeches," January 17, 1984,

Richard Darman files, Box 5–6, folder "Speechwriting, Office of (1)," Ronald Reagan Library.

A substantial literature has developed on Baker. For a biographical sketch, see Lawrence Barrett, *Gambling with History* (Garden City: Doubleday, 1983), chap. 21. For contemporary appraisals of Baker's performance as chief of staff, see Hedrick Smith, "The Presidential Troika," *New York Times Magazine,* April 19, 1981; "The Big 3," *Washington Post,* May 24, 1981, p. A1; "An Outsider Among the Insiders," *Washington Post,* July 11, 1982, p. A1; and John Kessel, "The Structures of the Reagan White House," *American Journal of Political Science,* 28 (May 1984): 231–58. For later evaluations of Baker, see Wallace Walker and Michael Reopel, "Strategies for Governance: Transition and Domestic Policymaking in the Reagan Administration," *Presidential Studies Quarterly* 16 (Fall 1986): 734–60; Martin Anderson, *Revolution,* updated ed. (Stanford: Hoover Institution Press, 1990), pp. 204–5; Lou Cannon, *President Reagan* (New York: Simon and Schuster, 1991), pp. 111–15; Ken Collier, "Behind the Bully Pulpit: The Reagan Administration and Congress," *Presidential Studies Quarterly* 26 (Summer 1996): 805–15; Fred Greenstein, "Reckoning with Reagan," *Political Science Quarterly* 115 (Spring 2000): 115–22; and David Cohen, "From the Fabulous Baker Boys to the Master of Disaster: The White House Chief of Staff in the Reagan and G. H. W. Bush Administrations," *Presidential Studies Quarterly* 32 (September 2002): 463–83. For the role and duties of a presidential chief of staff, see Samuel Kernell and Samuel Popkin, eds., *Chief of Staff* (Berkeley: University of California Press, 1986).

2. For examples of media theme planning by Deaver and his staff, see Memo from Frederick Ryan, "Excellence in Education Theme," May 9, 1983, Donald Regan Files, Box 1, folder "White House Transition Briefing Materials for Office of Scheduling, Advance, 1," Ronald Reagan Library; Memo from Frederick Ryan, "Presidential Theme Events," March 24, 1984, Donald Regan Files, Box 1, folder "White House Transition Briefing Materials for Offices of Scheduling and Advance, 3," Ronald Reagan Library; and Memo from Pamela Bailey, "90 Day Plan," January 10, 1984, Donald Regan Files, Box 1, folder "Regan-Deaver Breakfast, January 11, 1984," Ronald Reagan Library.

3. Richard Darman, *Who's in Control?* (New York: Simon and Schuster, 1996), pp. 120–23; Michael Deaver, *Behind the Scenes* (New York: William Morrow, 1987), p. 141; "Gergen: An Old Hand to Craft a New Message," *Los Angeles Times,* May 30, 1993, p. 1; Robert Rowland and John Jones, "'Until Next Week': The Saturday Radio Addresses of Ronald Reagan," *Presidential Studies Quarterly* 32 (March 2002): 85–89, 104–7. On the administration's media strategy and manipulation, see also "Mike Deaver, the Man Who Looks After the Man," *Washington Post,* March 8, 1981, p. K1; "Deaver Looks Out for No. 1: His Oval Office Chief," *New York Times,* December 10, 1981, B8; Tom Hamburger, "How the White House Cons the Press," *Washington Monthly,* January 1982; "Television's Role at the White House," *New York Times,* February 16, 1983, p. A20; Sidney Blumenthal, "Reagan the Unassailable," *New Republic,* September 12, 1983; "Key Presidential Buffer Looks Back," *New York Times,*

January 10, 1984, p. A18; "Master of the Media," *Newsweek*, June 18, 1984, p. 25; and Lee Sigelman and Cynthia Whissell, "'The Great Communicator' and 'The Great Talker,' on the Radio: Projecting Presidential Personas," *Presidential Studies Quarterly* 32 (March 2002): 137–46.

4. John Herbers, "The President and the Press Corps," *New York Times Magazine*, May 9, 1982, p. 45; Garry Wills, *Reagan's America* (Garden City: Doubleday, 1987), chaps. 40–41.

5. "The Making of a Chief of Staff," *New York Times*, February 8, 1982, p. A16; Cannon, *President Reagan*, p. 18; William Pemberton, *Exit with Honor* (Armonk, N.Y.: M. E. Sharpe, 1997), p. 92.

6. David Stockman, *The Triumph of Politics* (New York: Harper and Row, 1986), pp. 75, 76; Anderson, *Revolution*, p. 247. For Stockman's ideological journey, see *Triumph of Politics*, chap. 1. For Stockman's media stardom, additional details of his pre-1981 career, and comments about his self-absorption and manipulativeness, see Walter Shapiro, "The Stockman Express," *Washington Post Magazine*, February 8, 1981; "Meet David Stockman," *Newsweek*, February 16, 1981, pp. 24–25; Sidney Blumenthal, "The President's Cutting Edge," *New York Times Magazine*, March 15, 1981; and Barrett, *Gambling with History*, chap. 12.

7. Blumenthal, "The President's Cutting Edge," p. 91; Donald Regan, *For the Record* (New York: Harcourt Brace Jovanovich, 1988), p. 144; Paul Craig Roberts, *The Supply-Side Revolution* (Cambridge: Harvard University Press, 1984), pp. 74, 311.

8. For Reagan's proposals, see "Address Before a Joint Session of the Congress on the Program for Economic Recovery," *Public Papers*, pp. 108–15, and *New York Times*, February 19, 1981, pp. B5–9.

9. Larry Speakes, *Speaking Out* (New York: Charles Scribner's Sons, 1988), p. 220. For an example of Reagan's phone calls to congressmen and senators about the ERTA, see Max Friedersdorf, "Recommended Telephone Call, Seven House Democrats," April 23, 1981, Presidential Handwriting File, Series IV, Telephone Calls, Box 1, Folder 2, Ronald Reagan Library.

10. "Next on the Agenda," *Wall Street Journal*, July 31, 1981, p. 18; "Rest in Peace, New Deal," *Newsweek*, August 10, 1981, p. 16; "The Master Politician Has His Day," *Washington Post*, August 2, 1981, p. 1; William Greider, "Why Reagan's a Winner," *Washington Post*, August 8, 1981, p. E1. See also Martin Tolchin, "The Troubles of Tip O'Neill," *New York Times Magazine*, August 14, 1981.

11. Michael Mussa, "U.S. Monetary Policy in the 1980s," in *American Economic Policy in the 1980s*, ed. Martin Feldstein (Chicago: University of Chicago Press, 1994), pp. 103–4; Benjamin Friedman, *Day of Reckoning* (New York: Random House, 1988), p. 148; Martin Feldstein, "American Economic Policy in the 1980s: A Personal View," in *American Economic Policy*, ed. Feldstein, pp. 6–9; John Taylor, "Changes in American Economic Policy in the 1980s: Watershed or Pendulum Swing?" *Journal of Economic Literature* 33 (June 1995): 780.

12. Darman, *Who's in Control?* pp. 90–96; Stockman, *Triumph of Politics*, pp. 97, 124, 276–77, 397.

13. "The President Fights for Credibility," *Wall Street Journal,* August 31, 1981, p. 1; "Making It Work," *Time,* September 21, 1981, p. 38; "Reagan's Confidence Gap," *Newsweek,* September 21, 1981, p. 26; Walker and Reopel, "Strategies for Governance," p. 151; "Polarizing the Nation?" *Newsweek,* February 8, 1982, pp. 33–34; "Approval of Reagan and Economy Found Stable in Poll," *New York Times,* September 10, 1981, p. B11; "Support Slipping for Reagan Policy," *Washington Post,* November 25, 1981, p. 1; "Reagan's Pace in Poll Is Lagging Carter's," *New York Times,* January 10, 1982, p. 20; "Reagan Coalition Periled by Unease on Budget Deficit," *New York Times,* January 29, 1982, p. 1; "Reagan Steadies Position in Poll," *New York Times,* May 16, 1982, p. 23.

14. "Address Before a Joint Session of the Congress Reporting on the State of the Union," *Public Papers of the Presidents of the United States, Ronald Reagan, 1982* (Washington: U.S. Government Printing Office, 1983), p. 74; Don Fullerton, "Inputs to Tax Policy-Making: The Supply-Side, the Deficit, and the Level Playing Field," in *American Economic Policy,* ed. Feldstein, p. 187.

15. W. Elliot Brownlee and C. Eugene Steurle, "Taxation," in *The Reagan Presidency,* ed. W. Elliott Brownlee and Hugh Davis Graham (Lawrence: University Press of Kansas, 2003), pp. 165–68; Fullerton, "Inputs to Tax Policy-Making," pp. 189–90; James Poterba, "Federal Budget Policy in the 1980s," in *American Economic Policy,* ed. Feldstein, pp. 252–54. I am grateful to Ed Berkowitz for providing me with an early draft chapter from his book *Robert Ball and the Politics of Social Security* (Madison: University of Wisconsin Press, 2003).

16. "Reaganomics: The Facts," *National Review,* September 18, 1981, p. 1060; "Reign of Panic," *Wall Street Journal,* October 23, 1981, p. 26; Paul Craig Roberts, "The Budget Deficit Is a Red Herring," *New York Times,* February 14, 1982, sec. 3, p. 2; "Where Reaganomics Is Going Astray," *U.S. News and World Report,* p. 27; Jack Kemp, "Talking Back to the Skeptics," *National Review,* June 11, 1982, p. 688. See also "Supply Siders vs. Monetarists," *Business Week,* August 24, 1981, pp. 78–82; "Fed Policy Too Tight for Regan," *New York Times,* October 7, 1981, p. D1; Roberts, *Supply-Side Revolution,* pp. 174–77; and Regan, *For the Record,* chap. 10. For a monetarist evaluation of Volcker's policy, see Milton Friedman, "Lessons from the 1979–82 Monetary Policy Experiment," *American Economic Review* 74 (May 1984): 397–400.

17. Stockman, *Triumph of Politics,* p. 3; William Greider, "The Education of David Stockman," *Atlantic,* December 1981, pp. 38, 47, 46, 44, 54.

18. Alan Reynolds, "After Stockman," *National Review,* December 11, 1981, p. 1468; Roberts, *Supply-Side Revolution,* pp. 192, 193, 205; Stockman, *Triumph of Politics,* pp. 4–5; "Supply-Side Advocate Leaves the Treasury," *New York Times,* January 19, 1982, p. D1; Paul Craig Roberts, "The Stockman Recession: A Reaganite's Account," *Fortune,* February 22, 1982, pp. 56–70; Paul Craig Roberts, "Getting the Drift of Mr. Reagan's Economic Policy," *Wall Street Journal,* July 13, 1982, p. 32; "Reagan's Old Gang Heads for Exit Signs at the White House," *Wall Street Journal,* February 5, 1982, p. 48.

19. "Turn Back, Mr. President," *Wall Street Journal*, August 13, 1982, p. 16; Roberts, *Supply-Side Revolution*, p. 202; "Reagan's Brain Drain," *Wall Street Journal*, March 25, 1982, p. 28; "Thunder on the Right," *Time*, August 16, 1982, p. 25; "The Right-Wing Revolt," *Newsweek*, August 16, 1982, pp. 24–25; "Calling Plays for the Gipper," *Time*, August 23, 1982, p. 8. For additional claims that Baker had manipulated Reagan into supporting tax increases, see Regan, *For the Record*, chap. 10, and Joseph Sobran, "Reaganomics Without Reagan," *National Review*, September 3, 1982, pp. 1074–77.

20. Meese interview; Letter, Ronald Reagan to Ward Quaal, August 4, 1988, Presidential Handwriting File, Series II, Box 19, folder 334, Ronald Reagan Library. The Presidential Handwriting File at the Reagan Library contains hundreds of documents in Reagan's handwriting from throughout his administration that provide evidence of his attention and reaction to documents. For additional information on Reagan's engagement in policy and decision-making style, see Darman, *Who's in Control?* pp. 39–40; Regan, *For the Record*, chaps. 8, 10; Anderson, *Revolution*, pp. 241, 242; Edwin Meese, *With Reagan* (Washington: Regnery Gateway, 1992), pp. 20–21; and Deborah Strober and Gerald Strober, *Reagan* (Boston: Houghton Mifflin, 1998), chap. 4. For a useful guide to Reagan administration memoirs and their value as historical sources, see Charles Jones, "Mistrust but Verify: Memoirs of the Reagan Era," *American Political Science Review* 83 (September 1989): 981–88.

21. Leslie Gelb, "The Mind of the President," *New York Times Magazine*, October 6, 1985, p. 23; Letter, Ronald Reagan to Nackey Loeb, November 16, 1987, Presidential Handwriting File, Series II, Box 19, folder 311, Ronald Reagan Library.

22. "Short-Term Rates Fall, Bond Prices Soar amid Signs Fed Is Easing Its Credit Reins," *Wall Street Journal*, July 9, 1982, p. 3; "In Binge of Optimism, Stock Market Surges by Record 38.81 Points," *Wall Street Journal*, August 18, 1982, p. 1; "Interest Rates Are Likely to Drop Further in Next Few Months After Brief Increases," *Wall Street Journal*, August 30, 1982, p. 21. For the beginning of the recovery, see Eugene Becker and Norman Bowers, "Employment and Unemployment Improvements Widespread in 1983," *Monthly Labor Review*, February 1984.

23. Paul Craig Roberts, "Supply-Side Economics—Theory and Results," *Public Interest*, Fall 1988; Martin Feldstein, "Supply Side Economics: Old Truths and New Claims," *American Economic Review* 76 (May 1986): 28; Wallace Peterson and Paul Estenson, "The Recovery: Supply-Side or Keynesian?" *Journal of Post Keynesian Economics* 7 (Summer 1985): 447–62; Lawrence Chimerine and Richard Young, "Economic Surprises and Messages of the 1980s," *American Economic Review* 76 (May 1986): 32. See also Adrian Throop, "A 'Supply-Side' Miracle?" Federal Reserve Bank of San Francisco *Weekly Letter*, November 2, 1984, p. 1, and the articles by Allan Meltzer, Alfred Eichner, and Mark Miles in the symposium "Reagan's Economic Policies," *Journal of Post Keynesian Economics* 7 (Summer 1988): 527–66, and Herbert Stein, *Presidential Economics*, 3d ed. (Washington: American Enterprise Institute, 1994), pp. 277–78.

24. "Budget Study Finds Cuts Cost the Poor as the Rich Gained," *New York Times*, April 4, 1984, p. 1; "Census Data Show Result of Tax Cut," *New York Times*, July 13, 1984, p. A14; U.S. Census Bureau, *Poverty in the United States, 1988 and 1989* (Washington: U.S. Department of Commerce, 1991); U.S. Census Bureau, *The Changing Shape of the Nation's Income Distribution* (Washington: U.S. Department of Commerce, 2000), pp. 4, 7–8; Ana Revenga, "Exporting Jobs? The Impact of Import Competition on Employment and Wages in U.S. Manufacturing," *Quarterly Journal of Economics* 107 (February 1992): 257.

25. "The Reindustrializing of America," *Business Week*, June 30, 1980, pp. 58, 60; Andrew Hacker, "Where Have the Jobs Gone?" *New York Review of Books*, June 30, 1983, p. 27; Robert Reich, *The Next American Frontier* (New York: Times, 1983), p. 202; "Some Hard-Hit Areas Fail to Share Benefits of General Recovery," *Wall Street Journal*, March 28, 1984, p. 1.

A large literature developed during the early and mid-1980s on deindustrialization, inequality, and the perceived threat to the middle class. For the growing fear of deindustrialization, see Barry Bluestone and Bennett Harrison, *The Deindustrialization of America: Plant Closings, Community Abandonment, and the Dismantling of Basic Industry* (New York: Basic, 1982). On the fear that middle-class jobs were endangered, see Robert Kuttner, "The Declining Middle," *Atlantic*, July 1983; Lester Thurow, "The Disappearance of the Middle Class," *New York Times*, February 5, 1984, sec. 4, p. 3. On poverty and inequality, see Sheldon Danziger and Peter Gottschalk, "Do Rising Tides Lift All Boats? The Impact of Secular and Cyclical Changes on Poverty," *American Economic Review* 76 (May 1986): 405–10.

26. Rosenthal, "Nature of Occupational Employment Growth," pp. 46–49; Hacker, "Where Have the Jobs Gone?" p. 30.

For additional discussions and analyses of the types of jobs created during the 1980s, see Patrick McMahon and John Tschetter, "The Declining Middle Class: A Further Analysis," *Monthly Labor Review*, September 1986; Marvin Kosters and Murray Ross, "A Shrinking Middle Class?" *Public Interest*, Winter 1988; Maury Gittleman, "Earnings in the 1980s: An Occupational Perspective," *Monthly Labor Review*, July 1994, pp. 19–21; Neal Rosenthal, "The Nature of Occupational Employment Growth, 1983–1993," *Monthly Labor Review*, June 1995, pp. 46–49; and Edward Wolff, "Skills and Changing Comparative Advantage," *Review of Economics and Statistics* 85 (February 2003): 77–93.

27. Gittleman, "Earnings in the 1980s," pp. 19–21; Chinhui Juhn, Kevin Murphy, and Brooks Pierce, "Wage Inequality and the Rise in Returns to Skill," *Journal of Political Economy* 101 (June 1993): 410–42; Kevin Murphy and Finis Welch, "The Structure of Wages," *Quarterly Journal of Economics* 107 (February 1992): 286; Marvin Kosters, "Schooling, Work Experience, and Wage Trends," *American Economic Review* 80 (May 1990): 309, 311; Elizabeth Sawhill, "Poverty in the U.S.: Why Is It So Persistent?" *Journal of Economic Literature* 26 (September 1988): 1073–1119; David Cutler and Lawrence Katz, "Macroeconomic Performance and the Disadvantaged," *Brookings Papers on Economic Activity* 1991, no. 2 (1991): 1–74; Jared

Bernstein and Heidi Hartman, "Defining and Characterizing the Low-Wage Labor Market," in *The Low-Wage Labor Market: Challenges and Opportunities for Self-Sufficiency* (Washington: Department of Health and Human Services, 2000).

Economists have developed a substantial literature to explain the rise in inequality and demand for higher skills during the 1980s. For examples, see Barry Bluestone, McKinley Blackburn, and David Bloom, "Earnings and Income Inequality in the United States," *Population and Development Review* 13 (December 1987): 575–609; "The Impact of Schooling and Industrial Restructuring on Recent Trends in Wage Inequality in the United States," *American Economic Review* 80 (May 1990): 303–7; David Howell and Edward Wolff, "Trend in the Growth and Distribution of Skills in the U.S. Workplace, 1960–1985," *Industrial and Labor Relations Review* 44 (April 1991): 486–502; Lawrence Katz and Kevin Murphy, "Changes in Relative Wages, 1963–1987: Supply and Demand Factors," *Quarterly Journal of Economics* 107 (February 1992): 36–78; John Bound and George Johnson, "Changes in the Structure of Wages in the 1980s: An Evaluation of Alternative Explanations," *American Economic Review* 82 (June 1992): 371–92; Frank Levy and Richard Murnane, "U.S. Earnings Levels and Earnings Inequality: A Review of Recent Trends and Proposed Explanations," *Journal of Economic Literature* 30 (September 1992): 1333–81; Alan Krueger, "How Computers Have Changed the Wage Structure: Evidence from Microdata, 1984–1989," *Quarterly Journal of Economics* 108 (February 1993): 33–60; John Bound and George Johnson, "What Are the Causes of Rising Wage Inequality in the United States?" Federal Reserve Bank of New York *Economic Policy Review,* January 1995; Chinhui Juhn and Kevin Murphy, "Inequality in Labor Market Outcomes: Contrasting the 1980s and Earlier Decades," Federal Reserve Bank of New York *Economic Policy Review,* January 1995; David Brauer and Susan Hickok, "Explaining the Growing Inequality in Wages Across Skill Levels," Federal Reserve Bank of New York *Economic Policy Review,* January 1995; Richard Murnane, John Willett, and Frank Levy, "The Growing Importance of Cognitive Skill in Wage Determination," *Review of Economics and Statistics* 77 (May 1995): 251–66; "Symposium: Wage Inequality," *Journal of Economic Perspectives* 11 (Spring 1997): 21–96; Daron Acemoglu, "Technical Change, Inequality, and the Labor Market," *Journal of Economic Literature* 50 (March 2002): 7–72; and Thomas Piketty and Emmanuel Saez, "Income Inequality in the United States, 1913–1998," *Quarterly Journal of Economics* 118 (February 2003): 1–39. For a sociological perspective, see Michael Hout, "More Universalism, Less Structural Mobility: The American Occupational Structure in the 1980s," *American Journal of Sociology* 93 (May 1988): 1358–1400. For an extended critique of the effects of inequality on American society, see Robert Frank and Philip Cook, *The Winner-Take-All Society* (New York: Free Press, 1995).

28. Robert Topel, "Factor Proportions and Relative Wages: The Supply-Side Determinants of Wage Inequality," *Journal of Economic Perspectives* 11 (Spring 1997): 69–72; Steven Brint, "The Political Attitudes of Professionals," *Annual Review of Sociology* 11 (1985): 394–95, 408; "Optimism on Finances Is at High Level in Poll," *New York Times,* April 8, 1984, p. A26; "Most in Poll Say They're Better Off Than in

1980," *New York Times,* August 17, 1984, p. 1. See also Wilson Carey McWilliams, "Politics," *American Quarterly* 35 (Spring–Summer 1983): 29; Jerome Himmelstein and James McRae, Jr., "Social Issues and Socioeconomic Status," *Public Opinion Quarterly* 52 (Winter 1988): 492–512; and Finis Welch, "In Defense of Inequality," *American Economic Review* 89 (May 1999): 1–17. For statistics on the educational levels of the adult population and the labor force, see U.S. Bureau of the Census, *Statistical Abstract of the United States,* 1990 and 1995 editions; U.S. Bureau of the Census, *Educational Attainment in the United States: March 1979 and 1978* (Washington: U.S. Government Printing Office, 1980); and U.S. Bureau of the Census, *Educational Attainment in the United States: March 1989 and 1988* (Washington: U.S. Government Printing Office, 1991). See also Anne McDougall Young and Howard Hayghe, "More U.S. Workers Are College Graduates," *Monthly Labor Review,* March 1984; Anne McDougall Young, "One-Fourth of the Adult Labor Force Are College Graduates," *Monthly Labor Review,* February 1985; and Daniel Aaronson and Daniel Sullivan, "Growth in Worker Quality," Federal Reserve Bank of Chicago *Economic Perspectives,* Fourth Quarter, 2001.

29. "Batting Almost 1.000," *Newsweek,* August 27, 1984, p. 35; Andre Modigliani and Franco Modigliani, "The Growth of the Federal Deficit and the Role of Public Attitudes," *Public Opinion Quarterly* 51 (Winter 1987): 46–51; Alan Blinder and Douglas Hotz-Eakin, "Public Opinion and the Balanced Budget," *American Economic Review* 74 (May 1984): 144.

30. Alice Rivlin, "Reform of the Budget Process," *American Economic Review* 74 (May 1984): 133, 134; Michael Boskin, "Federal Government Deficits: Some Myths and Realities," *American Economic Review* 72 (May 1982): 301, 297; Steven Schier, "Deficits Without End: Fiscal Thinking and Budget Failure in Congress," *Political Science Quarterly* 107 (Autumn 1992): 411–33; "Frustrations of Forecasters," *New York Times,* July 2, 1984, p. D1. For additional views on the problems of budget making and measuring, see Alice Rivlin, "The Political Economy of Budget Choices: A View from Congress," *American Economic Review* 72 (May 1982): 351–55; Robert Eisner and Paul Pieper, "A New View of the Federal Debt and Budget Deficits," *American Economic Review* 74 (March 1984): 11–29; Robert Eisner, "Which Budget Deficit? Some Issues of Measurement and Their Implications," *American Economic Review* 74 (May 1984): 138–43; Paul Peterson, "The New Politics of Deficits," *Political Science Quarterly* 100 (Winter 1985–86): 575–601; and Robert Nelson, "The Economics Profession and the Making of Public Policy," *Journal of Economic Literature* 25 (March 1987): 49–91.

Economists still cannot agree upon precisely what effects the deficits of the 1980s had on the economy. See Preston Miller and William Roberds, "How Little We Know About Deficit Policy Effects," Federal Reserve Bank of Minneapolis *Quarterly Review,* Winter 1992, and Owen Humpage, "Do Deficits Matter?" Federal Reserve Bank of Cleveland *Economic Commentary,* June 15, 1993.

31. "Batting Almost 1.000," p. 34; "Complacency on Deficits?" *New York Times,* June 26, 1983, sec. 3, p. 1; "Do Large Deficits Matter?" *New York Times,* February 2,

1984, p. B7; Memo, Richard Wirthlin, "Debt and Budgets," November 18, 1982, WHORM Subject File FI004, folder 124683.

32. Peterson, "New Politics of Deficits," p. 600; Modigliani and Modigliani, "Growth of the Federal Deficit," pp. 472–73; Schier, "Deficits Without End," pp. 422, 428; "$200 Billion and Counting," *New York Times*, August 23, 1983, p. A22; William Niskanen, *Reaganomics* (New York: Oxford University Press, 1988), pp. 111–12.

33. "Public's Approval of Reagan in Poll Rising but Limited," *New York Times*, July 3, 1983, p. 1; "At Last—Off and Running," *Newsweek*, February 6, 1984, p. 17; "Address Before a Joint Session of the Congress Reporting on the State of the Union," in *Public Papers of the Presidents of the United States, Ronald Reagan, 1982* (Washington: U.S. Government Printing Office, 1983), p. 73; "Address Before a Joint Session of the Congress on the State of the Union," *Public Papers of the Presidents of the United States, Ronald Reagan, 1983*, Vol. 1 (Washington: U.S. Government Printing Office, 1984), pp. 104, 103.

34. Mark Shields, "The Reagan Difference," *Washington Post*, December 11, 1981, p. A23; Jack Citrin and Donald Green, "Presidential Leadership and the Resurgence of Trust in Government," *British Journal of Political Science* 16 (October 1986): 437, 450. See also "Poll Finds Trust in Government Edging Back Up," *New York Times*, July 15, 1983, p. 1; Richard Kirkland, "America on Top Again," *Fortune*, April 15, 1985; Seymour Martin Lipset and William Schneider, "The Confidence Gap During the Reagan Years, 1981–1987," *Political Science Quarterly* 102 (Spring 1987): 1–23; and Seymour Martin Lipset and William Schneider, *The Confidence Gap*, revised ed. (Baltimore: Johns Hopkins University Press, 1987).

35. "Assembly Plant for the Olympics," *New York Times*, January 6, 1984, p. A17; "Olympic Organizers Gear Up for a Frenetic Stretch Drive," *New York Times*, March 31, 1984, p. 1; "Ueberroth: Ruthless and Shy," *Los Angeles Times*, June 24, 1984, p. 1.

36. "More Than Olympic Flame Crosses America," *New York Times*, June 10, 1984, p. 1; "Torch Ignites Patriotic Response Across U.S.," *Los Angeles Times*, July 2, 1984, p. 1; "Patriotism: A Movable Feast," *Los Angeles Times*, July 4, 1984, sec. 2, p. 4; "Patriotism Is Back in Style," *U.S. News and World Report*, July 9, 1984, p. 58; "Feeling Proud Again," *Time*, January 7, 1985, p. 20. See also "America's Upbeat Mood," *Time*, September 24, 1984.

37. "Private Sponsoring of Games Appears to be Successful," *New York Times*, August 6, 1984, p. C11; "Success of Games in Los Angeles Likely to Change Future Olympics," *New York Times*, August 12, 1984, p. 1; "Parade-Goers Express Pride, Patriotism," *Washington Post*, August 15, 1984, p. A10; "Ticker Tape and Cheers Greet Olympic Medallists," *New York Times*, August 16, 1984, p. 1; "Olympic Surplus Put at $215 Million," *New York Times*, December 20, 1984, p. B13.

38. Adam Clymer, *Edward M. Kennedy* (New York: William Morrow, 1999; reprint, New York: Harper Perennial, 2000), pp. 325–32; Martin Tolchin, "The Troubles of Tip O'Neill," *New York Times Magazine*, August 14, 1981, p. 68; "Tip and

His Fleeced Flock," *Newsweek,* August 10, 1981, p. 22. For O'Neill's background and views, see John Farrell, *Tip O'Neill* (Boston: Little, Brown, 2001), chaps. 2, 3.

39. "Democrats in Congress Hunt for Policy Ideas to Counter Reagan's," *Wall Street Journal,* April 1, 1982, p. 1; Richard Reeves, "How New Ideas Shape Presidential Politics," *New York Times Magazine,* July 15, 1984, p. 29. See also Tom Wicker, "Democrats in Search of Ideas," *New York Times Magazine,* January 25, 1981; Morton Kondracke, "The Democrats' New Agenda," *New Republic,* October 18, 1982; and Kenneth S. Baer, *Reinventing Democrats* (Lawrence: University of Kansas Press, 2000), chaps. 1, 2.

40. Tom Hayden, "The Future Politics of Liberalism," *Nation,* February 21, 1981, p. 208; Andrew Kopkind, "The Return of Cold War Liberalism," *Nation,* April 23, 1983, pp. 503, 512.

41. On the Democrats' organization and factionalism, see Jo Freeman, "The Political Culture of the Democratic and Republican Parties," *Political Science Quarterly* 101 (Autumn 1986): 327–56.

42. "Democrats: An Aye for Business," *New York Times,* March 1, 1981, sec. 3, p. 4; Paul Tsongas, *The Road from Here* (New York: Alfred A. Knopf, 1981), p. 43. See also "The Man Who Put Neo in Neoliberal," *New York Times,* November 1, 1984, p. B12.

43. Charles Peters, "A Neoliberal's Manifesto," *Washington Monthly,* May 1983, pp. 9, 10, 11, 14; Paul Tsongas, "Update Liberalism or It's a '60s Relic," *New York Times,* June 30, 1980, p. A19; "ADA Debates Role of Liberalism in a Year of Losses and Budget Cuts," *New York Times,* June 15, 1980, p. 14; "Massachusetts' 'Other Senator' Urging a Realistic Liberalism," *New York Times,* October 6, 1981, p. A26. See also Charles Peters, "Where Neoliberals Stand," *New York Times,* January 4, 1984, p. A19.

44. "Neoliberals and the Fight for the Political Center," *New York Times,* October 26, 1983, p. B10; Tsongas, *Road from Here,* p. 10; Richard Reeves, "Old Wine in New Skins," *New York Times Book Review,* July 29, 1984, p. 12; Peters, "Where Neoliberals Stand"; Arthur M. Schlesinger, Jr., "Requiem for Neoliberalism," *New Republic,* June 6, 1983, p. 29. For the founding and history of the Democratic Leadership Council, see Baer, *Reinventing Democrats.*

45. "The Reindustrialization of America," pp. 57, 60, 86, 88, 102. For a general history of industrial policy, see Otis Graham, *Losing Time* (Cambridge: Harvard University Press, 1992).

46. Ira Magaziner and Robert Reich, *Minding America's Business* (New York: Harcourt Brace Jovanovich, 1982), p. 255. For biographic sketches of Magaziner and Reich, see Steven Pearlstein, "The Many Crusades of Ira Magaziner," *Washington Post Magazine,* April 18, 1993, and Mickey Kaus, "The Policy Hustler," *New Republic,* December 7, 1982.

47. Magaziner and Reich, *Minding America's Business,* p. 343; Felix Rohatyn, "Alternatives to Reaganomics," *New York Times Magazine,* December 5, 1982, p. 80; Felix Rohatyn, "Time for a Change," *New York Review of Books,* August 18, 1983, p. 49; Robert Reich, "Playing Tag with Japan," *New York Review of Books,* June 24,

1982, p. 37; Robert Reich, "Beyond Reaganomics," *New Republic,* November 18, 1981, p. 20; Robert Reich, *The Next American Frontier* (New York: Times, 1983), pp. 275, 281–82.

48. Robert Lawrence, "Is Trade Deindustrializing America? A Medium-Term Perspective," *Brookings Papers on Economic Activity* (1983): 157; Robert Crandall, "Can Industrial Policy Work?" *Washington Post Book World,* May 22, 1983, p. 8; Herbert Stein, "Don't Fall for Industrial Policy," *Fortune,* November 14, 1983, p. 64. For a summary of economists' criticism of industrial policy, see R. D. Norton, "Industrial Policy and American Renewal," *Journal of Economic Literature* 24 (March 1986): 1–40.

49. Robert M. Kaus, "Can Creeping Socialism Cure Creaking Capitalism?" *Harper's,* February 1983, p. 17; Robert Samuelson, "The Policy Peddlers," *Harper's,* June 1983, p. 62; Michael Kinsley, "The Double Felix," *New Republic,* March 26, 1984, p. 29. For other skeptical views of industrial policy, see Peter Schuck, "Industrial Policy's Obstacles," *New York Times,* September 6, 1983, p. A23; Simon Lazarus and Robert Litan, "The Democrats' Coming Civil War over Industrial Policy," *Atlantic,* September 1984.

50. "The Democrats' New Guru," *Newsweek,* February 28, 1983, p. 61; Sidney Blumenthal, "Drafting a Democratic Industrial Plan," *New York Times Magazine,* August 28, 1983, p. 57; "What Is Industrial Policy?" *Washington Post,* June 20, 1983, p. A10; "Industrial Policy," *New York Times,* March 30, 1984, p. B6.

51. "Industrial Referendum Pits Elite Against Skeptics in Rhode Island," *Washington Post,* June 8, 1984, p. A2; "Putting Industrial Policy to a Vote," *New York Times,* June 10, 1984, sec. 3, p. 4; "A 'New Idea' Fizzles on Launch," *Washington Post,* July 15, 1994, p. B5.

Reich and Magaziner's subsequent careers show that they learned little from their experiences. Reich continued to write about the social and political effects of economic change, becoming one of the country's most prominent liberal spokesmen on the issue. Appointed secretary of labor by President Clinton as a favor to liberal Democrats, he soon found his policy advice ignored. After leaving Washington, Reich published an engaging memoir of his experiences, *Locked in the Cabinet* (1997), which critics soon discovered to contain accounts of events that had never taken place. In 2002, Reich ran for governor of Massachusetts and was badly beaten in the Democratic primary. Magaziner, for his part, returned to his consulting practice, where he earned a reputation for providing mediocre advice. Appointed by Clinton in 1993 to develop a plan for a national health system, Magaziner—as in Rhode Island—produced an enormous report and proposed an unworkable plan. The plan died in the Democratic-controlled Congress and was in large part responsible for the party's catastrophic defeat in the 1994 elections. Magaziner remained an adviser to Clinton but never again was given a project of any importance.

52. Steven Gillon, *The Democrats' Dilemma* (New York: Columbia University Press, 1992), pp. 77, 284, 299; Walter Mondale, "The Re-Education of Walter Mondale," *New York Times Magazine,* November 3, 1982, p. 67.

53. Mondale, "Re-Education of Mondale," pp. 116, 111; Gillon, *Democrats' Dilemma,* p. 307. See also Gregg Easterbrook, "The Perpetual Campaign: Walter Mondale's Bid for the Presidency," *Atlantic,* January 1983.

54. Gillon, *Democrats' Dilemma,* p. 333; Jack W. Germond and Jules Witcover, *Wake Us When It's Over* (New York: Macmillan, 1985), p. 135.

55. "Mondale Unveils Detailed Proposal to Slash Deficit," *Washington Post,* September 11, 1984, p. 1; "Mondale Warns of 'Scary Future' in Reagan Election," *Los Angeles Times,* September 24, 1984, p. 6; "The Speech: Walter F. Mondale," *New York Times,* October 11, 1984, p. B13.

56. "Mondale, in Poll, Fails to Gain Lift from Convention," *New York Times,* August 14, 1984, p. 1; "Mondale Effort Starts Slowly," *Washington Post,* September 6, 1984, p. 1; "Mondale Finds Message Obscured," *Washington Post,* September 23, 1984, p. 1; TRB, "Walter, Walter, Everywhere," *New Republic,* October 29, 1984, p. 6.

57. Cannon, *President Reagan,* p. 483.

58. "Remarks Accepting the Presidential Nomination at the Republican National Convention in Dallas, Texas," in *Public Papers of the Presidents of the United States, Ronald Reagan, 1984,* vol. 2 (Washington: U.S. Government Printing Office, 1987), p. 1181; "Remarks and a Question-and-Answer Session at the University of Alabama in Tuscaloosa," in *Public Papers,* p. 1530; "Remarks at a Reagan-Bush Rally in Endicott, New York," in *Public Papers,* p. 1285; "President Uses Launch to Attack 'Pessimists,'" *Washington Post,* August 31, 1984, p. A3; "Blue-Collar Workers and Suburbanites Still Back President Firmly," *Wall Street Journal,* October 26, 1984, p. 1; "Going Strong in Farm Belt," *Washington Post,* October 20, 1984, p. 1.

59. "Mondale's Image Is a Victim of Television's Eye," *Washington Post,* October 5, 1984, p. A4; Gillon, *Democrats' Dilemma,* p. 373; Germond and Witcover, *Wake Us,* p. 462; "A Contrast on TV," *New York Times,* September 5, 1984, p. 20; "TV Ads Frame Election Choice," *Washington Post,* November 4, 1984, p. A7.

60. "In the Family Room, Mondale's TV Message Still Seems Muddled," *Washington Post,* September 24, 1984, p. A3; "The Medium and Mondale," *New York Times,* November 9, 1984, p. A22.

61. "Portrait of the Electorate," *New York Times,* November 8, 1984, p. A19; Everett Carll Ladd, "On Mandates, Realignments, and the 1984 Presidential Election," *Political Science Quarterly* 100 (Spring 1985): 9.

62. Haynes Johnson, "Campaigning Through the Camera's Eye," *Washington Post,* November 11, 1984, p. A3; Germond and Witcover, *Wake Us,* p. 539; Theodore Marmor, "The Lessons of Mondale's Defeat," *The Political Quarterly* 56 (April–June 1985): 166, 155.

63. "Poll Says Labor Endorsement May Have Negative Influence," *New York Times,* June 12, 1983, p. 32; "Labor's Effort for Mondale May Backfire," *Los Angeles Times,* October 23, 1984, p. 1; "Going Strong in the Farm Belt"; "Mondale Finds Message Obscured."

Chapter 3: Work and Life

1. David Stockman, *The Triumph of Politics* (New York: Harper and Row, 1986), p. 103.

2. "Reagan's War on Regulation," *Newsweek*, April 20, 1981, p. 77; Martin Anderson, *Revolution*, updated ed. (Stanford: Hoover Institution Press, 1990), p. 260.

3. John Gillroy and Robert Shapiro, "The Polls: Environmental Protection," *Public Opinion Quarterly* 50 (Summer 1986): 270–79; Steven Brint, "The Political Attitudes of Professionals," *Annual Review of Sociology* 11 (1985): 398; "Environmental Agency: Deep and Persisting Woes," *New York Times*, March 6, 1983, p. 1; "New EPA Chief Seeks More Funds," *New York Times*, December 6, 1983, p. A25; "Leaving a Righted Ship," *Time*, December 10, 1984, p. 37; Ed Rubenstein, "Regulation Redux," *National Review*, March 18, 1988, p. 22. For the ups and downs of regulatory reform during the Reagan years, see W. Kip Viscusi, "The Misspecified Agenda: The 1980s Reforms of Health, Safety, and Environmental Regulation," in *American Economic Policy in the 1980s*, ed. Martin Feldstein (Chicago: University of Chicago Press, 1994), pp. 453–504.

4. "Remarks at the Annual Meeting of the Boards of Governors of the World Bank Group and International Monetary Fund," in *Public Papers of the Presidents of the United States, Ronald Reagan, 1981* (Washington: U.S. Government Printing Office, 1982), p. 855. For the growing pressure to intervene in trade, see Pietro S. Nivola, "The New Protectionism: U.S. Trade Policy in Historical Perspective," *Political Science Quarterly* 101 (Winter 1986): 577–600; Paul Krugman, "Is Free Trade Passe?" *Journal of Economic Perspectives* 1 (Fall 1987): 131–44; Robert Baldwin, "The Political Economy of Trade Policy," *Journal of Economic Perspectives* 3 (Fall 1989): 119–35; and Ellis Krauss and Simon Reich, "Ideology, Interests, and the American Executive: Toward a Theory of Foreign Competition and Manufacturing Trade Policy," *International Organization* 46 (Autumn 1992): 857–97.

5. "U.S. and Japan Agree on Ceilings for Car Shipments Through 1983," *New York Times*, May 1, 1981, p. 1; "Reagan Vows to Seek Voluntary Steel-Import Curbs; Restraints Held Unlikely to Stem Decline of Industry," *Wall Street Journal*, September 18, 1984, p. 3; "Computer Chip Fight Is Settled; U.S., Japan Agree on Anti-Dumping Plan, More Access," *Los Angeles Times*, August 1, 1986, p. 1; "U.S. and Japan Resolve Dispute on Microchips," *New York Times*, August 1, 1986, p. 1. For an overview of Reagan-era trade restraints, see the untitled essay by Paula Stern in *American Economic Policy in the 1980s*, ed. Feldstein, pp. 666–83. For the ability of well-financed pressure groups to influence policy, see Gary Becker, "A Theory of Competition Among Pressure Groups for Political Influence," *Quarterly Journal of Economics* 98 (August 1983): 371–400.

6. Robert Feenstra, "Quality Change Under Trade Restraints in Japanese Autos," *Quarterly Journal of Economics* 103 (February 1988): 131–46; Elias Dinopoulos and Mordechai Kreinin, "Effects of the U.S.-Japan Auto VER on European Prices and on U.S. Welfare," *Review of Economics and Statistics* 70 (August 1988): 484–91; Steven Berry, James Levinshohn, and Ariel Pakes, "Voluntary Export Restraints on

Automobiles: Evaluating a Trade Policy," *American Economic Review* 89 (June 1999): 400–430; Christopher Singleton, "Auto Industry Jobs in the 1980s: A Decade of Transition," *Monthly Labor Review,* February 1992, p. 22; "Detroit Beware: Japan Is Ready to Sell Luxury," *Business Week,* December 9, 1985, p. 114; Robert Crandall, "The Effects of U.S. Trade Protection for Autos and Steel," *Brookings Papers on Economic Activity* (1987): 271–88; Jaime de Melo and David Tarr, "Welfare Costs of U.S. Quotas in Textiles, Steel, and Autos," *Review of Economics and Statistics* 72 (August 1990): 489–97; Stefanie Lenway, Randall Morck, and Bernard Yeung, "Rent Seeking, Protectionism, and Innovation in the American Steel Industry," *The Economic Journal* 106 (March 1996): 410–21; Kenneth Flamm, *Mismanaged Trade?* (Washington: Brookings Institution, 1996), pp. 292, 395–405. See also Lindley Clark, Jr., "There's No Way to Be a Little Protectionist," *Wall Street Journal,* September 25, 1984, p. 29; Murray Weidenbaum, "The Assault on International Trade," *National Review,* December 28, 1984, p. 33; and George Gilder, "Don't Let the Grinch Steal Christmas," *National Review,* April 24, 1987, p. 40.

7. Thomas Moore, "U.S. Airline Deregulation: Its Effects on Passengers, Capital, and Labor," *Journal of Law and Economics* 29 (April 1986): 13, 14, 11, 27; Severin Borenstein, "The Evolution of U.S. Airline Competition," *Journal of Economic Perspectives* 6 (Spring 1992): 60–65, 47, 51; James MacDonald and Linda Cavaluzzo, "Railroad Deregulation: Pricing Reforms, Shipper Responses, and the Effects on Labor," *Industrial and Labor Relations Review* 80 (October 1996): 81, 83; David Davis and Wesley Wilson, "Wages in Rail Markets: Deregulation, Mergers, and Changing Networks Characteristics," *Southern Economic Journal* 69 (April 2003): 865, 867; James Peoples, "Deregulation and the Labor Market," *Journal of Economic Perspectives* 12 (Summer 1998): 112.

8. Felix Rohatyn, "American Roulette," *New York Review of Books,* March 29, 1984, p. 12. For the legal and regulatory backgrounds to AT&T's divestiture, see Martha Derthick and Paul Quirk, *The Politics of Deregulation* (Washington: Brookings Insitution, 1985), pp. 174–202, and Richard Vietor, *Contrived Competition* (Cambridge: Harvard University Press, 1994), pp. 185–211.

9. For changes in phone rates and AT&T, see "Phone Rates Are in Midst of Upheaval," *New York Times,* October 10, 1983, p. 1; "Bell System Breakup Opens Era of Great Expectations and Great Concern," *New York Times,* January 1, 1984, p. A12; Jeremy Main, "Waking Up AT&T: There's Life After Culture Shock," *Fortune,* December 24, 1984; "One Year Later, the Debate over Bell Breakup Continues," *New York Times,* December 27, 1984, p. 1; William Johnston, "The Coming Glut of Phone Lines," *Fortune,* January 7, 1985; Kenneth Labich, "Was Breaking Up AT&T a Good Idea?" *Fortune,* January 2, 1989; William Taylor and Lester Taylor, "Postdivestiture Long-Distance Competition in the United States," *American Economic Review* 83 (May 1993): 185–90; and Eli Noam, "Assessing the Impacts of Divestiture and Deregulation in Telecommunications," *Southern Economic Journal* 59 (January 1993): 438–49. For AT&T's response to competition, see Vietor, *Contrived Competition,* pp. 202–33.

10. "Prospects: Deregulation Plus Five," *New York Times,* December 25, 1988, p. C1.

11. "The Raiders," *Business Week,* March 4, 1985, p. 83. For the development and performance of conglomerates, see David Ravenscraft and F. M. Scherer, *Mergers, Sell-Offs, and Economic Efficiency* (Washington: Brookings Institution, 1987); Andrei Shleifer and Robert Vishny, "Takeovers in the '60s and the '80s: Evidence and Implications," *Strategic Management Journal* 12 (1991): 51–59; Gerald Davis, Kristina Diekmann, and Catherine Tinsley, "The Decline and Fall of the Conglomerate Firm in the 1980s: The Deinstitutionalization of an Organizational Form," *American Sociological Review* 59 (August 1994): 547–70; Alfred Chandler, "The Competitive Performance of U.S. Industrial Enterprises Since the Second World War," *Business History Review* 68 (Spring 1994): 110–43; and Naomi Lamoreaux, Daniel Raff, and Peter Temin, "Beyond Markets and Hierarchies: Toward a New Synthesis of American Business History," *American Historical Review* 108 (April 2003): 423–24.

12. Robin Marris, "A Model of the 'Managerial' Enterprise," *Quarterly Journal of Economics* 77 (May 1963): 190; Henry Manne, "Mergers and the Market for Corporate Control," *Journal of Political Economy* 73 (April 1965): 112, 113; Phillip Areeda, "Antitrust Policy in the 1980s," in *American Economic Policy in the 1980s,* ed. Feldstein, pp. 573–600; Marc Eisner and Kenneth Meier, "Presidential Control Versus Bureaucratic Power: Explaining the Reagan Revolution in Antitrust," *American Journal of Political Science* 34 (February 1990): 276–77; "U.S. Is Easing '68 Antitrust Guidelines on Mergers," *New York Times,* June 15, 1982, p. 1; "New Antitrust Merger Guidelines Issued," *New York Times,* June 15, 1984, p. 1. On the Justice Department's merger guidelines, see "Symposium: 1982 Merger Guidelines," *California Law Review* 77 (March 1983), and Thomas Krattenmaker and Robert Pitofsky, "Antitrust Merger Policy and the Reagan Administration," *Antitrust Bulletin* 33 (Summer 1988): 211–32. For Milken, Drexel, and the development of the junk bond and takeover markets, the indispensable works are Connie Bruck, *The Predators' Ball* (New York: Simon and Schuster, 1988), and James Stewart, *Den of Thieves* (New York: Simon and Schuster, 1991). For several contemporary accounts of Milken and major figures in takeovers, see Joel Dreyfuss, "The Firm That Fed on Wall Street's Scraps," *Fortune,* September 3, 1984; Connie Bruck, "My Master Is My Purse," *Atlantic,* December 1984; "The Raiders," *Business Week,* March 4, 1985; and Aloysius Ehrbar, "Have Takeovers Gone Too Far?" *Fortune,* May 27, 1985.

13. George Baker, "Beatrice: A Study in the Creation and Destruction of Value," *Journal of Finance* 47 (July 1992): 1108; "Even Lawyers Gasp over the Stiff Fees of Wachtell Lipton," *Wall Street Journal,* November 2, 1988, p. 1. For a brief summary of various takeover methods, see Michael Jensen, "Takeovers: Folklore and Science," *Harvard Business Review,* November–December 1984.

14. Benjamin Stein, "Not Worthy of the Name?" *Barron's,* July 13, 1987, p. 32; Benjamin Stein, "Who Owns This Company Anyway?" *Barron's,* December 15, 1986, p. 8; "The Mergermakers' Spiraling Fees," *New York Times,* September 30, 1984, sec. 3, p. 6; "Where's the Limit?" *Time,* December 5, 1988, p. 67; Felix Rohatyn, "On a

Buyout Binge and a Takeover Tear," *Wall Street Journal,* May 18, 1984, p. 26; Robert Kuttner, "The Truth About Corporate Raiders," *New Republic,* January 20, 1986, p. 17; "Surge in Company Takeovers Causes Widespread Concern," *New York Times,* July 3, 1984, p. 1. For other examples of the debates regarding takeovers, see "Deal Mania" and "Do All These Deals Help or Hurt the U.S. Economy?" *Business Week,* November 24, 1986; Felix Rohatyn, "Blight on Wall Street," *New York Review of Books,* March 12, 1987; John Brooks, *The Takeover Game* (New York: E. P. Dutton, 1987); Walter Adams and James Brock, "Reaganomics and the Transmogrification of Merger Policy," *Antitrust Bulletin* 33 (Summer 1988): 309–59; and Robert Reich, "Leveraged Buyouts: America Pays the Price," *New York Times Magazine,* January 29, 1989.

15. Ford Worthy, "The Coming Defaults in Junk Bonds," *Fortune,* March 16, 1987; "The Bills Are Coming Due," *Business Week,* September 11, 1989; "Trading in Junk Bonds Collapses, While Treasurys Stage Big Rally," *Wall Street Journal,* October 16, 1989, p. C1; "Junk Gets Junkier, and That May Explain Bonds' Current Ills," *Wall Street Journal,* November 3, 1989, p. C1; Steven Kaplan and Jeremy Stein, "The Evolution of Buyout Pricing and Financial Structure in the 1980s," *Quarterly Journal of Economics* 108 (May 1993): 316. For Milken's central role in criminal behavior on Wall Street in the 1980s, see Stewart, *Den of Thieves.* For contemporary accounts of the collapse of the junk bond market and Drexel, see "After Drexel," *Business Week,* February 26, 1990, and Brett Fromson, "The Last Days of Drexel Burnham," *Fortune,* May 21, 1990.

16. "Deal Mania," p. 75; "Gulf's Managers Find Merger into Chevron Forces Many Changes," *Wall Street Journal,* December 5, 1984, p. 1; "People Trauma in Mergers," *New York Times,* November 19, 1985, p. D1; "Leveraged Buyouts Make Some Companies Tougher Customers," *Wall Street Journal,* September 15, 1988, p. 1. See also Myron Magnet, "What Merger Mania Did to Syracuse," *Fortune,* February 3, 1986. For the tendency of conglomerates to develop bloated work forces, see Richard Caves and Matthew Krepps, "Fat: The Displacement of Nonproduction Workers from U.S. Manufacturing Industries," *Brookings Papers on Microeconomics* (1993): 236–37.

17. Davis, Diekmann, and Tinsley, "Decline and Fall of the Conglomerate Firm," p. 547; Caves and Krepps, "Fat," pp. 271–72; Matthew Krepps, Sanjai Bhagat, Andrei Shleifer, and Robert Vishny, "Hostile Takeovers in the 1980s: The Return to Corporate Specialization," *Brookings Papers in Microeconomics* (1990): 40, 55–58; Frank Lichtenberg, *Corporate Takeovers and Productivity* (Cambridge: MIT Press, 1992), pp. 12–13, 129–33; Walter Kiechel, "Corporate Strategy for the 1990s," *Fortune,* February 29, 1988, p. 34; Michael Jensen, "Takeovers: Their Causes and Consequences," *Journal of Economic Perspectives* 2 (Winter 1988): 27; Andrei Shleifer and Robert Vishny, "Value Maximization and the Acquisition Process," *Journal of Economic Perspectives* 2 (Winter 1988): 11, 12.

Scholars have produced a large body of research describing the beneficial effects of the takeovers of the 1980s. Notable examples in addition to those cited above include

Alan Auerbach, ed., *Corporate Takeovers: Causes and Consequences* (Chicago: University of Chicago Press, 1988); Kenneth Martin and John McConnell, "Corporate Performance, Corporate Takeovers, and Management Turnover," *Journal of Finance* 46 (June 1991): 671–87; Michael Jensen, "The Modern Industrial Revolution, Exit, and the Failure of Internal Control Systems," *Journal of Finance* 48 (July 1993): 851; Linda Stearns and Kenneth Allan, "Economic Behavior in Institutional Environments: The Corporate Merger Wave of the 1980s," *American Sociological Review* 61 (August 1996): 699–718; Gregor Andrade, Mark Mitchell, and Erik Stafford, "New Evidence and Perspectives on Mergers," *Journal of Economic Perspectives* 15 (Spring 2001): 103–20; Bengt Holmstrom and Steven Kaplan, "Corporate Governance and Merger Activity in the United States: Making Sense of the 1980s and 1990s," *Journal of Economic Perspectives* 15 (Spring 2001): 121–44; and Dario Focarellie and Fabio Panetta, "Are Mergers Beneficial to Consumers? Evidence from the Market for Bank Deposits," *American Economic Review,* 93 (September 2003): 1152–71.

18. G. David Wallace, "America's Leanest and Meanest," *Business Week,* October 5, 1987, p. 78; Clifford Winston, "Economic Deregulation: Days of Reckoning for Microeconomists," *Journal of Economic Literature* 31 (September 1993): 1284. For more on the long-term benefits of deregulation, see Elizabeth Bailey, "Price and Productivity Change Following Deregulation: The U.S. Experience," *The Economic Journal* 96 (March 1986): 1–17; Sam Peltzman, "The Economic Theory of Regulation After a Decade of Deregulation," *Brookings Papers on Microeconomics* (1989): 1–41; Alfred Kahn, "Deregulation: Looking Backward, Looking Forward," *Yale Journal of Regulation* 7 (Summer 1990): 325–54; Clifford Winston, "U.S. Industry Adjustment to Economic Deregulation," *Journal of Economic Perspectives* 12 (Summer 1998): 89–110; Allen Kaufman and Ernest Englander, "Kohlberg Kravis Roberts & Co. and the Restructuring of American Capitalism," *Business History Review* 67 (Spring 1993); and Roger Sherman, "The Future of Market Regulation," *Southern Economic Journal* 67 (April 2001): 783–800.

19. Frank Levy, *The New Dollars and Dreams* (New York: Russell Sage Foundation, 1998), p. 76.

20. Adrian Throop, "A 'Supply-Side' Miracle?" Federal Reserve Bank of San Francisco *Weekly Letter,* November 2, 1984, p. 1; "High Technology Is Spurring Race to Retool in the Midwest," *New York Times,* December 22, 1985, p. 1.

Since the 1980s, economists and business scholars have generated a large body of literature on the connection between the rising use of computers and information technology and the demand for skilled workers. See Ann Bartel and Frank Lichtenberg, "The Comparative Advantage of Educated Workers in Implementing New Technology," *Review of Economics and Statistics* 69 (February 1987): 1–11; "Smart Machines, Smart Workers," *New York Times,* October 17, 1988, p. D1; Jerome Mark, "Technological Change and Employment: Some Results from BLS Research," *Monthly Labor Review,* April 1987; Ernst R. Berndt, Catherine Morrison, and Larry Rosenblum, "High-Tech Capital Formation and Labor Composition in U.S. Manufacturing Industries: An Exploratory Analysis," National Bureau of Economic

Research Working Paper No. 4010, March 1992; Mary Coleman and John Pencavel, "Changes in Work Hours of Male Employees," *Industrial and Labor Relations Review* 46 (January 1993): 262–83; Mary Coleman and John Pencavel, "Trends in Market Work Behavior of Women Since 1940," *Industrial and Labor Relations Review* 46 (July 1993): 653–76; Eli Berman, John Bound, and Zvi Griliches, "Changes in the Demand for Skilled Labor Within U.S. Manufacturing: Evidence from the Annual Survey of Manufactures," *Quarterly Journal of Economics* 109 (May 1994): 367–97; Mark Doms, Timothy Dunne, and Kenneth Troske, "Workers, Wages, and Technology," *Quarterly Journal of Economics* 112 (February 1997): 253–90; Michael Kiley, "The Supply of Skilled Labor and Skill-Biased Technological Progress," *Board of Governors of the Federal Reserve System, Finance and Economic Discussion Series,* 1997-45, September 1997; Claudia Goldin and Lawrence Katz, "The Origins of Technology-Skill Complementarity," *Quarterly Journal of Economics* 113 (August 1998): 694–732; David Thesmar and Mathias Thoenig, "Creative Destruction and Firm Organization Choice," *Quarterly Journal of Economics* 115 (November 2000): 1201–37; Daron Acemoglu, "Technical Change, Inequality, and the Labor Market," *Journal of Economic Literature* 49 (March 2002): 7–72; Hyunbae Chun, "Information Technology and the Demand for Educated Workers: Disentangling the Impacts of Adoption Versus Use," *Review of Economics and Statistics* 85 (February 2003): 1–8; and David Autor, Frank Levy, and Richard Murnane, "The Skill Content of Recent Technological Change: An Empirical Exploration," *Quarterly Journal of Economics* 118 (November 2003): 1279–1333.

21. "Growth in Jobs Since '80 Is Sharp, but Pay and Quality Are Debated," *New York Times,* June 8, 1986, p. 1; Richard Walton and Gerald Susman, "People Policies for the New Machines," *Harvard Business Review,* March–April 1987; Norm Alster, "What Flexible Workers Can Do," *Fortune,* February 13, 1989; David Kirkpatrick, "Smart New Ways to Use Temps," *Fortune,* February 15, 1988; "More Companies Use Free-Lancers to Avoid Cost, Trauma of Layoffs," *Wall Street Journal,* April 18, 1986, p. 23; Lewis Segal and Daniel Sullivan, "The Growth of Temporary Services Work," *Journal of Economic Perspectives* 11 (Spring 1997): 117–36.

For the effects of computers and information technology on workplace processes and organization, see Peter Nulty, "The Bar-Coding of America," *Fortune,* December 27, 1982; Michael Porter, "How Information Gives You Competitive Advantage," *Harvard Business Review,* July–August 1985; Walter Keichel, "Corporate Strategy for the 1990s," *Fortune,* February 29, 1988; Gene Bylinsky, "A Breakthrough in Automating the Assembly Line," *Fortune,* May 26, 1986; Lynda Applegate, James Cash, and D. Quinn Mills, "Information Technology and Tomorrow's Manager," *Harvard Business Review,* November–December 1988; Michael Hammer, "Reengineering Work: Don't Automate, Obliterate," *Harvard Business Review,* July–August 1990; Thomas Davenport and James Short, "The New Industrial Engineering: Information Technology and Business Process Redesign," *Sloan Management Review,* Summer 1990; Paul Milgrom and John Roberts, "The Economics of Modern Manufacturing: Technology, Strategy, and Organization,"

American Economic Review 80 (June 1990): 511–28; Paul Osterman, "How Common Is Workplace Transformation and Who Adopts It?" *Industrial and Labor Relations Review* 47 (January 1994): 173–88; Timothy Bresnahan, Erik Brynjolfsson, and Lorin Hitt, "Information Technology, Workplace Organization, and the Demand for Skilled Labor: Firm-Level Evidence," *Quarterly Journal of Economics* 117 (February 2002): 339–76; David Autor, Frank Levy, and Richard Murnane, "Upstairs, Downstairs: Computers and Skills on Two Floors of a Large Bank," *Industrial and Labor Relations Review* 55 (April 2002): 432–47; and Frank Levy, Anne Beamish, Richard Murnane, and David Autor, "Computerization and Skills: Examples from a Car Dealership," http://web.mit.edu/flevy/www/car-paper.html.

22. Bylinsky, "Breakthrough in Automating"; Thomas Holt and George Stalk, "Working Better and Faster with Fewer People," *Wall Street Journal,* May 15, 1987, p. 14; Brian Dumaine, "How Managers Can Succeed Through Speed," *Fortune,* February 13, 1989, p. 56. On improving productivity growth, see William Gullickson, "Multifactor Productivity in Manufacturing Industries," *Monthly Labor Review,* October 1992; Edward Dean and Mark Sherwood, "Manufacturing Costs, Productivity, and Competitiveness, 1979–1983," *Monthly Labor Review,* October 1994; Bart van Ark, "Manufacturing Prices, Productivity, and Labor Costs in Five Economies," *Monthly Labor Review,* July 1995; Christopher Sparks and Mary Grenier, "U.S. and Foreign Productivity and Unit Labor Costs," *Monthly Labor Review,* February 1997. For the understatement of productivity growth, see Paul David, "The Dynamo and the Computer: An Historical Perspective on the Modern Productivity Paradox," *American Economic Review* 80 (May 1990): 355–61; Erik Brynjolfsson and Lorin Hitt, "Beyond Computation: Information Technology, Organizational Transformation, and Business Performance," *Journal of Economic Perspectives* 14 (Fall 2000): 23–48; Sandra Black and Lisa Lynch, "How to Compete: The Impact of Workplace Practices and Information Technology on Productivity," *Review of Economics and Statistics* 83 (August 2001): 434–45; Mark Sieling, Brian Friedman, and Mark Dumas, "Labor Productivity in the Retail Trade Industry, 1987–99," *Monthly Labor Review,* December 2001; and Sandra Black and Lisa Lynch, "What's Driving the New Economy? The Benefits of Workplace Innovation," Federal Reserve Bank of San Francisco Working Paper 2003-23, October 2003; and Robert Gordon, "Why Was Europe Left at the Station When America's Productivity Locomotive Departed?" National Bureau of Economic Research Working Paper 10661, August 2004.

23. "Tales from the Digital Treadmill," *New York Times,* June 3, 1990, sec. 3, p. 1; Coleman and Pencavel, "Hours of Male Employees," pp. 281–82; Thomas Bailey, Peter Berg, and Carola Sandy, "The Effect of High-Performance Work Practices on Employee Earnings in the Steel, Apparel, and Medical Electronics and Imaging Industries," *Industrial and Labor Relations Review* 54 (March 2001): 525–43; and Sandra Black, Lisa Lynch, and Anya Krivelyova, "How Workers Fare When Employers Innovate," National Bureau of Economic Research Working Paper No. 9569, March 2003; Kevin Leicht and Mary Fennell, "The Changing Organizational Context of

Professional Work," *Annual Review of Sociology* 23 (1997): 215–31; Vicki Smith, "New Forms of Work Organization," *Annual Review of Sociology* 23 (1997): 315–39.

For the effects of workplace technology and reorganization on inequality, see Berman, Bound, and Griliches, "Changes in the Demand for Skilled Labor" ; Assar Lindbeck and Dennis Snower, "Reorganization of Firms and Labor Market Inequality," *American Economic Review* 86 (May 1996): 315–21; Doms, Dunne, and Troske, "Workers, Wages, and Technology"; Kiley, "Supply of Skilled Labor"; Goldin and Katz, "Origins of Technology-Skill Complementarity"; Dennis Snower, "Causes of Changing Earnings Inequality," Federal Reserve Bank of Kansas City *Proceedings*, August 1998, pp. 69–132; Bresnahan, Brynjolfsson, and Hitt, "Information Technology"; Acemoglu, "Technical Change"; Autor, Levy, and Murnane, "Upstairs, Downstairs"; Chun, "Information Technology and Demand"; and Autor, Levy, and Murnane, "Skill Content of Technological Change." For a skeptical view, see David Card and John DiNardo, "Skill-Based Technological Change and Rising Wage Inequality: Some Problems and Puzzles," *Journal of Labor Economics* 20 (October 2002): 733–83.

24. Sylvia Fava, "Beyond Suburbia," *Annals of the American Academy of Political and Social Science* 421 (September 1975): 11–12; "How to Pinpoint a City," *Washington Post*, March 8, 1987, p. A26; Joel Garreau, *Edge City* (New York: Random House, 1991; reprint, New York: Anchor, 1992), p. 29; Christopher Leinberger and Charles Lockwood, "How Business Is Reshaping America," *Atlantic*, October 1986, pp. 43, 45–46; Robert Fishman, *Bourgeois Utopias* (New York: Basic, 1987), chap. 7.

25. Neal Rosenthal, "The Nature of Occupatonal Employment Growth: 1983–1993," *Monthly Labor Review*, June 1995, pp. 46–47.

26. Paul Flaim and Ellen Sehgal, "Displaced Workers of 1979–1983: How Well Have They Fared," *Monthly Labor Review*, January 1985, p. 3; Diane Herz, "Worker Displacement Still Common in the Late 1980s," *Monthly Labor Review*, May 1991, pp. 4–5; Henry Farber, "The Incidence and Costs of Job Loss: 1982–1991," *Brookings Papers on Microeconomics* (1993): 80, 81, 102, 107, 110, 118. See also Louis Jacobson, Robert LaLonde, and Daniel Sullivan, "Earnings Losses on Displaced Workers," *American Economic Review* 83 (September 1993): 685–709.

27. Paul Swaim and Michael Podgursky, "Do More-Educated Workers Fare Better Following Job Displacement?" *Monthly Labor Review*, August 1989, pp. 43, 45; Michael Podgursky, "The Industrial Structure of Job Displacement, 1979–1989," *Monthly Labor Review*, September 1992, pp. 20, 24; Diane Herz, "Worker Displacement in a Period of Rapid Job Expansion: 1983–1987," *Monthly Labor Review*, May 1990, pp. 21, 31. See also Bruce Fallick, "A Review of the Recent Empirical Literature on Displaced Workers," *Industrial and Labor Relations Review* 50 (October 1996): 5–16.

28. James Smith and Finis Welch, "Race and Poverty: A Forty-Year Record," *American Economic Review* 77 (May 1987): 152–53; James Smith and Finis Welch, "Black Economic Progress After Myrdal," *Journal of Economic Literature* 27 (June 1989): 555–56; June O'Neill, "The Role of Human Capital in Earnings Differences

Between Black and White Men," *Journal of Economic Perspectives* 4 (Fall 1990): 29–30, 38; Lori Kletzer, "Job Displacement, 1979–1986: How Blacks Fared Relative to Whites," *Monthly Labor Review,* July 1991, p. 17; Amitabh Chandra, "Labor Market Dropouts and the Racial Wage Gap: 1940–1990," *American Economic Review* 90 (May 2000): 337; Joseph Meisenheimer, "Black College Graduates in the Labor Market, 1979 and 1989," *Monthly Labor Review,* November 1990, p. 18; "Experts Foresee a Social Gap Between Sexes Among Blacks," *New York Times,* February 5, 1989, p. 1; National Center for Education Statistics, *The Educational Progress of Black Students* (Washington: Department of Education, 1994), p. 14; John Bound and Richard Freeman, "What Went Wrong? The Erosion of Relative Earnings and Employment Among Young Black Men in the 1980s," *Quarterly Journal of Economics,* 107 (February 1992): 202, 208, 228, 230.

29. Robert Fairlie and Lori Kletzer, "Race and the Shifting Burden of Job Displacement: 1982–1993," *Monthly Labor Review,* September 1996, p. 20; Finis Welch, "Catching Up: Wages of Black Men," *American Economic Review* 93 (May 2003): 320–25; Mark Schneider and Thomas Phelan, "Black Suburbanization in the 1980s," *Demography* 30 (May 1993): 269–79; James Peoples and Lisa Saunders, "Trucking Deregulation and the Black/White Wage Gap," *Industrial and Labor Relations Review* 47 (October 1993): 23–35; Maury Gittleman and David Howell, "Changes in the Structure and Quality of Jobs in the United States: Effects By Race and Gender, 1973–1990," *Industrial and Labor Relations Review* 48 (April 1995): 430–31; Jacqueline Agesa, "The Impact of Deregulation on Employment and Discrimination in the Trucking Industry," *Atlanta Economic Journal* 26 (September 1998): 288–303; Kenneth Couch and Mary Daley, "The Improving Relative Status of Black Men," Federal Reserve Bank of San Francisco Working Paper 2004-02, January 2004; U.S. Census Bureau, *Racial and Ethnic Residential Segregation in the United States, 1980–2000* (Washington: U.S. Department of Commerce, 2002), chap. 5; "To Blacks, the Suburbs Prove Both Pleasant and Troubling," *New York Times,* May 20, 1985, p. 1; Glenn Loury, "Blacks' Share of U.S. Income," *New York Times,* August 7, 1985, p. D2; "Black Professionals Refashion Their Careers," *New York Times,* November 29, 1985, p. 1; Robert Hill, "The Black Middle Class Defined," *Ebony,* August 1987, pp. 30–32; "The Black Middle Class: Where It Lives," *Ebony,* August 1987, pp. 34–40; "How History Distributed Wealth, Races," *Washington Post,* November 29, 1987, p. A16; "In Georgia, a White Twin County of Prince George's Blacks," *Washington Post,* December 1, 1987, p. A15; "The Black Middle Class," *Business Week,* March 14, 1988, pp. 62–70; William O'Hare, "In the Black," *American Demographics,* November 1989, p. 24. For an overview of black economic status during the Reagan years, see U.S. Census Bureau, *The Black Population in the United States: March 1988* (Washington: Department of Commerce, 1989). For a definition of the black middle class, see William Julius Wilson, *The Declining Significance of Race,* 2d ed. (Chicago: University of Chicago Press, 1980), p. 129. For a thorough discussion of the growth of the underclass and its results, see William Julius Wilson, *The Truly Disadvantaged* (Chicago: University of Chicago Press, 1987), chaps. 1–4.

30. Richard Freeman, "Contraction and Expansion: The Divergence of Private Sector and Public Sector Unionism in the United States," *Journal of Economic Perspectives* 2 (Spring 1988): 74; Linda Bell, "Union Concessions in the 1980s," Federal Reserve Bank of New York *Quarterly Review*, Summer 1989, pp. 44–58; "Labor Unions Troubled by Drop in Numbers," *New York Times*, May 31, 1983, p. A16; "AFL-CIO Study Calls for Radical Solutions to Problems of Labor Unions," *New York Times*, February 22, 1985, p. 10. For a general history of organized labor and its troubles, see Nelson Lichtenstein, *State of the Union* (Princeton: Princeton University Press, 2002), especially chap. 6.

31. Peoples, "Deregulation and the Labor Market," pp. 111, 112, 114, 122–25, 126; Nancy Rose, "Labor Rent Sharing and Regulation: Evidence from the Trucking Industry," *Journal of Political Economy* 95 (December 1987): 1147–78; Randall Pozdena, "Airline Deregulation," Federal Reserve Bank of San Francisco *Newsletter*, March 9, 1984, p. 3; "Even Profitable Firms Press Workers to Take Permanent Pay Cuts," *Wall Street Journal*, March 6, 1984, p. 1; MacDonald and Cavalluzzo, "Railroad Deregulation," p. 90; "Once-Secure Phone Union Faces a Loss of Power from AT&T Split," *Wall Street Journal*, March 12, 1984, p. 31.

32. For the effects of changes in the immigration laws, see Steven Gillon, *That's Not What We Meant to Do* (New York: W. W. Norton, 2000), chap. 4, and Hugh Graham, *Collision Course* (New York: Oxford University Press, 2002), chap. 5. For immigrants and their motives, see Douglas Massey, "The New Immigration and Ethnicity in the United States," *Population and Development Review* 21 (September 1995): 631–52; George Borjas, "Does Immigration Grease the Wheels of the Labor Market?" *Brookings Papers on Economic Activity* (2001): 69–70, 118; "Flow of Third World Immigrants Alters Weave of U.S. Society," *New York Times*, June 30, 1986, p. 1; and Nicholas Lemann, "Growing Pains," *Atlantic*, January 1988.

33. George Borjas, "Immigrant and Emigrant Earnings: A Longitudinal Study," *Economic Inquiry* 27 (January 1989): 21–37; George Borjas, "The Economics of Immigration," *Journal of Economic Literature* 32 (December 1994): 1674, 1687; Robert Schoeni, "New Evidence on the Economic Progress of Foreign-Born Men in the 1970s and 1980s," *Journal of Human Resources* 32 (Fall 1997): 692–97, 702, 716; Peter Cattan, "The Growing Presence of Hispanics in the U.S. Work Force," *Monthly Labor Review*, August 1988, p. 13; Edward Funkhouser and Stephen Trejo, "The Labor Market Skills of Recent Male Immigrants: Evidence from the Current Population Survey," *Industrial and Labor Relations Review* 48 (July 1995): 798–801, 804–6; Don Mar, "Four Decades of Asian American Women's Earnings: Japanese, Chinese, and Filipino American Women's Earnings, 1960–1990," *Contemporary Economic Policy* 18 (April 2000): 231–33, 237; "Asians Galvanize Sales Activity in Flushing," *New York Times*, July 29, 1984, sec. 8, p. 1; "Suburbs Absorb More Immigrants, Mostly the Affluent and Educated," *New York Times*, December 14, 1986, p. 1; "Indians in U.S. Prosper in Their New Country, and Not Just in Motels," *Wall Street Journal*, January 27, 1987, p. 1; "Study Finds Less Bias Against Asian Workers," *New York Times*, July 18, 1988, p. D2.

34. Rita Simon and Jean Lanids, "Women's and Men's Attitudes About a Woman's Place and Role," *Public Opinion Quarterly* 53 (Summer 1989): 265–76; James Smith and Michael Ward, "Women in the Labor Market and in the Family," *Journal of Economic Perspectives* 3 (Winter 1989): 16; June O'Neill and Solomon Polachek, "Why the Gender Gap in Wages Narrowed in the 1980s," *Journal of Labor Economics* 11 (January 1993): 207, 209–11, 219–21, 225; Eric Eide, "College Major Choice and Changes in the Gender Wage Gap," *Contemporary Economic Policy* 12 (April 1994): 56; Gittleman and Howell, "Changes in the Structure and Quality of Jobs," pp. 432–33; Francine Blau and Lawrence Kahn, "Gender Differences in Pay," *Journal of Economic Perspectives* 14 (Fall 2000): 75–99; Sandra Black and Chinhui Juhn, "The Rise of Female Professionals: Are Women Responding to Skill Demand?" *American Economic Review* 90 (May 2000): 450–55; Finis Welch, "Growth in Women's Relative Wages and in Inequality Among Men: One Phenomenon or Two?" *American Economic Review* 90 (May 2000): 444–49; Francine Blau, "Trends in the Well-Being of American Women, 1970–1995," *Journal of Economic Literature* 36 (March 1998): 129; Bruce Weinberg, "Computer Use and the Demand for Female Workers," *Industrial and Labor Relations Review* 53 (January 2000): 290–308; Francine Blau and Andrea Beller, "Black-White Earnings over the 1970s and 1980s: Gender Differences in Trends," *Review of Economics and Statistics* 74 (May 1992): 279–80; Cattan, "Growing Presence of Hispanics," p. 13. See also Claudia Goldin, "The Rising (and then Declining) Significance of Gender," National Bureau of Economic Research Working Paper No. 8915, April 2002; Claudia Goldin, "From the Valley to the Summit: The Quiet Revolution That Transformed Women's Work," National Bureau of Economic Research Working Paper 10335, March 2004.

35. Smith and Ward, "Women in the Labor Market," pp. 18–22; Blau, "Trends in Well-Being," pp. 114–15, 151; Robert Wood, Mary Corcoran, and Paul Courant, "Pay Differences Among the Highly Paid: The Male-Female Gap in Lawyers' Salaries," *Journal of Labor Economics* 11 (July 1993): 417–41; Jane Waldfogel, "Understanding the 'Family Gap' in Pay for Women with Children," *Journal of Economic Perspectives* 12 (Winter 1998): 137–56; Cedric Herring and Karen Wilson-Sadberry, "Preference or Necessity: Changing Work Roles of Black and White Women, 1973–1990," *Journal of Marriage and the Family* 55 (May 1993): 314–25; "Women Gain, but at a Cost," *New York Times*, February 6, 1987, p. D2; "Bars to Equality of Sexes Seen as Eroding, Slowly," *New York Times*, August 20, 1989, p. 1; "Women's Gains on the Job: Not Without a Heavy Toll," *New York Times*, August 21, 1989, p. 1; and Larry Jones, Rodolfo Manuelli, and Ellen McGrattan, "Why Are Married Women Working So Much?" Federal Reserve Bank of Minneapolis Research Department Staff Report 317, June 2003.

36. For the easing of discrimination because of increased competition, see Orley Ashenfelter and Timothy Hannan, "Sex Discrimination and Product Market Competition: The Case of the Banking Industry," *Quarterly Journal of Economics* 101 (February 1986): 149–73; Felice Schwartz, "Executives and Organizations: Management Women and the New Facts of Life," *Harvard Business Review*,

January–February 1989; Coleman and Pencavel, "Women Since 1940," p. 675; Sandra Black and Elizabeth Brainerd, "Importing Equality?" Federal Reserve Bank of New York *Staff Reports* 74, April 1999; Sandra Black, "Investigating the Link Between Competition and Discrimination," *Monthly Labor Review*, December 1999; June O'Neill, "The Gender Gap in Wages, Circa 2000," *American Economic Review*, 93 (May 2003): 309–14; James Smith, "Assimilation Across the Latino Generations," *American Economic Review* 93 (May 2003): 315–19; Welch, "Catching Up"; Couch and Daly, "Improving Relative Status of Black Men."

37. "Adam Smith," *Paper Money* (New York: Summit, 1981), pp. 271–73. For the effects of inflation on stock values during the 1970s, see Martin Feldstein, "Inflation and the Stock Market," *American Economic Review* 70 (December 1980): 839–47; Lawrence Summers, "Inflation and the Valuation of Corporate Equities," National Bureau of Economic Research Working Paper No. 824, December 1981; Myron Gordon, "The Impact of Real Factors and Inflation on the Performance of the U.S. Stock Market from 1960 to 1980," *Journal of Finance* 38 (May 1983): 553–63; and Robert Pindyck, "Risk, Inflation, and the Stock Market," *American Economic Review* 74 (June 1984): 335–51.

38. "IRAs a Hit with Taxpayer," *New York Times*, April 15, 1983, p. D1.

39. "IRA Ownership," *Wall Street Journal*, July 30, 1985, p. 33; Jeffrey Laderman, "IRA Money Floods the Markets," *Business Week*, April 14, 1986, p. 34. Several economic studies have found that IRA contributions represented a net increase in savings. See R. Glenn Hubbard, "Do IRAs and Keoghs Increase Saving?" *National Tax Journal* 37 (March 1984): 43–54; Steven Venti and David Wise, "Have IRAs Increased U.S. Saving? Evidence from Consumer Expenditure Surveys," *Quarterly Journal of Economics* 105 (August 1990): 661–98; R. Glenn Hubbard and Jonathan Skinner, "Assessing the Effectiveness of Saving Incentives," *Journal of Economic Perspectives* 10 (Fall 1996): 73–90; James Poterba, Steven Venti, and David Wise, "How Retirement Savings Programs Increase Saving," *Journal of Economic Perspectives* 10 (Fall 1996): 91–112.

40. Robert Barsky and J. Bradford DeLong, "Bull and Bear Markets in the Twentieth Century," *Journal of Economic History* 50 (June 1990): 265–81; James Poterba and Andrew Samwick, "Stock Ownership Patterns, Stock Market Fluctuations, and Consumption," *Brookings Papers on Economic Activity* (1995): 295–357; Jay Ritter and Richard Warr, "The Decline of Inflation and the Bull Market of 1982–1999," *Journal of Financial and Quantitative Analysis* 37 (March 2002): 29–61; "Growing Interest in IRAs Prompts Big Marketing Battle for Investors," *Wall Street Journal*, April 13, 1984, p. 35; "Once-Cautious IRA Holders Take Aggressive Tack Managing Funds," *Wall Street Journal*, February 6, 1985; "Funds Strive to Secure Self-Directed IRAs," *Barron's*, February 18, 1985, p. 55; "Self-Directed IRAs Gaining in Popularity as Investors Seek a Wider Array of Options," *Wall Street Journal*, April 11, 1985; "Investors Place More IRA Assets in Stocks, Bonds," *Wall Street Journal*, January 2, 1986, p. 8.

41. Smith, *Paper Money*, p. 274; "Discounters Are Taking Ever Wider Slice of Broker Commissions, SIA Study Finds," *Wall Street Journal*, March 7, 1983, p. 20; "Is Wall Street Ready for Mayday 2?" *New York Times*, April 28, 1985, sec. 3, p. 1; Merton Miller, "Financial Innovation: The Last Twenty Years and the Next," *Journal of Financial and Quantitative Analysis* 21 (December 1986): 459; Ken Auletta, *Greed and Glory on Wall Street* (New York: Random House, 1986; reprint, New York: Warner, 1987), p. 40.

42. Tim Carrington, *The Year They Sold Wall Street* (Boston: Houghton Mifflin, 1985), chap. 11; Auletta, *Greed and Glory*, pp. 139–42; "Kidder's Road to Acquisition," *New York Times*, May 5, 1986, p. D1.

43. Sylvia Auerbach, "A Broker by Any Name . . ." *Barron's*, February 11, 1984, p. 18; "Merrill's New Bank Challenge," *New York Times*, April 11, 1984, p. D4; "Cash Management Accounts Proliferating as Banks, Brokers Vie for People's Money," *Wall Street Journal*, November 15, 1982, p. 31; Carol Loomis, "The Fight for Financial Turf," *Fortune*, December 28, 1981, pp. 54, 57; "Peddling Advice to the Middle Class," *New York Times*, November 7, 1982, sec. 3, p. 14; Alex Taylor, "Why Fidelity Is the Master of Mutual Funds," *Fortune*, September 1, 1986; Geoffrey Colvin, "Would You Buy Stocks Where You Buy Socks?" *Fortune*, July 9, 1984.

44. "Small Investors Surge Back into the Market; Many Buy New Issues," *Wall Street Journal*, March 24, 1983, p. 1; "Small Investors Are Going It Together," *New York Times*, December 22, 1985, sec. 4, p. 16; "Rally Luring Small Investors," *New York Times*, March 17, 1986, p. D1; "Market Luring Small Buyers," *New York Times*, January 20, 1987, p. D1; "Following Deregulation, You Need to Do More Homework Before Investing at Banks," *Wall Street Journal*, February 27, 1984, p. 29; Vartanig Vartan, "Assessing the Newsletters," *New York Times*, January 2, 1986, p. D4; Joseph Nocera, *A Piece of the Action* (New York: Simon and Schuster, 1994), p. 284. On the movement toward indirect ownership of stocks, see also Poterba and Samwick, "Stock Ownership Patterns," pp. 320–23.

45. "Those Strange Market Turns," *New York Times*, August 30, 1985, p. D1; "Wall Street's Computers Gain Power," *New York Times*, June 15, 1986, sec. 4, p. 4; "Wall Street's Tomorrow Machine," *New York Times*, October 19, 1986, sec. 3, p. 1. For the effects of market volatility, see James Poterba and Lawrence Summers, "The Persistence of Volatility and Stock Market Fluctuations," *American Economic Review* 76 (December 1986): 1142–51; Sean Becketti and Gordon Sellon, "Has Financial Market Volatility Increased?" Federal Reserve Bank of Kansas City *Economic Review*, June 1989, pp. 17–30.

46. Leonard Silk, "Running Uphill on Eggs," *New York Times*, February 4, 1987, p. D2; John Curran, "Don't Climb Off the Bull Yet," *Fortune*, August 3, 1987, p. 195; "Speculative Fever Ran High in the 10 Months Prior to Black Monday," *Wall Street Journal*, December 11, 1987, p. 1.

47. "Small Investors Seize the Moment, Hunt for Deals," *New York Times*, October 22, 1987, p. D16; Phillip Mack, "Recent Trends in the Mutual Fund

Industry," *Federal Reserve Bulletin*, November 1993, p. 1006; "Main Street's View of the Crash Is Far from Wall Street's," *Wall Street Journal*, December 30, 1987, p. 1; Poterba and Samwick, "Stock Market Fluctuations," p. 295; William Sheeline, "Why the Crash Left Few Traces," *Fortune*, October 24, 1988, p. 81; David Runkle, "Why No Crunch from the Crash?" Federal Reserve Bank of Minneapolis *Quarterly Review*, Winter 1988; Diana Henriques, "Hopeful Sign," *Barron's*, March 6, 1989, p. 16.

48. Mack, "Recent Trends," p. 1001; Ana Aizcorbe, Arthur Kennickell, and Kevin Moore, "Recent Changes in U.S. Family Finances: Evidence from the 1998 and 2001 Survey of Consumer Finances," *Federal Reserve Bulletin*, January 2003, pp. 8–13; Milton Marquis, "Shifting Household Assets in a Bear Market," Federal Reserve Bank of San Francisco *Economic Letter*, March 28, 2003.

49. Arthur Kennickell and Janice Shack-Marquez, "Changes in Family Finances from 1983 to 1989: Evidence from the Survey of Consumer Finances," *Federal Reserve Bulletin*, January 1992, pp. 5, 6–7; Edward Wolff, "Recent Trends in the Size Distribution of Household Wealth," *Journal of Economic Perspectives* 12 (Summer 1998): 134; Poterba and Samwick, "Stock Ownership Patterns," pp. 326–29; John Weicher, "The Rich and the Poor: Demographics of the U.S. Wealth Distribution," Federal Reserve Bank of St. Louis *Review*, July–August 1997, pp. 29–30. See also Wojciech Kopczuk and Emmanuel Saez, "Top Wealth Shares in the United States, 1916–2000: Evidence from Estate Tax Returns," National Bureau of Economic Research Working Paper 10399, March 2004.

50. On pension plan changes, see David Bloom and Richard Freeman, "The Fall in Private Pension Coverage in the United States," *American Economic Review* 82 (May 1992): 539–45; William Even and David MacPherson, "Why Did Male Pension Coverage Decline in the 1980s?" *Industrial and Labor Relations Review* 47 (April 1991): 439–53; Olivia Mitchell and James Moore, "Can Americans Afford to Retire? New Evidence on Retirement Saving Adequacy," *Journal of Risk and Insurance* 65 (September 1998): 371–400; Leora Friedberg and Michael Owyang, "Not Your Father's Pension Plan: The Rise of 401(k) and Other Defined Contribution Plans," Federal Reserve Bank of St. Louis *Review*, January–February 2002, pp. 23–34; and David Zalewski, "Retirement Insecurity in the Age of Money-Manager Capitalism," *Journal of Economic Issues* 36 (June 2002): 349–56.

51. For the end of Regulation Q, see R. Alton Gilbert, "Requiem for Regulation Q: What It Did and Why It Passed Away," Federal Reserve Bank of St. Louis *Review*, February 1986, pp. 22–37.

52. For summaries of the S&L industry and its collapse, see R. Dan Brumbaugh and Andrew Carron, "Thrift Industry Crisis: Causes and Solutions," *Brookings Papers on Economic Activity* (1987): 349–88, and Lawrence White, "A Cautionary Tale of Deregulation Gone Awry: The S&L Debacle," *Southern Economic Journal* 59 (January 1993): 496–514. On the costs of cleaning up the S&Ls, see Joyce Manchester and Warwick McKibbin, "The Macroeconomic Consequences of the Savings and Loan Debacle," *Review of Economics and Statistics* 76 (August 1994): 579–84.

53. For criminal behavior in the S&Ls, see K. Calavita, R. Tillman, and H. Pontell, "The Savings and Loan Debacle, Financial Crime, and the State," *Annual Review of Sociology* 23 (1997): 19–38. For a popular treatment of the S&Ls, see Martin Mayer, *The Greatest-Ever Bank Robbery* (New York: Collier, 1990).

54. Barbara Ehrenreich, "Is the Middle Class Doomed?" *New York Times Magazine,* September 7, 1986, p. 44. For other descriptions of declining or stagnant income during the 1980s and its implications, see Joan Berger, "The False Paradise of a Service Economy," *Business Week,* March 3, 1986, p. 78; ". . . And Flat Productivity at Home," *Washington Post,* May 4, 1986, p. C6; "Warning: The Standard of Living Is Slipping," *Business Week,* April 20, 1987, pp. 46, 50; Norman Jones, "It's Time for America to Wake Up," *Business Week,* November 16, 1987, p. 158; Jeff Faux, "The Party's Over, but Who Pays?" *Nation,* January 30, 1988, p. 128; "Workers' State," *Nation,* September 19, 1988, p. 187; Laura D'Andrea Tyson, "Behind the Rosy Numbers Lurks Decline," *New York Times,* October 9, 1988, sec. 3, p. 3; "Are You Better Off?" *Time,* October 10, 1988.

55. Berger, "False Paradise," p. 78; Peter Klenow, "Measuring Consumption Growth: The Impact of New and Better Products," Federal Reserve Bank of Minneapolis *Quarterly Review,* Winter 2003, pp. 14, 16; Michael Boskin et al., "Consumer Prices, the Consumer Price Index, and the Cost of Living," *Journal of Economic Perspectives* 12 (Winter 1998): 6, 9; Leonard Nakamura, "Is the U.S. Economy Really Growing Too Slowly? Maybe We're Measuring Growth Wrong," Federal Reserve Bank of Philadelphia *Business Review,* March–April 1997, p. 10. For additional discussions of measurement problems in income and consumption data, see Daniel Slesnick, "The Standard of Living in the United States," *Review of Income and Wealth* 37 (December 1991): 363–86; Zvi Griliches, "Productivity, R&D, and the Data Constraint," *American Economic Review* 84 (March 1994): 1–23; William Nordhaus, "Quality Change in Price Indexes," *Journal of Economic Perspectives* 12 (Winter 1998): 59–68; Robert Fogel, "Catching Up with the Economy," *American Economic Review* 89 (March 1999): 1–21; Michael Boskin, "Economic Measurement: Progress and Challenges," *American Economic Review* 90 (May 2000): 247–52; Bruce Hamilton, "Using Engel's Law to Estimate CPI Bias," *American Economic Review* 91 (June 2001): 619–30; and Dora Costa, "Estimating Real Income in the United States from 1888 to 1994: Correcting CPI Bias Using Engel Curves," *Journal of Political Economy* 109 (December 2001): 1288–1310.

56. Neal Rosenthal, "The Shrinking Middle Class: Myth or Reality?" *Monthly Labor Review,* March 1985, pp. 3–5, 10; Michael Horrigan and Steven Haugen, "The Declining Middle-Class Thesis: A Sensitivity Analysis," *Monthly Labor Review,* May 1988, pp. 3–4, 9–10; and Mary Daly, "The 'Shrinking' Middle Class?" Federal Reserve Bank of San Francisco *Economic Letter,* 97-07, March 7, 1997.

57. Kennickell and Shack-Marquez, "Changes in Family Finances," pp. 10, 16; Dora Costa, "Less of a Luxury: The Rise of Recreation Since 1888," National Bureau of Economic Research Working Paper 6054, June 1997; Leonard Silk, "How Well Off Are Workers? *New York Times,* September 2, 1988, p. D2; Robert Hamrin, "Sorry

Americans—You're Still Not 'Better Off,'" *Challenge,* September–October 1988, p. 50.

58. "As Steel Jobs Dwindle, Blue Collar Families Face Vexing Changes," *Wall Street Journal,* August 8, 1986, p. 1; "Families, Singles, Yuppies: Who Are the Middle Class?" *Wall Street Journal,* March 9, 1987, p. 23; John Burnett and Alan Bush, "Profiling the Yuppies," *Journal of Advertising Research* 26 (April–May 1986): 32; "The Year of the Yuppie," *Newsweek,* December 31, 1984. On the increasing variety and quality of consumer goods and the benefits to buyers, see Kenneth Labich, "The Innovators," *Fortune,* June 6, 1988; W. Michael Cox and Richard Alm, "The Right Stuff," Federal Reserve Bank of Dallas *1998 Annual Report,* pp. 3–26; Mark Bils and Peter Klenow, "The Acceleration in Variety Growth," *American Economic Review* 91 (May 2001): 274–80; Mark Bils and Peter Klenow, "Quantifying Quality Growth," *American Economic Review,* 91 (September 2001): 1006–30; and Amil Petrin, "Quantifying the Benefits of New Products: The Case of the Minivan," *Journal of Political Economy* 110 (August 2002): 705–30.

59. Maureen Boyle Gray, "Consumer Spending on Durables and Services in the 1980s," *Monthly Labor Review,* May 1992, p. 25.

60. Petrin, "Case of the Minivan," pp. 717, 726–27; Geoffrey Paulin, "Consumer Expenditures on Travel, 1980–1987," *Monthly Labor Review,* June 1990, pp. 56–59.

61. "Dining Chic to Chic," *Wall Street Journal,* April 21, 1986, p. 18D; "New American Eating Pattern: Dine Out, Carry In," *New York Times,* October 30, 1985, p. C1; Ruth Hamel and Tim Schreiner, "Yeast, Hops, Barley, and Profits," *American Demographics,* April 1988, pp. 45–47; "Brew Pubs Pour into Restaurant Market, Creating Their Own Beers and Ambiance," *Wall Street Journal,* February 22, 1990, p. B1.

62. Robert Avery, Gregory Elliehausen, and Arthur Kennickell, "Changes in Consumer Installment Debt: Evidence from the 1983 and 1986 Surveys of Consumer Finances," *Federal Reserve Bulletin,* October 1987, pp. 761, 768; Kennickell and Shack-Marquez, "Changes in Family Finances," pp. 15–16; Peter Yoo, "Charging Up a Mountain of Debt: Accounting for the Growth of Credit Card Debt," Federal Reserve Bank of St. Louis *Review,* March–April 1997, pp. 6–7.

63. Labich, "Innovators," pp. 51, 52, 64; "Masters of Innovation," *Business Week,* April 10, 1989, p. 58; Edward McLaughlin, "Supermarketing Success," *American Demographics,* August 1985, p. 35.

64. George Sternlieb and James Hughes, "The Demise of the Department Store," *American Demographics,* August 1987, pp. 31–33; "Losing Sales, Big Retailers Adopt Specialty Stores' Marketing Tactics," *Wall Street Journal,* January 13, 1986, p. 29; Richard Stevenson, "Watch Out Macy's, Here Comes Nordstrom," *New York Times Magazine,* August 27, 1989, pp. 34, 40; Stanley Angrist, "Entrepreneur in Short Pants," *Forbes,* March 7, 1988, pp. 84–85; "Computer Users Shop at Home Over the Phone," *Wall Street Journal,* February 25, 1985, p. 35.

65. John Huey, "Wal-Mart: Will It Take Over the World?" *Fortune,* January 30, 1989; "Is Wal-Mart Good for America?" *New York Times,* December 7, 2003, sec. 4,

p. 1; "With Big Selection and Low Prices, 'Category Killer' Stores Are a Hit," *Wall Street Journal*, June 17, 1986, p. 31; Susan Caminiti, "The New Champs of Retailing," *Fortune*, September 24, 1990, pp. 85–86; "Bookshop 'Superstore' Reflects the Latest Word in Retailing," *Wall Street Journal*, February 23, 1987, p. 27; Kyle Bagwell, Garey Ramey, and Daniel Spulber, "Dynamic Retail Price and Investment Competition," *RAND Journal of Economics* 28 (Summer 1997): 207–27; Thomas Holmes, "Bar Codes Lead to Frequent Deliveries and Superstores," *RAND Journal of Economics* 32 (Winter 2001): 708–25; Nicholas Verchaver, "Scanning the Globe," *Fortune*, May 31, 2004; Walter Levy, "The End of an Era: A Time for Retail Perestroika," *Journal of Retailing* 65 (Fall 1989): 390; "It's Expansion Lagging, Sears Now Struggles to Stay Independent," *Wall Street Journal*, November 2, 1988, p. 1; "Sears Cutting Prices by as Much as 50% in a Shift of Strategy," *New York Times*, February 24, 1989, p. 1; "A Tough Spring for the 'Big 7,'" *New York Times*, April 27, 1985, p. 31; "Piece by Piece, the Big Stores Rebuild," *New York Times*, September 21, 1986, sec. 3, p. 1.

66. Charles Lockwood and Christopher Leinberger, "Los Angeles Comes of Age," *Atlantic*, January 1988, p. 33; Robert Fishman, "Megalopolis Unbound," *Wilson Quarterly*, Winter 1990, pp. 27, 28, 30; "Shallow Roots: New Suburbs Tackle City Ills While Lacking a Sense of Community," *Wall Street Journal*, March 26, 1987, p. 1; "Shallow Roots: Young and Old Alike Can Lead Lonely Lives in New U.S. Suburbs," *Wall Street Journal*, March 27, 1987, p. 1.

67. "A Rural Landscape, but an Urban Boom," *New York Times*, August 8, 1987, p. 1; Avijit Ghosh and Sara McLafferty, "The Shopping Center: A Restructuring of Post-war Retailing," *Journal of Retailing* 67 (Fall 1991): 255, 256.

68. David Birch, "From Suburb to Urban Place," *Annals of the American Academy of Political and Social Science* 421 (September 1975): 25–37; Fishman, "Megalopolis," p. 30; Irving Welfeld, *Where We Live* (New York: Simon and Schuster, 1988), pp. 99, 100; Witold Rybczynski, "The New Downtowns," *Atlantic*, May 1993, p. 101; David Boyd, "From 'Mom and Pop' to Wal-Mart: The Impact of the Consumer Goods Pricing Act of 1975 on the Retail Sector in the United States," *Journal of Economic Issues* 31 (March 1997): 223–32; "Neighborhood Groceries Fading Away in Face of High Costs, Big Competition," *Wall Street Journal*, December 7, 1988, p. B2; "Arrival of Discounter Tears the Civic Fabric of Small-Town Life," *Wall Street Journal*, April 14, 1987, p. 1; "How Wal-Mart Hits Main St.," *U.S. News and World Report*, March 13, 1989, pp. 53–55; William Kowinski, *The Malling of America* (New York: William Morrow, 1985), p. 204; William Sharpe and Leonard Wollock, "Bold New City or Built-up 'Burb? Redefining Contemporary Suburbia," *American Quarterly* 46 (March 1994): 15, 12, 11; Juliet Schor, *The Overworked American* (New York: Basic, 1991), pp. 107, 124. See also Peter Muller, "The Suburban Transformation of the Globalizing American City," *Annals of the American Academy of Political and Social Science* 551 (May 1997): 44–58; Edward Glaeser, Jed Kolko, and Albert Saiz, "Consumer City," *Journal of Economic Geography* 1 (January 2001): 27–50; and, for criticisms of the idea that malls could form new downtowns, Lizabeth Cohen, *A Consumers' Republic* (New York: Knopf, 2003), chap. 6.

69. On the satisfactions to be gained from consumption, see Stanley Lebergott, *Pursuing Happiness* (Princeton: Princeton University Press, 1993).

70. "Why There Are No Issues," *New York Times*, May 3, 1988, p. A34.

Chapter 4: Second Term

1. Donald Regan, *For the Record* (New York: Harcourt Brace Jovanovich, 1988), pp. 219–20; Lou Cannon, *President Reagan* (New York: Simon and Schuster, 1991), pp. 551–52, 555–60.

2. Joseph Nocera, *A Piece of the Action* (New York: Simon and Schuster, 1994), pp. 152–53; "Donald Regan Will Sell Both Tax, Budget Cuts as Treasury Secretary," *Wall Street Journal*, December 12, 1980, p. 1; Regan, *For the Record*, pp. 229–30, 242; "Regan," *Washington Post*, February 13, 1985, p. C1; Memo from Roger Porter, "White House Organization I: Overview," January 19, 1985, Donald Regan Files, Box 2, folder "White House Organization Memos, Porter to Regan," Ronald Reagan Library; Memo from Roger Porter, "White House Organization IV: Office of the Chief of Staff," January 23, 1985, Donald Regan Files, Box 2, folder "White House Organization Memos, Porter to Regan," Ronald Reagan Library; Edwin Meese, interview by the author, Washington, D.C., January 7, 2004.

3. David Cohen, "From the Fabulous Baker Boys to the Master of Disaster: The White House Chief of Staff in the Reagan and G. H. W. Bush Administrations," *Presidential Studies Quarterly* 32 (September 2002): 472; Richard Darman, *Who's in Control?* (New York: Simon and Schuster, 1996), p. 171. For contemporary reporting on Regan's problems as chief of staff, see "Regan Expected to Seek New White House Style," *Washington Post*, January 14, 1985, p. 1; "Feisty, Outspoken Regan Faces Tough Challenge Walking Political Mine Fields as Chief of Staff," *Wall Street Journal*, February 21, 1985, p. 64; "White House Aide Regan Gains Job Security by Mending Ways," *Washington Post*, October 20, 1985, p. A5; Bernard Weinraub, "How Donald Regan Runs the White House," *New York Times Magazine*, January 5, 1986; and "The Stormy Siege of Don Regan," *Washington Post*, December 5, 1986, p. C1. Nancy Reagan came to detest Regan and they traded barbs in their memoirs. For examples, see Regan, *For the Record*, 70–79, and Nancy Reagan, *My Turn* (New York: Random House, 1989), chap. 16.

4. "99th Congress Opens Somberly in Deficit Shadow," *New York Times*, January 4, 1985, p. A17; "President's Popularity High Despite Doubts on Policies," *Washington Post*, January 20, 1985, p. 1; "Reagan's Achievements Pose Hard Tests for Second Term," *New York Times*, January 20, 1985, p. 1; Carl Van Horn, "Fear and Loathing on Capitol Hill: The 99th Congress and Economic Policy," *PS* 19 (Winter 1986): 23–29.

5. "Drive to End Deficits: Odd Bedfellows," *New York Times*, October 10, 1985, p. B18; "Budget-Balancing Bill Is Signed in Seclusion," *New York Times*, December 13, 1985, B8; John Hoadley, "Easy Riders: Gramm-Rudman-Hollings and the Legislative Fast Track," *PS* 19 (Winter 1986): 30–36. The amendment had a third

sponsor, Senator Fritz Hollings (D-S.C.), but it was almost always referred to as Gramm-Rudman. The best short history of the passage of Gramm-Rudman is by Representative Mike Synar (D-Okla.), who was on the conference committee and then led a successful court challenge to the law. See Mike Synar, Vincent LoVoi, and Donald Pongrace, "Congressional Perspective on the Balanced Budget and Emergency Deficit Control Act of 1985," *Pace Law Review* 7 (Spring–Summer 1987): 675–94. For an explanation of Gramm-Rudman's automatic cutting mechanisms, see Harry Havens, "Gramm-Rudman-Hollings: Origins and Implementation," *Public Budgeting and Finance* 6 (Autumn 1986): 4–24.

6. Bill Bradley, "The Gramm-Rudman Plan: 'Congress at Its Worst,'" *Washington Post*, October 9, 1985, p. A19; Richard Gephardt, "Voodoo Politics Takes Center Stage," *New York Times*, October 27, 1985, sec. 3, p. 2; Michael Barone, "The Deficit Panic: If We Won't Pay Now, Why Will We Later?" *Washington Post*, October 27, 1985, p. B1; Irving Kristol, "Congressional Right Has It Wrong," *Wall Street Journal*, November 18, 1985, p. 30; Memo from Dennis Thomas, "Future Strategy," September 25, 1985, Dennis Thomas Files, Box 7, folder "Regan Memorandums, July–Dec 85, 2"; Memo from Dennis Thomas, "Gramm-Rudman/Tax Reform," December 3, 1985, Dennis Thomas Files, Box 7, folder "Regan Memorandums, July–Dec 85, 2"; "Gramm-Rudman Stays Alive Despite Host of Uncertainties," *Washington Post*, October 28, 1985, p. A3; "Letter from Washington," *National Review*, November 15, 1985, p. 15; "A Bad Idea Whose Time Has Come," *New Republic*, December 30, 1985, p. 7; Darrell West, "Gramm-Rudman-Hollings and the Politics of Deficit Reduction," *Annals of the American Academy of Political and Social Science* 499 (September 1988): 99; Kate Stith, "Rewriting the Fiscal Constitution: The Case of Gramm-Rudman-Hollings," *California Law Review* 76 (May 1988): 655.

7. *Bowsher v. Synar*, 478 U.S. 714; Robert Reischauer, "Taxes and Spending Under Gramm-Rudman-Hollings," *National Tax Journal* 43 (September 1990): 226–27; "Budget Panels' Chairmen Ready to Forget Law's Deficit Goal," *New York Times*, February 24, 1987, p. 1; "Congress Is Ready to Ignore Deficit During Election '88," *Wall Street Journal*, February 19, 1988, p. 12; "Frustration Is Deepening over the Deficit," *New York Times*, June 28, 1987, sec. 4, p. 5; Benjamin Friedman, "Gramm-Rudman: A Sham," *New York Times*, October 13, 1986, p. A19. For additional commentaries on the constitutional aspects of Gramm-Rudman, see William Banks and Jeffrey Straussman, "Bowsher v. Synar: The Emerging Judicialization of the Fisc," *Boston College Law Review* 28 (June 1987): 659–88, and Eric Richards, "The Gutting of Gramm-Rudman: Implications for Bureaucrats, Budgets, and the Balance of Power," *New England Law Review* 22 (August 1987): 1–30. For economists' views on Gramm-Rudman's effectiveness, see Preston Miller, "Gramm-Rudman-Hollings' Hold on Budget Policy: Losing Its Grip?" Federal Reserve Bank of Minneapolis *Quarterly Review*, Winter 1989, pp. 11–12, 21; Edward Grimlich, "U.S. Federal Budget Deficits and Gramm-Rudman-Hollings," *American Economic Review* 80 (May 1990): 79, 80.

8. "Reagan's Critics," *New York Times,* October 22, 1987, p. D13; "Stock Market Crash Makes Budget Accord, Tax Rise More Likely," *Wall Street Journal,* October 23, 1987, p. 1; "Budget Deficit Up in '88, Despite Forecast of Drop," *New York Times,* October 29, 1988, p. 6; John Ellwood, "The Politics of the Enactment and Implementation of Gramm-Rudman-Hollings: Why Congress Cannot Address the Deficit Dilemma," *Harvard Journal on Legislation* 25 (Summer 1988): 574; and Guido Tabelline and Alberto Alesina, "Voting on the Budget Deficit," *American Economic Review* 80 (March 1990): 37–49. See also Daniel Patrick Moynihan, "How Reagan Created the Crash," *New York Times,* November 1, 1987, sec. 4, p. 25.

9. Regan, *For the Record,* p. 195. For an overview of the problems of the tax system in the early 1980s and previous proposals and efforts at reform, see Joseph A. Pechman, "Tax Reform: Theory and Practice," *Journal of Economic Perspectives* 1 (Summer 1987): 11–15. For a brief overview of why reform was considered hopeless, see David Beam, Timothy Conlan, and Margaret Wrightson, "Solving the Riddle of Tax Reform: Party Competition and the Politics of Ideas," *Political Science Quarterly* 105 (Summer 1990): 193–95.

10. "Address Before a Joint Session of the Congress on the State of the Union, January 25, 1984," http://www.reagan.utexas.edu/resource/speeches/1984/ 12584e.htm; "Address to the Nation on Tax Reform," http://www.reagan.utexas .edu/resource/speeches/1985/52885c.htm. For the Treasury's tax plan, see *Tax Reform for Fairness, Simplicity, and Economic Growth* (Washington: Department of the Treasury, 1984). For Baker's changes, see Memo from James Baker, "Fundamental Tax Reform," n.d., but probably May 1, 1985, Presidential Handwriting File, Series II, Box 12, folder 180–81, "(4/26/85–5/5/85)," Ronald Reagan Library.

11. Letter, Ray Patterson to Ronald Reagan, June 10, 1985, WHORM Subject File FI010-02, Income Tax, folder 316100–316303, Ronald Reagan Library.

12. The full story of the politics and personalities behind the Tax Reform Act is lengthy and convoluted. WHORM Subject File FI010-02, Income Tax, and the Presidential Handwriting File, Series IV, contain scores of memos and Reagan's phone call notes describing the White House effort on tax reform. The standard— and fascinating—account of the tax reform effort is Jeffrey Birnbaum and Alan Murray, *Showdown at Gucci Gulch* (New York: Random House, 1987).

13. Charles McLure, "The 1986 Act: Tax Reform's Finest Hour or Death Throes of the Income Tax?" *National Tax Journal* 41 (September 1988): 303; Regan, *For the Record,* p. 286; "The Tax Revolt Lives," *National Review,* September 12, 1986, p. 18; "Why It's Real Reform," *Wall Street Journal,* August 19, 1986, p. 28; "Tax Transformation," *New York Times,* August 19, 1986, p. A26; "Judging This Congress," *Washington Post,* August 18, 1986, p. A16; "The Next Tax Reform," *New Republic,* September 15 and 22, 1986, p. 5; Edward Yorio, "The President's Tax Proposals: A Major Step in the Right Direction," *Fordham Law Review* 53 (May 1985): 1255–98; Edward Yorio, "Equity, Efficiency, and the Tax Reform Act of 1986,"

Fordham Law Review 55 (March 1987): 395–458; Pechman, "Theory and Practice," pp. 18, 21.

14. Joseph Pechman, "The Future of the Income Tax," *American Economic Review* 80 (March 1990): 1–20; Joel Slemrod, "Do Taxes Matter? Lessons from the 1980s," *American Economic Review* 82 (May 1992): 252; Alan Auerbach and Joel Slemrod, "The Economic Effects of the Tax Reform Act of 1986," *Journal of Economic Literature* 35 (June 1997): 518–28.

15. David Broder, "Malignant Deficits," *Washington Post,* July 21, 1985, p. G7; "Citing Chronic Deadlock, Panel Urges Altering Political Structure," *New York Times,* January 11, 1987, p. 1; Lloyd Cutler, "The Cost of Divided Government," *New York Times,* November 22, 1987, p. 27; David Beam, Timothy Conlan, and Margaret Wrightson, "Solving the Riddle of Tax Reform: Party Competition and the Politics of Ideas," *Political Science Quarterly* 105 (Summer 1990): 193–217.

16. Birnbaum and Murray, *Gucci Gulch,* pp. 103–7, 182–91; Fred Barnes, "Senator Hackwood," *New Republic,* May 5, 1986, p. 12; Fred Barnes, "Bradley's Triumph," *New Republic,* June 2, 1986, p. 11; Robert McIntyre, "Get on Board," *New Republic,* June 2, 1986, pp. 14–16; James Wilson, "Does the Separation of Powers Still Work?" *Public Interest,* Winter 1986, p. 47.

17. Franco Modigliani, "Reagan's Economic Policies: A Critique," *Oxford Economic Papers* 40 (September 1988): 425; Benjamin Friedman, *Day of Reckoning* (New York: Random House, 1988), p. 5; Edythe Miller, "Economic Efficiency, the Economics Discipline, and the 'Affected-with-a-Public-Interest' Concept," *Journal of Economic Issues* 24 (September 1990): 719; John Taylor, "Changes in American Economic Policy in the 1980s: Watershed or Pendulum Swing?" *Journal of Economic Literature* 33 (June 1995): 783; Alan Meltzer, "Economic Policies and Actions in the Reagan Administration," *Journal of Post Keynesian Economics* 10 (Summer 1988): 537; Owen Humpage, "Do Deficits Matter?" Federal Reserve Bank of Cleveland *Economic Commentary,* June 15, 1993, p. 1.

For other evaluations of Reagan's economic performance, see Wallace Peterson, "The Macroeconomic Legacy of Reaganomics," *Journal of Economic Issues* 22 (March 1988): 1–15; Alfred Eichner, "The Reagan Record: A Post Keynesian View," *Journal of Post Keynesian Economics* 10 (Summer 1988): 541–55; Samuel Bowles, David Gordon, and Thomas Weisskopf, "Business Ascendancy and Economic Impasse: A Structural Retrospective on Conservative Economics, 1979–1987," *Journal of Economic Perspectives* 3 (Winter 1989): 107–34; Robert Alexander, "A Keynesian Defense of the Reagan Deficit," *American Journal of Economics and Sociology* 48 (January 1989): 47–54; Preston Miller and William Roberts, "How Little We Know About Deficit Policy Effects," Federal Reserve Bank of Minneapolis *Quarterly Review,* Winter 1992, pp. 2–11.

18. "Yankee Doodle Magic," *Time,* July 7, 1986, p. 13; Ann Dowd, "What Managers Can Learn from Manager Reagan," *Fortune,* September 15, 1986, pp. 36, 41.

19. Dowd, "What Managers Can Learn," p. 33; "Fraud Was Rampant at HUD, Ex-Reagan Official Tells Congress," *New York Times,* May 1, 1989, p. 1; "Aides and Critics Call Pierce a Loyal but Detached Chief," *New York Times,* June 18, 1989, p. 1; "Former Housing Secretary Won't Be Charged in Investigation," *New York Times,* January 11, 1995, p. A17. See also Charles Moore and Patricia Hoban-Moore, "Some Lessons from Reagan's HUD: Housing Policy and Public Service," *PS* 23 (March 1990): 13–18. On Reagan's passive management style, see Lou Cannon, *President Reagan* (New York: Simon and Schuster, 1991): pp. 181–85, and William Pemberton, *Exit with Honor* (Armonk, N.Y.: M. E. Sharpe, 1997), pp. 110–11.

20. "Travels with Deaver," *New York Times,* September 18, 1985, p. B8; "Foreigners Hiring Reagan's Ex-Aides," *Washington Post,* February 16, 1986, p. 1; "Independent Counsel Requested by Deaver; Meese Disqualifies Self," *Washington Post,* April 29, 1986, p. 1; "U.S. Indicts Deaver on Perjury Charges," *Washington Post,* March 19, 1987, p. 1; "U.S. Probes $1 Million Stock Transfer to Nofziger," *Washington Post,* November 4, 1986, p. A6; "Counsel Asked for Inquiry on Nofziger," *Washington Post,* January 17, 1987, p. 1; "Nofziger Indicted on 6 Ethics Counts," *Washington Post,* July 18, 1987, p. 1; "Deaver Is Found Guilty of Lying About Lobbying," *Washington Post,* December 17, 1987, p. 1; "Meese Critics to Raise Ethics Points as Confirmation Hearings Resume," *New York Times,* January 27, 1985, p. 18; "Prosecutor Studying Actions of Meese While in the Cabinet," *New York Times,* October 16, 1987, p. 1; "Pipeline Revelations Show Meese Willing to Do Favors," *Washington Post,* March 2, 1988, p. 1; "The Misadventures of E. Robert Wallach," *New York Times Magazine,* June 19, 1988; James McKay, *Report of Independent Counsel, in re Edwin Meese III* (Washington: United States Court of Appeals for the District of Columbia Circuit, July 5, 1988), p. 50; "Meese Announces Resignation, Says Probe 'Vindicated' Him," *Washington Post,* July 16, 1988, p. 1; "From Grant to Reagan, Scandals Seem to Hit Republican Presidents," *Wall Street Journal,* July 16, 1987, p. 1. See also Fred Barnes, "Why Can't Conservatives Govern?" *American Spectator,* May 1988, p. 14.

21. The events in Iran-Contra, the investigation, and the outcome of the prosecutions are in Lawrence Walsh, *Final Report of the Independent Counsel for Iran/Contra Matters,* vol. 1 (Washington, D.C.: United States Court of Appeals for the District of Columbia Circuit, August 4, 1993). For a short account of the Iran-Contra schemes, see Pemberton, *Exit with Honor,* chap. 9. For a longer, more detailed account, see Cannon, *President Reagan,* chaps. 19–20. The most complete, detailed account is in Theodore Draper, *A Very Thin Line* (New York: Hill and Wang, 1991).

22. "46% Approve of Reagan's Work, Down 21 Points," *New York Times,* December 2, 1986, p. 1; "Poll Finds Wide Skepticism over Reagan's Handling of Iran Affair," *Washington Post,* January 23, 1987, p. A8; Letter, Ronald Reagan to Nackey Loeb, December 4, 1986, Presidential Handwriting File, Series II, Box 17, folder 268 (12/3/86–12/8/86), Ronald Reagan Library; *Report of the President's Special Review Board,* February 26, 1987, p. 4-1; "Reagan Concedes 'Mistake' in Arms-for-Hostage Policy; Takes Blame, Vows Changes," *New York Times,* March 5, 1987, p. 1; "President

Asserts He Is Moving Away from Iran Affair," *New York Times,* March 6, 1987, p. 1. See also Richard Brody and Catherine Shapiro, "Policy Failure and Public Support: The Iran-Contra Affair and Public Assessment of President Reagan," *Political Behavior* 11 (December 1989): 353–69.

23. *Report of the President's Special Review Board,* p. 4-11.

24. Memo, Dennis Thomas, "Iran Working Group," December 15, 1986, Dennis Thomas Files, Box 6, "Regan Memorandum File, 1986, Oct.–Dec.," Folder 1, Ronald Reagan Library; Memo, Dennis Thomas, "Iran," December 23, 1986, Dennis Thomas Files, Box 6, "Regan Memorandum File, 1986, Oct.–Dec.," Folder 1, Ronald Reagan Library; Memo, Donald Regan, "Advancing the Agenda—Seeking Peace/Quest for Excellence," February 13, 1987, Presidential Handwriting File, Series II, Box 17, Folder 279, Ronald Reagan Library; "High-Level Efforts to Replace Regan Are Reported," *New York Times,* December 11, 1986, p. 1; "White House Losing Politics Aide Daniels," *Washington Post,* February 1, 1987, p. 1; Regan, *For the Record,* p. 372.

25. Cohen, "Fabulous Baker Boys," pp. 464, 480; David Eisenhower, "Fighting the President's Final Battles," *New York Times Magazine,* September 6, 1987; "Reagan's Agenda Being Pared Down for Rest of Term," *New York Times,* January 12, 1987, p. 1; "Public Skeptical on State of the Union," *New York Times,* January 27, 1987, p. 1; "Reagan: What Next?" *National Review,* March 27, 1987, p. 16; "Howard Baker Team Has Buoyed President, but Difficulties Loom," *Wall Street Journal,* May 7, 1987, p. 1; "Visibly Aged and Hurt by Hearing, Reagan Tries Hard to Rebound," *Wall Street Journal,* August 12, 1987, p. 1; "As the End Nears, the Bailout Begins," *New York Times,* October 2, 1987, p. 32; "Administration Seems Increasingly Paralyzed in Wake of Bork Fight," *Wall Street Journal,* October 16, 1987, p. 1; John McLaughlin, "Reagan's No-Risk Regimen," *National Review,* November 6, 1987, p. 26; Paul Gigot, "On Baker's Watch, 'Consensus' Was a Lot Like Defeat," *Wall Street Journal,* June 17, 1988, p. 26.

26. Draper, *Very Thin Line,* pp. 30–33, 114–16. For biographical details on McFarlane, North, and Poindexter, see Robert Timberg, *The Nightingale's Song* (New York: Simon and Schuster, 1995).

27. On both sides' hopes and fears regarding Supreme Court appointments, see "Reagan Appointments to the Federal Bench Worry U.S. Liberals," *Wall Street Journal,* September 6, 1985, p. 1; "Cuomo Sees Peril in Picking Judges on Ideology Basis," *New York Times,* August 12, 1986, p. 1; and "Democrats Plan Closer Scrutiny of Reagan's Judicial Appointments," *Wall Street Journal,* March 6, 1987, p. 1.

28. Richard Vigilante, "Who's Afraid of Robert Bork?" *National Review,* August 28, 1987, p. 25.

29. Kennedy quoted in Ethan Bronner, *Battle for Justice* (New York: W. W. Norton, 1989), p. 99; "Grass-Roots Activists Mobilize Against Bork," *Washington Post,* August 3, 1987, p. A3; Ruth Bamberger, "Why Common Cause Opposed the Bork Nomination," *PS* 20 (Autumn 1987): 876–80. An extensive literature has

developed on the Bork nomination and its effects. Bronner provides the most detailed and insightful narrative of events. Congress, Senate, Committee on the Judiciary, *Nomination of Robert H. Bork to be an Associate Justice of the United States Supreme Court,* 100th Cong., 1st sess., October 13, 1987, also is indispensable. For additional details on Kennedy's role in leading the opposition to Bork, see Adam Clymer, *Edward M. Kennedy* (New York: William Morrow, 1990), pp. 416–28. Bork's version of the nomination fight is in Robert Bork, *The Tempting of America* (New York: Free Press, 1990), chaps. 14–18. For scholarly views of Bork and the nomination, see Peter Phillips, "A Study of Robert Bork," *Arizona State Law Journal* 19 (Summer 1987): 425–53; Ronald Dworkin, "The Bork Nomination," *New York Review of Books,* August 13, 1987, reprinted in *Cardozo Law Review* 9 (October 1987): 101–13; Stephen Carter, "The Confirmation Mess," *Harvard Law Review* 101 (April 1988): 1185–1201; Morton Horwitz, "The Bork Nomination and American Constitutional History," *Syracuse Law Review* 39 (1988): 1029–39; Stephen Griffin, "Politics and the Supreme Court: The Case of the Bork Nomination," *Journal of Law and Politics* 5 (Spring 1989): 551–604; Richard Hodder-Williams, "The Strange Story of Judge Robert Bork and a Vacancy on the United States Supreme Court," *Political Studies* 36 (December 1988): 613–37; Lawrence Marshall, "Intellectual Feasts and Intellectual Responsibility," *Northwestern University Law Review* 84 (Spring–Summer 1990): 832–50; David Danelski, "Ideology as a Ground for the Rejection of the Bork Nomination," *Northwestern University Law Review* 84 (Spring–Summer 1990): 900–920; and L. A. Powe, "From Bork to Souter," *Willamette Law Review* 27 (Fall 1991): 781–801.

30. Dworkin, "The Bork Nomination," pp. 101, 113; Anthony Lewis, "Bork and History," *New York Times,* September 10, 1987, p. A31. Ann Dowd, "Winning One from the Gipper," *Fortune,* November 9, 1987, p. 125.

31. Memo, John Tuck, "Summary of Senator Baker's Communications Activities and Meetings on Behalf of Judge Bork," October 14, 1987, Howard Baker Files, Box 1, folder "Judge Bork, Nomination of, 1," Ronald Reagan Library; Memo, Arthur Culvahouse, "Bork Confirmation Status Report," September 8, 1987, WHORM Subject File FG051, Box 4, folder 506700–508899, Ronald Reagan Library; "How Reagan's Forces Botched the Campaign for Approval of Bork," *Wall Street Journal,* October 7, 1987, p. 1; Bronner, *Battle for Justice,* p. 200; Powe, "Bork to Souter," pp. 786–91; William Ball, "Recommended Telephone Call for the President," September 30, 1987, Presidential Handwriting File, Series IV, Telephone Calls, Box 10, folder 187, Ronald Reagan Library; Judiciary Committee, *Nomination of Robert H. Bork,* p. 97.

32. Suzanne Garment, "The War Against Robert H. Bork," *Commentary,* January 1988, p. 21; Horwitz, "The Bork Nomination," pp. 1029, 1038–39; "Letter from Washington," *National Review,* November 6, 1987, p. 14; "The Bork Disaster," *National Review,* November 6, 1987, p. 16; Ronald Dworkin, "From Bork to Kennedy," *New York Review of Books,* December 12, 1987, p. 36; Griffin, "Politics and the Supreme Court," p. 551; Bentsen quoted in Bronner, *Battle for Justice,* p. 291. For

conservative views of the Supreme Court's reluctance to overturn key cases, see "Has the Supreme Court Gone Too Far?" *Commentary,* October 2003.

33. Dowd, "Winning One," p. 128; Danelski, "Ideology as a Ground," p. 916; Ayo Ogundele and Linda Keith, "Reexamining the Impact of the Bork Nomination to the Supreme Court," *Political Research Quarterly* 52 (June 1999): 403–20; Carter, "Confirmation Mess," pp. 1193–94.

34. For early discussions of the constitutional and practical problems created by the Ethics in Government Act, see Victor Kramer and Louis Smith, "The Special Prosecutor Act: Proposals for 1983," *Minnesota Law Review,* 66 (July 1982): 969–83, and Constance O'Keefe and Peter Safirstein, "Fallen Angels, Separation of Powers, and the Saturday Night Massacre: An Examination of the Practical, Constitutional, and Political Tensions in the Special Prosecutor Provisions of the Ethics in Government Act," *Brooklyn Law Review* 49 (Fall 1982): 113–47. See also Robert Solloway, "The Institutionalized Wolf: An Analysis of the Unconstitutionality of the Independent Counsel Provisions of the Ethics in Government Act of 1978," *Indiana Law Review* 21 (1988): 955–82.

35. *Morrison v. Olson,* 487 U.S. 654, pp. 713, 730. For analyses of *Morrison v. Olson,* see Stephen Carter, "The Independent Counsel Mess," *Harvard Law Review* 102 (November 1988): 105–41, and Allan Moore, "Separation of Powers and the Independent Counsel Act," *Harvard Journal of Law and Public Policy* 12 (Winter 1988): 259–74. I am indebted to Professor Todd Peterson for his explanation of the Court's reasoning in Morrison.

36. Walsh, *Final Report,* pp. xiii–xiv, 372, 558–59; Herbert Miller and John Elwood, "The Independent Counsel Statute: An Idea Whose Time Has Passed," *Law and Contemporary Problems* 62 (Winter 1999): 123, 125; Gregory Smith, "The Independent Counsel in the Iran/Contra Affair: Why Gordon Liddy Went to Jail, and Oliver North Went to Disneyland," *American Criminal Law Review* 29 (Summer 1992): 1262. For an angry memoir by a target of Walsh's investigation who believes his prosecution was entirely political, see Elliott Abrams, *Undue Process* (New York: Free Press, 1993).

37. "GOP Conservatives, After 8 Years in Ascendancy, Brood Over Lost Opportunities, Illusory Victories," *Wall Street Journal,* August 17, 1988; R. Emmett Tyrell, "The Coming Conservative Crack-Up," *American Spectator,* September 1987, p. 18.

38. Meese interview; Robert Bork, "Only the Start," *National Review,* August 5, 1988, p. 35.

39. Paul Gigot, "Guerrilla Gingrich Lights a Fire Under the GOP," *Wall Street Journal,* August 19, 1988, p. 10; William Bennett, "Completing the Reagan Revolution," *Vital Speeches,* August 1, 1986, p. 610; Irving Kristol, "Don't Count Out Conservatism," *New York Times Magazine,* June 14, 1987, p. 32. For other comments on conservatives' views of the Reagan era and the future of the movement, see "Reagan: Truman or Eisenhower?" *National Review,* December 5, 1986, p. 16; John McLaughlin, "Iran and the GOP," *National Review,* May 22, 1987, p. 24; "High Tide for Conservatives, but Some Fear What Follows," *New York Times,* October 13, 1987,

p. 1; Fred Barnes, "Thou Shalt Not Commit Conservatism," *American Spectator,* February 1988, pp. 14–15; Irving Kristol, "The Reagan Revolution That Never Was," *Wall Street Journal,* April 19, 1988, p. 34; "The Reagan Legacy," *National Review,* August 5, 1988, pp. 35–38; and Terry Eastland, "Wanted: Energy in the Executive," *American Spectator,* November, 1988, pp. 14–16; Grover Rees, "The Next Bork," *National Review,* December 9, 1988, pp. 33–34; Tom Bethell, "Guidelines for President Bush," *American Spectator,* January 1989, pp. 11–13.

40. "7 Vying to Lead the Democrats Somewhere," *New York Times,* January 15, 1985, sec. 4, p. 4; "Conservative Shift Is Sought as Democrats Meet to Pick Chief," *New York Times,* January 30, 1985, p. B12; "Democrats Remain in the Doldrums," *Washington Post,* February 3, 1985, p. 1.

41. "Democrats' Revamping," *New York Times,* April 12, 1985, p. A14; Paul Barrett, "The Caucus-Happy Democrats," *Washington Monthly,* April 1985, pp. 25–29; "Kirk to Seek Cancellation of Midterm Convention," *Washington Post,* May 10, 1985, p. A2; "Democratic Chairman Reaffirms Party's Political Philosophy," *Washington Post,* May 3, 1986, p. A7; "Democratic Left Seeks to Halt Rightward Drift," *Washington Post,* May 3, 1986, p. A7. Many of Kuttner's articles, edited and expanded, may be found in Robert Kuttner, *The Life of the Party* (New York: 1987).

42. Peter Petre, "A Liberal Gets Rich Yet Keeps the Faith," *Fortune,* August 31, 1987; Jefferson Morley, "The Washington Intellectual," *New Republic,* August 11, 1986, pp. 10, 11, 14; "The New Republic, Longtime Liberal Stronghold, Drifts Toward the Right as Conservatives Cheer," *Wall Street Journal,* March 6, 1985, p. 64; "Dejected U.S. Liberals Search for a Way Back, but Idea They're Dead May Prove Unwarranted," *Wall Street Journal,* April 15, 1986, p. 64.

43. Lester Thurow, *The Zero-Sum Solution* (New York: Simon and Schuster, 1985), pp. 48–51, 60–66, 38–42, 153–57, 207–28, 262–98, 381.

44. Robert Reich, *Tales of a New America* (New York: Times, 1987), pp. 8–19, 119–20, 140, 170–71, 242, 235–53.

45. Arthur M. Schlesinger, Jr., *The Cycles of American History* (Boston: Houghton Mifflin, 1986), pp. 24, 32, 45, 46–47.

46. Felix Rohatyn, "On the Brink," *New York Review of Books,* June 11, 1987, p. 3; Felix Rohatyn, "What Next?" *New York Review of Books,* December 3, 1987, pp. 3, 4–5; Felix Rohatyn, "Restoring American Independence," *New York Review of Books,* February 18, 1988, pp. 8, 9, 10.

47. "Competitiveness Panel Reports on U.S. Lag," *New York Times,* February 14, 1985, p. D1; Robert Kuttner, "Must We Lose the Industrial World Series?" *Business Week,* November 17, 1986, p. 23; Michael Porter, "Why U.S. Business Is Falling Behind," *Fortune,* April 28, 1986, p. 260; "Can America Compete?" *Business Week,* April 20, 1987.

48. Robert Reich, "The New 'Competitiveness' Fad," *New York Times,* January 14, 1987; "The Clamor for 'Competitiveness,'" *New York Times,* January 12, 1987, p. A14; Robert Herzstein, "Competitiveness—Not Just a Buzzword," *New York Times,* January 21, 1987, p. A31.

49. Paul Kennedy, *The Rise and Fall of the Great Powers* (New York: Random House, 1987; reprint, New York: Vintage, 1989), pp. xii, 529, 534.

50. Peter Schmeisser, "Is America in Decline?" *New York Times Magazine,* April 17, 1988, p. 66; Edward Luttwak, "Why Do the Mighty Fall?" *Washington Post Book World,* December 27, 1987, p. 2; David Landes, "Power Shortage," *New Republic,* February 29, 1988, p. 38. Other major works from this period on the connections between economics, strategy, and national decline are Mancur Olson, *The Rise and Decline of Nations* (New Haven: Yale University Press, 1982), William McNeill, *The Pursuit of Power* (Chicago: University of Chicago Press, 1982), and David Calleo, *Beyond American Hegemony* (New York: Basic, 1987). For a cross-section of the debate about Kennedy's arguments, see Michael Howard, "Imperial Cycles: Bucks, Bullets, and Bust," *New York Times Book Review,* January 10, 1988; James Joll, "The Cost of Bigness," *New York Review of Books,* February 4, 1988; Max Lerner, "No More 'Number Ones' in a New World," *Wall Street Journal,* February 19, 1988, p. 17; Evan Thomas, "Is America in Decline?" *Newsweek,* February 22, 1988; George Will, "The Task of the Body Politic Is to Choose a Nation's Destiny, Not Adjust to One," *Los Angeles Times,* March 7, 1988, sec. 2, p. 7; W. W. Rostow, "Beware of Historians Bearing False Analogies," *Foreign Affairs,* Spring 1988; "The Ascent of Books on Decline of U.S.," *New York Times,* April 10, 1988, sec. 4, p. 4; Daniel Patrick Moynihan, "Debunking the Myth of Decline," *New York Times Magazine,* June 19, 1988; Samuel Huntington, "The U.S.—Decline or Renewal?" *Foreign Affairs,* Winter 1988–89; Charles Kupchan, "Empire, Military Power, and Economic Decline," *International Security* 13 (Spring 1989): 36–53; and Patrick Reagan, "Strategy and History: Paul Kennedy's *The Rise and Fall of the Great Powers,*" *Journal of Military History* 53 (July 1989): 291–306.

51. Lou Cannon, *President Reagan,* p. 675; Albert Hunt, "Democrats' Win, Sans an Agenda, No Help in '88," *Wall Street Journal,* November 6, 1986, p. 12; Michael Barone, "A Small Uptick for the Out Party," *Washington Post,* November 6, 1986, p. A19; Richard Cohen, "Issue-less and Leaderless," *Washington Post,* November 6, 1986, p. A19; Mark Penn and Douglas Schoen, "Reagan's Revolution Hasn't Ended," *New York Times,* November 9, 1986, sec. 4, p. 23.

52. John Farrell, *Tip O'Neill* (Boston: Little, Brown, 2001), pp. 568–70; Thomas O'Neill, "My Own View of Our Country," *Vital Speeches,* June 1, 1985, p. 484; "'Synfuel' Backers Plan Assault on Reagan Cuts," *Wall Street Journal,* February 18, 1981, p. 29; Paul West, "The Wright Stuff," *New Republic,* October 14, 1985, p. 25; Gregg Easterbrook, "The Business of Politics," *Atlantic,* October 1986, p. 33; Steven Waldman, "The Man Who Would Be Speaker," *Washington Monthly,* March 1986, pp. 28, 32, 33; "Farewell to a Quartet of Kings on the Hill," *Time,* November 10, 1986, p. 28; "Bob and Jim Play a Duet," *Newsweek,* February 9, 1987, p. 29; "Jim Wright: Pork-Barrel Politician as Statesman," *Newsweek,* November 30, 1987, p. 26.

53. West, "Wright Stuff," pp. 24–25; "Speaker's Royalty: 55 Percent," *Washington Post,* September 24, 1987, p. 1; "Wright Received Preferential Treatment as Investor," *Washington Post,* May 21, 1989, p. A8; "Wright to Resign Speaker's Post, House Seat," *Washington Post,* June 1, 1989, p. 1.

54. Philip Stern, "The Tin Cup Congress," *Washington Monthly*, May 1988, p. 26; U.S. Department of Commerce, Bureau of the Census, *Statistical Abstract of the United States, 1990* (Washington, 1990), p. 266.

55. Easterbrook, "Business of Politics," p. 36, Bob Secter, "Power in the House," *Los Angeles Times Magazine*, January 11, 1987, p. 22; "Coelho Mixes Democratic Fund-Raising, Political Matchmaking," *Washington Post*, December 1, 1985, p. A17.

56. "For $5,000 a Year, Welcome to the Speaker's Club," *New York Times*, March 24, 1983, p. B14; Craig Carter, "The Democrats' New Money-Raising Champ," *Fortune*, January 6, 1985, p. 71; Robert Kuttner, "Ass Backward," *New Republic*, April 22, 1985, p. 21; Easterbrook, "Business of Politics," p. 29.

57. "Rep. Coelho Makes Money, and Waves, for the Democrats," *Wall Street Journal*, June 14, 1983, p. 1; Farrell, *Life of the Party*, pp. 647–50; Secter, "Power," p. 12; Kuttner, "Ass Backward," p. 18; Kuttner, *Life of the Party*, p. 63; Jack Beatty, "People's Party Sold to High Rollers," *Los Angeles Times*, June 2, 1989, sec. 2, p. 7.

58. "Coelho Campaign Listed as Junk Bonds Buyer," *Washington Post*, April 13, 1989, p. 1; "Coelho Confirms Profiting in 1986 Drexel Bond Issue," *Wall Street Journal*, April 14, 1989, p. 6; "Money Has Big Role in Coelho's Career," and "Stunned Democrats Try to Regroup," *Washington Post*, May 28, 1989, p. 1; "Gore Strategist Controversial," *Los Angeles Times*, April 16, 2000, p. A3.

59. For Dukakis's biography and personality, see "Dukakis: Liabilities into Assets," *Boston Globe*, November 4, 1974, p. 26; "Grim Dukakis Backers Try to Figure Out Why," *Boston Globe*, September 20, 1978, p. 23; "Please Remain Calm," *New Republic*, October 7, 1978, pp. 5–6; Robert Turner, "Into the Loser's Circle," *Boston Globe*, January 20, 1981, p. 15; "Taking the Measure of Michael Dukakis," *Boston Globe*, March 17, 1987, p. 12; and Fox Butterfield, "Dukakis," *New York Times Magazine*, May 8, 1988.

60. "If Dukakis Wins . . . ," *Boston Globe*, September 12, 1982, p. A33; "Issue of Corruption Hurt King, Polls Show," *Boston Globe*, September 15, 1982, p. 28; "Dukakis Gaining National Admirers, Some Say White House, He Talks State House," *Boston Globe*, February 16, 1986, p. 1; "Dukakis Masters the Political Game," *Boston Globe*, March 23, 1986, p. A21; Charles Kenney, "Massachusetts Makes a Comeback," *Boston Globe Magazine*, May 18, 1986; Jon Keller, "Dukakis in Office," *New Republic*, July 4, 1988; Robert Kuttner, "Dukakonomics," *New Republic*, July 18, 1988. For the promotion of Dukakis as a potential president, see David Broder, "Party on the Mend?" *Washington Post*, May 26, 1982, p. A23; "A Success Story in the Industrial Cradle," *Washington Post*, October 31, 1982, p. 1; "New Welfare Strategy Works in Massachusetts," *Washington Post*, August 9, 1985, p. A3; Fred Barnes, "Dukakis Rising," *New Republic*, April 14, 1986, pp. 13–15; and David Broder, "'New Deal-Making' Politics," *Washington Post*, February 10, 1986, p. 1. For background to the Massachusetts Miracle, see Edward Glaeser, "Reinventing Boston," National Bureau of Economic Research, Working Paper No. 10166, December 2003.

61. "Dukakis Gaining National Admirers"; Butterfield, "Dukakis," p. 92; Peter Goldman and Tom Matthews, *The Quest for the Presidency, 1988* (New York: Simon and Schuster, 1989), pp. 69–74.

62. "Dukakis Says He Will Run for President," *New York Times,* March 17, 1987, p. A16; "Dukakis Opens Presidential Quest Stressing His Record as Governor," *New York Times,* April 30, 1987, p. B8; "A Call to Meet the Challenges of 'The Next American Frontier,'" *New York Times,* January 4, 1988, p. 12; "Democrats Repackage Liberalism, Proposing Cheaper Government," *Wall Street Journal,* April 25, 1988, p. 1; "More Wealth Than Meets the Eye Lies Behind Frugal Dukakis Image," *New York Times,* July 6, 1988, p. 1; "Dukakis Works at Warmth, Yet Tries to Keep His Cool," *New York Times,* August 8, 1988, p. 1.

63. Goldman and Matthews, *Quest for the Presidency,* pp. 106–13; "Two Top Aides to Dukakis Resign as One Admits Role in Biden Tape," *New York Times,* October 1, 1987, p. 1; "The Tape: What Sin?" *New York Times,* October 2, 1987, p. A16; "The High Price of Hesitancy," *Boston Globe,* October 1, 1987, p. 1.

64. Goldman and Matthews, *Quest for the Presidency,* pp. 174, 335–42; "She's More Than Most Can Manage," *Los Angeles Times,* June 4, 1988, p. 1.

65. The most complete biography on Bush is Herbert Parmet, *George Bush* (New York: Scribner, 1997). For a detailed study of Bush's prepresidential career, see Nathan Ray, "His Biggest Asset: George Bush's Pre–Vice Presidential Career, 1970–1977" (Ph.D. diss., Texas A&M University, 2002).

66. "The Bush Problem," *National Review,* February 28, 1986, p. 18; "Letter from Washington," *National Review,* April 5, 1985, p. 15; Robert Dornan, "Stop Beating Around the Bush," *National Review,* November 6, 1987, p. 32; "Moderate Conservatives Bush and Dole Woo a Right Wing that Doesn't Quite Trust Them," *Wall Street Journal,* January 28, 1988, p. 52. For conservative views of Bush, see also "Yes, Virginia, the 1988 Race Is Under Way," *National Review,* October 14, 1985, p. 14; "Soul of the Party," *Wall Street Journal,* July 1, 1987, p. 22; and Richard Brookhiser, "Bush on the Brink," *National Review,* February 5, 1988.

67. "Bush Sharpens Image and Positions Himself in the GOP Mainstream," *Wall Street Journal,* December 31, 1987, p. 1; "Aides Fret, but Bush Has to 'Be Me,'" *New York Times,* August 8, 1988, p. B5.

68. "Bush Weak on Law, Dukakis Asserts," *New York Times,* August 24, 1988, p. 1; "Bush Attacks Democrats on Crime Policies," *Washington Post,* October 7, 1988, p. A18; "Bush Plies Northeast for Votes," *Washington Post,* October 1, 1988, p. A3; "Bush Steps Up Attack on Dukakis as Liberal," *Washington Post,* September 30, 1988, p. A8. Poll figures are from Goldman and Matthews, *Quest for the Presidency,* pp. 419–22.

69. "Massachusetts, the Stigma State," *Washington Post,* February 1, 2004, p. D1; Elizabeth Drew, *Election Journal* (New York: William Morrow, 1989), pp. 275–82; "Dukakis Remains on Course, Dismissing Polls and Advice," *New York Times,* July 11, 1988, p. 1; "Dukakis Campaign Fights Slump with New Look and Sharper Edge,"

New York Times, September 9, 1988, p. 1; "Campaign Ads: Emotional vs. Cerebral," *Washington Post*, September 27, 1988, p. A6; "Dukakis Ads: Blurred Signs, Uncertain Path," *New York Times*, October 19, 1988, p. 1; "In War of Negative Ads, Bush May Have the Edge," *Washington Post*, October 14, 1988, p. A21; "Dukakis Hits Foreign Ownership," *Washington Post*, October 8, 1988, p. 1; David Nyhan, "How Dukakis Is Self-Destructing," *Boston Globe*, October 16, 1988, p. A31.

70. "The Democrats Recast Party to Recapture Lost Suburban Vote," *Wall Street Journal*, July 19, 1988, p. 1; "Rivals on Different Paths to Win Middle-Class Vote," *New York Times*, September 29, 1988, p. 1; "'Misery Index' Sets Up Challenge for Dukakis," *Washington Post*, September 19, 1988, p. A8; "In Budget Crisis, Fallout Hit Dukakis," *Boston Globe*, June 26, 1988, p. 1; "'88 Budget Gap Widens, Yet Again, to $450m," *Boston Globe*, July 3, 1988, p. 1; "Budget Could Be Costly for Dukakis," *Boston Globe*, July 11, 1988, p. 1; "Dukakis's Strong Suit Turns a Bit Weak," *New York Times*, May 4, 1988, p. B8; "Dukakis Still Faces Fiscal Headaches," *Washington Post*, August 4, 1988, p. A8.

71. "Dukakis Asserts He Is a 'Liberal,' but in Old Tradition of His Party," *New York Times*, October 31, 1988, p. 1; "Challenge for Dukakis—2," *Boston Globe*, December 2, 1988, p. 18.

72. C. Vann Woodward, "Referendum on Reagan," *New York Review of Books*, December 22, 1988, p. 14; "For Dukakis, a Challenge to Be Likable," *Washington Post*, October 3, 1988, p. A24; Drew, *Election Journal*, p. 326. For voters' evaluations of the candidates and issues, see J. Merrill Shanks and Warren Miller, "Partisanship, Policy, and Performance: The Reagan Legacy in the 1988 Election," *British Journal of Political Science* 21 (April 1991): 133, 150, 158; Leonard P. Stark, "Predicting Presidential Performance from Campaign Conduct: A Character Analysis of the 1988 Election," *Presidential Studies Quarterly* 22 (Spring 1992): 295–308; and Tali Mendelberg, "Executing Hortons: Racial Crime in the 1988 Presidential Campaign," *Public Opinion Quarterly* 61 (Spring 1997): 134–57.

73. "Dukakis, in Bombshell, Rules Out Reelection Bid," *Boston Globe*, January 4, 1989, p. 1; "As Financial Gloom Deepens, Dukakis Enters Political Eclipse," *Boston Globe*, April 3, 1989, p. 1; "State Hits Bottom in Bond Rating," *Boston Globe*, November 16, 1989, p. 1; "Dukakis Plight Elicits Mixed Reviews," *Boston Globe*, July 20, 1989, p. 17.

Chapter 5: If Things Are So Good, Why Do I Feel So Bad?

1. Lisa McGirr, *Suburban Warriors* (Princeton: Princeton University Press, 2001), p. 53. For discussions of popular support for conservative views, see Leo Ribuffo, *The Old Christian Right* (Philadelphia: Temple University Press, 1983); Leo Ribuffo, "Why Is There So Much Conservatism in the United States and Why Do So Few Historians Know Anything About It?" *American Historical Review* 99 (April 1994): 438–49; and Leonard Moore, "Good Old-Fashioned New Social History and the Twentieth-Century American Right," *Reviews in American History* 24 (December 1996). For anger on social issues turning people toward conservatism during the

1970s, see Jonathan Rieder, *Canarsie* (Cambridge: Harvard University Press, 1985); J. Anthony Lukas, *Common Ground* (New York: Alfred A. Knopf, 1985); Ronald Formisano, *Boston Against Busing* (Chapel Hill: University of North Carolina Press, 1991); and Samuel Freedman, *The Inheritance* (New York: Simon and Schuster, 1996).

2. "Reagan Backs Evangelicals in Their Political Activities," *New York Times,* August 23, 1980, p. 8; "Ultraconservative Evangelicals a Surging New Force in Politics," *New York Times,* August 17, 1986, p. 1; "'Christian New Right's' Rush to Power," *New York Times,* August 18, 1980, p. B7; "Rev. Falwell Inspires Evangelical Vote," *New York Times,* August 20, 1980; "A Tide of Born-Again Politics," *Newsweek,* September 15, 1980, p. 28. For a history of the rise of the religious right and its activities during the Reagan years, see Matthew Moen, *The Christian Right and Congress* (Tuscaloosa: University of Alabama Press, 1989). For shorter overviews of the Christian conservative politics, see Leo Ribuffo, "God and Contemporary Politics," *Journal of American History* 79 (March 1993): 1515–33, and Leo Ribuffo, "Liberals and That Old-Time Religion," *Nation,* November 29, 1980.

3. Jerry Falwell, *Listen, America!* (Garden City: Doubleday, 1980), p. 243; Robert Novak, "The Test of a President-Elect," *National Review,* November 28, 1980, p. 1444; Norman Podhoretz, "The New American Majority," *Commentary,* January 1981, p. 27; Allan Carlson, "Radical Liberals, Illiberal Families," *American Spectator,* April 1981, p. 19.

4. "Ultraconservative Evangelicals a Surging New Force in Politics"; Michael Lienesch, "Right-Wing Religion: Christian Conservatism as a Political Movement," *Political Science Quarterly* 97 (Fall 1982): 403, 404; Jeffrey Brudney and Gary Copeland, "Evangelicals as a Political Force: Reagan and the 1980 Religious Vote," *Social Science Quarterly* 65 (December 1984): 1079.

5. Seymour Martin Lipset and Earl Raab, "The Election and the Evangelicals," *Commentary,* March 1981, p. 25; Harold Brown, "The Road to Theocracy?" *National Review,* October 31, 1980, p. 1328; Kathleen Beatty and B. Oliver Walter, "Fundamentalists, Evangelicals, and Politics," *American Politics Quarterly* 16 (January 1988): 43–59; Lee Sigelman and Stanley Presser, "Measuring Public Support for the New Christian Right: The Perils of Point Estimation," *Public Opinion Quarterly* 52 (Autumn 1988): 325–37; Matthew Moen, "From Revolution to Evolution: The Changing Nature of the Christian Right," *Sociology of Religion* 55 (Fall 1994): 350; Jeffrey Hadden, "The Rise and Fall of American Televangelism," *Annals of the American Academy of Political and Social Science* 527 (May 1993): 126–27; "Bakker, Evangelist, Resigns His Ministry over Sexual Incident," *New York Times,* May 21, 1987, p. 1; "Swaggert Says He Has Sinned; Will Step Down," *New York Times,* February 22, 1988, p. 1; see also Andre Prevos, "Television as Religion, Religion as Television? The Case of the PTL," *Journal of Popular Culture* 24 (Winter 1990): 113–29. On the divisions among Christian conservatives and their strength, see Brudney and Copeland, "Evangelicals as a Political Force"; Ribuffo, "God and Contemporary Politics"; and Phillip Hammond, Mark Shibley, and Peter Solow, "Religion and Family Values in Presidential Voting," *Sociology of Religion* 55 (Fall 1994): 277–90.

6. Tom Smith, "The Sexual Revolution," *Public Opinion Quarterly* 54 (Autumn 1990): 415-35; Lucky Tedrow and E. R. Mahoney, "Trends in Attitudes Toward Abortion: 1972-1979," *Public Opinion Quarterly* 43 (Summer 1979): 183; Jacqueline Scott, "Conflicting Beliefs About Abortion: Legal Approval and Moral Doubts," *Social Psychology Quarterly* 52 (December 1989): 325; Michelle Dillon, "Argumentative Complexity of Abortion Discourse," *Public Opinion Quarterly* (Autumn 1993): 305-14; Alan Yang, "Trends: Attitudes Toward Homosexuality," *Public Opinion Quarterly* 61 (Autumn 1997): 477-507; Thomas Wilson, "Trends in Tolerance Toward Rightist and Leftist Groups, 1976-1988," *Public Opinion Quarterly* 58 (Winter 1994): 539-56; Leonie Huddy, Francis Neely, and Marily Lafay, "Trends: Support for the Women's Movement," *Public Opinion Quarterly* 64 (Autumn 2003): 309-50; Steven Brint, "The Political Attitudes of Professionals," *Annual Review of Sociology* 11 (1985): 396, 401; Norval Glenn, "Social Trends in the United States: Evidence from Sample Surveys," *Public Opinion Quarterly* 51 (Supplement: 50th Anniversary Issue): S115, S117, S124; William Schneider, "Being Good or Being Free," *Los Angeles Times,* July 20, 1986, sec. 5, p. 1; Jerome Himmelstein and James McRae, "Social Issues and Socioeconomic Status," *Public Opinion Quarterly* 52 (Winter 1988): 506. For an extensive analysis of individualism in the United States during the 1980s, see Robert Bellah et al., *Habits of the Heart* (Berkeley: University of California Press, 1985). For the religious right's problems in dealing with Congress, see Moen, *Christian Right,* chaps. 5-9.

7. Joseph Sobran, "The Politics of AIDS," *National Review,* May 23, 1986, pp. 22, 24; Terry Teachout, "Gay Rights and Straight Realities," *National Review,* November 11, 1983, pp. 1412, 1411; Ralph de Toledano, "The Homosexual Assault," *National Review,* August 10, 1984, p. 51.

8. "Rep. Bauman in Court," *Washington Post,* October 3, 1980, p. 1; "Conservatives Are Leaving Bauman Camp," *Washington Post,* October 7, 1980, p. 1; William F. Buckley, Jr., "The Ordeal of Robert Bauman," *National Review,* October 31, 1980, p. 1349; John Woolman (pseud.), "A Conservative Speaks Out for Gay Rights," *National Review,* September 12, 1986, pp. 29-30; Marvin Liebman, letter to William F. Buckley, Jr., and response, reprinted in Marvin Liebman, *Coming Out Conservative* (San Francisco: Chronicle, 1992), pp. 257-61.

9. Tony Schwartz, "The TV Pornography Boom," *New York Times Magazine,* September 13, 1981, p. 44; "Pornography Industry Finds Big Profits in New Markets," *Boston Globe,* February 13, 1983, p. 1; "Battle on Pornography Spurred by New Tactics," *New York Times,* July 3, 1984, p. A8; "Porn King Expands His Empire with Aid of Businessman's Skills," *Wall Street Journal,* May 8, 1985, p. 1; "Risque Business," *Wall Street Journal,* April 21, 1986, p. 20D; Attorney General's Commission on Pornography, *Final Report* (Washington: Department of Justice, 1986), pp. 284-90; Smith, "Sexual Revolution," p. 417.

10. "Battle on Pornography Spurred by New Tactics"; "The Dubious Porn War Alliance," *Washington Post,* September 1, 1985, p. C1; "Debate Persists on Rights and Smut," *New York Times,* November 21, 1984, p. A17; "Pornography Foes Lose New

Weapon in Supreme Court," *New York Times,* February 25, 1986, p. 1. For a concise statement of MacKinnon's legal theory on pornography, see Catharine MacKinnon, "Not a Moral Issue," *Yale Law and Policy Review* 2 (Spring 1984): 321–45. For additional legal discussions and the history of the Indianapolis ordinance and a similar effort in Minneapolis, see Note, "Anti-Pornography Laws and First Amendment Values," *Harvard Law Review* 98 (December 1984): 460–81; Marilyn Maag, "The Indianapolis Pornography Ordinance: Does the Right to Free Speech Outweigh Pornography's Harm to Women?" *University of Cincinnati Law Review* 54 (1985): 249–69; and Paul Brest and Ann Vandenberg, "Politics, Feminism, and the Constitution: The Anti-Pornography Movement in Minneapolis," *Stanford Law Review* 39 (February 1987): 607–61. The federal district court decision on the Indianapolis ordinance is *American Booksellers Association, Inc., v. Hudnut,* 598 F. Supp. 1316 (1984).

11. Edwin Meese, interview by the author, Washington, D.C., January 7, 2004; "Meese Names Panel to Study How to Control Pornography," *New York Times,* May 21, 1985, p. A21; "Justice Dept. Pornography Study Finds Material Tied to Violence," *New York Times,* May 14, 1986; "Researchers Dispute Pornography Report on Its Use of Data," *New York Times,* May 17, 1986, p. 1; "'Adult' Magazines Lose Sales as 8,000 Stores Forbid Them," *New York Times,* June 16, 1986, p. 1; "Panel Calls on Citizens to Wage National Assault on Pornography," *New York Times,* July 10, 1986, p. 1; Attorney General's Commission, *Final Report,* pp. 324, 346–47; Schneider, "Being Good"; "X-Rated Industry in a Slump," *New York Times,* October 5, 1986, sec. 3, p. 6; "Justice Dept. Plans Anti-Racketeering Drive Against Pornographers," *New York Times,* January 12, 1988, p. A16; "20 Indicted in Pornography Case," *New York Times,* July 2, 1988, p. 8; Terry Teachout, "The Pornography Report That Never Was," *Commentary,* August 1987.

12. Meese interview; David O'Brien, "Federal Judgeships in Retrospect," in *The Reagan Presidency,* ed. W. Elliott Brownlee and Hugh Davis Graham (Lawrence: University Press of Kansas, 2003), pp. 333–34; Sheldon Goldman, "Reagan's Second Term Judicial Appointments: The Battle at Midway," *Judicature* 70 (April–May 1987): 324–39; Christopher Smith and Rhomas Hensley, "Unfulfilled Aspirations: The Court-Packing Efforts of Presidents Reagan and Bush," *Albany Law Review* 57 (1994): 1111–17; John Jenkins, "Mr. Power," *New York Times Magazine,* October 12, 1986, p. 89; "Reagan Choices Alter the Makeup and Views of the Federal Courts," *Wall Street Journal,* February 1, 1988, p. 1. Records of Reagan's phone calls to judicial nominees are in the Presidential Handwriting File, Series IV, Ronald Reagan Library. See also Timothy Tomasi and Jess Velona, "All the President's Men? A Study of Ronald Reagan's Appointments to the U.S. Courts of Appeals," *Columbia Law Review* 87 (May 1987): 766–93.

13. George Kannar, "The Constitutional Catechism of Antonin Scalia," *Yale Law Journal* 99 (April 1990): 1316; "Reagan Justice," *Newsweek,* June 30, 1986, pp. 14–21; "Reagan's Mr. Right," *Time,* June 30, 1986, pp. 24–33; Antonin Scalia, "Common-Law Courts in a Civil-Law System: The Role of the United States Federal Courts in

Interpreting the Constitution and Laws," in *A Matter of Interpretation,* ed. Amy Gutmann (Princeton: Princeton University Press, 1997), p. 25. For Scalia's explanation of originalism, see Antonin Scalia, "Morality, Pragmatism, and the Legal Order," *Harvard Journal of Law and Public Policy* 9 (Winter 1986): 123–27; Antonin Scalia, "Originalism: The Lesser Evil," *Cincinnati Law Review* 57 (1989): 849–65; and Antonin Scalia, "The Rule of Law as a Law of Rules," *University of Chicago Law Review* 56 (Fall 1989): 175–88.

Scholars are making an industry out of writing about Scalia and the implications of his views. See Richard Brisbin, Jr., "The Conservatism of Antonin Scalia," *Political Science Quarterly* 105 (Spring 1990): 1–29; Alex Kozinski, "My Pizza with Nino," *Cardozo Law Review* 12 (June 1991): 1583–91; George Kannar, "Strenuous Virtues, Virtuous Lives: The Social Vision of Antonin Scalia," *Cardozo Law Review* 12 (June 1991): 1845–67; L. Benjamin Young, Jr., "Justice Scalia's History and Tradition: The Chief Nightmare in Professor Tribe's Anxiety Closet," *Virginia Law Review* 78 (March 1992): 581–619; Jeffrey Rosen, "The Leader of the Opposition," *New Republic,* January 18, 1993; Jeffrey Rosen, "Originalist Sin," *New Republic,* May 5, 1997; David Zlotnick, "Justice Scalia and His Critics: An Exploration of Scalia's Fidelity to His Constitutional Methodology," *Emory Law Journal* 48 (Fall 1999): 1377–1429.

14. Stephen Wermiel, "O'Connor: A Dual Role—An Introduction," *Women's Rights Law Reporter* 13 (Summer–Fall 1991): 130–31; "Judge O'Connor, Cont'd," *National Review,* August 7, 1981, p. 881; "The Lessons of Mrs. O'Connor," *National Review,* October 16, 1981, p. 1182; Thomas Haggard, "Mugwump, Mediator, Machiavellian, or Majority? The Role of Justice O'Connor in the Affirmative Action Cases," *Akron Law Review* 24 (Summer 1990): 47–87; Christopher Smith, "Supreme Court Surprise: Justice Anthony Kennedy's Move Toward Moderation," *Oklahoma Law Review* 45 (Fall 1992): 468, 473; Smith and Hensley, "Unfulfilled Aspirations," p. 1129. For a brief portrait of Scalia and his role on the Court, see "In Re Scalia the Outspoken v. Scalia the Reserved," *New York Times,* May 2, 2004, p. 1. On areas of agreement among Kennedy, O'Connor, and Scalia, see Stephen Gottlieb, "Three Justices in Search of a Character," *Rutgers Law Review* 49 (Fall 1996): 219–83. I am grateful to Todd Peterson for helping me understand the ideological and personal dynamics of the Court's conservatives.

15. *Webster v. Reproductive Health Services,* 492 U.S. 490 (1989), pp. 526, 532; *Planned Parenthood of Southeastern Pennsylvania v. Casey,* 505 U.S. 833 (1992), pp. 867, 998. For an example of O'Connor distancing herself from Scalia in an issue not related to abortion, see *Burnham v. Superior Court of California, County of Marin,* 495 U.S. 604 (1990), pp. 628–40.

16. James Nuechterlein, "The Feminization of the American Left," *Commentary,* November 1987, p. 43; George Gilder in "The American '80s: Disaster or Triumph?" *Commentary,* September 1990, p. 18.

17. Meese interview; J. Harvie Wilkinson III, "Is There a Distinctive Conservative

Jurisprudence?" *University of Colorado Law Review* 73 (Fall 2002): 1392–93; Kozinski, "My Pizza," p. 1588.

18. Wilson, "Trends in Tolerance," pp. 550–53.

19. "Ward Blames Reagan for Poor Racial Climate," *New York Times*, January 20, 1988, p. B3; Richard Lowy, "Yuppie Racism," *Journal of Black Studies* 21 (June 1991): 446; Reginald Wilson, "Developing Leadership: Blacks in Graduate and Professional Schools," *Journal of Black Studies* 19 (December 1988): 167; "Wave of Conservatism Makes Life Tougher for America's Blacks," *Ebony*, January 1982, p. 31; Walter Leavy, "What's Behind the Resurgence of Racism in America?" *Ebony*, April 1987, p. 132; Laura Randolph, "Black Students Battle Racism on College Campuses," *Ebony*, December 1988, p. 126; "Stereotypes Haunt Black Achievement," *Los Angeles Times*, January 9, 1989, p. 1. For a selection of the vast literature on changing racial attitudes, see William Julius Wilson, *The Declining Significance of Race* (Chicago: University of Chicago Press, 1978); Thomas Pettigrew, "New Black-White Patterns: How Best to Conceptualize Them?" *Annual Review of Sociology* 11 (1985): 329–46; Glenn Firebaugh and Kenneth Davis, "Trends in Antiblack Prejudice, 1972–1984: Region and Cohort Effects," *American Journal of Sociology* 94 (September 1988): 251–72; Charlotte Steeh and Howard Schuman, "Young White Adults: Did Racial Attitudes Change in the 1980s?" *American Journal of Sociology* 98 (September 1992): 340–67; Steven Tuch, Lee Sigelman, and Jason MacDonald, "Race Relations and American Youth, 1976–1995," *Public Opinion Quarterly* 63 (Spring 1999): 109–48; and Clem Brooks, "Civil Rights Liberalism and the Suppression of a Republican Political Realignment in the United States, 1972 to 1996," *American Sociological Review* 65 (August 2000): 483–505.

20. For a brief history of civil rights policy from the mid-1960s through the early 1990s, see Hugh Davis Graham, "Race, History, and Policy: African Americans and Civil Rights Since 1964," *Journal of Policy History* 6 (1994): 12–39. For the concise histories of affirmative action and race relations, see Steven Gillon, *That's Not What We Meant to Do* (New York: W. W. Norton, 2000), chap. 3; Gary Gerstle, *American Crucible* (Princeton: Princeton University Press, 2001), chaps. 7–8 and epilogue; and Hugh Davis Graham, *Collision Course* (New York: Oxford University Press, 2002), chap. 4. For thoughtful and skeptical commentary on affirmative action, especially in its early years, see Nathan Glazer, *Affirmative Discrimination* (Cambridge: Harvard University Press, 1975), and Nathan Glazer, *Ethnic Dilemmas* (Cambridge: Harvard University Press, 1983), chaps. 9–11.

21. Public opinion on affirmative action is best summarized by Charlotte Steeh and Maria Krysan, "Affirmative Action and the Public, 1970–1995," *Public Opinion Quarterly* 60 (1996): 128–58. See also Lawrence Bobo and James Kluegel, "Opposition to Race-Targeting: Self-Interest, Stratification Ideology, or Racial Attitudes?" *American Sociological Review* 58 (August 1993): 443–64; James Kuklinski et al., "Racial Prejudice and Attitudes Toward Affirmative Action," *American Journal of Political Science* 41 (April 1997): 402–19; Martin Gilens, Paul Sniderman, and

James Kuklinski, "Affirmative Action and the Politics of Realignment," *British Journal of Political Science* 28 (January 1998): 159–83; and Murat Iyigun and Andrew Levin, "What Determines Public Support for Affirmative Action?" *Southern Economic Journal* 69 (January 2003): 612–27. For the issue of who benefits from affirmative action, see James Smith and Finis Welch, "Affirmative Action and Labor Markets," *Journal of Labor Economics* 2 (April 1984): 269–301; Jonathan Leonard, "Employment and Occupational Advance Under Affirmative Action," *Review of Economics and Statistics* 66 (August 1984): 377–85; Jonathan Leonard, "Affirmative Action as Earnings Redistribution: The Targeting of Compliance Reviews," *Journal of Labor Economics* 3 (July 1985): 363–84; Jonathan Leonard, "What Was Affirmative Action?" *American Economic Review* 76 (May 1986): 359–63; James Smith and Finis Welch, "Black Economic Progress After Myrdal," *Journal of Economic Literature* 27 (June 1989): 555–57; John Donohue and James Heckman, "Continuous Versus Episodic Change: The Impact of Civil Rights Policy on the Economic Status of Blacks," *Journal of Economic Literature* 29 (December 1991): 1603–43; and Harry Holzer and David Neumark, "Assessing Affirmative Action," *Journal of Economic Literature* 38 (September 2000): 483–568.

22. "Reagan Wins Endorsement of a Major Klan Group," *New York Times*, July 31, 1980, p. B10; "Race Issue in Campaign: A Chain Reaction," *New York Times*, September 27, 1980, p. 8; "Quotas in Hiring Are Anathema to President Despite Minority Gains," *Wall Street Journal*, October 24, 1985, p. 1; Milton Friedman, *Capitalism and Freedom* (Chicago: University of Chicago Press, 1962), chap. 7; George Gilder, *Wealth and Poverty* (New York: Basic, 1981; reprint, San Francisco: ICS Press, 1993), p. 150; William Bradford Reynolds, "The Reagan Administration and Civil Rights: Winning the War Against Discrimination," *University of Illinois Law Review* (1986): 1020; Virginia duRivage, "The OFCCP Under the Reagan Administration: Affirmative Action in Retreat," *Labor Law Journal* 36 (June 1985): 364. See also Terry Eastland, "Towards a New Policy on Equality," *Wall Street Journal*, April 17, 1981, p. 20.

23. "Wave of Conservatism Makes Life Tougher for America's Blacks," *Ebony*, January 1982, p. 31; Joel Selig, "The Reagan Justice Department and Civil Rights: What Went Wrong," *University of Illinois Law Review* (1985): 790; Drew Days III, "Turning Back the Clock: The Reagan Administration and Civil Rights," *Harvard Civil Rights–Civil Liberties Law Review* 19 (Summer 1984): 309; Hugh Davis Graham, "Civil Rights Policy," in *The Reagan Presidency*, ed. Brownlee and Graham, p. 284.

24. Daniel Seligman, "Affirmative Action Is Here to Stay," *Fortune*, April 19, 1982, p. 162; Anne Fisher, "Businessmen Like to Hire by the Numbers," *Fortune*, September 6, 1985, p. 28; Frank Dobbin and John Sutton, "The Strength of a Weak State: The Rights Revolution and the Rise of Human Resources Management Divisions," *American Journal of Sociology* 104 (September 1998): 455–56; "Firms Prod Managers to Keep Eye on Goal of Equal Employment," *Wall Street Journal*, May 17, 1982, p. 1; Peter Robertson, "Why Bosses Like to Be Told to Hire Minorities,"

Washington Post, November 10, 1985, p. D1; "Affirmative Action: After the Debate, Opportunity," *Business Week,* April 13, 1987, p. 37; "Rethinking Weber: The Business Response to Affirmative Action," *Harvard Law Review,* 102 (January 1989): 658, 662, 668–69. See also Frank Dobbin, John Sutton, John Meyer, and W. Richard Scott, "Equal Opportunity Law and the Construction of Internal Labor Markets," *American Journal of Sociology* 99 (September 1993): 396–427.

25. For brief histories of the Immigration Act of 1965 and its consequences, see Gillon, *That's Not What We Meant to Do,* chap. 4, and Graham, *Collision Course,* chap. 5. For an overview of the recent arguments and literature on immigration, see Christopher Jencks, "Who Should Get In?" *New York Review of Books,* November 29, 2001, and December 20, 2001.

26. Bureau of the Census, *The Hispanic Population of the United States: March 1988* (Washington: Department of Commerce, 1989), p. 2; Mary Waters and Karl Eschbach, "Immigration and Ethnic and Racial Inequality in the United States," *Annual Review of Sociology* 21 (1995): 433; Bureau of the Census, *The Black Population in the United States: March 1988* (Washington: Department of Commerce, 1989), p. 1. For recent black and Hispanic population data, see Bureau of the Census, *The Black Population in the United States: March 2002* (Washington: Department of Commerce, 2003), Bureau of the Census, *The Hispanic Population in the United States: March 2002* (Washington: Department of Commerce, 2003). As of 2002, the Asian population had increased to 12.5 million according to Bureau of the Census, *The Asian and Pacific Islander Population in the United States: March 2002* (Washington: Department of Commerce, 2003).

27. Thomas Muller, "Immigration Policy and Economic Growth," *Yale Law and Policy Review* 7 (1989): 114–16; George Borjas, *Friends or Strangers* (New York: Basic, 1990), chap. 5; Kristin Butcher and David Card, "Immigration and Wages: Evidence from the 1980s," *American Economic Review* 81 (May 1991): 292–96; David Cutler and Lawrence Katz, "Macroeconomic Performance and the Disadvantaged," *Brookings Papers on Economic Activity* (1991): 1–74; Isabel Sawhill, "Poverty in the U.S.: Why Is It So Persistent?" *Journal of Economic Literature* 26 (September 1988): 1073–1119; William Julius Wilson and Robert Aponte, "Urban Poverty," *Annual Review of Sociology* 11 (1985): 231–58; Bruce Klein and Philip Rones, "A Profile of the Working Poor," *Monthly Labor Review,* October 1989. Borjas has recently revised his estimates to incorporate data from the 1990s and reports that immigration has depressed wages, although the effects are mainly concentrated on high school dropouts. See George Borjas, "The Labor Demand Curve *Is* Downward Sloping: Reexamining the Impact of Immigration on the Labor Market," *Quarterly Journal of Economics* 118 (November 2003): 1335–74.

28. Bob Suzuki, "Asian Americans as the 'Model Minority,'" *Change,* November–December 1989; "Asian-Americans Question Ivy League's Entry Policies," *New York Times,* May 30, 1985, p. B1.

29. Linda Matthews, "When Being the Best Isn't Good Enough," *Los Angeles Times Magazine,* July 19, 1987, pp. 23–26; "Many Top Students Are Losing UC

Campus Bid," *Los Angeles Times,* February 12, 1988, p. 3; James Gibney, "The Berkeley Squeeze," *New Republic,* April 11, 1988, pp. 16, 17; "Surge in Enrollment Poses Tricky Problem for U. of California," *Chronicle of Higher Education,* July 13, 1988, p. A17; "U.S. Probing Possible Asian Bias at UCLA, Berkeley," *Los Angeles Times,* November 18, 1988, p. 3; "UC Berkeley Faculty Panel Finds No Pattern of Asian Bias in Admissions," *Los Angeles Times,* February 28, 1989, p. 3; "UC Berkeley Apologizes for Policy That Limited Asians," *Los Angeles Times,* April 7, 1989, p. 3.

30. Raphael Sonenshein, "The Dynamics of Biracial Coalitions: Crossover Politics in Los Angeles," *Western Political Quarterly* 42 (June 1989): 345–46; Byran Jackson, Elisabeth Gerber, and Bruce Cain, "Coalitional Prospects in a Multi-Racial Society: African-American Attitudes Toward Other Minority Groups," *Political Research Quarterly* 47 (June 1994): 280, 282; Michael Thornton and Yuko Mizuno, "Economic Well-Being and Black Adult Feelings Toward Immigrants and Whites, 1984," *Journal of Black Studies* 30 (September 1999): 15–44.

31. "*Ebony* Interview with the Rev. Jesse Jackson," *Ebony,* June 1981, pp. 155, 157–58; "Jackson: Playing to the Camera," *Washington Post,* December 27, 1987, p. 1; Marshall Frady, *Jesse* (New York: Random House, 1996), p. 325. Frady's biography is the best overall treatment of Jackson to date. For additional information on Jackson's place in the American political-religious tradition, see Michael McTighe, "Jesse Jackson and the Dilemmas of a Prophet in Politics," *Journal of Church and State* 32 (Summer 1990): 585–607, and Gary Wills, *Under God* (New York: Simon and Schuster, 1990; reprint, New York: Touchstone, 1991), chaps. 20–23.

32. Frady, *Jesse,* pp. 305–10; "Jackson Declares Formal Candidacy," *New York Times,* November 4, 1983, p. B5; "A Provocative Candidate," *New York Times,* November 4, 1983, p. B5; "He Seeks New Road to Power," *Washington Post,* January 19, 1984, p. 1; "Jackson: Tax Reform and Public Jobs," *New York Times,* April 22, 1984, p. F2; "Playboy Interview: Jesse Jackson," *Playboy,* June 1984; Steven Gillon, *The Democrats' Dilemma* (New York: Columbia University Press, 1992), p. 352; Gary Wills, "New Votuhs," *New York Review of Books,* August 18, 1988, pp. 4–5; Wills, *Under God,* pp. 258–65; "Jesse Jackson: Black Charisma on the Campaign Trail," *Ebony,* August 1984. For additional views of Jackson's 1984 run, see Adolph Reed, *The Jesse Jackson Phenomenon* (New Haven: Yale University Press, 1986), and Lucius Barker and Ronald Walters, eds., *Jesse Jackson's 1984 Presidential Campaign* (Urbana: University of Illinois Press, 1989).

33. "Peace with American Jews Eludes Jackson," *Washington Post,* February 13, 1984, p. 1; "Jackson and the Jews," *New Republic,* March 19, 1984, pp. 9–10; "Rainbow's End," *New Republic,* April 30, 1984, p. 7; "Jackson and Farrakhan Sought Unity," *New York Times,* June 30, 1984, p. 6; "Jackson Charges He Was Ignored for the No. 2 Spot," *New York Times,* July 11, 1984, p. 1; "Jewish Leaders Criticize Jackson; The Democrats Are Also Warned," *New York Times,* July 11, 1984, p. A17; Gillon, *Democrats' Dilemma,* pp. 350–51.

34. "Three Years Later, Jackson Is Haunted by Anti-Semitism of Farrakhan," *New York Times,* June 13, 1987, p. 6; "3 Democrats Lead," *New York Times,* March 9, 1988,

p. 1; "Jackson's Winning Ways Transform Candidate, Voters," *Washington Post,* March 15, 1988, p. 1; "Jackson Share of Votes by Whites Triples in '88," *New York Times,* June 13, 1988, p. B7; Wills, *Under God,* pp. 258, 365; McTighe, "Dilemmas of a Prophet," p. 590; "Friction Arises over Jackson's Campaign Role," *Washington Post,* September 2, 1988, p. A9; "Dukakis' Black Support Lags Mondale's," *Washington Post,* October 21, 1988, p. A8; "Black Turnout Drops from 1984," *Washington Post,* November 10, 1988, p. A49; Katherine Tate, "Black Political Participation in the 1984 and 1988 Presidential Elections," *American Political Science Review* 85 (December 1991): 1171–72.

35. Juan Williams, "Divided We Fell: Race and the '88 Election," *Washington Post,* November 20, 1988, p. D1. For more on Jackson's tragic aspect, see Gary Wills, "A Tale of Three Leaders," *New York Review of Books,* September 19, 1996.

36. Edwin Diamond, "The Sound Bites and the Fury," *New York,* March 28, 1988; "Sharpton: Fast and Loose," *Village Voice,* May 24, 1988, p. 11. For additional information on Sharpton's background, see Playthell Benjamin, "Jive at Five," *Village Voice,* July 27, 1988.

37. Diamond, "Sound Bites," pp. 36–39; Edwin Diamond, "The Brawley Fiasco," *New York,* July 18, 1988, p. 23; Stanley Crouch, "Three Buckets of Jive," *New Republic,* July 11, 1988, p. 15; "Evidence Points to Deceit by Brawley," *New York Times,* September 27, 1988, p. 1; "'We the Grand Jury': Text of Its Conclusions in the Tawana Brawley Case," *New York Times,* October 7, 1988, p. B4.

38. "Court Suspends Maddox for Refusal to Testify at Grievance Hearing," *New York Times,* May 22, 1990, p. B1; "Court Panel Bars Maddox for 5 More Years," *New York Times,* August 3, 1994, p. B3; "State Appellate Court Disbars an Advocate of Civil Rights," *New York Times,* January 27, 1995, p. B3; "Sharpton Runs for Presidency, and Influence," *New York Times,* December 5, 2003, p. 1; "On Dr. King's Day, Mrs. Clinton Sees Race Intersect Politics," *New York Times,* January 18, 2000, p. B1; "Homage That Comes with Perils," *New York Times,* January 18, 2000, p. B1; "Sharpton's Bid Renews Queries over Finances," *New York Times,* January 10, 2004, p. 1; "U.S. Panel Votes to Deny Tax Money for Sharpton," *New York Times,* May 2, 2004, p. A12.

39. Enrollment data from U.S. Census Bureau, *School Enrollment: Social and Economic Characteristics of Students, October 1981 and 1980* (Washington: U.S. Department of Commerce, 1985), p. 72; U.S. Census Bureau, *School Enrollment: Social and Economic Characteristics of Students, October 1989* (Washington: U.S. Department of Commerce, 1991), p. 47; and http://www.census.gov/population/socdemo/school/tabA-7.pdf. "Endowments Buoyed by Rises in Value of Stocks, Bonds," *Chronicle of Higher Education,* December 8, 1982, p. 3; "Size of Faculty Is Up at 30 Pct. of Colleges, Holds Steady at 55 Pct., Survey Finds," *Chronicle of Higher Education,* August 3, 1983, p. 19; "College Endowments Return a Record 42 Pct. in One Year," *Chronicle of Higher Education,* November 16, 1983, p. 1; "Jean Mayer's Decade at Tufts: A Stamp of Passion," *New York Times,* June 8, 1986, p. 54; Christopher Knowlton, "How the Richest Colleges Handle Their Billions," *Fortune,*

October 26, 1987. For a brief history of the universities since 1945, see Thomas Bender, "Politics, Intellect, and the American University, 1945–1995," *Daedalus* 126 (Winter 1997): 1–38.

40. Fran Schumer, "A Question of Sex Bias at Harvard," *New York Times Magazine,* October 18, 1981; "Harvard Reverses Tenure Decision," *New York Times,* January 8, 1985, p. A11; Shirley Clark and Mary Corcoran, "Perspectives on the Professional Socialization of Women Faculty," *Journal of Higher Education* 57 (January–February 1986): 20–43; Ana Lomperia, "Are Women Changing the Nature of the Academic Profession?" *Journal of Higher Education* 61 (November–December 1990): 643–77; Sylvia Hurtado, "The Campus Racial Climate," *Journal of Higher Education* 63 (September–October 1992): 560–64; Francine Blau and Lawrence Kahn, "Gender Differences in Pay," *Journal of Economic Perspectives* 14 (Fall 2000): 89–90.

41. John Higham, *History,* updated ed. (Baltimore: Johns Hopkins University Press, 1989), pp. 238–40, 246–50, 261; Peter Novick, *That Noble Dream* (New York: Cambridge University Press, 1988), chaps. 13–16; Thomas Bender, "Whole and Parts: The Need for Synthesis in American History," *Journal of American History* 73 (June 1986): 120–36; Bernard Bailyn, "The Challenge of Modern Historiography," *American Historical Review* 87 (February 1982): 2–3, 6–7; William Leuchtenburg, "The Historian and the Public Realm," *American Historical Review* 97 (February 1992): 1–18. The problem of the lost audience for historians continues to this day; see "Lessons We May Be Doomed to Repeat," *Washington Post,* January 11, 2004, p. D1.

42. George Dieter, "The Big Shift in Students' Majors: Its Impact on Colleges and Society," *Chronicle of Higher Education,* October 20, 1980, p. 56; National Center for Education Statistics, *Chartbook of Degrees Conferred, 1969–70 to 1993–94* (Washington: Department of Education, 1998), tables 26 and 34; "Concern over Departments' Resources Found Widespread Among Professors," *Chronicle of Higher Education,* November 23, 1983, p. 19; "Most New Faculty Members Seem Resigned to Wide Disparities in Starting Salaries," *Chronicle of Higher Education,* March 2, 1984, p. 27; "Resources for Faculty Travel, Clerical Help and Research Aid Reported Holding Steady," *Chronicle of Higher Education,* June 12, 1985, p. 21; "For Good or Ill, the Reagan Presidency Has Brought Profound Change to American Higher Education," *Chronicle of Higher Education,* November 8, 1988, pp. A22, A24, A26; Scott Kerlin and Diane Dunlap, "For Richer, for Poorer," *Journal of Higher Education* 64 (May–June 1993): 350.

43. Howard Bowen and Jack Schuster, *American Professors* (New York: Oxford University Press, 1986), pp. 121–26; "Tenured Professors May Lose Jobs as Michigan Retrenches," *Chronicle of Higher Education,* March 2, 1981, p. 5; "Ethnic Studies Often a Victim of Budget Cuts," *Chronicle of Higher Education,* April 25, 1984, p. 1; Bowen and Schuster, *American Professors,* chaps. 7, 8; Kerlin and Dunlap, "For Richer," p. 371; Sheila Slaughter, "Retrenchment in the 1980s," *Journal of Higher Education* 64 (May–June 1993): 271, 272. For data on the numbers of degrees awarded each year, broken down by field, see *Chartbook of Degrees Conferred.*

44. For explanations of, and introductions to, postmodernism and deconstruction, see Jacques Derrida, *Of Grammatology* (Paris: Les Editions de Minuit, 1967; translation, Baltimore: Johns Hopkins University Press, 1976); Harold Bloom et al., *Deconstruction and Criticism* (New York: Seabury Press, 1979); Terry Eagleton, *Literary Theory,* 2d ed. (Minneapolis: University of Minnesota Press, 1996), chap. 4; David Lehman, *Signs of the Times* (New York: Poseidon, 1991); and Terry Eagleton, *The Illusions of Postmodernism* (Oxford: Blackwell, 1996). For useful background on the spread of deconstruction, see Michele Lamont, "How to Become a Dominant French Philosopher: The Case of Jacques Derrida," *American Journal of Sociology* 93 (November 1987): 584–622, and Colin Campbell, "The Tyranny of the Yale Critics," *New York Times,* February 9, 1986. For criticisms of deconstruction, see Michael Wood, "Deconstructing Derrida," *New York Review of Books,* March 3, 1977; Richard Rorty, "Philosophy as a Kind of Writing: An Essay on Derrida," *New Literary History* 10 (Autumn 1978): 141–60; Denis Donoghue, "Deconstructing Deconstruction," *New York Review of Books,* June 12, 1980; and John Searle, "The Word Turned Upside Down," *New York Review of Books,* October 27, 1983.

45. For the politics of deconstruction, see Eagleton, *Literary Theory,* p. 125; Murray Edelman, "Political Language and Political Reality," *PS* 18 (Winter 1985): 10–19; Stephen White, "Poststructuralism and Political Reflection," *Political Theory* 16 (May 1988): 186–208; Mark Lilla, "The Politics of Jacques Derrida," *New York Review of Books,* June 25, 1998. For the de Man affair, see "Yale Still Feeling Loss of Revered Professor," *New York Times,* February 25, 1984, p. 26; "Yale Scholar Wrote for Pro-Nazi Newspaper," *New York Times,* December 1, 1987, p. B1; Geoffrey Hartman, "Blindness and Insight," *New Republic,* March 7, 1988; Jonathan Culler, "It's Time to Set the Record Straight About Paul de Man and His Wartime Articles for a Pro-Fascist Newspaper," *Chronicle of Higher Education,* July 13, 1988, p. B1; James Atlas, "The Case of Paul de Man," *New York Times Magazine,* August 28, 1988; Denis Donoghue, "The Strange Case of Paul de Man," *New York Review of Books,* June 29, 1989; and Lehman, *Signs of the Times.*

46. Elaine Showalter, "Twenty Years On: *A Literature of Their Own* Revisited," *Novel* 31 (Summer 1998): 405; Bonnie Zimmerman, "What Has Never Been: An Overview of Lesbian Feminist Literary Criticism," *Feminist Studies* 7 (Fall 1981): 451–75; Peter Shaw, "Feminist Literary Criticism," *American Scholar,* Autumn 1988, pp. 504–11. On politics and literature, see Robert Warshow, "The Legacy of the '30s," in Robert Warshow, *The Immediate Experience* (Garden City: Doubleday, 1962).

For further background on women's literary studies, see Elaine Showalter, "Women and the Literary Curriculum," *College English* 32 (May 1971): 855–62; Elaine Showalter, *A Literature of Their Own* (Princeton: Princeton University Press, 1977); Deborah McDowell, "New Directions for Black Feminist Criticism," *Black American Literature Forum* 14 (Winter 1980): 153–59; Naomi Schor, "Female Paranoia: The Case for Psychoanalytic Feminist Criticism," *Yale French Studies,* 62 (1981): 204–19; Karen Keener, "Out of the Archives and into the Academy: Opportunities for Research and Publication in Lesbian Literature," *College English* 44 (March 1982):

301–13; Lillian Robinson, "Treason Our Text: Feminist Challenges to the Literary Canon," *Tulsa Studies in Women's Literature* 2 (Spring 1983): 83–98; Elaine Showalter, "Women's Time, Women's Space: Writing the History of Feminist Criticism," *Tulsa Studies in Women's Literature* 3 (Spring–Autumn 1984): Adalaide Morris, "Dick, Jane, and American Literature: Fighting with Canons," *College English* 47 (September 1985): 467–81; Toril Moi, *Sexual/Textual Politics: Feminist Literary Theory* (New York: Methuen, 1985), 29–43; Laurie Finke, "The Rhetoric of Marginality: Why I Do Feminist Theory," *Tulsa Studies in Women's Literature* 5 (Autumn 1986): 251–72; Ellen Messer-Davidow, "The Philosophical Bases of Feminist Literary Criticism," *New Literary History* 19 (Autumn 1987): 65–103; Elizabeth Kolbert, "Literary Feminism Comes of Age," *New York Times Magazine,* December 6, 1987; and Elaine Showalter, "American Gynocriticism," *American Literary History* 5 (Spring 1993): 111–28. For criticism of the political aspects of women's literary studies by a well-known conservative intellectual, see Carol Iannone, "Feminism and Literature," *New Criterion,* November 1985, and Carol Iannone, "Feminism vs. Literature," *Commentary,* July 1988.

47. Slaughter, "Retrenchment," pp. 250, 251; Harland Bloland, "Postmodernism and Higher Education," *Journal of Higher Education* 66 (September–October 1995): 528, 529; Steven Watts, "The Idiocy of American Studies: Poststructuralism, Language, and Politics in the Age of Self-Fulfillment," *American Quarterly* 43 (December 1991): 627, 652. On the self-absorption of would-be radicals, see also Louis Menand, "Radicalism for Yuppies," *New Republic,* March 17, 1986, and Mark Lilla, "The Politics of Jacques Derrida," *New York Review of Books,* June 25, 1998. For the academic left since the 1960s and its attraction to deconstructionism, see John Patrick Diggins, *The Rise and Fall of the American Left* (New York: W. W. Norton, 1992), chaps. 7–9; Russell Jacoby, *The Last Intellectuals* (New York: Noonday, 1987), chap. 6; and John Searle, "The Storm over the University," *New York Review of Books,* December 5, 1990. For portrayals and criticisms of literary feminism and deconstructionism in the popular media, see Irving Howe, "The Treason of the Critics," *New Republic,* June 12, 1989; Anne Matthews, "Deciphering Victorian Underwear and Other Seminars," *New York Times Magazine,* February 10, 1992.

48. George Sher and William Bennett, "Moral Education and Indoctrination," *Journal of Philosophy* 79 (November 1982): 665–77; William Bennett, "Reviving the Humanities," *Washington Post,* April 15, 1983, p. A21; William Bennett, "The Shattered Humanities," *Wall Street Journal,* December 31, 1982, p. 10; "Humanities Chief Assails Programs of Graduate Study," *Chronicle of Higher Education,* February 29, 1984, p. 10; "Humanities Endowment Tilting Toward Classics," *Washington Post,* July 16, 1984, p. A9; Congress, Senate, Committee on Labor and Human Resources, *Hearing on William J. Bennett, of North Carolina, to be Secretary of Education,* 99th Cong., 1st Sess., January 28, 1985, p. 55. For more on Bennett's background, see Edward Fiske, "Reagan's Man for Education," *New York Times Magazine,* December 22, 1985.

49. Barbara Vobejda, "Colleges and Universities Ask What Does It Mean to Be an Educated Person?" *Washington Post Book World,* August 7, 1988, p. 4; Jeffrey Hart, "Wimmin Against Literature," *National Review,* September 30, 1988, p. 43; Henry Giroux and Harvey Kaye, "The Liberal Arts Must Be Reformed to Serve Democratic Ends," *Chronicle of Higher Education,* March 29, 1989, p. A44; Carol Camp Yeakey, "Social Change Through the Humanities: An Essay on the Politics of Literature and Culture in American Society," *New Literary History* 21 (Autumn 1990): 849. The debate about the canon quickly developed a large literature. For examples, see Allan Bloom, *The Closing of the American Mind* (New York: Simon and Schuster, 1987); Daniel Rossides, "Knee-Jerk Formalism," *Journal of Higher Education* 58 (July–August 1987): 404–29; Joe Weixlmann, "Dealing with the Demands of an Expanding Literary Canon," *College English* 50 (March 1988): 273–83; James Atlas, "The Battle of the Books," *New York Times Magazine,* June 5, 1988; Morris, "Dick, Jane"; Searle, "Storm over the University"; Tim Brennan, "The Education Debate: A Postmortem," *American Literary History* 4 (Winter 1992): 629–48; and Ellen Messer-Davidow, "Manufacturing the Attack on Liberalized Higher Education," *Social Text* 36 (Autumn 1993): 40–80.

50. "Students at Dartmouth Face off Across Widening Political Divide," *New York Times,* January 24, 1986, p. 1; "At Dartmouth, the Right Borrows the Protest Mantle of the Left," *New York Times,* February 13, 1986, p. A14; "Dartmouth: A Microcosm," *New York Times,* October 8, 1986, p. A15; "Racial Tensions Rekindled as Charges Fly at Dartmouth," *Boston Globe,* March 2, 1988, p. 1; "Sides Detail Confrontation at Dartmouth," *Boston Globe,* March 6, 1988, p. 43; "Newspaper at Dartmouth Sparks Racial Protest," *Chronicle of Higher Education,* March 9, 1988, p. A2; "Dartmouth President Blasts Conservative Campus Paper for 'Poisoning' the College's Intellectual Atmosphere," *Chronicle of Higher Education,* April 6, 1988, p. A27; "Dartmouth Divided," *Boston Globe,* April 3, 1988, p. 69; "Judge Ends Suspension of 2 Dartmouth Students," *Chronicle of Higher Education,* January 11, 1989, p. A2; John Casey, "The Clash of '89," *New York Times Magazine,* February 26, 1989, p. 29.

51. "In Dispute on Bias, Stanford Is Likely to Alter Western Culture Program," *New York Times,* January 19, 1988, p. A12; Isaac Barchas, "Stanford Would Toss Intellectual Heritage to the Winds," *Wall Street Journal,* January 21, 1988, p. 30; "Stanford Debates Its View of Western Culture," *Los Angeles Times,* February 3, 1988, p. 3; Lynne Cheney, "The Stanford Reading List Debate," *Washington Post,* February 16, 1988, p. A19; "Problem of Knowledge at Stanford," *Washington Post,* March 7, 1988, p. A13; "Bennett Draws Fire in Stanford Talk Assailing Course Change," *Los Angeles Times,* April 19, 1988, p. 3; William Bennett, "Why the West?" *National Review,* May 27, 1988, p. 37. See also Mary Louise Pratt, "Humanities for the Future: Reflections on the Western Culture Debate at Stanford," *South Atlantic Quarterly* 89 (Winter 1990): 7–25.

52. Michigan's speech code is excerpted in *Doe v. University of Michigan,* 721 F. Supp. 852 (1989), p. 856; Lee Dembart, "At Stanford, Leftists Become Censors,"

New York Times, May 5, 1989, p. A35; "Students Protest Policy to Limit Speech Practices," *New York Times,* September 17, 1989, p. 61; "Free Speech at Tufts: Zoned Out," *New York Times,* September 27, 1989, p. A29; "Tufts Drops Speech Restriction Policy, Saying It Was Open to a Legal Challenge," *Boston Globe,* October 5, 1989, p. 44; "A Din on the Campus," *Boston Globe,* October 8, 1989, p. A25; "Parties on Ethnic Themes Are Halted," *New York Times,* October 14, 1990, p. 39; "Hate Speech Code at U. of Wisconsin Voided by Court," *Chronicle of Higher Education,* October 23, 1991, p. 1. For legal arguments supporting speech codes, see Charles Lawrence, "If He Hollers Let Him Go: Regulating Racist Speech on Campus," *Duke Law Journal* 1990 (June 1990): 431–83; Lawrence White, "Hate-Speech Codes That Will Pass Constitutional Muster," *Chronicle of Higher Education,* May 25, 1994, p. A48; and Alice Ma, "Campus Hate Speech Codes: Affirmative Action in the Allocation of Speech Rights," *California Law Review* 83 (March 1995): 693–732. See also Chester Finn, "The Campus: 'An Island of Repression in a Sea of Freedom,'" *Commentary,* September 1989.

53. Carl Schorske, "Secretary Bennet and His Conservative Supporters Are the New Fundamentalists of Western Culture," *Chronicle of Higher Education,* June 1, 1988, p. B1. On the entry of Jews into higher education, see Diana Trilling, *The Beginning of the Journey* (New York: Harcourt Brace, 1993).

54. James Davison Hunter, *Culture Wars* (New York: Basic, 1991), p. 42; Midge Decter, "Ronald Reagan and the Culture War," *Commentary,* March 1991, p. 44. See also Peter Steinfels, "Metaphors Are Flying About a Civil War in American Culture, but Are They Reaching Too Far?" *New York Times,* December 7, 1991, p. 10. On multiculturalism, see Arthur M. Schlesinger, Jr., *The Disuniting of America* (New York: W. W. Norton, 1992), and John Patrick Diggins, *On Hallowed Ground* (New Haven: Yale University Press, 2000). For political correctness, see "The Rising Hegemony of the Politically Correct," *New York Times,* October 28, 1990, p. E1; Nat Hentoff, "Speaking Truth to 'Politically Correct' Students," *Village Voice,* November 22, 1990, p. 24; John Leo, "The Academy's New Ayatollahs," *U.S. News and World Report,* December 10, 1990, p. 22; and "Academic Group Fighting the 'Politically Correct Left' Gains Momentum," *Chronicle of Higher Education,* December 12, 1990, p. 1. By the early 1990s, writing books on the culture wars had become a small industry for conservatives. For a representative selection of their work, see Bloom, *Closing of the American Mind;* Charles Sykes, *Profscam* (Washington: Regnery Gateway, 1988); Robert Bork, *The Tempting of America* (New York: Free Press, 1990); Roger Kimball, *Tenured Radicals* (New York: Harper and Row, 1990); and Dinesh D'Souza, *Illiberal Education* (New York: Free Press, 1991). D'Souza, it is worth noting, was an editor of the *Dartmouth Review.* For a rejoinder to these books from the left, see Ellen Messer-Davidow, "Manufacturing the Attack on Liberalized Higher Education," *Social Text* 36 (Autumn, 1993): 40–80.

55. Alan Wolfe, *One Nation, After All* (New York: Viking, 1998), p. 129; Dennis Chong, Herbert McClosky, and John Zaller, "Patterns of Support for Democratic and Capitalist Values in the United States," *British Journal of Political Science* 13

(October 1983): 401–40; Steven Brint, "'New-Class' and Cumulative Trend Explanations of the Liberal Political Attitudes of Professionals," *American Journal of Sociology* 90 (July 1984): 30–71; Robert Shapiro and Harpreet Mahajan, "Gender Differences in Policy Preferences: A Summary of Trends from the 1960s to the 1980s," *Public Opinion Quarterly* 50 (Spring 1986): 42–61; Glenn, "Social Trends"; John Robinson and John Fleishman, "Ideological Identification: Trends and Interpretations of the Liberal-Conservative Balance," *Public Opinion Quarterly* 52 (Spring 1988): 134–45; Jerome Himmelstein and James McRae, Jr., "Social Issues and Socioeconomic Status," *Public Opinion Quarterly* 52 (Winter 1988): 492–512; Tom Smith, "Liberal and Conservative Trends in the United States Since World War II," *Public Opinion Quarterly* 54 (Winter 1990): 479–507; Michael Moffatt, "College Life," *Journal of Higher Education* 62 (January–February 1991): 44–61; Irene Taviss Thomson, "Individualism and Conformity in the 1950s vs. the 1980s," *Sociological Forum* 7 (September 1992): 497–516; Thomas Wilson, "Trends in Tolerance Toward Rightist and Leftist Groups, 1976–1988," *Public Opinion Quarterly* 58 (Winter 1994): 539–56; Daniel Bell, "The Disunited States of America," *Times Literary Supplement*, June 9, 1995, p. 16; Paul DiMaggio, John Evans, and Bethany Bryson, "Have Americans' Social Attitudes Become More Polarized?" *American Journal of Sociology* 102 (November 1996): 690–755.

INDEX